Sunset

Western Garden Annual

1999 EDITION

By the Editors of *Sunset Magazine* and Sunset Books

Euphorbia *'Palustris'* with purple Siberian irises (page 250).

Sunset Publishing Corporation ■ **Menlo Park, California**

SUSANNE WEIHL

SUNSET BOOKS

VP, Sales
Richard A. Smeby
Editorial Director
Bob Doyle
Production Director
Lory Day
Art Director
Vasken Guiragossian

STAFF FOR THIS BOOK

Managing Editor
Suzanne Normand Eyre
Contributing Editors
Philip Edinger
Helen Sweetland
Production Assistance
Cornelia Fogle
Linda Bouchard
Indexer
Pamela Evans
Production Coordinator
Patricia S. Williams

SUNSET PUBLISHING CORPORATION

President/Chief Executive Officer
Stephen J. Seabolt
VP, Chief Financial Officer
James E. Mitchell
VP, Consumer Marketing Director
Robert I. Gursha
VP, Manufacturing Director
Lorinda Reichert
VP, Editor-in-Chief, Sunset Magazine
Rosalie Muller Wright
Managing Editor
Carol Hoffman
Senior Editor, Gardening
Kathleen Norris Brenzel

Month-by-month in the Garden

Now a 6-year-long tradition, this *Western Garden Annual* comprises the entire previous year's output of *Sunset Magazine* garden and outdoor living articles. In each of the 12 chapters—one for each month of 1998—you will find all garden-related material from each of the regional editions of the magazine.

Just as in the magazine, each month begins with the Garden Guide material: short pieces that feature events, plants, tools, and innovations relevant to Western garden activities for that month. The Garden Notebook features present the personal observations of the *Sunset* garden editors who cover the Western gardening scene. Separate Checklists for each region detail garden activities appropriate to each month. The month's feature-length articles and photos conclude each chapter's offerings.

Throughout these chapters, plant performance and gardening activities are keyed to numbered climate zones. These 24 zones, covering the 11 contiguous Western states, are fully described and mapped in the sixth edition (1995) of the *Sunset Western Garden Book*.

Front cover: New hybrid tea rose 'Sunset Celebration'. Cover design: Vasken Guiragossian. Photographer: Norman A. Plate.

Back cover: Blue catmint and pink and coral diascias with 'Sunset Celebration' rose. Photographer: Norman A. Plate.

Endpapers: (hardcover edition): Wildflowers in Northern California's Bear Valley. Photographer: Graham Osborne.

All material in this book originally appeared in the 1998 issues of *Sunset Magazine*.

Sunset Western Garden Annual was produced by Sunset Books. If you have comments or suggestions, please let us hear from you. Write us at:

Sunset Books
Garden Book Editorial
80 Willow Road
Menlo Park, CA 94025

Contents

A Perfectly Western Year

East is east and west is west—this phrase may be timeworn, but it conveniently expresses Sunset's *raison d'être*. From its inception exactly 100 years ago as an inducement to westward-bound travelers, *Sunset Magazine* has kept its focus on the aspects of geography and lifestyle that make the Western states not simply unique but truly special. Within Alaska and the territory generally bounded by Canada, Mexico, the Pacific Ocean, and the Rocky Mountains, Western residents have it all: the scenic gamut of ocean, beaches, mountains, and deserts; cutting-edge urban centers; world-class agricultural regions; year-round recreation opportunities to suit all tastes and skills; climates to satisfy sun worshippers, alpine enthusiasts, and fog aficionados.

The realm of gardening perfectly displays the diversity of opportunities open to denizens of the West—where dramatic and varied topographies combine with a complex mix of climates that can host everything but truly jungle-steamed plants. The regional editions of *Sunset Magazine* address these different climate regimes, providing timely and inspiring monthly grist for the gardening mill suited to new gardeners as well as old hands.

The year 1998 presented a typically Western potpourri of information to inspire and energize all readers with a yen for hands-in-the-dirt experience. January opened the year with a feature article on Western native plants that have earned their spurs in gardens worldwide; December closed it with an all-you-need-to-know survey of the selection and care of living Christmas trees. In between, readers were treated to feature material on tasty new fruit varieties, the complete care and feeding of roses, a specialist's assortment of species geraniums, espalier as garden sculpture, plant introductions from notable Western plantspersons, decorative European garden pottery, the lowdown on Alaskan gardening, reproducing the tropical paradise look, low-chill peonies for the West—and more!

As usual, each month also supplied a checklist of garden tasks to address as well as newsworthy bulletins on upcoming events, imaginative products for the garden, noteworthy plant trends in the trade, and innovative solutions to specific garden or landscape problems.

But this summary is a mere glance at the year's composition. Round the hedge and follow the garden path through all 315 pages to view the entire landscape of offerings.

Incandescent California poppies (Eschscholzia californica) *is one of the Western native plants that has won a worldwide following. See pages 20–26 for other cherished Western exports.*

English primroses are treasured winter bloomers throughout the West. For details on the Sweetheart primula series, new this season, see page 10.

January

gardenguide

Plant a fruiting arbor

■ Pleaching trees—weaving branches together to form a hedge or an arbor—is a garden technique we associate with formality. (Think of the grand gardens of Europe, with their avenues of lindens and hornbeams that look like hedges on stilts.) But you can use the same technique to create a rustic arbor like the one pictured at right.

To fashion this living structure, Agatha Youngblood of Rancho Santa Fe, California, planted eight 'Anna' apple trees 4½ feet apart in a circle about 12 feet across. Then she trained their branches to form a leafy roof, creating a living gazebo. (If she had it to do over again, Youngblood would expand the circle of trees to 14 feet across.)

Plastic tape secures the top of each tree to a wire, which is in turn affixed to a center pole. The apple trees' straight trunks and long flexible branches take to this treatment quite well, says Youngblood.

Roman chamomile forms a fragrant carpet beneath the apple tree circle, thriving in the dappled light. Though the primary purpose of the pleached arbor is shelter, says Youngblood, the apples are a tasty bonus.

— *Sharon Cohoon*

GLENN CORMIER

PLANT PROFILE
Brambly beauty

■ During the growing season, *Rubus cockburnianus* isn't a particularly auspicious-looking plant. But in winter, this Chinese bramble is a hauntingly beautiful sight, with its bare, chalk-white branches standing tall against a background of dark evergreens, brown beds, or snow. The leafless plant generates such a high degree of winter interest that the Royal Horticultural Society gave it an Award of Garden Merit.

R. cockburnianus grows in a vase shape to 9 feet tall. The stems have prickly thorns. From spring through autumn, the plant is covered with leaves, each made up of seven to nine oblong, serrated leaflets. Small purple-pink flowers with numerous stamens (reminiscent of single roses) appear in June, followed by black fruits. This plant is hardy in all Northwest climate zones. It takes full sun or partial shade and

grows best in moist, acid soil.

You'll sometimes find this bramble at specialty nurseries and plant society sales. Heronswood Nursery (7530 N.E. 288th St., Kingston, WA 98346; 360/297-4172) sells *R. c.* 'Aureus', a variety with brilliant yellow spring foliage that fades to lime-yellow. — *Steven R. Lorton*

gear

Even with heavy leather gauntlets on, gardeners all too often end up with nasty scratches on their arms after tangling with thorny rose canes. Tender forearms are particularly vulnerable. To the rescue are Green-Best's ArmSavers—nifty slip-on sleeves made of tough ballistic nylon that protect the entire forearm from above the elbow to the wrist. Elastic around the top keeps the sleeves in place, and soft cotton cuffs allow them to slide comfortably under work gloves. Pop on a pair for protection when carrying firewood, too. If ArmSavers aren't available at your local nursery center, order them directly from the company. *$12.95; (650) 323-3533.* — *S. C.*

NEW PLANTS
Meet the 1998 All-America winners

■ Each year since 1932, a few garden-worthy plants have been named All-America Selections. This year, a vegetable, a culinary herb, and two flowers won the honors. Look for these newcomers in seed catalogs and as nursery plants this spring.

'Bright Lights' Swiss chard (pictured at left). This seed blend bears plants with stems in a rainbow of glowing colors—ruby red, yellow, orange, pink, violet, white—and delicious green or burgundy leaves. Plants reach about 20 inches tall.

'Prism Sunshine' petunia. This plant bears 3-inch-wide flowers with sunny yellow centers fading to a paler shade around the edges.

'Sweet Dani' lemon basil. Nibble one of its chartreuse leaves and you'll think you bit into a lemon: this basil makes a tasty garnish for sliced tomatoes and salads.

'Victorian Rose' impatiens. Resembling miniature roses when they first unfold, the buds open to semidouble flowers 1 to 2 inches across. The deep rose-colored blooms appear earlier than on many other impatiens. — *Tracy Jan*

PLANT PROFILE
A sweetheart of a primrose

■ English primroses are treasured winter bloomers throughout the West, and for good reason: gray weather simply does not diminish the jewel-like glow of their many-colored flowers. Other than their attractiveness to snails, these plants have only one major shortcoming: a rain-induced mold called botrytis can sometimes cut short their bloom period.

The Sweetheart primula series, new this season, is the culmination of a 30-year effort by breeders, such as Kirin of Japan, to correct this fault. In trials across the country, Sweetheart demonstrated superior tolerance to botrytis, according to Twyford Plant Laboratories, an American subsidiary of Kirin.

Sunset was one of those test growers, and we were impressed with the series. Despite heavy rains during the first two months after transplanting, we didn't lose a single primrose to botrytis. And we were delighted with the plants' rosebudlike double petals and their better-than-average rebloom rate.

Sweetheart primroses should be available in a range of colors (including valentine red, pictured on page 6) at nurseries this month. — *S. C.*

How to plant a bare-root rose

■ Dig a planting hole broad and deep enough to accommodate the roots easily without cramping, bending, or cutting them to fit. Make a firm cone of soil in the hole. Spread the roots over the cone, positioning the plant at the same depth at which (or slightly higher than) it grew in the field, with the bud union above the surrounding soil (use a stick to check the level).

Fill in with backfill nearly to the hole's top, firming it with your fingers. Then add water. If the plant settles, raise it to the proper level. Fill the hole with remaining soil. ◆

Pacific Northwest Garden Notebook

BY STEVEN R. LORTON

According to Japanese folklore, there are three friends of winter: the pine, the bamboo, and the flowering plum. In addition to admiring these plants' beauty in the winter garden, the Japanese attach symbolic meaning to them. The pine signifies long life and family love (its needles radiate from a common center). The bamboo stands for integrity and purity (it grows straight, and the woody fiber inside is pure white). The flowering plum represents grace and sweetness (it has a statuesque form and sweetly scented blossoms). I grow all three of these plants, and you won't find better friends.

As for pines, I appreciate their evergreen foliage and rugged bark, and I like the sound the wind makes as it blows through their needles. Long-needled species like Jeffrey pine make the most memorable murmur. But for all-around beauty and good sound, you can't beat *Pinus contorta,* our native shore pine. Rarely exceeding 30 feet in height, *P. contorta* is a well-behaved, drought-tolerant plant; its dark green needles and compact form make it useful as a background, screen, or windbreak. *P. contorta* is hardy throughout the Northwest.

I also admire bamboo for its musical talent as well as the rhythmic motion it brings to a garden when it sways in the winter wind. My favorite is black bamboo (*Phyllostachys nigra*), whose black stems and plumes of evergreen foliage glisten like onyx and jade in cold, wet weather. Although black bamboo is a running type that can spread aggressively,

I have mine contained on a natural shelf along a pond. *P. nigra* is hardy in *Sunset* climate zones 4 through 7.

My third friend, Japanese flowering plum (*Prunus mume*), will greet me with fragrant blossoms later this month. The longest-lived of all flowering fruit trees, *P. mume* continues blooming well into February in zones 4 through 7, and even later in zones 2 and 3. Mine has white double flowers; it's probably *P. m.* 'Rosemary Clarke' but I can't say for sure, since the plant wasn't tagged when I got it.

that's a good question ...

Q: Many *Magnolia grandiflora* trees broke down under last winter's heavy snows. Is there any way to prevent this?

— *Jessie Egersett, Seattle*

A: With its big, leathery leaves, the Southern magnolia can gather a heavier load of snow than its branches can bear. When the snow falls, shake your tree to lighten its load. Also, encourage the tree to develop a dense, sturdy crown that will shed snow better. In the fall, after bloom, cut long new shoots back by half. Next spring the tree will form multiple branches, making a thicker thatch to stand up to snow.

Northern California Garden Notebook

BY LAUREN BONAR SWEZEY

*j*anuary hits me with a thud. Holidays have ended, partying has come to a screeching halt, and I am suddenly faced with the daunting prospect of cleaning up the garden I neglected while getting ready for Christmas.

Last winter, I banished the post-holiday blues by tidying my perennial beds. My plants were looking pretty ragged—as perennials usually do in midwinter—but my pruning shears worked wonders. In just a few days, I transformed my garden from wild-looking to neat.

Don't be afraid to drastically prune plants. I usually cut back catmint, dead nettle, and diascia by about two-thirds. Then I clean out dead growth underneath the plants. My 'Wargrave Pink' geranium sometimes needs a bit of clipping, though I groom it heavily in late summer. I also cut back penstemon, salvia, and yarrow to within 4 to 6 inches off the ground. But I wait until spring (just before the plants' first flush of growth) to take my shears to *Artemisia* 'Powis Castle'. Pruning that big gray mound of foliage in January would leave a bare spot in the garden for too long.

GARDENS AND SEMINARS IN SACRAMENTO

If it's gardening information and inspiration you're looking for, you'll find plenty of both at the Northern California Home & Landscape Expo January 30 through February 1 at the Cal Expo Fairgrounds in Sacra-

mento. The expo's UC Master Gardeners Seminars will include presentations by industry professionals on a wide range of topics. Workshops will focus on dried flowers, container gardening, bonsai, topiaries, and fountains. The seminars and workshops are offered throughout the three-day event at no extra charge. Master Gardeners are also on hand to answer gardening questions.

The Sacramento Area Landscape Design Competition runs in conjunction with the show and features professionally designed garden displays that offer attendees plenty of ideas for their own gardens.

Expo hours are 1 to 8 January 30, 10 to 8 January 31, and 10 to 6 February 1. Admission costs $5. Call (800) 343-1740 for more information.

(Editor's note: dates and times in this article were valid for 1998; they will vary from year to year.)

that's a good question ...

Q: I want to plant some bare-root prune trees. How long do I have to get it done? All of January? February?
— *Occidental, California*

A. Bare-root fruit-tree-planting season in Northern California generally starts in early January and lasts until the weather starts warming up in late winter. In cool, coastal areas, you may have until early March to plant. But the weather can heat up earlier in inland areas, and bare-root planting may end in late February. When bare-root season ends, nurseries pot up the trees, so there's still an opportunity to plant them later in the season.

Southern California Garden Notebook

BY SHARON COHOON

Yikes, spikes!" So began one of the first messages I received addressed to the Garden Notebook. "My backyard contains as many blades as a sword-swallower's suitcase," the memo read. Or words to that effect. "What can I plant that will soften all those sharp edges?" I wrote a sympathetic response, confessing to a fatal weakness for flaxes, grasses, and all things spiky myself, and suggesting some softer, more relaxed plants to counteract all that bristly activity.

Then I stepped outside and assessed my own garden. Pretty edgy out there. That e-mail correspondent could have been describing my own yard. Turns out he was. The message originated from my husband's computer on the other side of the wall from mine. I just didn't recognize his new on-line handle. He waited until I stopped putting in broad-leafed plants before confessing that he was the sender.

How's the balance in your garden, by the way? Maybe you lean toward yin instead of yang and have ended up with too many round mounds. A few spikes could jazz things up. Or perhaps you've overloaded on variegated foliage—another pitfall of mine—and need to replace some of those busy patterns with sensible solids. January is an excellent time for a garden inventory. Blooms are sparse, and there are few distractions. Decide what you need to add or subtract to improve the picture, and devise a planting plan.

FOR THOSE LULLS BETWEEN STORMS

Two ways to take advantage of back-to-back winter storms: First, broadcast leftover annual seeds during a lull. Damp soil from the first rain and new moisture from the next create ideal germination conditions. Second, feed lawns and planting beds. Plants will be well watered from the first rain, so fertilizer won't burn them, and the next storm will water it in.

that's a good question ...

Q: "I bought an Asian pear tree on impulse last year, and my wife says I wasted my money," writes Phil Chenier of Huntington Beach. "She says it will never set fruit. Is she right?"

A: My bet's with your wife. Even if El Niño behaves as predicted and we have a wetter winter than usual, it isn't likely to be chilly enough for pears in your mild location. Deciduous fruit trees all require a minimum number of chill hours during winter to set fruit. Chill hours are the total number of hours during dormancy when temperatures are below 45°. The number of chill hours required varies with the type of fruit. Asian pears require 450 chill hours, hard to achieve in your coastal climate. You'll have better luck with a fruit tree with a 250 to 300 chill-hour requirement. Try 'Panamint' or 'Desert Dawn' nectarines, for instance, 'Desertgold' or 'Bonita' peaches, 'Santa Rosa' plum, or 'Anna' apple.

MARINA THOMPSON

Westerner's Garden Notebook

BY JIM McCAUSLAND

When I look out on my winter garden, with its leafless trees standing stark against the sky (beds of annuals still lying dormant in seed packets on the kitchen table), I get the urge to plant something—and watch it grow quickly—right on my windowsill. That's when I head to the grocery store for produce that quickly reverts back to plant form: avocado, fresh ginger root, pineapple, and sweet potato. Growing these tropical wonders is a fun way for kids to learn about plants. Treat them as short-term experiments, unless you can provide the conditions and space to sustain their growth (a greenhouse is ideal).

Avocado. After eating the avocado, I wash the seed and let it dry for a few days. Then I insert toothpicks around the seed's equator and set it, pointed end up, half-submerged in a glass full of water. Roots and growth start in a few weeks.

Ginger. I buy fresh common ginger (*Zingiber officinale*) and plant the thick root (actually a rhizome) in damp potting soil. Heat, humidity, and lots of water make it sprout and grow.

Pineapple. This bromeliad is easy. I just cut off its leafy top with about an inch of fruit attached and set it in a saucer of water, where it roots like magic.

Sweet potato. I slice a sweet potato in two and set the halves cut side down in an inch of water to sprout. Soon they're covered with pretty, heart-shaped leaves that remind me of morning glory foliage, which they should since both plants are in the *Convolvulaceae* family.

A GARDEN FULL OF INSECT LIFE—AND STRIFE

Any book that illuminates the garden's animal life makes a welcome addition to Southwest garden literature, and *In a Desert Garden: Love & Death Among the Insects,* by John Alcock (Norton, New York, 1997; $27.50), fits the bill.

Alcock, a biology professor at Arizona State University, walks the reader through his own garden's transformation from a "bermuda-grass desert" into a rich, varied blend of ornamental plants and vegetables that attract birds and both beneficial and troublesome bugs. Along the way, he tells what happens to beneficial insects you buy (many fly away) and how to make an effective desert compost pile (trench it).

FENCE-BUILDING SEASON

Setting fence posts is hard work that is best done on a mild day during the cold season—as long as the ground isn't frozen. I use a posthole digger to form a 20-inch-deep hole in the ground. Then I set the post in the hole, pour one 50-pound sack of dry concrete around it, add water, and stir the mix with the post itself.

After making sure that the post is standing straight and its front and back sides are parallel to the fence line, I mound the concrete up about an inch above ground level, smooth it, and let it dry for two days.

With the posts now firmly set in concrete, I nail on 2-by-4 cross-braces and attach the facing boards.

that's a good question ...

Q: How much water does it take to leach the salts out of the potting soil around my house plants?

A: Here's a simple formula I found in "Mastering the Mojave," a newsletter published for the University of Nevada Reno's Clark County Master Gardeners: To wash away the salts, just estimate the volume of soil you want to leach (a quart, for example) and pour three times that much water through.

Pacific Northwest Checklist

PLANTING & SHOPPING

☑ **BARE-ROOT STOCK. Zones 4–7:** Shop for bare-root berries, fruit and shade trees, grapes, ornamental shrubs and roses, and perennial vegetables (asparagus, horseradish, and rhubarb). Plant them whenever the soil is workable. If you can't plant right away, keep the roots from drying out by heeling in plants: place them on their sides in a shallow trench and cover with moist sawdust or soil.

☑ **HARDY PERENNIALS.** For frost-tolerant perennials such as columbine, delphinium, hellebore, veronica, and viola, start seeds now in coldframes or greenhouses. Set plants outside when they develop one or two true sets of leaves, but not more than a month before the last frost.

☑ **ORDER SEEDS.** Look through catalogs and order seeds now so you won't be stuck with substitutions later in the season.

☑ **WINTER-BLOOMING SHRUBS. Zones 4–7:** Visit a nursery and you'll be amazed at all the shrubs in bloom this month, including hybrid camellias, cornelian cherry *(Cornus mas), Prunus subhirtella* 'Autumnalis', stachyurus, wintersweet, and witch hazel. Plant shrubs immediately or slip them into decorative pots for display on a deck or patio.

MAINTENANCE

☑ **CARE FOR HOUSE PLANTS.** Water regularly, but fertilize only those plants bearing blooms or fruit. Snip off faded leaves. If plants are dusty, set them in the shower and rinse under tepid water. If the old potting mix is crusty, use a large serving spoon to remove an inch or two of soil (stop digging when you start uncovering roots), then replace with fresh mix.

☑ **PRUNE FRUIT TREES AND ROSES. Zones 4–7:** On a day when temperatures are well above freezing, prune roses and deciduous fruit trees. Use sharp-bladed tools to make clean cuts. Prune hybrid tea roses to a vase shape made from the three to five strongest canes. Remove dead, diseased, crossing, and close parallel branches from fruit trees, then prune for form. In zones 1–3, hold off on pruning fruit trees until early spring.

PEST & WEED CONTROL

☑ **OVERWINTERING PESTS.** Spray dormant oil on deciduous trees and shrubs, including fruits, ornamentals, and roses, to control overwintering insects.

☑ **SLUGS.** Whenever there's a warm spell, slugs wake up and start nibbling. Poison bait and handpicking are the most effective methods at this time of year. Place the bait near slugs' hiding places—under rocks, pavers, and large pots; along house foundations; and in dense ground covers like ivy. Keep children and pets well away from the bait.

Northern California Checklist

PLANTING

☑ **ORDER SEEDS.** Thumb through catalogs such as Nichols Garden Nursery (541/928-9280), Redwood City Seed Company (650/325-7333), and Shepherd's Garden Seeds (860/482-3638). Order varieties you can't find on seed racks. Zones 7–9, 14–17: Sow seeds of cool-season vegetables such as chard, lettuce, and spinach for planting out in February. Zones 1–2: Sow seeds of cool-season crops such as broccoli and cauliflower six to eight weeks before the soil can be worked.

☑ **PLANT BARE-ROOT.** Zones 7–9, 14–17: It's prime time for buying and planting dormant roses, shrubs, fruit and shade trees, and vines. Bare-root plants cost less and adapt more quickly than container plants.

☑ **PLANT BERRIES.** Zones 7–9, 14–17: Blackberries, raspberries, and strawberries are all available bare-root this month. 'Olallie' blackberries are taste treats—the huge, 1½-inch-long berries are sweet and succulent, and the plant is well adapted to Northern California. 'Sequoia' strawberries are also rich in flavor.

☑ **SHOP FOR INSTANT COLOR.** Zones 7–9, 14–17: For midwinter bloom, buy 4-inch-size instant color (smaller plants will just sit until spring). Stuff plants into containers or set them out in flower beds. Try calendula, candytuft, cineraria, dianthus, English daisies, English and fairy primroses, Iceland poppies, pansies, snapdragons, stock, and violas.

Sunset
CLIMATE ZONES
☐ Mountain (1-2)
☐ Valley (7-9)
☐ Inland (14)
☐ Coastal (15-17)

DEBRA LAMBERT

MAINTENANCE

☑ **CARE FOR GIFT PLANTS.** Zones 7–9, 14–17: Snip off spent blossoms on blooming plants and move hardier types such as azaleas, cineraria, cyclamen, cymbidiums, and miniature Christmas trees to protected spots outside. Keep tender plants such as amaryllis and kalanchoe indoors in a well-lighted spot. Water regularly. Repot if plants are rootbound and dry out quickly. Fertilize amaryllis and azaleas after bloom finishes. Feed cymbidiums with half-strength fertilizer every week or so; other plants should be fertilized every two to four weeks. Zones 1–2: Keep all plants indoors until after the last hard freeze.

☑ **FEED CITRUS.** Zones 7–9, 14–17: Six to eight weeks before they bloom, give citrus trees one feeding according to their age: give two-year-old trees (trees planted last season) ¼ pound of actual nitrogen; three-year-old trees ½ pound; four-year-old trees ¾ pound; five-year-old trees 1 pound; and trees more than five years old 1 to 1½ pounds. Or divide the total fertilizer into two feedings (January and February); for very sandy soil, divide it into once-a-month feedings from late winter through summer.

☑ **PROTECT PLANTS FROM FROST.** Zones 7–9, 14–17: If weather forecasts predict dry, still, clear nights and frost, water all plants well. Move tender container plants such as citrus, cymbidiums, hibiscus, and mandevilla beneath overhangs or into the garage. Protect other frost-tender plants with burlap or cloth coverings; do not let the cover touch the leaves. Remove covers first thing in the morning.

PEST CONTROL

☑ **SPRAY ROSES.** Zones 7–9, 14–17: To control overwintering insects such as aphids, mites, and scale, spray roses with a dormant oil.

Southern California Checklist

PLANTING

☑ **BUY BARE-ROOT PLANTS.** January is bare-root planting time in all mild-weather climates. Take advantage of it. Bare-root plants are not only less expensive than leafed-out ones, but also take hold more quickly. Shop for roses, stone fruit and deciduous shade trees, strawberries and cane berries, and artichokes, asparagus, and other perennial vegetables. Plant them immediately if possible. If the soil is too wet to plant right away, cover the roots with soil or plant temporarily in containers.

☑ **PLANT COOL-SEASON COLOR.** If the soil isn't soggy from rain, there's still time to plant Iceland poppies, pansies, primulas, and other winter annuals, especially along the coast. Low-desert gardeners (zone 13) can also plant petunias.

☑ **PLANT SUMMER BULBS.** Nurseries are well stocked with calla, canna, crinum, dahlia, gladiolus, lily, nerine, tigridia, and other summer-blooming bulbs. If you live in a frost-free area, this is also a good time to replant into the garden those amaryllis bulbs you forced during the holidays or received as gift plants. They won't bloom this spring but should next year.

Sunset
CLIMATE ZONES

1-3 7-9 11 13 14-24

DEBRA LAMBERT

☑ **PLANT WINTER VEGETABLES.** Germination will be slow, but it's still possible to start cool-season crops from seed—especially endives, lettuces, and other greens. Also try beets, carrots, peas, and radishes. Set out broccoli, brussels sprouts, and cabbage seedlings.

MAINTENANCE

☑ **BEGIN PRUNING DORMANT PLANTS.** Start with roses. Cut out all dead wood, crossing branches, and twiggy growth, leaving five to seven strong canes. Deciduous fruit trees should be pruned now, too. Apricots, peaches, and plums all require different pruning. Consult a good reference book and/or attend a fruit-tree pruning demonstration at an arboretum before proceeding. Hold off pruning trees, shrubs, and vines that flower in early spring; wait until after bloom to shape them.

☑ **FEED CITRUS.** In frost-free areas, fertilize citrus this month; inland, wait until February. Where frost lingers, wait until March to avoid damage to new growth. Water first; a day later, sprinkle slow-release ammonium sulfate over entire root area, then water to wash into soil. Wait two months, then apply a second feeding.

PEST & WEED CONTROL

☑ **APPLY DORMANT SPRAY.** Spray roses and deciduous flowering and fruit trees with horticultural oil to smother overwintering insects such as mites, scale, and sawfly larvae. For fungal diseases such as peach leaf curl or brown rot, mix lime sulfur or fixed copper into the oil. Spray the branches, crotches, trunk, and ground beneath the tree's drip line. Hold off spraying if rain is forecast or temperatures are expected to drop below 0°.

☑ **MANAGE WEEDS.** Mulch flower and vegetable beds to keep ahead of weeds encouraged by winter rains. Keep on top of areas seeded with wildflowers. Hand-pull or carefully hoe emerging weeds.

Mountain Checklist

Sunset
CLIMATE ZONES
☐ 1-3   ☐ 10-11

PLANTING & SHOPPING

☑ **INDOOR COLOR.** For a splash of winter color indoors, shop nurseries and floral shops for cyclamen, Johnny-jump-ups, pansies, and primroses. Set potted plants in a bright, cool spot.

☑ **ORDER SEEDS, PLANTS.** To ensure the best selection, place catalog orders early for seeds and plants, particularly if you want specialty varieties like Chinese vegetables, rare plants, or antique roses. Start seeds indoors about five weeks before the date of the last frost in your area.

☑ **START HARDY PERENNIALS.** In milder parts of the intermountain West, start seeds of perennials such as delphinium, hellebore, veronica, and viola in a coldframe or greenhouse. Transplant seedlings when they have at least two sets of true leaves; in coldest areas, wait until the ground thaws and soil can be worked.

MAINTENANCE

☑ **CARE FOR HOUSE PLANTS.** Check soil often, and water when the top of the soil has dried out. Examine plants regularly for signs of aphids, mealy bugs, scale insects, and spider mites; one of the first signs on leaves and pot rims is the sticky "honeydew" exuded by feeding insects. Rinse infested plants with lukewarm water in the shower, then spray with insecticidal soap.

☑ **CARE FOR LIVING CHRISTMAS TREES.** After the holidays, move the tree outside as soon as possible. Start it off in a place that's shaded from midday and afternoon sun, moving it into full sun after a couple of weeks. If your tree is among the varieties that thrive in your area, plant it after the ground thaws; otherwise, keep the tree in the container and protect it from prolonged hard frost.

☑ **CHECK STORED BULBS, PRODUCE.** Inspect corms, tubers, and produce for shriveling and rot. Reverse shriveling by sprinkling on a little water. Discard any items that show signs of decay, except dahlia tubers: for these, cut out bad spots, dust with sulfur, and store apart from the rest.

☑ **FEED WILD BIRDS.** When winter diminishes their natural food supply, birds seek out backyard feeders. Insect-eating birds go for suet and peanut butter; seed-eaters prefer sunflower seeds, cracked corn, millet, and mixed birdseed.

☑ **KNOCK SNOW OFF EVERGREENS.** If you live in an area that gets heavy snow, knock or sweep it off the branches of evergreen shrubs and trees before its accumulated weight breaks or disfigures them.

☑ **MAINTAIN TOOLS.** Spring will be here before you know it. Get ready for it now by sharpening blades of shovels, hoes, and mowers. Rub down wood handles with linseed oil. Hone or replace the blades of pruning shears.

☑ **PRUNE TREES, SHRUBS.** In the mildest parts of the intermountain West, start pruning when daytime temperatures are well above freezing. Use sharp-bladed tools to make clean cuts. Remove dead, diseased, crossing, and close parallel branches, then prune for shape.

Southwest Checklist

PLANTING

☑ **BARE-ROOT STOCK.** Nurseries offer bare-root berries, fruit trees, grapes, roses, and shade and flowering trees now. Before you buy, decide what you want to grow and dig the planting hole. To keep bare roots from drying out, ask nursery staff to pack them in damp peat moss or sawdust and wrap them for the trip home.

☑ **BULBS.** If you've chilled crocus, hyacinth, and tulip bulbs in the refrigerator for six weeks, take them out and plant now in amended soil; water well. Shoots should emerge in a month or two.

☑ **VEGETABLES.** Zones 12–13: Start seeds of eggplant, melons, peppers, and tomatoes indoors now for transplanting outside when the weather warms up. Also set out short-day onions.

☑ **WINTER COLOR.** Zones 10–13: Nurseries offer a big selection of cool-season flowers, including bachelor's buttons, calendulas, cinerarias, cyclamen, English daisies, pansies, primroses, snapdragons, sweet alyssum, and wallflowers.

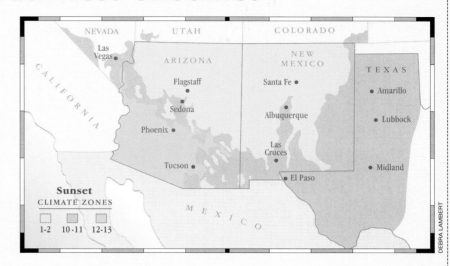

Sunset
CLIMATE ZONES
1-2   10-11   12-13

DEBRA LAMBERT

MAINTENANCE

☑ **CARE FOR CITRUS TREES.** Apply fertilizer now, so nutrients will be available when citrus starts to bloom. Water trees first, then apply ammonium sulfate a day later at the following rates for mature, full-size trees: 2½ pounds for grapefruit trees; 4 pounds for oranges and tangerines; and 5 pounds for lemons. Water again after feeding. If temperatures below 28° are forecast, cover trees at night with a cloth (old sheets are fine); uncover them in the morning. When temperatures drop below 25° for longer than two hours, most citrus fruits are damaged. Pick and juice damaged fruit within 24 hours.

☑ **PRUNE ROSES.** For hybrid tea roses, prune plants back to the three to five strongest canes. Cut back top growth by about a third.

☑ **WATER.** Zones 12–13: If winter rains are sporadic, deep-water trees and shrubs every two or three weeks.

PEST CONTROL

☑ **HOUSE PLANT PESTS.** Examine plants regularly for signs of aphids, mealy bugs, scale insects, and spider mites; one of the first on leaves and pot rims is the sticky "honeydew" exuded by feeding insects. Rinse infested plants with tepid water in the shower, then spray with insecticidal soap.

☑ **OVERWINTERING INSECTS.** Spray dormant deciduous trees and shrubs with horticultural oil to kill insects, eggs, and larvae.

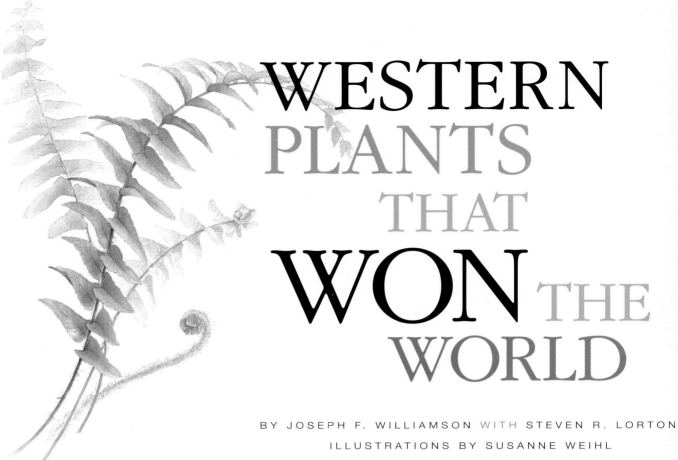

WESTERN PLANTS THAT WON THE WORLD

BY JOSEPH F. WILLIAMSON WITH STEVEN R. LORTON

ILLUSTRATIONS BY SUSANNE WEIHL

Sword fern

Polystichum munitum
Sunset climate zones
4–9, 14–24

From California to Alaska to Montana, this lush green native fern with leathery fronds grows naturally in forests. In the eastern United States, it is most widely used in the Appalachian Mountains, the Hudson Valley, interior New England, and coastal Maine. It's also a favorite in England, where it carpets the ground in woodland plantings. It can take dry or moist soil and shade or some sun.

■ We take them for granted in our gardens. We neglect them, and they thrive anyway. We treat some of them as intruders, removing them from the soil when and if they reseed too readily. Nevertheless, many of the West's native plants are so attractive, durable, and endearing that they have been adopted by gardeners around the world.

These are the real heroes of Western horticulture. Give them a mild climate like ours and they make themselves at home. California poppy, Oregon grape, and coast redwood may be Western namesakes, but they're all just as happy in such places as Australia, Britain, Israel, and New Zealand.

Which of these plants have earned the widest acclaim abroad? Our interviews with garden experts in other mild-climate regions of the world led us to the following 20. They all make splendid garden plants, but save the very largest ones for expansive landscapes.

These 20 plants, native to the western United States, have captivated gardeners around the world. Here's why you should consider growing one or more of them

Wild lilac
Ceanothus
Zones 1–9, 14–24
These beautiful ground-hugging to tree-tall shrubs come mostly from California's dry, rocky slopes. In March and April, they bear flowers in shades of indigo to sky blue above glossy dark green leaves. In Europe, a few of the western U.S. species were hybridized to produce named varieties that are hardier and sometimes handsomer than our originals. These plants do best in sunny locations in well-drained soil and, once established, cannot tolerate summer water.

California fuchsia

Zauschneria (*Epilobium*)
Zones 5–6, 8–9, 14–24

Originally from Arizona, Southern California, and Baja California, this shrubby perennial adapts to all but the coldest climates. Large quantities of orange-red flowers shaped like slender, flaring tubes make a big show and attract hummingbirds from midsummer until frost. It needs full sun and excellent drainage; not for tailored gardens.

MARION BRENNER

Bush anemone
Carpenteria californica
Zones 5–9, 14–24

John C. Frémont discovered this handsome evergreen shrub during the 1840s in its native Sierra Nevada foothills between the Kings and San Joaquin rivers in California. Gertrude Jekyll popularized this summer-blooming plant in England around 1885 when she used it in a garden she designed. It thrives in full sun or part shade and, once established, needs little or no water on the coast (some water inland).

Flannel bush
Fremontodendron californica
Zones 7–24

This rambling shrub, an other discovery by John C Frémont during his travels i the 1840s, is native to th foothills of the Sierr Nevada, to the Coast Range and to the mountains c Southern California. Ga deners in colder climate overseas commonly put where it can bask in the sun even growing it against sunny wall to show off it yellow flowers in summer.

THEODORE PAYNE: WESTERN PLANTS' GREATEST CHAMPION

Long before Westerners paid any attention to our native flora, many of our plants were already at home in England. And it was an Englishman, Theodore Payne, who introduced us to the beauty of our own flowers, shrubs, and trees.

Payne arrived in Southern California in 1893. On long walks in the Santa Ana Mountains, he fell in love with the poppies, lupines, and tidytips that carpeted the land, and he began propagating them.

"There's charm and grace in a milkweed, in a wild parsnip, in a buttercup," he insisted, at a time when most Californians regarded these plants as little more than fodder for cattle.

Undaunted by popular opinion, Payne opened his own nursery. He sold seeds of Western plants in Europe and, in 1906, published a catalog listing 56 varieties of wildflowers.

Gradually, he turned "humble" plants into superstars. "One summer on a trip to Catalina Island, I found a brown seed stalk of giant buckwheat (St. Catherine's lace)," he told a reporter in 1948. "The natives said, 'Just another weed.' But I brought some seeds back anyway and planted them. Later that 'weed' was exhibited at the Santa Barbara Flower Show and people went wild over its lacy flowers. It captured the fancy of growers and found its rightful niche."

Payne died in 1963, but his legacy lives on. He introduced into cultivation 400 to 500 species of Western plants, saving many of them from extinction as housing developments began to wipe out their habitats.

In 1960, the Theodore Payne Foundation, a nonprofit organization for the propagation and preservation of native California flora, was formed. Today, it

sells more than 600 specie of plants at its 23-acre sit in L.A. County. It fills see orders for gardeners as fa away as China and Israel.

During March and Apri the plants are in pea bloom, and along the site' Flowerhill trails, you'll se dazzling wildflowers.

In the nursery at the bas of the hills, plants ar

Gaillardia

All zones

Named for a French botanist in the 1700s, gaillardia is native to the western and central United States. In summer, it bears handsome yellow to rust flowers that are reminiscent of the warm hues of a Southwestern blanket; it's a standout in borders and bouquets. *G. pulchella* is an annual; *G. grandiflora,* developed from the native species, is perennial. Both take full sun and light watering.

grouped by habitat—riparian or chaparral. There's also a bookstore, reference library, and picnic area. Membership (from $20) entitles you to a quarterly newsletter and a 10 percent discount on plants and books. March through May, a wildflower hotline (818/768-3533) offers advice on the best viewing areas in Southern California.

The foundation is at 10459 Tuxford St., Sun Valley, CA 91352, off La Tuna Canyon Rd.; (818) 768-1802. Open 8:30–4:30 Wed-Sun. Seed and plant lists cost $1.

— *Kathleen N. Brenzel*

RICHARD SHIELL

JANET LOUGHREY

California poppy
Eschscholzia californica
All zones

The state flower of California, this beautiful, silky-petaled poppy grows wild in low elevations all over the West. It has also naturalized in lands overseas. Many named varieties now exist, with different heights, compactness, and flower colors (gold, orange, red, pink, white). They bloom most heavily in midspring; in a flower bed, deadhead regularly to extend the season of both flowers and fresh foliage. Give plants full sun; start them from seed in place in fall or early spring.

Pacific Coast iris
Iris douglasiana
Zones 4–24

Native to the Pacific Coast from mid-Oregon to Santa Barbara County, these elegant plants bloom in spring. Stems carrying flowers in a broad range of rich colors grow 1 to 2 feet tall among strappy evergreen leaves 1½ to 2 feet long. An English seed catalog calls it "an aristocratic plant from California." This iris is most at home in meadow, woodland, and rock garden plantings.

NORMAN A. PLATE

Oregon grape
Mahonia aquifolium
Zones 1–21
The state flower of Oregon, this mahonia comes from the Coast Ranges and inland foothills from British Columbia to Northern California. It does much to delight gardeners in similar climates around the world: takes sun or shade and aridity, withstands frost, and produces beautiful yellow flowers March to May.

Matilija poppy
Romneya coulteri
All zones
This robust perennial, discovered by Irish botanist Thomas Coulter in the 1830s, grows naturally in just a few Coast Range arroyos from Santa Barbara to northern Baja. But it takes well to a variety of climates and has been a favorite in the British Isles and New Zealand for many years.

Godetia, farewell-to-spring
Clarkia amoena
All zones
Native from California to British Columbia, these sprawling plants bear papery, cup-shaped pink or lavender blooms during spring and early summer. Flowers of new strains come in a rainbow of sherbet colors. Gardeners abroad and in the eastern United States have told us that Westerners don't appreciate or use godetias enough. Maybe so. An early catalog of the Theodore Payne Foundation calls godetias "the most beautiful of the late-flowering wild flowers" and recommends that they "find a place in every garden." These reliable annuals take full sun and moist soil.

RICHARD SHELL

Western azalea
Rhododendron occidentale
Zones 4–24
These deciduous shrubs, which grow wild in the mountains and foothills of California and Oregon, grow to 10 feet tall. In late spring and early summer, they display fragrant clusters of beautiful, big, funnel-shaped flowers. The plant succeeds mightily in England, where it was introduced in 1851.

Beard tongue
Penstemon
Zones vary by species
Many kinds, mostly from Western mountains to the desert, are available in nurseries (*P. palmeri* is shown above). Gardeners in the Midwest and South now grow these tough, attractive plants. As a group, penstemons are mostly drought-tolerant and pest- and disease-free, but they must have soil with excellent drainage.

POSTCARDS FROM HOME

In Seville, in the middle of summer, I once made the mistake of visiting the Plaza de España at high noon. In the blistering heat, I quickly realized why Spain shuts down for siestas. Sunlight glared off the plaza and the surrounding edifices, and I could almost feel the heat from the pavement penetrating the soles of my shoes. To cool off, I ducked into the surrounding park. And there, in the shadowy canopy of tall trees, I got the eerie feeling I'd arrived back in the American West. This place felt like California.

The trees that cast welcome shade I recognized as California natives—*Washingtonia robusta* and California sycamore (*Platanus racemosa*). They grew beside other plants that favor Mediterranean climates—lemon, crape myrtle, and oleander.

I suppose I shouldn't have been surprised by my discovery: plants from California and the Southwest were often cultivated in the Spanish missions, then found their way back to the plazas and gardens of Spain.

I'm not a Californian. I live in Seattle, where I grow some of these plants. But seeing them in Spain was as good as receiving postcards from home. In fact, to find *any* Western plant in a faraway garden and trace it back to its source is to follow a thrilling, if not swashbuckling, romp through history. — *S. R. L.*

RICHARD SHIELL (3)

Our Lord's candle
Yucca whipplei
Zones 2–24

Native to Southern California mountains, the California coast, and Baja California, this plant forms a stemless cluster of rigid, needle-tipped gray-green leaves. It sends out tall flower spikes—just once (usually in spring)—then dies. Today's travelers might see it growing in the milder temperate climates around the world; it can withstand temperatures as low as 27°.

Coral bells
Heuchera sanguinea
All zones

One of the prettiest Western native perennials, this species comes from Arizona and Mexico. Its flowers are tiny but numerous atop wiry stems. From late spring into summer, they form clouds of blossoms that float above rounded leaves. Plants grow throughout the rest of the United States, except in the Deep South. And they're popular in England.

Lewisia
Zones 1–7, 14–17

Several species are native to the mountains from Montana to Washington to Northern California. *L. rediviva* (bitterroot) is the state flower of Montana. In spring, these beautiful plants bear white to pink daisylike blooms above fleshy leaves. Plants can be difficult; they need excellent drainage (mulch around their crowns with small gravel). They thrive in some winter cold but not too much; plants need full sun to light shade, and light watering once established. Gardeners in most of Britain, as well as interior New England and Appalachia, have adopted this handsome-flowered alpine.

MICHAEL S. THOMPSON

Celebrity trees

Arizona cypress
Cupressus arizonica
Zones 5, 8–24

This spreading conifer (to 40 ft. tall) comes from the arid basin regions of the Southwest, at elevations of 3,000 to 8,000 feet. Wherever it goes, it withstands what it has always experienced in its home range: heat, cold, aridity, and wind. It makes a good windbreak plant because it grows fast and strong right in the face of those winds. It is known and used in the southeastern U.S. magnolia belt, and is a favorite in Australia, New Zealand, Britain, and elsewhere.

California fan palm and Mexican fan palm
Washingtonia filifera and *W. robusta*
Zones 8–10 (warmer parts),
11–24

Canyon springs and moist spots in Arizona, California, and northern Mexico are home to these skinny-trunked palms that seem never to stop getting taller. *W. filifera* grows fast to 60 feet, and *W. robusta* to 100 feet with a more slender trunk. *Washingtonia* palms grow in coastal resorts in Devon, England, and in Seville, Spain, where they have become popular street trees. They thrive wherever warm coastal currents moderate the climate.

Coast redwood
Sequoia sempervirens
Zones 4–9, 14–24

This sweetheart of a huge tree grows naturally in parts of the Coast Ranges from Curry County, Oregon, to Monterey County, California. It performs well at sea level and low elevations in mild climates around the world. With early vertical growth, it shoots up at a rate of 4 feet a year, then slows down some after 15 to 20 years. Showy varieties include 'Aptos Blue' (blue-green foliage), 'Santa Cruz' (light green foliage), and 'Filoli' (as blue as blue spruce). Another type of redwood—*Sequoiadendron giganteum*—grows at Kew Gardens near London, and holds a place in the hearts of many British gardeners as one of the most majestic trees in the world.

Coast silktassel
Garrya elliptica
Zones 5–9, 14–21

This pretty, broad-leafed evergreen tree-shrub (to 20 ft. tall) grows wild from western Oregon to San Luis Obispo, California, in chaparral and thickets and on dry slopes and ridges. It displays pendulous light green catkins for weeks in winter. It seems more loved in England and parts of Australia than at home. In climates colder than California's, it's usually grown in south- and west-facing positions where it can get sun and be protected from wind. ◆

Pure white 'Nuccio's Gem', one of the Nuccio family's hybrids, has formal double flowers with petals arranged in neat swirls around the centers.

Growing great camellias

It's easier than you might think, says Julius Nuccio, whose family has grown them commercially for 63 years

BY SHARON COHOON

"Camellias are like kids," says second-generation nursery-man Julius Nuccio. "They grow up better if you don't hover over them all the time." Don't smother them. Don't drown them. And never overfeed them. Remember those three rules, says Nuccio, and camellia care is a breeze.

Nuccio ought to know. He's the son of Joe Nuccio and the nephew of Julius Nuccio. The senior Nuccios opened Nuccio's Nurseries in Alhambra, California, in 1935. They started the business as a general nursery but quickly decided to specialize in their favorite plants, camellias and azaleas. They introduced their first hybrid camellia in 1950, the year they moved the nursery to nearby Altadena, and have since developed more than 100 others. Their sons—Julius, Tom, and Jim—carry on the tradition.

So what kind of care *do* camellias need? The Nuccios share their advice.

Plant high. Camellias need a lot of oxygen, says Julius. They'll suffocate if their roots can't breathe. Plant them in loose soil, and keep soil and mulch away from their trunks. Dig a hole twice as wide and 1½ times as deep as the rootball. Mound some soil at the bottom of the hole—enough so the top of the rootball is at least an inch or two above the ground. Place the plant on top and fill the hole with equal parts native soil, peat moss, and perlite. Substitute oak leaf mold for peat if you can find it at a nursery, and add compost if you have it. (Use the same blend for pots—potting soil is too light.)

Tamp the soil mixture firmly, making sure the root crown remains slightly above soil level. Create a water basin around the plant with surplus soil. Fill the basin with water.

Water as needed. Camellias like moist but not soggy conditions. "Give them a deep soaking when you water," Julius advises, "but then let the first couple of inches of soil dry out before you water again." Water less in winter, more in summer. Be guided by weather and soil conditions, he says, not set schedules.

Fertilize in spring and summer. Next to smothering and drowning, overfeeding is the offense most frequently committed against camellias, according to the Nuccios. Although it may seem natural to reward a plant with a hefty dose of fertilizer for producing buds and flowers, resist the temptation with camellias, which are actually dormant from September through March. Fertilizing camellias then is a waste of time and money. Wait to feed camellias until they begin actively growing again in April.

Use an acid plant food with a low nitrogen content. Cottonseed meal is a cool fertilizer—released gradually by bacterial action in the soil—so the risk of fertilizer burn is minimal. "Plus, it's inexpensive," says Julius. Apply half the recommended dosage, and water plants before feeding. Feed the plants again in June, and once more in August. Then stop.

Watch for diseases. Camellia blight, a fungal disease that causes the center of the flower to turn brown and rot, is a nuisance. "Mostly it's a headache for growers and hobbyists, not homeowners with only two or three shrubs," says Julius. If blight occurs, pick infected flowers from plants and dispose of all fallen petals and flowers.

Protect plants from sun. Camellias don't like afternoon sun. Plant them where they'll get morning sun and afternoon shade, or dappled light throughout the day. Sasanquas are the exception, says Julius. "They can take full sun even in hot, dry climates." Despite their delicate appearance, camellias can survive considerable cold. Sasanquas and Japonicas can endure temperatures as low as 5° to 10°. Reticulatas, though, are tender.

… and enjoy them. Camellia care, in summary, is a lot like parenthood: get plants off to a good start, then stop babying them.

SHOPPING FOR CAMELLIAS?
Nuccio's sells camellias by mail as well as at the nursery at 3555 Chaney Trail, Altadena. For a free catalog, write to Box 6160, Altadena, CA 91003, or call (818) 794-3383. ◆

In the living room, a 10-foot-tall pigmy date palm lends an airy tropical flavor, which is accented by bromeliads around its base (*Guzmania* 'Tutti-Frutti', an *Aechmea* hybrid, and *Tillandsia xerographica*).

JAMIE HADLEY

Interior design—with plants

Professional tips for decorating with indoor plants

BY LAUREN BONAR SWEZEY

When Davis Dalbok walks into a room, he doesn't just casually admire it. He scrutinizes every detail—fabric and wall colors, the height of the ceiling, the intensity of daylight washing through windows. All these factors weigh heavily on his decorating decisions, just as they would for an interior designer. But Dalbok's point of view is different—he decorates with plants, not furnishings.

Dalbok, an interior plantsman and owner of Living Green, a plant and design store in San Francisco, works with palms, orchids, bromeliads, and other lush vegetation from around the globe.

He uses them like living sculptures. "Decorating with house plants has come a long way since the '70s, when every home had a Boston fern," says Dalbok. "Now, house plants are more exotic, and an integral part of interior design."

To view some of Dalbok's latest work, we visited the home of interior designer Tricia Rissmann in Oakland. As the photos on these pages show, Dalbok used plants in bold yet simple designs for the main living areas and in striking, often surprising, small arrangements for tabletops and counters. Use Dalbok's guidelines at right to inspire your house-scaping designs.

A DESIGNER'S GUIDE TO HOUSE-SCAPING

• *Consider the desired look or style.* Does the room need a sculptural focal point (a pigmy date palm, for example)? Or something more neutral (like a bamboo palm) that won't compete with the decor? Do you want a plant that's spiky or soft, bold or delicate, exotic or formal? "When you get down to it, it's all a matter of personal taste," says Davis Dalbok.

• *Choose contrasting or complementary colors.* The basic foliage may be dark green, light green, gray, or variegated. Add other foliage (caladiums, coleus) and flowers that are richly colored. Match them with the decor or contrast with existing colors.

• *Analyze environmental factors.* Consider air circulation, temperature, proximity of heating vents, and—most important—the quality of light. Most house plants don't thrive in low light, but a few tolerate it. "The troopers of low light are cast-iron plant, *Dracaena fragrans, D. deremensis* 'Janet Craig', *D. massangeana,* pothos, and spathiphyllum," says Dalbok.

• *Plan for growth.* Select plants that won't quickly outgrow the space. Some fast-growing plants (ficus) can be pruned once a year or so. Others (fishtail or pigmy date palm) can't be pruned because of their growth habit, and must be replaced when they outgrow a space.

• *Consider height for effect.* Even if you have a high ceiling, you may not want to draw attention to it, so you might select a tree that only reaches two-thirds of the way up.

• *More isn't necessarily better.* Instead of filling a room with dozens of plants, which can be a maintenance nightmare, display one or two specimen plants for simple drama, then top a table with an accent arrangement.

• *Don't crowd plants.* They should look comfortable in their spaces. Choose narrow, upright

TOP: Two *Dracaena marginata* plants, in antique red brass urns, add graceful symmetry to the dining room. On the table, in a bronze bowl from India, *Oncidium* bursts over *Tillandsia juncea*.

ABOVE: Making a splash on a bath counter, a ceramic seashell from Vietnam is filled with sculptural *Tillandsia*, including *T. caput-medusae*, *T. chiapensis*, *T. harrisii*, *T. juncea*, and *T. meridionalis*.

LEFT: Displayed on a small table, white *Dendrobium* and *Tillandsia tectorum* make an elegant pair in a gunmetal-colored ceramic planter.

plants for tight spaces; use sprawling plants only in wide, open areas.

• *Underplant for added interest.* Grow small plants beneath taller ones. "I try to create the illusion that smaller plants are springing forth from the base of the tall one," says Dalbok. He prefers long-blooming plants such as orchids (which can flower for two months) and bromeliads, including flowering tillandsias (whose blooms can hold for as long as six months). For greenery, Dalbok depends on ferns, elephant's ear (*Alocasia*), creeping fig, and plants with colorful foliage.

• *Choose a suitable container.* "Containers should be an artful element of the design," says Dalbok. "Take signals from the interior's color and style. Any vessel that can contain a plant will work. We've used everything from old, battered copper cauldrons to antique wooden drums from Java." ◆

Clematis vines climb a twiggy trellis shaped like a four-panel screen. For details on this eye-catching structure, see page 36.

February

gardenguide

Dawn redwood: leafless sculpture in winter (left), lush foliage in summer.

This redwood bares its branches

■ Evergreens are so widespread in the West that gardeners are often startled when a conifer drops its needles and goes naked in the winter. Yet we have a strong selection of deciduous conifers, including bald cypress (*Taxodium distichum*), dawn redwood (*Metasequoia glyptostroboides*), and larches (*Larix* species).

Dawn redwood, shown here in Lakewold Gardens south of Tacoma, is the most popular, and for good reason. This tree puts on a four-season show. In spring, its delicate branchlets bear needles that emerge pale chartreuse, deepen to bright green in summer, then turn coppery orange in au-

tumn before dropping to expose the tree's conical branch structure and handsome, reddish-brown bark.

In the landscape, dawn redwood makes a dramatic state-ment, whether standing alone on a lawn or planted among other evergreens. It's also a good candidate for a quick screen: dawn redwood can produce 4 to 6 feet of growth in a year, eventually reaching a height of 80 to 90 feet. This tree is hardy in *Sunset* climate zones 3 through 7. It requires little, if any, pruning. Now, while the dawn redwood is dormant, is an ideal time to plant. Nurseries offer trees in 1-, 5-, and 15-gallon cans. — *Steven R. Lorton*

seed pans

During Victorian times, gardeners filled the conservatories of English estates with exotic plants. Most of these plants weren't available at nurseries and so were often started from seed sown in handmade terra-cotta seed pans. Today, these practical pans are being reproduced in England in two sizes. The large pans (10½ inches long, 6½ inches wide, and 2½ inches deep) are perfect for sowing seeds of flowers and vegetables that you need in quantity. The small ones (7¾ by 4½ by 2¼ inches) are best for starting seeds of specialty plants or vegetables. The pans, available by mail from Kinsman Company (800/733-4146), cost $9.95 (large) and $6.95 (small), plus shipping. — *Lauren Bonar Swezey*

NEW ROSES

Give her Romantica

■ Just in time for Valentine's Day, Romantica roses are destined to win the hearts of many gardeners. These sturdy, disease-resistant plants were developed in France by the House of Meilland and introduced in the United States by the Conard-Pyle Company.

"Romantica roses are very modern in habit and color, and old-fashioned in fragrance and look," says Jacques Ferare, assistant vice president for Conard-Pyle.

The first six introductions in the series have the controlled growth habit of Hybrid Tea (HT) or Floribunda (F) roses. Plants re-

bloom freely. Shop for these roses at full-service nurseries, or order by mail from Wayside Gardens (800/845-1124).

'Abbaye de Cluny' (HT, 5 feet tall): apricot with yellow highlights. *'Auguste Renoir'* (HT, 6 feet tall): deep pink, cup-shaped bloom. *'Frederic Mistral'* (HT, 6 feet tall): medium pink, full hybrid-tea bloom. *'Guy de Maupassant'* (F, 6 feet tall): carmine pink, many-petaled flowers. *'Toulouse Lautrec'* (HT, 5 feet tall): very full, lemon yellow flowers. *'Yves Piaget'* (HT, 5 feet tall): mauve pink, peony-shaped flowers. — *L. B. S.*

Perennial perfection in Vail

■ In winter, Barbara DeVoe's plants sleep beneath a blanket of snow 4 to 6 feet deep, which insulates them against the bitter cold. Perched on a steep hillside above Vail, Colorado, her garden is a virtual catalog of the best perennials for the high Rockies. And for good reason: DeVoe pretests many plants that are eventually grown in the Betty Ford Alpine Garden, where she has served as director of operations. "When they do well for me at 9,000 feet, they usually don't have problems 600 feet lower in Vail," she says.

Despite the diversity of her private collection, DeVoe weaves the plants into a cohesive tapestry. "When I plant, I'm thinking about how colors will blend," she explains, "and I try to work with heights, so that things stay balanced." Her rear garden is shown here. The shortest plants, mostly Irish and Scotch moss, carpet the flagstone path. Slightly taller plants, including geraniums, *Heuchera,* lady's-mantle, *Lamium maculatum,* and sweet woodruff crowd along the path. Farther back, columbines, Maltese cross, phlox, Russell lupines, and Shasta daisies compete for space with everything from poppies to veronica. Her favorite plants are gentians and primroses.

— *Jim McCauslan*

CHAD SLATTERY

Waves of shrubs transform a slope

■ When Dingeman and Rebecca Kalis step out onto the stone patio that perches above the softly shrouded slope of their Pasadena, California, garden, they see a valley below and foothills in the distance through the silvery frames of eucalyptus trunks. With a vista like this to enjoy, the Kalises figured their garden ought to be simple, so it would complement rather than compete with the view. Because it wasn't simple, they called in landscape architect Denis Kurutz to fix it.

Kurutz first stripped away the existing terraces, restoring the site's former slope, then replaced the lawn and ivy with pillowy plants whose rounded shapes echo the contours of the nearby foothills. He planted breath of heaven (*Coleonema pulchrum*), New Zealand tea tree (*Leptospermum scoparium*) and strawberry guava (*Psidium cattleianum*) in waves that run down slope (in colder inland areas—*Sunset* climate zone 14—strawberry guava needs a sheltered location). A carpet of autumn moor grass (*Sesleria autumnalis*) knits everything together.

During sunny months the subtle variations in the foliage texture of these grasses and shrubs are pleasing enough. But when the skies turn leaden and rain clouds obscure the view, these shrubs kick into bloom. It a rare garden that peaks in late winter, but pumping up the color for the season makes perfect sense at this site.

— *Sharon Cohoo*

GARDEN DESIGN

Capture the spirit of the desert

"I looked for the gnarliest, oldest tree I could find," says landscape architect Christy Ten Eyck. She found the ideal candidate—a littleleaf palo verde (*Cercidium microphyllum*)—and it became the focal point of this planting in Paradise Valley, Arizona. The tree's twisted branches and lacy foliage cast light shade that perfectly suits the plants beneath it—an assortment of flowering perennials, including sunny yellow desert-marigold (*Baileya multiradiata*)

and red and pink penstemon (*P. eatonii* and *P. parryi*, respectively). Designed to capture the spirit of the desert, this composition could be re-created anywhere in *Sunset* climate zones 11 through 13, which include Las Vegas, Phoenix, and Tucson.

Just as splashes of flowers enliven this garden, cobalt blue window frames relieve the subdued earth tones of the adobe house. Ten Eyck chose blue-toned plants to establish a visual link

between the landscape and the structure. *Salvia chamaedryoides* (foreground) presents an attractive combination of bright blue flowers and silvery foliage.

Creosote bushes (*Larrea tridentata*) are planted throughout the landscape; their yellow flowers appear sporadically all year. On days when raindrops spatter the bushes, their leaves release the musky creosote odor that is the scent of the desert itself. — *Judy Mielke*

Tougher breeds of blueberries

■ Blueberries are finicky about winter temperatures. If winters are warm, plants don't get enough chill to set fruit. If it gets too cold, they freeze and die. Recently, breeders have released varieties better suited to these temperature extremes.

Where winters are cold (*Sunset* zones 1–3), try one of these extra-hardy deciduous varieties. 'Chippewa' grows 3 to 4 feet tall and produces 4 to 7 pounds of fruit. 'Northsky' is hardy to -40°, grows 18 inches tall, and yields 1 to 2 pounds of fruit.

Where winters are milder, consider 'Sunshine Blue' (shown at right). It requires only 150 chill hours—with temperatures below 45°—to set fruit. This evergreen plant is compact (less than 4 feet), hardy to 10°, and yields up to 10 pounds of berries at maturity.

All three varieties are available by mail from Raintree Nursery (360/496-6400).—*S.C.*

Twiggy trellis for clematis

■ What can you do with a very narrow planting bed that's snuggled up against a blank stucco wall? Kent Gordon England of Campbell, California, may have hit upon the perfect solution: a twiggy trellis that's as interesting to look at as the vine it supports (see photograph on page 30).

England designed the 8-foot-tall trellis of birch prunings. Shaped like a four-panel screen, it embellishes two stucco walls in the corner of an elevated brick patio.

The vertical branches of the trellis are spaced 30 inches apart. To allow twining room behind them for vines, they're attached to 1½-inch-long birch-plug spacers that have been screwed into the wall. White-barked birch branches form a horizontal grid; starting 32 inches from the ground, they're spaced about 2 feet apart, and ar screwed to the vertical branches. Th trellis's arching tops are formed by bu dles of delicate, whiplike birch twig held together (and to the framework with copper wire.

Clematis vines climb the trellis; flo ering perennials such as coral bell Swan River daisies, and 'Moonshin yarrow grow at their feet.

The trellis was built by Whiteh Landscape of Cupertino, California.
— *Peter O. Whitel*

CURTIS ANDERSON

Give your spade an edge

■ A sharp edge helps a spade slid through soil, sod, and roots with r markable ease. Most spades are u sharpened when you buy them, hov ever, and work about as well as a butt knife on steak.

You can sharpen spades with a inch bench grinder (about $60). Or u a mill bastard file (less than $10) hand-sharpen spades, as shown her Follow the blade's original bevel, an file away from the tool head. When t edge is sharp, rub oil over the rest the blade to protect it from rust. —*J. l*

Pacific Northwest Garden Notebook

BY STEVEN R. LORTON

Last February, I was glad to welcome Alaska readers back to the Pacific Northwest edition of *Sunset,* and I invited them to write and tell us about their gardens. The response was overwhelming, and the gardens were so intriguing that I decided to take a grand garden tour around the state. I can confidently report that Alaskans garden like they live: with rambunctious abandon and on a scale to match the size of the West's largest state—all 591,004 square miles of it.

Now it's February again, and in Alaska the snow is piled high and the thermometer rarely climbs above 0°. But neither snow nor freezing cold can stop Alaska gardeners from pursuing their passion.

In Anchorage, for example, Jerry McEwen is probably busy making plant labels, building trellises in his workshop, and knocking snow off his lilac standards so they won't break under the weight. On nights when the moon is full, Jerry's winter garden is dazzling; the moonshine reflected by the snow is brighter than the sunlight at high noon this time of year.

In Willow, north of Anchorage, Les Brake is poring over seed catalogs and getting his grow-light system ready; he'll sow seed in flats by midmonth. Meanwhile, at the Willow Public Library, Ann Dixon is guiding patrons (some of whom come in on skis or snowmobiles) to the hefty collection of garden books.

In Homer, at the southern end of the Kenai Peninsula, Sue Klinker is starting annual poppies in her greenhouse now for transplanting outside in mid-May. Local garden columnist Rosemary Fitzpatrick is advising readers to note the places where snow piles up the most because those will be the last spots to warm up in spring.

Throughout the state, gardeners are hoping to avoid visits from moose, who come to nibble the tender young shoots of trees and shrubs. But Bud Sherfield of Chickaloon puts these huge mammals in perspective: "You've got your slugs down there; we've got moose up here."

The fact is, Alaska's gardeners don't let winter stop them. They work year-round to perfect their gardens. So if you've succumbed to a case of the winter blahs, think about your fellow gardeners in Alaska, and get up, get out, and get going!

that's a good question ...

Q: Will *Sunset* be having a lecture series again this year at the Northwest Flower and Garden Show? I'd like to come.
— *Peggie Garrison, Juneau*

A: Yes. For the 10th year in a row, *Sunset* will sponsor a series of more than 100 lectures and demonstrations covering a wide range of horticultural topics. This show runs February 4 through 8 at the Washington State Convention Center in Seattle. The presentations are given continuously during show hours: 9 A.M. to 9:30 P.M. Wednesday through Saturday, 9 to 7 Sunday. For more information, call (800) 229-6311.

(Editor's note: dates and times in this article were valid for 1998; schedules will vary from year to year.)

Northern California Garden Notebook

BY LAUREN BONAR SWEZEY

Sometime around the first of January, I get thoroughly fed up with my bedraggled roses and declare to my family that the next weekend will be devoted to pruning them. But no matter how determined I am, I never seem to get to it until February. Fortunately, my roses don't seem to care. February's still a great month to prune roses (and any other deciduous tree or shrub).

When I finally do get out in the garden, I always arm myself with shears and my favorite Garden Rose Gloves—made of cotton, they're coated with a dense, rubberlike material that resists thorns. To find a local source or order by mail, call De Van Koek (800/992-1220).

What you'll never find in my garden is that gunky black pruning sealer. Years ago, I learned that using it to seal wounds does more harm than good. So when I heard about NuBark Natural Rose Stick Pruning Sealer and NuBark Pruning Sealer Paste, both made of lanolin, beeswax, and other natural compounds, I wondered if I should recommend them for pruning cuts on woody plants. They sounded better than the sticky black stuff. According to Alison Berry, associate professor of environmental horticulture at UC Davis, these products might help prevent wounds from drying out in some tree species, but the effect on most plants would be minor.

A much better solution is to prune correctly during the dormant season. Follow the guidelines on pages 50–51 and the pruning cuts should heal readily without a sealer.

VIDEOS TO DREAM BY

February is a wonderful time to design your spring garden. But beautiful landscaping first takes inspiration, then a good plan. I love to browse through books, but I've discovered two videos that really bring gardens to life: *The Great Gardens of England,* which features Hidcote Manor, Mottisfont Abbey, and Sissinghurst Castle, and *English Cottage and Country Gardens.* Both videos are produced by the Larkspur Company. For more information, write Box 938, Larkspur, CA 94977; or call (800) 772-4884.

The cinematography in these videos is gorgeous, and I find plenty of design and planting ideas for my own garden. I particularly enjoy the visits to each cottage garden and listening to the owners discuss their achievements.

The videos can be purchased directly from the producer for $19.95 each (plus tax and shipping).

that's a good question ...

Q: I'm looking for a specialty retail nursery that sells a wide variety of ornamental grasses. — *Los Altos, California*

A. Baylands Nursery (1165 Weeks St., East Palo Alto, CA 650/323-1645) sells more than 50 kinds of ornamental grasses. To find other specialty nurseries, check out *Where on Earth: A Guide to Specialty Nurseries and Other Resources for California Gardeners,* by Barbara Stevens and Nancy Conner (Heyday Books, Berkeley, CA, 1997; $12.95, 510/549-3564).

Southern California Garden Notebook

BY SHARON COHOON

Every cloud, wrote some Pollyanna, has a silver lining. But when the storms roll in and the snails slide out, it's hard not to be grumpy. When those leaf-munching mollusks emerge, the urge to annihilate the lot on the spot is powerful. But before you reach for your snail bait, read on.

Snails and slugs are like house cats, contends Leland Miyano. Without a powerful lure to draw them away, they stick close to home. Snail bait contains such an enticement. It's what lures snails to their death. So when you set it out, says Miyano, you're attracting your neighbors' snails as well as your own to the deadly feast. And the ones you don't slay may stay.

Miyano, a Honolulu landscape designer, artist, amateur botanist, and horticultural writer, knows his gastropods. He maintains a veritable arboretum of endemic Hawaiian and rescued rain-forest plants in his home garden in the rain-swept hills of Kahaluu—slug paradise, surely—without using any chemicals.

Instead of relying on snail bait, suggests Miyano, conduct search-and-destroy missions. Find out where the enemies sleep—often not the same place they feed—and harvest them. (In my yard, for instance, fortnight lilies, which never show chomp marks, are a favorite snail hideout.) Also try not to plant things snails relish (succulents, for instance) en masse. "Slugs follow each other's trail scents to these favored spots," he says. Finally, before transferring nursery plants to your own garden, check them for stowaways. Since mollusks don't wander far, says Miyano, any strays you miss can be rounded up on the next walk-through.

STILL TOO WET TO PLANT?

Banish the need-to-dig blues with the garden video *An American Gardener at the Chelsea Flower Show,* narrated by Lew Whitney of Roger's Gardens in Newport Beach. Great behind-the-scenes tidbits, and no crowds. It costs $29.95 at Roger's, an additional $4.95 if ordered by mail (888/357-7469). Or pick up *The Sensuous Garden,* by Montagu Don (Simon & Schuster, New York, 1997; $32.50). Delicious photos, charming text. I particularly like Don's parting sentence: "Gardening is like sex: if everyone involved is happy, then you are doing it right."

that's a good question ...

Q: Do I have to live without roses in Tehachapi?

A: "No," says Ed Sampson, owner and chief horticulturist of the Mourning Cloak Ranch and Botanical Garden in Tehachapi. Roses bloom beautifully here, in spite of the strong winds and near-zero winter temperatures. Rugosa roses are the safest choice, but many David Austins do just fine, and so does 'Iceberg'. Sampson propagates the unpatented roses he's had the most success with and sells them, as well as patented varieties, on February 7 and 8 at the garden. For details, call (805) 822-1661.

MARINA THOMPSON

Westerner's Garden Notebook

BY JIM McCAUSLAND

every February, I prowl the countryside looking for damp places where pussy willows grow. When I locate a stand, I cut a handful of the catkin-covered twigs, which are as soft and furry as a rabbit's toes. I bring the cuttings back home and arrange them in a vase of water. As the catkins gradually open, they whisper spring to me.

Kept in water, the catkins quickly turn gold with pollen. If you want to keep them furry and pollen-free, display them in a dry vase (once they dry out, they'll keep for years). Only male willows bear catkins, so not every plant produces the irresistible fuzzy twigs. Classic catkins come from *Salix discolor,* a shrub or small tree (to 25 feet tall) that grows across the northern tier of the United States. Farther south, scouler willow (*S. scouleriana*) also produces catkins, but this tree gets too big (to 50 feet tall) for most gardens.

If you'd rather buy than forage a willow for your garden—one that's been selected for the beauty of its catkins—pick up a French pussy willow (*S. caprea*), with its pinkish-gray catkins, or perhaps the rose-gold pussy willow (*S. gracilistyla*).

But before you plant a pussy willow in your yard, remember that its roots are capable of invading water and sewer lines. It may be wiser to admire cuttings in a vase.

CITRUS BY THE BOOK

Having grown up grazing on kumquats, lemons, and oranges from neighborhood trees, I was glad to see *Citrus,* by Lance Walheim (Ironwood Press, Tucson, 1996; $16.95, 888/601-

0824). Whether you grow citrus outdoors or in the house, o you're simply a citrus fruit aficionado, this book will satisf your appetite with solid information and luscious pho tographs. Walheim, a frequent contributor to *Sunset* and a ci rus rancher, knows his stuff. He puts each kind of citrus fru into perspective and offers plant selection advice keyed to Ar zona's deserts. For the low desert (Phoenix area), Walheir recommends 'Valencia' oranges, lemons, grapefruit, or pun meloes (pummelo-grapefruit hybrids 'Oroblanco' and 'Melc gold' show promise). For the intermediate desert (Tucson try more cold-hardy mandarins like 'Fairchild', 'Fremont', o 'Fortune'. For the coldest parts of the Southwest, he suggest growing dwarf citrus like calamondins, kumquats, lemons, o limes in pots indoors in winter, outdoors in summer.

A WELL-ILLUSTRATED GUIDE TO INDOOR PLANTS

My favorite pictorial books about plants, bar none, are thos done by Roger Phillips and Martyn Rix. Their previous worl on bulbs, perennials, and trees have proved indispensable t me, so I was delighted to pick up their latest two-volume se *Indoor and Greenhouse Plants* (Random House, New Yor 1997; $29.95 each). These large-format paperbacks contai an exquisite collection of photographs. I most appreciate th information Phillips and Rix provide on each plant's nativ range. For example, when you know that *Ficus benjamina* home turf extends from India to the Philippines, where grows "in rocky places by streams in rainforest and on e posed rocks," you understand why this tree is so shade-tole ant, water-loving, and adaptable to poor soil when it's grow indoors.

that's a good question ...

Q: How should I orient my vegetable garden?

A. A standard rectangular bed should run along an east-west axis. The goal is to give sun-loving plants as much light as possible. Put tall plants like corn, beans, and staked tomatoes on the north side, shorter ones like squash and peppers on the south. Remember that in summer the sun swings across the southern sky for most of the day, so plants tend to cast shadows to the north; that's why tall ones should go at the north rear of the garden.

Pacific Northwest Checklist

PLANTING & SHOPPING

☑ **BARE-ROOT STOCK. Zones 4–7:** Trees, shrubs, vines, and cane berries can all be planted. It's best to put them in the ground as soon as you get them, but if you can't, pack the roots in damp compost, sawdust, or soil, and keep them out of direct sun. In zones 1–3, bare-root planting comes later in the spring.

☑ **FLOWERING SHRUBS, TREES.** Shop nurseries for winter-blooming shrubs and trees, including coast silk-tassel (*Garrya elliptica*), Cornelian cherry (*Cornus mas*), February daphne (*D. mezereum*), fragrant winter hazel (*Corylopsis glabrescens*), *Stachyurus praecox,* and wintersweet (*Chimonanthus praecox*).

☑ **PEAS. Zones 4–7:** You can plant peas outside this month. Give them a head start by soaking seeds in water overnight, then place them between layers of damp paper towels on a cookie sheet and set in a warm place. Use a spray bottle of water to keep the towels damp. Once the peas have sprouted, plant them.

☑ **PRIMROSES.** Blooming plants in 4-inch pots will be everywhere this month. In zones 4–7, you can plant them outdoors in beds or pots. Or grow them indoors, repotted, or with their plastic pots grouped in a handsome container and topped with moss. Keep plants evenly moist to prolong bloom. Fill the sink with water and let potted plants soak overnight once a week or so.

MAINTENANCE

☑ **CHECK STORED BULBS.** Look over the bulbs you've been storing through the winter. If any are shriveled, sprinkle a bit of water on them to rehydrate them. If any show signs of rot, toss them out. Dahlia tubers are the exception: cut out the bad spots, dust wounds with sulfur, and store tubers apart from the rest.

☑ **FEED HOUSE PLANTS.** Days are short, light is low, and most house plants are dormant now. In general, house plants should be fed from April through October. The exceptions are plants that are in bloom or fruit; feed these monthly with a complete liquid house plant food mixed to manufacturer's directions, or every other week with the same food mixed to half-strength.

☑ **PRUNE ROSES. Zones 4–7:** George Washington's birthday is the traditional time for pruning roses. Remove injured or dead canes, cut the remaining ones back to 6 to 8 inches long, then prune plants so canes form a vase shape. Each cut cane should have one strong, outward-facing bud. In zones 1–3, wait until April to prune.

DEBRA LAMBERT

PEST & WEED CONTROL

☑ **BATTLE SLUGS.** When the temperature rises, slugs crawl out to eat—primroses are a prime target. Spread bait around plants and rocks, in ground covers, and along the foundation of the house. Make sure children and pets can't get at the poison bait.

☑ **WEED.** The weeds you pull now will never get the chance to steal soil nutrients from valuable plants. ◆

Northern California Checklist

PLANTING

☑ **BUY FLOWERING PLANTS. Zones 7–9, 14–17:** Nurseries should have a good selection of early-spring-blooming shrubs and vines. Try azalea, camellia, Carolina jessamine, daphne, flowering quince, forsythia, hardenbergia, heath, or primrose jasmine.

☑ **PLANT BARE-ROOT LILACS. Zones 7–9, 14–17:** The most economical way to purchase lilacs is to buy them bare-root. Call around to nurseries this month to find out who still sells bare-root plants. If you can't find them bare-root, buy them in containers, a form that most nurseries carry this time of year.

☑ **PLANT GLADIOLUS. Zones 7–9, 14–17:** For gladiolus from spring through fall, begin planting corms this month and make successive plantings every 15 to 25 days through July.

☑ **PLANT VEGETABLES. Zones 7–9, 14–17:** Set out artichokes and asparagus, and seedlings of broccoli, cabbage, cauliflower, celery (only in zones 15–17), green onions, kohlrabi, and lettuce. Sow seeds of beets, carrots, chard, lettuce, peas, and spinach. Indoors, sow seeds of eggplant, pepper, and tomato using bottom heat (from a heating coil, or set containers on a water heater until seeds germinate, then move them into bright light); allow six to eight weeks for seedlings to reach transplant size.

Sunset
CLIMATE ZONES
- ☐ Mountain (1-2)
- ☐ Valley (7-9)
- ☐ Inland (14)
- ☐ Coastal (15-17)

DEBRA LAMBERT

☑ **START VEGETABLES. Zones 1–2:** To get a jump on the season, start seeds of broccoli, cabbage, and cauliflower indoors or in a greenhouse at the end of the month. When seedlings are ready to plant (in six to eight weeks) and the ground can be worked, set them out and drape with floating row covers.

☑ **START SPECIALTY TOMATOES. Zones 7–9, 14–17:** Some of the tastiest varieties for Northern California are 'Brandywine', 'Gardener's Delight', 'Green Grape', and 'Stupice' (available from Tomato Growers Supply Co., 941/768-1119). Start seeds this month for planting outside during April.

MAINTENANCE

☑ **CUT BACK WOODY PLANTS. Zones 7–9, 14–17:** To stimulate new, lush growth on artemisia, butterfly bush, fuchsia, and Mexican bush sage, cut back woody stems close to the ground. If left unpruned, plants get leggy and scraggly-looking.

☑ **MAINTAIN HUMMINGBIRD FEEDERS.** Change nectar every three to four days and wash feeders thoroughly each time. To make nectar, in a pan mix 4 parts water with 1 part granulated sugar. Heat to dissolve the sugar, then cool. Store leftovers in the refrigerator.

☑ **RECYCLE GARDEN CONTAINERS.** Many nurseries reuse plastic flats and containers or return them to growers. Instead of throwing them away after setting out plants, ask your nursery if it takes them back. If it doesn't, you can probably take the ones that have a 1 or a 2 marked on the bottom to your local recycling center.

PEST CONTROL

☑ **SPRAY FOR PEACH LEAF CURL. Zones 7–9, 14–17:** Around mid- to late February, when buds are beginning to swell on your peach trees but before any green foliage appears, apply a dormant spray to prevent peach leaf curl. This fungus distorts peach leaves and destroys the fruit. Use lime sulfur with a spreader-sticker to improve coverage; do not spray when rain is predicted to fall within 36 hours. ◆

Southern California Checklist

PLANTING

☑ **PLANT PERENNIAL WILDFLOW-ERS.** In the low desert (zone 13), it's time to set out coreopsis, evening primrose, penstemon, salvia, and *Tagetes lemmonii.*

☑ **PLANT SUMMER BULBS.** If you get glads into the ground now in zones 14–24, they'll bloom before thrips attack and disfigure foliage and flowers. Nurseries are well stocked with gladiolus corms this month. Other summer bulbs to look for and plant now are callas, crinums, dahlias, daylilies, glory lilies, tigridia, and tuberoses.

☑ **PLANT FOR WINTER COLOR.** In frost-free areas it's not too late to set out winter bedding plants. If the soil is too soggy, plant in containers. Good candidates include African daisies, calendulas, cineraria, dianthus, Iceland poppies, lobelia, pansies, primroses, snapdragons, and violas.

☑ **SHOP FOR WINTER-BLOOMING SHRUBS.** Select camellias and azaleas at nurseries while in flower, but resist planting them if the ground is still soggy. Wait until the soil dries out enough to be crumbly, then plant. Other winter-blooming shrubs to look for include *Erica canaliculata,* Geraldton waxflower, and New Zealand tea tree (*Leptospermum scoparium*). February is also an excellent time to add to your orchid collection—cymbidiums are in peak bloom this month.

Sunset
CLIMATE ZONES
1-3 7-9 11 13 14-24

DEBRA LAMBERT

MAINTENANCE

☑ **DRAIN STANDING WATER.** If water is pooling around plants, dig small, temporary trenches to let the water flow away. Few plants tolerate soggy roots for very long.

☑ **FINISH DORMANT-SEASON PRUNING.** Before spring growth appears, finish pruning stone-fruit trees, rosebushes, grapes, and other deciduous shrubs, trees, and vines. Consult a good pruning reference for specific instructions for each plant.

☑ **FEED PERMANENT PLANTS.** Feed ground covers, roses, shrubs, perennials, and trees. One quick method is to scatter all-purpose granular fertilizer before a storm is expected and let the rain do the watering-in. For more gradual feeding, apply a slow-release food such as cottonseed meal, bonemeal, or well-rotted manure.

☑ **TEND LAWNS.** Cool-season lawns such as tall fescue and ryegrasses grow quickly this time of year. Cut them frequently, weather permitting, with mower blades set low—$1\frac{1}{2}$ to $1\frac{3}{4}$ inches. Feed the lawns this month, too.

PEST AND WEED CONTROL

☑ **APPLY DORMANT SPRAY.** To eliminate a lot of pesky problems later this spring, spray deciduous plants with horticultural oil. Spray rosebushes early this month, before they leaf out, to smother mites, sawfly larvae, scale, and other overwintering insects. To prevent peach leaf curl and other fungal diseases in deciduous fruit trees, add lime sulfur or fixed copper to the oil, following label directions, and spray trees before flower buds open. Spray branches, crotches, trunk, and the ground beneath the tree's drip line.

☑ **CONTROL CRABGRASS.** To prevent seeds of crabgrass and other annual weeds from germinating later this spring, apply a preemergence herbicide to lawns early this month.

☑ **TRAP GOPHERS.** The reproductive season is just beginning for gophers, so trapping now means fewer to deal with this summer. ◆

Mountain Checklist

PLANTING & SHOPPING

☑ **BARE-ROOT PLANTS.** If the soil can be worked where you live, you can plant bare-root stock. Nurseries carry small fruits like grapes and strawberries; cane fruits like blackberries and raspberries; all kinds of ornamental, fruit, and shade trees; and even vegetables like asparagus and horseradish.

☑ **HARDY PERENNIALS.** In milder parts of the intermountain West, start seeds of delphinium, hellebore, veronica, and viola in a coldframe or greenhouse for transplanting when at least two sets of true leaves appear (and when ground can be worked).

☑ **SEED.** Place your seed orders for spring planting this month, before suppliers run out of popular and unusual varieties.

☑ **VEGETABLES.** Indoors or in a greenhouse, start the seeds of cool-season vegetables such as broccoli, cabbage, cauliflower, Chinese vegetables, kale, and lettuce about six weeks before planting time in your region. In many areas, indoor sowing should be done late this month.

☑ **WILDFLOWERS.** Sow seeds of hardy wildflowers in prepared, weed-free soil. Most will bloom this season, but some of the perennials and biennials common to most wildflower mixes won't bloom until their second growing season.

Sunset
CLIMATE ZONES
☐ 1-3   ☐ 10-11

DEBRA LAMBERT

MAINTENANCE

☑ **CHECK STORED BULBS, PRODUCE.** Look over stored corms, tubers, and produce for shriveling and rot. You can usually rehydrate shriveled bulbs by sprinkling them with a little water. Discard any that show signs of decay except dahlia tubers: cut the bad spots out of those, dust with sulfur, and store apart from the rest.

☑ **CLEAN HOUSE PLANTS.** Sponge dust off big leaves. For small plants in pots, cover the soil with plastic wrap, then spray the plants with lukewarm shower water. Prune yellowing and dead leaves. If plants are losing too many leaves, insufficient light is likely the problem: consider installing artificial light.

☑ **FROST PROTECTORS.** In the coldest parts of the West, late frost can come anytime and nip tender seedlings. Order cloches or row covers now so you'll have them when you need to cover plants.

☑ **PREPARE BEDS.** As soon as the ground can be worked, dig or till compost or other organic matter into the soil to prepare flower and vegetable beds for spring planting. If spring comes late in your area, you can even dig in manure that's not fully rotted yet; by planting time, it will have aged enough to fertilize plants without burning them.

☑ **PRUNE TREES, SHRUBS.** Start pruning when daytime temperatures are well above freezing. First remove dead, crossing, and closely parallel branches, then prune for shape.

☑ **WASH SEED-STARTING CONTAINERS.** Before you start spring-blooming vegetables and flowers, wash pots and flats with a mild mixture of household bleach and water.

PEST CONTROL

☑ **HOUSE PLANTS.** Inspect leaves for aphids, telltale webs of spider mites, and the sticky honeydew that signals scale insects. Spray pests off leaves with lukewarm water; scrape off scale insects if necessary. If you spray with an insecticide, first cover the plant with a plastic garment cover (the kind you get from dry cleaners) to confine the spray. ◆

Southwest Checklist

PLANTING

☑ **BARE-ROOT STOCK.** Plant bare-root grapes, strawberries, blackberries, and raspberries; all kinds of ornamental, fruit, and shade trees; and even vegetables like asparagus and horseradish.

☑ **GROUND COVERS, VINES.** Zone 11 (Las Vegas): Set out Hall's honeysuckle and *Vinca major* or *V. minor*. Zones 12–13: Set out these as well as perennial verbena, star jasmine, and trailing indigo bush (*Dalea greggii*).

☑ **PERENNIAL WILDFLOWERS.** Zones 1–2, 10–11: You can still scatter wildflower seed mixes now for bloom this summer. Zones 12–13: Set out desert marigold, evening primrose, paperflower (*Psilostrophe cooperi*), penstemon, and salvia for bloom this spring.

☑ **VEGETABLES.** Zones 1–2: Order seed now for sowing when the weather warms up. Zones 10–11: Start seeds of cool-season crops (broccoli, cabbage, cauliflower, Chinese vegetables, and lettuce) indoors after midmonth. Zones 12–13: Start seeds of warm-season crops, including cucumbers, eggplant, melons, peppers, squash, and tomatoes, indoors for transplanting when danger of frost is past. Sow seeds of root crops (beets, carrots, radishes), peas, and spinach in prepared soil.

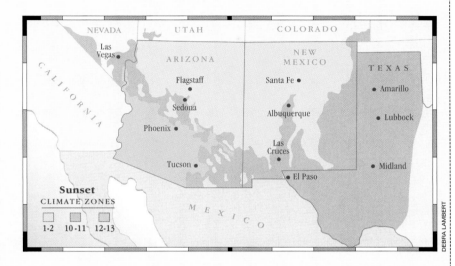

MAINTENANCE

☑ **FEED BEARDED IRISES.** Late in the month, scratch a complete fertilizer into the soil over iris rhizomes; water it in well.

☑ **FEED CITRUS.** If you didn't feed citrus last month, scatter a complete fertilizer over the entire root zone of each tree; water it in thoroughly.

☑ **FEED ROSES.** On a late-February day when nighttime temperatures are forecast to remain above freezing, water established plants, let the soil drain, apply a complete fertilizer, and water again.

☑ **FEED WINTER RYEGRASS.** Zones 12–13: Apply 2½ pounds of ammonium sulfate per 1,000 square feet of lawn and water it in well.

☑ **MAINTAIN DRIP SYSTEMS.** Clean or replace your drip system's filters and check each emitter. When you find one that can't be unclogged, install a new emitter next to it.

☑ **PREPARE SOIL.** Get beds ready for spring planting by digging compost or other organic matter into the soil. If the soil is very alkaline in your garden, you can adjust its pH and increase fertility by adding 2 pounds of ammonium phosphate and 3 pounds of soil sulfur per 100 square feet.

PEST CONTROL

☑ **CONTROL APHIDS.** Zones 12–13: Check new growth for aphids. When you see them, blast them off with a jet of water and if necessary follow up with a spray of insecticidal soap. ◆

Glorious Roses

Beautiful roses win hearts. Gardeners, lovers, photographers, and flower breeders are all smitten by shapely buds that open into flawless, perfectly formed blooms. So it's no wonder that rose growing has flowered into such a high art, with new varieties becoming the toast of the rose world every year. •While roses reign as the West's most popular cut flowers, for some gardeners, growing them means just one thing—trouble. But you don't need an arsenal of sprays, dusts, and tools to grow them successfully. If you follow the directions developed by *Sunset* and other rosarians over the years, you, too, can grow them well. •Roses do make a few demands, though, and better care always translates into more attractive flowers and healthier foliage. Just remember the four basics: Buy plump, healthy bare-root plants in winter. Plant in good soil, following guidelines on page 50. Water and feed regularly. Prune properly. •Success starts with choosing an adaptable, trouble-free variety. The introduction of our Centennial rose, 'Sunset Celebration', adds to the selection of award-winning performers. This beauty is disease-resistant, and hardy enough to handle just about any climate. It makes a handsome addition to the garden, whether you grow it singly or among other flowering perennials, in garden beds or containers. — *Jim McCausland*

Are picture-perfect roses difficult to grow? Not if you follow our guidelines. You can plant our own 'Sunset Celebration', and other roses, this month

NORMAN A. PLATE

'SUNSET CELEBRATION': VITAL STATISTICS

The plants
- About 4 feet tall.
- Bushy, with deep-green foliage.
- Excellent disease resistance.

The flowers
- $4\frac{1}{2}$ to $5\frac{1}{2}$ inches in diameter, with 25 to 30 petals in a formal spiral.
- Color varies by climate—richer peach in cool climates and lighter apricot in warm climates. But our many test plants at *Sunset* headquarters produced colors across the range.
- Fragrance is sweetly fruity.
- Excellent for cutting. Long stems. Vase life—one of the longest for apricot-colored roses—is about seven days.

THE MAKING OF A PRIZEWINNER

■ Ten years ago, 'Sunset Celebration' was just a nameless seedling. Then hybridizer Gareth Fryer of Knutsford, England, selected it out of the thousands of roses started from seed.

The lovely chameleonlike hybrid tea, whose colors vary from rich peach to apricot-umber burnished with cream, is the result of a cross between an unnamed seedling and medium-yellow 'Pot O' Gold'. Fryer named it 'Fryxotic' (an international code name that it will always retain). But after this rose arrived in the United States, where it won the All-America Rose Selections (AARS) award for 1998, it was renamed 'Sunset Celebration' for the U.S. market, in honor of *Sunset Magazine's* 100th anniversary.

"The great thing about 'Sunset Celebration' is that it captures what everyone likes in a hybrid tea," says Tom Carruth of Weeks Roses, the American agent for the rose, "but it does it on an attractive plant that looks good in the landscape. This plant pumps out such great quantities of fragrant flowers, it will make a lot of home gardeners happy."

The rose also won nine international awards, including the Golden Rose of the Hague award and the Golden Rose award. Very few roses amass such honors in a wide array of climates, says Carruth.

'Sunset Celebration' is more than just another pretty rose. Its beauty should endure for decades.
— *Lauren Bonar Swezey*

Rose & perennial partnerships

■ Roses are party animals. When surrounded by agreeable companions, they take on a special glow they don't exhibit when grown alone. Take the example pictured in photo above right. The cool blue spikes of 'Indigo Spires' salvia tickling the roses' ribs make the apricot blossoms appear even warmer.

Good rose companions need to be more than visually compatible, however. They need to tolerate the roses' regular irrigation and feeding, but they shouldn't compete for them. That rules out plants programmed for summer dormancy like California ceanothus, as well as water-siphoners like willows. Plants with aggressive root systems like mint or red valerian (*Centranthus ruber*) should also be avoided. And eliminate plants that attract diseases you're trying to keep off your roses.

Pictured above left are two good rose companions, campanula and Santa Barbara daisy. Other perfect perennials to pair with roses: asters, bearded irises, catmint (*Nepeta faassenii*), delphiniums, feverfew (*Chrysanthemum parthenium*), foxglove (*Digitalis*), garden penstemon (*P. gloxinioides*), nicotiana, phlox, scabiosa, Shasta daisy, true geraniums, verbena, and yarrow (*Achillea*). — *Sharon Cohoon*

OTHER PRETTY PARTNERSHIPS

- A trio of white roses—'Iceberg', 'Class Act', and 'Sally Holmes'— with gray-leafed snow-in-summer and white-flowered veronica and nicotiana.

- A simple hedge of pink 'Bonica' roses edged with baby-blue 'Peter Pan' agapanthus.

- Apricot-cinnamon-gold 'Singin' in the Rain' with a skirt of yarrow in mixed pastels and a few sunny yellow 'Little Maid' kniphofia spikes popping through.

- 'Lavender Pinocchio' and 'Blueberry Hill' backed with bronze fennel or purple smokebush (*Cotinus coggygria*) and fronted with a wide ruffle of *Geranium himalayense* 'Baby Blue'.

Medley in apricot: 'Sunset Celebration' rose presides above *Verbena* 'Peaches & Cream' (front), *Salvia* 'Salsa Salmon Bicolor', and taller *S. coccinea* 'Brenthurst'. Design: Bud Stuckey.

How to plant a bare-root rose

1

SOAK THE ROSE in a bucket of water. Dig a hole 2 feet wide, 1½ feet deep. Make a firm cone of soil in the hole.

2

SPREAD THE ROOTS over the soil cone. Cut back long roots so they fit without bending.

3

SET THE PLANT so the bud union (graft) is just above the soil level, or just below it if temperatures will drop to 10°. Use a shovel handle to gauge soil level.

4

PULL BACKFILL into the hole, firming it over the roots with your hands to stabilize the plant.

5

SLOWLY FILL the hole with water to soak and settle the soil, then finish backfilling.

6

MILD CLIMATES: When growing season begins, make a ridge of soil around the hole to form a watering basin.
COLD CLIMATES: Protect the rose from cold or drying wind by partly covering the plant with soil as shown. After leaves emerge, shape the soil into a basin.

WHEN THINGS GO WRONG

• BLACK SPOT

Problem: Small, fringed, black-to-brown spots on leaves come first, then leaves yellow and drop off. Symptoms of this fungus disease start at the bottom of the plant, then work their way up. Common in warm, humid weather.

Solution: Remove and discard infected leaves. To reduce infection, try a baking soda–oil spray (mix 2 teaspoons baking soda and 2 teaspoons summer oil in a gallon of water). Use often to protect new growth.

• POWDERY MILDEW

Problem: Patches of white fungal filaments and spores disfigure leaves, buds, and stems. Thrives in humid air but—unlike other rose diseases— needs dry foliage to become established.

Making th

Make cuts at a 45° angle about ¼ inch above an outward-facing growth bud. Make a clean cut without ripping the bark. Don't leave stubs.

right   wrong

Solution: Overhead watering (in the early morning) may wash off fungal spores and reduce infection. Baking soda–oil sprays can also be effective (see black spot). For the worst cases, spray with a fungicide such as triforine or benomyl.

• RUST

Problem: Small rust-colored spots form on leaf undersides. Leaf tops show yellow mottling; in advanced cases, leaves yellow and drop. Warm days, cool nights, and moisture encourage this fungus disease, which is spread by spores.

Solution: Keep fallen leaves picked up, and during winter, pick off any rust-infected leaves that remain on the plant. During the growing season, spray foliage with a wettable sulfur, or a fungicide such as triforine.

• APHIDS

Problem: Small green, red, pink, or black oval insects cluster on new leaves, leaf undersides, and buds, distorting them by sucking plant juices.

Solution: If infestations are light, do nothing; beneficial insects such as ladybugs will feed on them. For heavier infestations, dislodge the pests with a strong spray of water from a hose, or spray with insecticidal soap.

• SPIDER MITES

Problem: Barely visible, spiderlike insects hang out on leaf undersides, often weaving delicate webs. They suck plant juices, turning the leaves stippled yellow.

Solution: Spray leaves with water in early morning. For heavy infestations, spray with insecticidal soap or summer oil.

How to prune a rose

REMOVE ALL DEAD WOOD and all weak, twiggy branches (darkened in drawing). Make cuts flush with the bud union (the swelling at the base of the plant).

CUT ALL BRANCHES THAT CROSS through the center. This opens up the plant and gives it a vase shape. In hot climates, some rosarians just shorten center-crossing branches, so leaves will shade the bud union from the scorching summer sun.

IN MILD CLIMATES, shorten the remaining healthy growth by about one-third.
IN COLD-WINTER CLIMATES, where freeze damage occurs, remove all dead and injured stems. This may result in a shorter bush.

roper cuts

Dotted lines show where to cut a rose at different times during the growing season. Always cut above a five-leaflet leaf.

three-leaflet leaf

five-leaflet leaf

early-season cut

hook

peak-season cut

ILLUSTRATIONS BY MARINA THOMPSON

Rose care calendar

The best roses get the best care at the right time.
Use this calendar as your guide for what to do when.

JAMIE HADLEY

JANUARY

Sunset climate zones 4–9, 12–24

- Plant bare-root roses (see page 50). Ask the nursery to wrap the roots to keep them from drying out, then plant immediately when you get home. (Or temporarily place them on their sides in a shallow trench and cover them with moist sawdust or soil to keep roots from drying out until you can plant them.) Set them in well-drained soil in a spot that gets six to eight hours of sunlight. If soil is sandy or heavy clay, amend it with organic matter such as fir bark or compost.
- Prune plants when temperatures are well above freezing. Prune hybrid teas to a vase shape made from the strongest three to five canes (see page 51).
- Spray established plants when they're dormant to kill overwintering insects such as aphids and scale and to control diseases such as mildew. Use horticultural oil either alone or mixed with lime sulfur or fixed copper.

FEBRUARY

Zones 4–9, 12–24

- Finish planting bare-root roses.
- Complete pruning.
- If you haven't already done so, apply dormant sprays to control aphids, black spot, and mildew. Use horticultural oil with lime sulfur or fixed copper.
- In the low desert (zone 13) after midmonth, feed established roses with a complete fertilizer or commercial rose food, following package directions, when buds begin to swell. Water first, let drain, spread the fertilizer around each plant, then water again.

Zones 10–11 (high deserts)

- Plant bare-root roses.

MARCH

Zones 4–24

- As soon as buds begin to swell, feed roses with a high-nitrogen fertilizer such as 20-10-10, or a commercial rose food. Continue feeding every four to six weeks until October.

APRIL

Zones 1–3 (cold climates)

- Plant bare-root roses (as instructed on page 50).
- Prune dormant plants.

Zones 4–24

- Apply mulch to save water, smother weeds, and keep soil cooler. Spread 1 to 3 inches (depending on size of plant) of bark chips, compost, wood shavings, or other organic material. Leave a circle of bare soil around the plant's base.
- Blast aphids off plants with a jet of water from a hose. If infestations are heavy, spray with insecticidal soap.

MAY

Zones 1–3

- Fertilize roses with high-nitrogen plant food.
- Finish pruning roses.

Zones 4–24

- Water when rain has been minimal. This is especially important for anything you planted this year and for plants in pots and under house eaves.
- Apply high-nitrogen fertilizer.
- Remove spent flowers. Cut blooms above a five-leaflet leaf (see detail, page 51).

JUNE–JULY–AUGUST

All zones

- Feed, water (especially on hot days), weed, and mulch. Remove faded blooms.
- To eliminate aphids and spider mites from roses, spray plants with water, then apply insecticidal soap.
- Clean up fallen leaves. If they're diseased, discard them (don't compost them).

SEPTEMBER

All zones

- Continue removing spent flowers.
- Renew mulch if necessary.

Zones 4–24

- Feed roses after their fall bloom flush. Use a complete liquid fertilizer at half dose.
- Irrigate plants as needed.

OCTOBER

All zones

- Continue deadheading and watering.

NOVEMBER

All zones

- Clean up fallen leaves and petals.
- Knock down watering basins.
- Continue deadheading faded flowers.

Zones 1–3

- Protect plants from winter cold by mounding soil around them. Make sure the soil is high enough to cover the bud union. Then surround each plant with a wire cylinder weighted down at the base with rocks or bricks, and fill in with straw or leaves. Keep protected through winter.

DECEMBER

Zones 7–24

- To control overwintering insects and plant diseases, spray roses this month or next with horticultural oil, oil and lime sulfur, or oil and fixed copper.

Zone 13

- Plant bare-root roses as soon as they appear in the nurseries. ◆

Polar bear pansies

Frost won't faze these beauties if you give them proper care

BY JIM McCAUSLAND

In a window box, Universal Plus and Accord pansies peek through frosted panes.

JAMES CARRIER

If you judged pansies only by their velvety, tissue-thin flowers, you might assume they were, well, pansies. The delicate-looking blooms belie the plant's tough, frost-resistant nature.

Just how much cold can a pansy stand? At Territorial Seeds's trial grounds in Oregon, several varieties of pansies endured 6° during one cold snap; all recovered and rebloomed.

Although most pansy series and mixes on the market can survive freezing temperatures, a few groups have distinguished themselves in recent winter trials. The Accord blotch and clear mixes, the Atlas mix, the Clear Sky series, the Rally mix, the Ultima series, and the Universal Plus blotch and clear

More pansies that shine in winter cold

In trials over two successive winters, Allan Armitage evaluated more than 150 varieties of pansies and mixes from 22 series. Plants were exposed to minimum temperatures of 10° for different lengths of time. In addition to the groups named above, these pansies turned in outstanding individual performances: Bingo (yellow, blotched light rose), Delta (yellow, blotched violet), Fama (blue, white, lilac, orange, silver-blue), Glory (bicolored blue 'Glory Beaconsfield', blue, sherbet, and blotched forms of rose, white, yellow), Happy Face (yellow), Imperial (purple-and-yellow), Maxim (blue, orange, yellow, red-and-yellow), bicolored blue 'Paramount Beaconsfield', and Skyline (white-and-purple).

mixes all performed well above average in the trials conducted by Allan Armitage, professor of horticulture at the University of Georgia. "In general, smaller-flowered pansies do better [in winter cold] than large-flowered kinds like Majestic Giants, which get beat up in bad weather and don't recover quickly," says Armitage. Individual pansies that did well in the trials are listed in the box at left.

CHOOSE FACES, CLEAR COLORS, OR TINTED SHADES

Pansies (*Viola wittrockiana*) were originally hybridized to get bigger flowers with faces (blotched). Over the years, many clear (unblotched) pansies have also been developed; Clear Sky is a current example. Many popular kinds, including Delta and Universal Plus, come in both clear and blotched forms. You'll also find tinted and bicolored flowers, including the so-called antique shades seen in the Imperial strain.

Clear pansies should be your first choice for massing in beds, where their solid colors have more impact than blotched varieties. Pansies with faces are best seen up close—in pots or window boxes—to appreciate their markings.

WHAT PLANTS NEED TO THRIVE

Pansies are usually sold in flower, having been forced into bloom in a commercial greenhouse. They'll continue growing, budding, and flowering if your soil temperature is at least 45°. If it's much cooler than that, pansies just sit and wait for warmer weather.

They prefer at least a half-day of sun, except in hot climates (see below). Pansies benefit from good nutrition: Before planting, amend the bed with two 1-cubic-foot sacks of well-rotted manure per square yard of soil. Once bloom starts, feed plants every two weeks with a half-strength solution of liquid fertilizer. Keep plants well watered. Pinch off fading blooms and leggy stems.

During cold weather, you can speed flower development by covering plants with cloches or floating row covers.

In the West's colder climates, buy plants in 4-inch pots, since mature pansies will become established and bloom sooner than seedlings. In hot climates, set pansies in filtered shade, and choose strains like Maxim or Universal Plus, which tolerate both heat and cold.

Pansies are technically short-lived perennials. But because they bloom most vigorously in their first year, many gardeners treat them as annuals. ◆

New flavors

Pluots, and white-fleshed peaches and nectarines

BY LAUREN BONAR SWEZEY

'Flavor King' pluot (an apricot-plum hybrid) looks like a plum but is sweeter.

'Flavor Supreme' pluot has green skin and beautiful, sweet red flesh.

for stone fruits

ong the tastiest new fruits you can grow. Plant them this winter

PHOTOGRAPHS BY JAMES CARRIER

'Dapple Dandy' pluot has
bright, mottled skin and
succulent, sweet-spicy flesh.

'Arctic Queen' nectarine has
bright, smooth skin and
intensely sweet flesh.

When it comes to stone fruits, flavor is everything. We want our apricots, nectarines, peaches, and plums to taste tangy-sweet or sweet, and we want them juicy. That's why new varieties of these fruits regularly come and go. Very few introductions actually revolutionize fruit breeding and fruit flavor. But pluots (apricot-plum hybrids) and new varieties of white-fleshed peaches and nectarines, developed by stone-fruit breeder Zaiger Genetics in Modesto, California, have changed all that.

These fruits break all standards for flavor. In taste tests, they're the fruits people choose over tree-ripened apricots, yellow peaches, and most plums, says Craig Minor, wholesale sales manager at Dave Wilson Nursery in Hickman, California.

We couldn't resist tasting these new fruits at *Sunset*. Our tasters' favorite varieties, along with some of their comments, are listed at right. Now is the time to plant one of these outstanding trees in your own garden.

PLUOT: A SWEET TASTE TREAT

Bite into a sweet, succulent, tree-ripened pluot (pronounced *plu*-ott) and your mouth tingles with pleasure as aroma, flavor, texture, and sugar-acid balance come together.

The Zaigers introduced their first pluot—a cross between plums and apricots, and hybrids of the cross—just nine years ago. "Pluots have a higher sugar content than either plums or apricots," says Leith Zaiger Gardner, general manager and daughter of Floyd Zaiger, who developed the fruit. "They've also lost the sour characteristics of plums. The skins aren't as puckery. "

Appearance differs by variety. Some pluots are greenish, others are purplish like plums, and one is yellow.

NEW PEACHES AND NECTARINES: SUPERSWEET OR SWEET-TART

Give anyone a tree-ripened 'Arctic Supreme' peach or 'Heavenly White' nectarine and it will elicit a big "Wow!" Like the best of the best yellow

Where to buy trees
If you can't find one of these fruit trees, have your nursery order it from Dave Wilson Nursery. Or order them by mail from Bay Laurel Nursery, Atascadero, CA; (805) 466-3406.

'Arctic Supreme' peach has fuzzy skin and juicy, sweet-tart flesh.

Sunset picks

Pluots
'Dapple Dandy': "Slightly spicy, almost cinnamony." "Sweet-tart and juicy." Harvest: August.
'Flavor King': "Almost tropical-tasting." "Strong plum aftertaste." Harvest: August.
'Flavor Supreme': "Tastes like a plum, but tartness is softened." "Complex flavors." Harvest: June.

Peaches & nectarines
Balanced-acid
'Arctic Supreme' peach (semi-freestone): "Perfect balance between sweet and tart." "Real peachy flavor." Harvest: late July to mid-August.
'Heavenly White' nectarine (freestone): "Excellent sweet-tart balance." "Very floral." Harvest: mid-July to early August.
'Arctic Glo' nectarine (clingstone): "Wonderful sharp, intense flavor." "Good balance." "Smooth texture." Low chill. Harvest: late June to late July.
'Snow Queen' nectarine (freestone): "Perfumy." "Sweet, but not too sweet." Low chill. Harvest: mid-June to mid-July.

Subacid
'Arctic Queen' nectarine (freestone): "Very sweet and floral." "Almost too sweet." "Strong nectarine flavor." Harvest: August.

peaches and nectarines, the white-fleshed varieties are simply sublime—sweeter, more delicately flavored, and more aromatic than many yellow-fleshed kinds.

As a group, white-fleshed peaches and nectarines aren't new. 'Babcock' peach has been around for years. Like other old white varieties, its fruits bruise more easily than yellow types, so they don't often show up in markets. When they do, they're usually immature (hard) and tasteless. (Gardeners have better luck with these varieties than commercial growers do, since they can handle the fruits with care.)

But new developments by Zaiger Genetics have led to some tremendous improvements in flavor and, in some cases, durability. Now gardeners can choose between subacid and balanced-acid white peaches and nectarines—much like choosing between sweet and tart apples. Subacid fruits taste very sweet (which only a few of our tasters preferred), while balanced-acid fruits have a more favored sweet-tart flavor. Unlike the balanced-acid types, the subacids can be harvested while slightly firm; at that stage they're already fairly sweet.

TREES ARE EASY TO GROW

Pluot trees grow more like plum than apricot trees. They are easier to grow than other stone fruits, adapting to a wide variety of soils and climates. If you can grow 'Santa Rosa' plum in your climate (*Sunset* zones 2–3, 7–12 and 14–23), you can grow pluots. But in the low desert and in Southern California's mildest coastal areas, pluot trees don't get enough winter chill to produce fruit.

Pluot harvest lasts about four weeks. All varieties become sweeter if they hang on the tree as long as possible within their harvest range.

Peaches and nectarines grow well in cooler climates, from Northern California to the Pacific Northwest. 'Arctic Glo' and 'Snow Queen' also grow in most areas of Southern California, except directly on the coast. ◆

Out with the lawn, in with the flowers

A Northwest front yard gets a total face-lift

BY JIM McCAUSLAND

His old front yard was about as soulless as a landscape can be. But for Joel Potthoff of Bothell, Washington, the 1,800-square-foot space had one thing in its favor: unlimited potential. With that in mind, he tore out everything but an electric lamppost, and started over.

An old concrete walkway and the lawn were the first things to go. Potthoff, who is head groundskeeper at Lake Washington Technical College, smothered the lawn under a layer of soil. Then he tilled in 15 cubic yards of topsoil and compost, raising the level of the garden by almost 20 inches. He laid a new brick path from the street to the house, where it meets a series of steps and landings that form a spacious entry area outside the front door.

Potthoff planted deciduous trees, including maples and a dawn redwood (*Metasequoia glyptostroboides*), and flowering shrubs such as *Lavatera maritima*. He also planted a row of *Cupressocyparis leylandii* 'Castlewellan'; its golden foliage forms an evergreen privacy screen on one side of the garden.

Then he filled the area between the trees and shrubs with long-blooming perennials, including coreopsis, delphinium, gaillardia, geranium, monarda, *Rudbeckia fulgida* 'Goldsturm', and Shasta daisy. "I really packed the plants in, so there would be no room for weeds," he says.

In the entry area, Potthoff placed benches and raised planter boxes along the steps and on the landings. Most of the planters hold summer annuals, but one contains a small maple that provides winter interest as well.

The whole project cost around

BEFORE: A bare lawn, a few dull shrubs, and a lonely lamppost.
AFTER (top): The lamppost is all but hidden in a sea of flowers and greenery.

RIGHT: The elevated entry area is lined by planters filled with geraniums, felicia, petunias, and a small Japanese maple (top center).

$4,500 ($3,000 for materials, $1,500 for plants) and took about 100 hours, with the work spread over several months from February through summer. Potthoff is pleased with his new landscape. "It's a pretty private garden for the city," he says.

KEEPING THE GARDEN SHARP

The plants are irrigated by soaker hoses operated by automatic timers. They get a dose of granular organic fertilizer

JAMES F. HOUSEL (2)

(5-5-5) every spring and summer, and monthly applications of liquid fertilizer during the growing season. It takes six to eight hours a week to keep the garden looking sharp. Light pruning and deadheading of faded flowers is about all that's needed. "I really don't have to pull weeds," says Potthoff. ◆

The stiff, fleshy leaves of *Aloe polyphylla* spiral outward—either clockwise or counterclockwise—from a central rosette. For more on this rare succulent, see page 62.

March

gardenguide

Fresh twist on a summer classic

New morning glory with a tie-dyed look

■ 'Tie Dye', a morning glory vine imported from Japan, is as splashy as the T-shirts Grateful Dead fans used to wear to the group's concerts. Each funnel-shaped flower is a glorious swirl of blue-violet against pale lavender-blue. And no two blooms are marked quite the same.

To add to the novelty, this *Ipomoea* has silvery white splotches on its big, heart-shaped leaves. It may sound over-the-top on paper, but everyone who walked through the test garden at *Sunset's* headquarters last summer smiled at this divine vine.

Grow 'Tie Dye' as you would any annual morning glory. Sow seeds directly into the ground in a sunny spot after danger of frost has passed. (To speed germination, notch them with a knife or soak them in warm water for two hours before planting.) Water them regularly until the vines take off, then less frequently.

Seed is available through Park Seed Company, 1 Parkton Ave., Greenwood, SC 29647; (800) 845-3369. Catalog is free.

— *Sharon Cohoon*

tools

■ For centuries, women had no choice but to use heavy, thick-handled gardening tools made for men. But that's changing. Manufacturers have recently developed tools that are easier for women to use. Lady Gardener shovels, cultivators, and rakes, for example, have slender wood handles that give small hands a firmer, more comfortable grip. Their tempered-steel heads are lighter and more compact than those of conventional tools. Short-handled models (shown), 18 inches long and weighing about 1 pound each, are ideal for light tasks in cultivated ground or raised beds. Long-handled models measure 4 to 4½ feet and weigh 2 to 3½ pounds. Lady Gardener tools ($13 to $15 each) are sold at garden, home improvement, and hardware stores. For details, call UnionTools at (800) 888-4196, or check its Web site: info.ut@uniontools.com. — *Tracy Jan*

SHOWY FOLIAGE

Let's hear it for 'Golden Ears'

■ Most gardeners grow common geraniums (*Pelargonium*) for their showy flowers. But some geraniums are more celebrated for their leaves than their flowers. 'Golden Ears' is a perfect example.

We discovered this beauty (pictured at right) at Pergola nursery in Soquel. The leaf is a striking dark bronze edged with chartreuse yellow.

'Golden Ears' is a Stellar geranium, a series that was developed in Australia and named for its small, deeply cut, almost star-shaped leaves and star-burst flowers. This hybrid from Vancouver, British Columbia, produces a prolific show of bright orange-red blooms. Its mounding foliage grows about a foot tall and looks wonderful planted next to green- or yellow-foliage plants. It also makes a fine container plant for an indoor windowsill.

Plant 'Golden Ears' geraniums in full sun in coastal climates or in bright shade in hot, inland areas. Cover the plants when temperatures drop to 28° for an extended period (more than just a few hours).

Look for 'Golden Ears' at your nursery. If you can't find it, ask the nursery to order it for you from Moran Nursery in Watsonville (wholesale only). 'Golden Ears' is also available by mail from New Leaf Nurseries in Vista (760/726-9269). — *Lauren Bonar Swezey*

A polite zucchini

■ A single zucchini plant can elbow its way through an entire vegetable garden—unless, that is, it's the new, truly compact 'Spacemiser' zucchini.

Developed by Petoseed Company, 'Spacemiser' is the first hybrid zucchini in many years bred specifically for home gardens. It takes up about one-third less space than a standard zucchini plant, and is very open, making the fruits easy to find and pick. It's also highly productive, out-yielding many other varieties.

The zucchinis are handsome, too—dark green with yellow flecking—and can be harvested in the baby stage (about 3 inches long) or when they're more mature (about 6 inches for optimum tenderness).

Order seeds from Vermont Bean Seed Company, Garden Lane, Fair Haven, VT 05743; (803) 663-0217. — *L. B. S.*

A gem of an aloe

■ Alan Beverly never dreamed that he would succeed as a stand-in for the malachite sunbird, the only natural pollinator of *Aloe polyphylla* (pictured on page 58). Beverly, a landscape designer and owner of Ecoscape in Santa Cruz, California, first gathered seeds of this rare succulent in the Drakensberg Mountains of southern Africa in 1978. But, without the help of the malachite sunbird, it took him 17 years to propagate the plant he now sells as the "Gem of the Drakensberg."

And what a gem it is. *A. polyphylla* has stiff, fleshy leaves that spiral outward from the center of a rosette. Half of the plants that Beverly grows spiral in a clockwise direction; the others spiral counterclockwise. Mature plants reach 2 feet tall and 3 feet across; in spring, they produce a 3-foot-tall stalk topped with salmon-coral flowers. Unlike *Aloe vera* and its other heat-loving cousins, *A. polyphylla* prefers cooler temperatures and is hardy to 10°.

Beverly recommends that the plant be grown in a 50-50 mix of potting soil and lava rock. It does best in a large container with thick sides or a raised bed to keep roots cool.

Two- or three-year-old plants of *A. polyphylla* are sold bare-root for $20 each, plus $15 shipping (for one or two plants). You can specify whether you want a clockwise or a counterclockwise spiral. To order, call Ecoscape at (408) 459-8106, or visit www.scruz.net/~ecoscape.

— *Pam Cornelison*

Planting from cell-packs

■ Many plants, including summer annuals, are available in cell-packs at nurseries this month. Here's how to get these plants off to a good start. 1) Turn cell-pack upside down and poke plants out by pushing on the bottom of the individual cell with your thumb; let gravity help. If plant is tight, run a knife between container and soil. 2) Lightly separate matted roots. If there's a pad of coiled roots at the bottom, cut it off so roots will grow into soil. 3) Without squeezing roots, position plant in a generous planting hole, fill in around the roots with soil, press lightly to firm, and water gently.

Pacific Northwest Garden Notebook

BY STEVEN R. LORTON

One morning the phones rang fast and furious in my Seattle neighborhood. The reason? A new owner had moved into an old house and immediately decided to have a perfect pair of 30-year-old street trees cut down. The rationale? The property needed more light, and the sidewalk was showing signs of buckling.

Meanwhile, those of us who love our street trees were in a state of shock. We'll survive, but it will be a long time before the busy street beyond is again screened from view.

In all the neighborhood hubbub, the sagest comment came from a 40-year resident: "Well, it's done. Let's all just pretend a hurricane came through and move on."

But this particular storm need never have happened if Seattle's street-tree ordinances had stronger teeth. Every community needs clearly defined legislation to regulate the selection, planting, care, and *removal* of the trees that make up a healthy, diverse urban forest. Portland, for example, has enacted model street-tree ordinances. It's up to citizens to ensure that their city governments have solid regulations.

But ordinances aside, new property owners ought to use common sense. Refrain from making any big changes in the landscape, especially in public spots, for a year after moving in. Given some time, you're likely to see the wisdom of the existing plantings. If you do decide to remove plants, seek good advice from a reliable and objective source.

When you think about it, the leafy canopy rising above sidewalks and streets really belongs to the community. Elegant trees lining avenues take years—decades—to grow. The options are unthinkable: rows of horticultural lollipops lining our streets—or no trees at all. Let's grow together for the common good.

that's a good question ...

Q: I've heard you should plant trees in fall. I missed my chance. Must I wait seven or eight more months?
— *Leo Adams, Yakima*

A: You don't have to wait. Although fall is considered the best time for planting trees, early spring comes in a close second. In the coldest Northwest climates (*Sunset* climate zones 1 through 3), you should get trees in the ground as soon as the soil thaws.

MARINA THOMPSON

Northern California Garden Notebook

BY LAUREN BONAR SWEZEY

*t*welve years ago, Kay Forster, Nancy Conner, and other dedicated garden lovers came together to inaugurate what would become an internationally recognized event: the San Francisco Landscape Garden Show. I remember the first shows and their gardens vividly—Living Green's towering Mayan ruin, Topher Delaney's undulating walls with neon lights.

This year, the 13th show moves to the Cow Palace in San Francisco, and to an earlier date, March 26 through 29. The new producers—Duane Kelly, founder of the Northwest Flower & Garden Show, along with Garden Expositions—chose the site for its size and ample parking.

The event features 27 display gardens, horticultural exhibits, the ever-popular marketplace, and more than 100 seminars. It promises to be an exciting show.

Admission costs $12.50 (ages 11 and under free). A portion of the ticket sales benefits Friends of Recreation and Parks in San Francisco. For details, call (800) 829-9751.

(Editor's note: dates and times in this article were valid for 1998; schedules will vary from year to year.)

PERENNIALS GALORE

Emerisa Gardens has been producing an amazing array of perennials, herbs, and ornamental grasses for the nursery trade for eight years. Now the owners—a family headed by former UC Cooperative Extension agent Muchtar Salzmann—have opened a retail section. The Nursery at Emerisa Gardens has one of the largest selections of 4-inch perennials in Northern California, including 50 varieties of salvia and 30 of lavender.

The nursery (555 Irwin Lane, Santa Rosa; 707/525-9644) is open 10–5 Tue-Fri, 9–6 Sat, March-October.

that's a good question ...

Q: I just read in a baby book that privet trees are poisonous. We have one in our backyard. Do I have to worry about all of the droppings (leaves, berries, twigs)? — *Elaine Johnson, Palo Alto*

A: According to "Know Your Plants ... Safe or Poisonous?"—a brochure developed by Elise Stone of the California Poison Control System and Ann King of UC Cooperative Extension—privet is considered a minor toxin. The sap may cause a rash or skin irritation in some people, and ingestion of the plant may cause minor illness, such as vomiting or diarrhea. The brochure also categorizes the toxicity of almost 200 other landscape plants, house plants, and trees and seeds; suggests treatment for exposure; and lists the California Poison Control System number (800/876-4766). For a free brochure, call (650) 726-9059.

Southern California Garden Notebook

BY SHARON COHOON

I have only one complaint with Carole Saville's new book, *Exotic Herbs:* I wish I'd owned it a year ago. Since I didn't, I'll have to plant Cuban oregano (*Plectranthus amboinicus*) again. Also East Indian  love basil (*Ocimum gratissimum*), a woody shrub bearing little resemblance to its culinary cousins. Though both herbs smelled intriguing, I was too intimidated to cook with them. The fleshy leaves of the oregano were unlike any herb I'd used before, and the coarse texture of the basil obviously ruled out using it raw in pesto. Since I never did figure out how to use either herb in the kitchen, I eventually yanked them both out of the garden. Now I learn that the Cuban oregano would have been super in bean and shellfish soups. And the excuse I was looking for to hang onto that gangly-looking but heavenly-smelling love basil—just a few good recipes—is right here in Saville's book. (Baked apples and herb honey with fresh berries.) There's no edible herb you're likely to stumble across that food and garden writer and herb maven Saville hasn't discovered first. She's tested and tasted and cultivated and cooked with it already. Go buy *Exotic Herbs: A Com-* *pendium of Exceptional Culinary Herbs* (Henry Holt & Company, New York, 1997; $35).

MARK YOUR CALENDARS

One plant-oriented activity you could enjoy this month, the 53rd Annual Santa Barbara International Orchid Show, March 20 through 22, has displays, demonstrations, 65 vendors, and the chance to tour nurseries that aren't generally open to the public; call (805) 967-6331 for details.

(Editor's note: dates and times in this article were valid for 1998; schedules will vary from year to year.)

that's a good question ...

Q: "My Hawaiian snow bush lost lots of leaves, and the ones that are left are muddy green," customers complain to Evelyn Weidner at Weidners' Gardens in Encinitas every spring. "What's wrong?"

A: Losing leaves in winter is normal behavior for a Hawaiian snow bush in our climate, says Weidner. To rejuvenate the plant, cut it back by as much as half, provide some balanced fertilizer, and move it to a brighter spot if it's growing in a container, she says. (Hawaiian snow bush can take as much as four hours of full morning sun and even more along the coast.) The plant will leaf out again in warmer weather, and the new foliage will be mostly pink and white.

Westerner's Garden Notebook

BY JIM McCAUSLAND

*t*here I stood last summer with a stake in my left hand, some twine in my right hand, and a scowl on my face. I felt like the stake was in my heart: I'd just cracked a delphinium stem while trying to bend it straight and tie it to a 4-foot length of bamboo. To make matters worse, I'd done the same thing to a sprawling tomato stem a few minutes earlier. As an unwitting horticriminal, I confess that I've also been guilty of impaling dahlia tubers and lily bulbs by staking plants too late. The lesson is simple: stake everything at planting time, when the stems are supple and you know where the underground parts (bulbs, tubers, roots) are.

I prefer to use green bamboo stakes. They're sharp, have just the right combination of stiffness and flexibility, and are less visible than most other kinds of stakes. After all, you want to show off the plant, not the stake that supports it. But an acquaintance of mine in Holland learned about the disadvantages of camouflage when she leaned over and poked her eye on just such a bamboo stake. Having learned from her lesson, I put corks over the ends of my bamboo stakes.

GENERIC MOWER BLADE IS A DUD

After paying $65 for a lawn mower tune-up last season, I was dismayed when the machine worked worse than ever, refusing to bag even short, dry grass. I saw the problem when I checked the blade: the original had been replaced by a generic model—one whose aerodynamics weren't good enough to blow the grass into the bag. Installing a new original-brand blade solved the problem.

that's a good question ...

Q: Three years ago we planted two ocotillos in our yard. Both were about 7 feet tall and had no leaves. One of the plants is thriving, while the other has not produced any leaves, though its stems are green and firm to the touch. How can we encourage it to grow some leaves? — *Joe and Rhonda Chambers, Albuquerque*

A: Be patient. Ocotillos vary greatly from plant to plant as to when they leaf out and how long their foliage lasts, says Mary Irish, horticulturist at Desert Botanical Garden in Phoenix. Moving plants on intensifies their finicky foliage habits. As long as your ocotillo has healthy green canes, stick with it; it should eventually develop a regular leafing pattern.

Q: I've heard that sprouts are very nutritious. What kinds are there, and how do you grow them at home?

A: There are literally dozens of kinds of seeds that make tasty sprouts. Use only those seeds intended for eating, not ones pretreated with pesticides for planting (pretreated seeds must be marked as such). If you want traditional stingy sprouts, soak 3 tablespoons of alfalfa, radish, cabbage, or clover seed (or a mix) in a cup of water in a widemouthed jar covered with clean cotton cloth. After six hours, drain the water and put the jar upside down in a light place. Flush and drain the jar twice a day until sprouts are 1½ to 3 inches long. For crunchy sprouts, presoak green peas or lentils for about 12 hours, then eat them when the sprouts are about ½ inch long.

Pacific Northwest Checklist

PLANTING

☑ **BULBS, CORMS, TUBERS.** Zones 4–7: Plant summer-blooming bulbs (acidanthera, callas, crocosmia, gladiolus, ranunculus, and tigridia) from midmonth on. If a hard frost is predicted, cover bulb beds with 1 inch of organic mulch.

☑ **CAMELLIAS.** Zones 4–7: Nurseries have a supply of plants in bloom. Buy now and slip them into decorative containers near a window or on a deck while in flower. When blooms fade, get the plants in the ground.

☑ **LAWNS.** Throughout the Northwest, now is the ideal time to start a new lawn. First, spade and rake the top 6 to 12 inches of soil to a fine consistency and amend it with organic matter. Next, lay sod or rake in a seed mix of bent, blue, fescue, and rye grasses. In zones 4–7, bluegrass should be the predominant seed. Water the newly planted lawn regularly.

☑ **SOW COOL-SEASON CROPS.** Zones 4–7: Sow seeds of beets, carrots, chard, lettuce, peas, radishes, spinach, and most members of the cabbage family.

☑ **START WARM-SEASON CROPS.** Zones 1–7: Start seeds for tomatoes, peppers, and other heat-loving crops indoors—on windowsills or in greenhouses. When the weather warms, transplant the seedlings outdoors.

MAINTENANCE

☑ **CLEAN BEDS.** Follow up on your fall cleanup efforts by going over beds again this month. Rake up and dispose of wind-downed debris. Cut back perennials that you may have left standing to provide winter interest. Pull weeds that have sprouted. Give beds a top dressing with fresh compost or soil. You may want to blast moss and slime off paving with a pressure washer.

☑ **DIVIDE PERENNIALS.** Zones 4–7: Dig, divide, and replant summer- and fall-blooming perennials early this month. In zones 1–3, wait until April to do this job. Wherever you garden, wait until autumn to divide spring-flowering perennials (if you divide them now, you'll miss a year of bloom).

☑ **FERTILIZE LAWNS.** Zones 1–7: Start your lawn feeding program this month. Use a fertilizer with a 3-1-2 ratio of nitrogen, phosphorus, and potassium. Apply ½ pound of actual nitrogen per 1,000 square feet of turf. Water it in thoroughly.

☑ **PRUNE CLEMATIS.** Zones 4–7: Cut back summer-flowering clematis now. After pruning, scatter a handful of fertilizer at the base of plants (10-10-10 is a good choice). In zones 1–3, do this job after danger of a hard frost has passed. In all zones, prune back spring-flowering varieties as soon as they finish blooming.

PEST CONTROL

☑ **SLUGS.** Whatever your method (handpicking, beer traps, or poison bait), go after slugs now. ◆

Northern California Checklist

PLANTING

☑ **PLANT CITRUS.** Zones 7–9, 14–17: For fast establishment, purchase young trees in 5-gallon cans. Try 'Washington' orange, 'Eureka' or 'Meyer' lemon, 'Oroblanco' grapefruit-pummelo hybrid, or 'Moro' blood orange. In zones 15–17, try 'Trovita' orange, which not only sweetens better than other oranges in cool temperatures, but also does well in heat. In zones 7–9, wait until the end of the month to plant.

☑ **PLANT STRAWBERRIES.** Zones 7–9, 14–17: Select a site in full sun with well-drained soil. Set plants in the ground so the base of the crown (the area from which the leaves rise) is level with the soil; roots should barely be covered. Mulch the soil, water regularly, and keep the bed free of weeds.

☑ **PLANT SUMMER BULBS.** Zones 7–9, 14–17: Calla, canna, dahlia, gladiolus, and tigridia bulbs are available at nurseries this month. Plant in well-drained soil or containers (use only dwarf varieties of cannas in containers); mix a balanced fertilizer into the soil before planting.

☑ **START VEGETABLES.** Zones 7–9, 14–17: Make successive sowings of these spring vegetables right in the ground: beets, carrots, lettuce, peas, radishes, spinach, Swiss chard, and turnips. Set out broccoli, cauliflower, and cabbage seedlings. Plant potato tubers. If last frost has passed, you can also start planting the first warm-season crops when they appear in nurseries. Most need warm (at least 60°) soil to thrive. To give plants a boost, plant through black plastic and use floating row covers.

Sunset
CLIMATE ZONES
☐ Mountain (1-2)
☐ Valley (7-9)
☐ Inland (14)
☐ Coastal (15-17)

DEBRA LAMBERT

MAINTENANCE

☑ **CARE FOR HERBS.** Zones 7–9, 14–17: To rejuvenate perennial herbs such as mint and sage, cut back old or dead growth on established plants, then fertilize and water the plants to stimulate new growth. Also set out fresh plants of herbs, such as mint, oregano, parsley, rosemary, sage, and thyme, in loose, well-drained soil. You'll find them at nurseries this month in cell-packs and 2- to 4-inch pots.

☑ **CHECK DRIP SYSTEMS.** Zones 7–9, 14–17: Flush out sediment from filters and check screens for algae (clean the screens with a toothbrush, if necessary). Turn on the water and check to make sure all emitters are dripping; clean or replace clogged ones. (If you can't get an emitter out, install a new one next to it.) Check for leaks in the lines and repair them if necessary.

PEST CONTROL

☑ **WASH APHIDS OFF ROSES.** Zones 7–9, 14–17: As the weather warms, aphids start appearing on succulent new growth and rosebuds. To control them in the least toxic way possible, blast aphids off with a strong jet of water from the hose. If water doesn't control them, spray with insecticidal soap (you can also use a more toxic control, such as malathion).

☑ **CONTROL MOSQUITOES.** Zones 7–9, 14–17: Mosquitoes breed in standing water left in birdbaths, buckets, old pots, and ponds. Dump out or drain the water from pots and saucers. Clean birdbaths regularly. In ponds, float doughnut-shaped briquets on the water (one per 100 square feet of surface area), which release *Bacillus thuringiensis israeliensis* for more than 30 days (available from Peaceful Valley Farm Supply; 530/272-4769). ◆

Southern California Checklist

PLANTING

☑ **PLANT AZALEAS AND CAMELLIAS.** Select plants while they're still in flower, and plant them as soon as possible. Plants are dormant while in bloom, but they begin growing again soon after flowering. Amend the soil well with organic material and a soil acidifier such as oak leaf mold or peat moss. Plant both azaleas and camellias a bit high so that the tops of the rootballs are an inch or so aboveground after the soil settles.

☑ **PLANT PERENNIALS.** Nurseries are well stocked with blooming perennials. And, next to fall, early spring is the best time to get them started in the garden. So start shopping. Good choices include campanula, columbine, coral bells, daylilies, delphinium, diascia, geraniums, geum, *Pelargonium,* penstemon, salvia, scabiosa, Shasta daisies, thalictrum, verbena, and yarrow.

☑ **REPLACE WINTER ANNUALS.** As the weather warms, replace fading winter-spring annuals with summer bedding plants. Choices include ageratum, amaranth, begonia, coleus, impatiens, lobelia, marigolds, nasturtium, nicotiana, petunias, phlox, salpiglossis, and verbena. In the high desert (zone 11), set out marigolds, petunias, and zinnias late this month.

☑ **SOW FLOWER SEEDS.** Coastal gardeners (zones 22–24) can sow seeds of aster, cleome, lobelia, lunaria, marigold, nasturtium, nicotiana, sunflower, and zinnia in flats or directly in the garden. Inland gardeners (zones 18–21) should wait until at least midmonth. In colder areas, sow seeds of alyssum, calendula, candytuft, clarkia, and larkspur.

Bishop

NEVADA

CALIFORNIA

San Luis
Obispo

Bakersfield

• Tehachapi

Santa
Barbara

• Lancaster

Los Angeles

• Palm Springs

Sunset
CLIMATE ZONES

1-3 7-9 11 13 14-24

• San Diego

MEXICO

DEBRA

MAINTENANCE

☑ **FEED PERMANENT PLANTS.** Ground covers, shrubs, perennials, and ornamental and fruit trees are putting out new growth now and will benefit from the application of an all-purpose balanced fertilizer. Wait until flowering ends to feed azaleas and camellias; they are dormant while in bloom. California natives and drought-tolerant Mediterranean plants are also exceptions. Don't feed them; they're slowing down prior to their summer dormancy.

☑ **FEED LAWNS.** Apply high-nitrogen fertilizer to warm- and cool-season turf grasses.

PEST CONTROL

☑ **CONTROL APHIDS.** Tender new plant growth attracts these sucking pests. Dislodge aphids with a strong blast of water from a hose or, if blossoms are delicate, mist plants with insecticidal soap. You can also strip aphids from plants by hand.

☑ **PREPARE FOR WHITEFLIES.** Set out yellow sticky cards (available in most nurseries) around abutilon, fuchsia, and other plants that are susceptible to these pests.

☑ **MANAGE SNAILS.** Control now to reduce their numbers for the rest of the year. Handpick—you'll often find them hiding under strap-leafed plants like agapanthus and clivia. Trap them by allowing them to collect on the underside of a slightly elevated board. Or set out commercial snail bait. Surround trunks of citrus trees and tender seedlings with copper barriers. The snails receive a mild shock when they come in contact with the copper, and don't proceed farther. ◆

Mountain Checklist

PLANTING

☑ **BARE-ROOT STOCK.** Early this month, set out bare-root plants of small fruits like grapes, raspberries, and strawberries; vegetables like asparagus and horseradish; and all kinds of fruit and shade trees. Bare-root plants cost less than those sold in containers and adapt more quickly to native garden soil. It's essential to bring home nursery plants with their bare roots wrapped in damp cloth or sawdust: if they dry out, they die

☑ **LAWNS.** You can overseed an old lawn or plant a new one this month. To overseed, first rough up the soil and sow it with the same kind of grass that was already growing there. Otherwise the texture and color of the new grass will contrast with the old. For a new lawn, till 2 inches of organic matter into the top 8 inches of soil before you sow. Keep all newly sown areas well watered until the grass is tall enough to mow.

MAINTENANCE

☑ **FEED BERRIES.** Established blackberries, blueberries, and raspberries can all use a dose of high-nitrogen fertilizer or well-aged manure this month. But hold off feeding new plantings until their roots have taken hold.

☑ **FEED EVERGREENS.** Sprinkle high-nitrogen fertilizer over the root zones around plants and water it in thoroughly.

Sunset
CLIMATE ZONES
☐ 1-3   ☐ 10-11

DEBRA LAMBERT

☑ **FEED ROSES.** Pick a day when nighttime temperatures are forecast to remain above freezing. Water established plants, let the soil drain, apply a complete fertilizer, and then water again.

☑ **FEED SHRUBS.** As soon as early-flowering shrubs have finished blooming, feed them with a high-nitrogen fertilizer. Do this on a mild day when temperatures are well above freezing.

☑ **INSTALL IRRIGATION SYSTEMS.** Install drip-irrigation systems or lay ooze-type soaker hoses in beds before plants leaf out.

☑ **PREPARE BEDS.** Once the soil has thawed, dig compost or well-aged manure into planting beds. If you have really bad soil, till 4 to 6 inches of organic matter into the top foot of soil. Rake amended beds, water them and let them settle for a week before planting.

☑ **START COMPOSTING.** As you get the garden in shape for planting, use the weeds you pull to start a compost pile. Layer green weeds with dry leaves, straw, or sawdust. Keep the pile damp and turn it weekly with a pitchfork. The compost should be ready in a few weeks.

PEST & WEED CONTROL

☑ **APHIDS.** In small numbers, these sucking insects do relatively little damage to plants. But when populations build up, they can do great harm. Watch tender new growth carefully; when you see a population develop, blast them off with hose water or spray with insecticidal soap.

☑ **WEEDS.** Hoe them now while they're young and shallow-rooted. If you wait until they form deep taproots, they'll sprout—and you'll weed—again. If weeds germinate between the time you prepare a flower bed and plant, hoe them lightly without disturbing more than the top ½ inch of soil. If you hoe any deeper, or till more, you'll just bring up a fresh batch of weed seeds.. ◆

Southwest Checklist

PLANTING

☑ **ANNUALS.** Zones 12–13: Set out warm-season flowers such as black-foot daisies (*Melampodium*), celosia, gomphrena, lisianthus, Madagascar periwinkle, marigolds, portulaca, and salvia.

☑ **CITRUS TREES.** Zone 12 (Tucson): Set out mandarins like 'Fairchild', 'Fortune', and 'Fremont'. Zone 13 (Phoenix, Yuma): Plant grapefruits, grapefruit-pummelo hybrids ('Oroblanco', 'Melogold'), lemons, and sweet oranges ('Marrs', 'Trovita', 'Valencia').

☑ **GROUND COVERS.** Zones 12–13: Set out aptenia, calylophus, dwarf rosemary, lantana, Mexican evening primrose, verbena, and vinca.

☑ **PERENNIALS.** Zones 10–13: Aster, autumn sage (*Salvia greggii*), chrysanthemums, coreopsis, feverfew, gerbera, helianthus, hollyhock, penstemon, Shasta daisies, and statice can all go in now.

☑ **SUMMER BULBS.** Zones 10–13: Shop for caladium, canna, and crinum this month, but wait until the soil warms to 65° before planting. Set out dahlia and gladiolus after danger of frost is past.

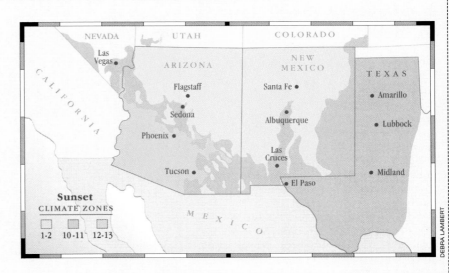

☑ **VEGETABLES.** Zones 10–11: Plant cool-season crops like broccoli, cabbage, carrots, cauliflower, kohlrabi, lettuce, potatoes, radishes, and spinach right away. Zones 12–13: Sow asparagus beans, black-eyed peas, bush and lima beans, cucumbers, melons, soybeans, summer squash, and sweet corn. Set out plants of peppers and tomatoes now.

☑ **VINES.** Zones 10–13: Plant hardy vines like Boston ivy, Carolina jessamine, Japanese honeysuckle, Lady Banks' rose, silver lace vine, trumpet creeper (*Campsis radicans*), Virginia creeper, and wisteria.

MAINTENANCE

☑ **DIVIDE PERENNIALS.** Zones 10–13: Dig and divide clumping perennials such as bearded iris, chrysanthemums, and daylilies.

☑ **MAINTAIN DRIP SYSTEMS.** Clean algae and sediment from drip tubing and emitters (a solution of water and either bleach or vinegar will help clear them out), replace any clogged emitters you can't clear, and clean all filters.

☑ **MULCH PLANTS.** Zones 12–13: After soil has warmed, spread 3 to 4 inches of organic mulch around roses, shrubs, and trees, and in rows between flowers and cool-season vegetables. Mulch warm-season vegetables next month.

☑ **TRIM ORNAMENTAL GRASSES.** When new growth appears, cut back the old grass to keep clumps from looking ratty. ◆

Bring on the butterflie.

They'll set up housekeeping
in your garden if you provide
the right plants

BY SHARON COHOON

■ It's no secret. The key to a wildly successful
butterfly garden is providing lots of caterpillar
food. Period.

Sure, if you have nectar plants in your garden, adult butterflies flitting through the
neighborhood will drop in for a quick drink.
But if you don't have food to offer future prog-
eny, the butterflies won't stay. A quick sugar fix
and the females are gone, continuing their
search for the specific plants they depend on
to nourish their caterpillar offspring. And
where there are no females, males don't linger.

If, on the other hand, you also have plants in
your garden that caterpillars can feed on, the females will stay to lay their eggs. And you've got
a front-row seat for the butterfly's remarkable
rite of passage from egg to caterpillar to chrys-
alis to winged adult. Witness this metamorpho-
sis a few times, gardeners attest, and you'll start
thinking of yourself as a butterfly grower rather
than a gardener; of caterpillars as endangered
species rather than threats to your plants; and
of defoliated plants as a lepidopteran triumph
rather than a horticultural defeat.

Adding host plants for caterpillars definitely
increases the total number of butterflies in
your garden. And, as Louise Hallberg discovered when she retired and took up butterfly
gardening, it can add to the variety of butterflies there as well. Hallberg was used to seeing
pipevine swallowtails on her property in Sebastopol, California. Back in the '20s, her
mother had planted California Dutchman's
pipe, their caterpillar food plant, and the vine
had slowly multiplied, covering fences and
scrambling up trees and luring in hundreds of
egg-bearing pipevine swallowtails each spring.
But monarchs are new to Hallberg's garden.
They didn't arrive until she planted milkweed a
few years ago. By letting weedy dock and sorrel
return to her pasture, she has recently at-
tracted purplish coppers. And she's hoping the

LEFT: A Western tiger swallowtail sips from summer phlox (*P. paniculata*).

ABOVE: Monarch caterpillar dines on milkweed (*Asclepias*), its host plant.

RIGHT: Cocktail hour at a butterfly weed for a gulf fritillary.

ABOVE: Louise Hallberg releases a monarch butterfly she reared from a caterpillar.

FRANCE RUFFENACH

RIGHT: Monarch caterpillar starts to enfold itself in a pupal case; two weeks later, the adult monarch is about to emerge.

BELOW: A monarch rests on a gloriosa daisy, a favorite nectar plant of many butterflies.

addition of some canyon live oaks this year will bring back California sisters.

Adding caterpillar plants to our gardens not only lures butterflies but also helps them, says Jeff Glassberg, president of the North American Butterfly Association (NABA), a nonprofit organization that promotes public awareness and conservation of butterflies. It extends their shrinking habitat and can even bring a species back from the brink. The atala, a beautiful metallic blue hairstreak butterfly, is a good example, says Glassberg. Once common in Florida, then believed to be extinct, the species has staged a comeback. The cycad, its host plant, has become a popular landscaping specimen in the state, so now there's plenty of atala caterpillar food to go around.

FROM FEAR & LOATHING TO FOSTER PARENTING

Since caterpillar plants are the best way to attract butterflies, why are gardeners so reluctant to add them

ROBERT & LINDA MITCHELL (2)

to their gardens? They confuse voracious with omnivorous, says Mark Dimmitt, associate director of science fo the Arizona-Sonora Desert Museum They watch gulf fritillary caterpillar vigorously chomping away at passio vines and think they're going to de nude the entire garden.

But caterpillars are actually quit picky eaters. Species like cabbag whites that feed on many plants—any thing in the brassica family—are rare Dimmitt says. Most caterpillars hav evolved to depend on only one or tw host plants and eat nothing else. Th blame for nibbles out of your othe plants belongs elsewhere, he says.

Gardeners also don't realize ho many natural predators caterpillar have, says San Francisco butterfl enthusiast Barbara Deutsch. Bird pick them off b the score. Spiders wasps, mantids, liz ards, and rodent eat them. And par asites finish o most of the rest. I fact, says Deutsch the odds agains any single caterpil lar making it to winged adulthood ar slim. Once they learn this, butterfly gar deners often feel compelled to inter cede. They start rescuing eggs and rear ing caterpillars and releasing adults t improve the butterfly population' long-term chances. "You start out think ing caterpillars are going to eat up al your plants," she says, "but you end up *wishing* for caterpillars."

GETTING TO KNOW BUTTERFLIES

The following tools can help you ge to know butterflies.

A good identification book—*Na tional Audubon Society Field Guide t North American Butterflies* or *A Field Guide to Western Butterflies* (from th Petersen field guide series), for in stance—is essential.

A pair of binoculars brings the exquis ite detail in butterflies' wings into clos focus. NABA's Glassberg recommends pair at least 7X power that focuses t less than 6 feet. For a reprint of hi binocular product review, send a sel addressed, stamped envelope to NABA

DANIEL WRAY/NATURAL SELECTION

4 Delaware Rd., Morristown, NJ 07960.

The Butterfly Book: An Easy Guide to Butterfly Gardening, Identification, and Behavior, by Donald and Lillian Stokes and Ernest Williams (Little, Brown and Company, Boston, 1991; $12.95), is still one of the best primers on butterfly gardening on the market. *Butterfly Gardeners' Quarterly* (Box 30931, Seattle, WA 98103) is also well worth its $8 annual cost.

NABA has a good Web site for additional information on butterfly gardening and identification: *www.naba.org.* ◆

RICHARD SHIELL

Getting started

Sunset gardener Bill Blum is a recent convert to butterfly gardening. He got good advice from veterans like Hallberg and Deutsch before installing his first butterfly garden at a local community plot. In its very first season, his 300-square-foot garden was a big hit with painted ladies, buckeyes, checkerspots, and skippers. Here's how to duplicate his success.

DO RESEARCH. Find out which butterflies are common in your area, then plant the host plants they feed on in their caterpillar stage. Some butterfly identification books contain maps showing the regional distribution of common butterflies and list their host plants. Blum, for instance, relied on John Steiner's pamphlet, "Butterflies of the San Francisco Bay Region" (to order, send 55 cents and a self-addressed, stamped envelope to the San Francisco Bay Wildlife Society, Box 524, Newark, CA 94560). A good resource for Southwest gardeners is *Desert Butterfly Gardening,* published by the Arizona Native Plant Society and Sonoran Arthropod Studies Institute (to order, send $3 to the institute, Box 5624, Tucson, AZ 85703; 520/883-3945).

PLANT NECTAR PLANTS. Choose kinds that thrive in your area and provide blooms from early spring to first frost. Butterfly bush (*Buddleia*), lantana, purple coneflower, coreopsis, and black-eyed Susan show up as top nectar plants in every reference, for good reason. But regional butterflies seem to develop their own preferences. Spicy jatropha, which doesn't appear on anyone's list, is irresistible to many butterflies in Southern California, for instance. Pay attention to the plants that butterflies land on in nurseries and at private and public gardens and plant those things.

PROVIDE WATER. In Blum's garden, a big rock with a natural indentation was a drinking fountain for butterflies. Shallow puddles are also good.

SHELTER YOUR GARDEN FROM WIND. Butterflies prefer warm, sunny spots. If your garden isn't protected from prevailing winds by a fence or wall, add some tall shrubs such as butterfly bush.

AVOID USING PESTICIDES. Butterflies are insects. Any insecticide that rids your garden of pests will kill them, too. That includes the bacterial insecticide *Bacillus thuringiensis.* BT is fatal to all caterpillars, not just those gnawing on your brassicas. But if damage control is absolutely necessary, look for organic solutions. Row covers, for instance, are as effective as BT in protecting cabbage crops.

ABOVE: Goldenrod, asters, phlox, and other nectar plants fill this flower field at Mourning Cloak Ranch and Botanical Garden in Tehachapi, California.

BELOW: A butterfly garden in a pot. Blue buddleia and orange lantana provide nectar for adults; parsley is fodder for anise swallowtail caterpillars; and fescue grass feeds skippers. Design: Bud Stuckey and Bill Blum.

NORMAN A. PLATE

In search of the true geraniums

Grower Robin Parer believes species geraniums deserve a spot in every garden

BY LAUREN BONAR SWEZEY

In the heart of Northern California's Marin County, along a steep, narrow, winding road, is an unusual nursery called Geraniaceae. You would not expect a nursery so far off the beaten track to be a great success, but this one is, partly because of the unique plants grown here, but mostly due to its owner's dedication to one fascinating genus—*Geranium*. Robin Parer owns Geraniaceae, and the nursery's name hints at her specialty: hardy geraniums.

Parer grows more than 300 hybrids, selected color forms, and species of true *Geranium*. Don't confuse these hardy plants with those other "geraniums," which actually belong to the genus *Pelargonium*. Many of Parer's geraniums will grow outdoors even in the coldest climates.

She discovered the plants during an extended stay in England. "When I saw the diversity of geraniums available, I thought, 'This is something I could do.'" Parer got started in the early

Geranium phaeum 'Lily Lovell' bears blossoms about 1 inch across with white eyes.

G. riversleaianum 'Mavis Simpson' plays off 'Silver Carpet' lamb's ears and pink blooms of 'The Fairy' polyantha rose.

1980s, when few people in the United States were offering these geraniums for sale. Ever since, she's been "preaching the gospel about hardy geraniums" at garden society meetings. Apparently, her passion has rubbed off. Hardy geraniums have been steadily rising in popularity as gardeners have come to recognize their value as practical plants with few problems.

True geraniums don't bear the big, showy blooms that pelargoniums do. "Geranium flowers aren't enormous. They've retained the quality of a wildflower, even though they've been hy-

bridized. There are lots of color forms, leaf shapes, and sizes. In fact, there's a geranium for every spot in the garden," Parer says. She recommends that geraniums be grown as fillers around structural plants (shrubs and taller perennials). "I always tell my customers to grow them for their attractive foliage. Then the flowers will be a bonus." Ten of Parer's favorite plants are described on page 80.

You can visit Parer's nursery, Geraniaceae, by calling (415) 461-4168 for an appointment. Request a mail-order catalog ($4) or check it out on the Web at www.freeyellow.com/members/

SAXON HOLT (2)

Robin Parer stands beside her all-time favorite, *G. maderense*, shown in detail at top. This species forms flower heads 2½ feet across.

geraniaceae. You can also order a number of these geraniums from Digging Dog Nursery (Box 471, Albion, CA 95410; 707/937-1130) and Heronswood Nursery (7530 N.E. 288th St., Kingston, WA 98346; 360/297-4172).

CARING FOR GERANIUMS

A good rule of thumb is to plant them in locations that get morning sun and afternoon shade, particularly in hot, inland climates.

Before planting, mix compost or other organic amendment into the soil. Keep soil moist but not wet. Hardy geraniums don't need additional fertilizer, unless they're grown in a container.

After the first flush of bloom, give plants (except *G. maderense*) a light haircut to remove bedraggled foliage, and mulch the plants; within a few weeks, they'll put on a flush of new leaves and flowers.

10 best geraniums

FOR BEDS AND BORDERS

G. magnificum. Large (2-inch-wide) violet-blue flowers with deep purple veins; dark green, quilted foliage. Plants reach 18 inches tall and 30 inches wide. Massive bloom in early spring, followed by sporadic flowers. Robin Parer's comments: "Wonderful with blue or purple columbine." *Sunset* climate zones 3–9, 14–24.

G. sanguineum striatum. Pale pink flowers with dark pink veins; deep green, divided leaves. 10 inches tall by 30 inches wide. Particularly heat-tolerant. Slow to establish; best by third year. "Delicate, pretty foliage." Zones 3–24.

G. wallichianum 'Buxton's Variety'. Clear blue flowers with white centers; medium-green foliage faintly blotched with light green. 15 inches tall by 36 inches wide. Blooms midsummer to fall (year-round in mild areas); flowers fade to pink in hot climates. "The flower color is irresistible." Zones 3–9, 14–24.

SCRAMBLERS AND SPILLERS

These look best growing through shrubs or over banks and walls.

G. 'Ann Folkard'. Purplish magenta flowers with black eyes; chartreuse foliage. 12 inches tall by 48 inches wide. Blooms from spring to late fall. Can be grown in containers. "Dynamite with *Heuchera* and *Lonicera nitida* 'Baggesen's Gold' honeysuckle." Zones 3–9, 14–24.

G. 'Frances Grate'. Pale mauve flowers; leaves gray-green above, silvery beneath. 15 to 18 inches tall by 36 inches wide. Blooms from spring through fall. Very heat-tolerant. "The plant develops into a great billowy mound." Zones 5–9, 14–24.

G. riversleaianum 'Mavis Simpson'. Medium-pink flowers; gray-green leaves. 18 inches tall by 48 inches wide. Blooms from spring through fall. "Tops for Southern California." Zones 5–9, 14–24.

THREE MADE FOR LIGHT SHADE

G. maderense. Luminous rose-pink blooms with paler veins develop on rounded flower heads 2½ feet wide; enormous (19-inch-wide) green, divided leaves. 48 inches tall by 60 inches wide. Flowers open over a four- to five-week period in spring. Biennial or short-lived perennial (central stem dies after bloom, but offsets form new plants; also self-seeds). "Looks wonderful even when not in bloom." Zones 15–24.

G. oxonianum 'Winscombe'. Pale pink flowers that fade to darker pink; medium-green foliage. 18 inches tall by 24 inches wide. Flowers appear spring through summer. "I love the multicolor effect." Zones 5–9, 14–24.

G. phaeum 'Lily Lovell'. Dark blue-maroon flowers with a white eye; medium-green foliage. Upright growth to 18 inches tall by 24 inches wide. Blooms come in flushes on elongated stems. Doesn't like sun. "Beautiful flower color." Zones 1–9, 14–24.

GROUND COVER

G. cantabrigiense 'Biokovo'. White flowers with pink flush and yellow anthers; small, medium-green leaves. 8 inches tall by 30 inches wide. Blooms in spring and fall. This evergreen plant spreads by rhizomatous roots. "Excellent ground cover. It's rambunctious—don't plant it next to your delicate little treasures." Zones 3–9, 14–24. ◆

CURTIS ANDERSON

Connoisseur flowers freshen the palette

Six uncommon plants add distinction to summer beds and borders

BY LAUREN BONAR SWEZEY

Annuals play an important role in any garden, brightening borders, bringing a spark to perennial beds during a downtime, or making a dramatic show on their own. But what if you want to move beyond the ho-hum world of marigolds and petunias? When that urge struck us last spring, we hit the seed catalogs and selected several uncommon annuals and tender perennials grown as annuals. The following six plants were standouts in *Sunset's* test garden for their striking flowers and forms.

Bells-of-Ireland (*Moluccella laevis*). Showy, apple green calyxes resembling bells surround whorls of white flowers on upright stalks. Good cut flowers (can be dried). Blooms summer. Full sun.

China aster (*Callistephus chinensis*). Many-petaled flowers come in several forms (anemone- and peony-flowered, pompom, ostrich feather) in shades of crimson, lavender, pink, purple, and white. Plants grow 1 to 3 feet tall. Blooms late summer. Good cut flowers. Full sun.

Dwarf morning glory 'Royal Ensign' (*Convolvulus tricolor*). The 2-inch-wide trumpet-shaped flowers are a deep purplish blue with white-and-yellow throats. Unlike other morning glories, this one is not a vine but a bush that grows 12 to 18 inches tall. Blooms summer to fall. Full sun.

Nicotiana sylvestris. Intensely fragrant, tubular white flowers appear on 5-foot stalks. Lyre-shaped leaves form a rosette. Tender perennial grown as an annual. Blooms summer. Full sun or partial shade.

Salvia coccinea. Bears 6- to 12-inch-long flower spikes in red, pink, or coral shades on bushy, 2- to 3-foot-tall plants with small, fuzzy leaves. 'Coral Nymph' and 'Lady in Red' are particularly compact varieties. Tender perennial grown as an annual. Blooms spring to fall. Attracts hummingbirds. Full sun.

Spider flower (*Cleome hassleran* or *C. spinosa*). Airy clusters of pink or white flowers are borne atop 4- to 6-foot-tall stems. Shrubby plant spreads to 5 feet wide; keep it on the dry side to avoid rampant growth. Blooms late summer to fall. Cut flower heads make intriguing accents in arrangements. Full sun.

SOURCES

China aster, *Nicotiana sylvestris, Salvia coccinea,* and spider flower are sometimes sold in containers at specialty nurseries. Most of the flowers listed can be grown from seed, sold by these sources: ***Shepherd's Garden Seeds*** (30 Irene St., Torrington, CT 06790; 860/482-3638) and ***Thompson & Morgan*** (Box 1308, Jackson, NJ 08527; 800/274-7333). Both catalogs are free.

Homegrown paprika beats the bottled spice

For superior quality, sow and grind your own peppers

BY LAUREN BONAR SWEZEY

ABOVE: 'Paprika Supreme' bears showy 4- to 6-inch-long pods on 18-inch-tall plants. Fully reddened pods are ready to harvest.

LEFT: Strung up in a warm spot, paprika peppers dry quickly.

I f you think of paprika merely as a cosmetic—for adding a bit of color to stuffed eggs or potato salad— you probably haven't tasted the real thing. *Paprika* means pepper in Hungarian, and mild, thin-walled peppers are the source of the spice. Hungarian cooks use a rich aromatic version in goulash, *paprikás csirke* (paprika chicken), and other traditional dishes.

In America, many people "don't understand the difference between real paprika that you can grow in the garden and the musty stuff that's sold in jars," says Rosalind Creasy, landscape designer and author of *Cooking from the Garden.* Creasy has been cultivating paprika peppers since a seed grower convinced her that they merited a place in the garden and kitchen. She reaches for her paprika when she wants to pep up chili, chicken, eggs, guacamole, even her lima bean casserole.

Grow your own peppers from seed and you, too, can produce superior paprika. Last season, we tried four kinds in *Sunset's* test garden. After drying them, we ground the peppers and compared their flavors. The tasters preferred the 'Kalosca' pepper, with 'Paprika Supreme' coming in a distant second. But all four rated well above the commercial powder found on most spice racks. Here are the tasters' comments.

'Hungarian'. Mildly sweet, with medium-red color.

'Kalosca'. Unbelievably sweet, with an intense aroma. Complex flavor, lingering aftertaste. Gorgeous orange-red when ground.

'Paprika Supreme'. Sweet, intense, musky flavor like a sun-dried tomato. Dark red.

'Papri Mild II'. Very mild, with a pretty color.

SEED SOURCES

Shepherd's Garden Seeds, 30 Irene St., Torrington, CT 06790; (860) 482-3638. Sells 'Kalosca'. Free catalog.

Southern Exposure Seed Exchange, Box 170, Earlysville, VA 22936; (804) 973-4703. Sells 'Hungarian'. Catalog $2.

Tomato Growers Supply Company, Box 2237, Fort Myers, FL 33902; (941) 768-1119. Sells 'Paprika Supreme' and 'Papri Mild II'. Free catalog. ◆

Growing tips

Like other peppers, paprika types thrive in warm weather. Sow seeds six to eight weeks before transplant time. Keep the potting soil temperature above 80° if possible (use a heating cable or set pots on a water heater). After seeds germinate, move containers into bright light and keep the soil moist.

When seedlings are ready to transplant, acclimate them to outdoor light by setting them in partial shade for a few days, then moving them into brighter light. Pick a planting site in full sun and amend the soil with organic matter. In cool climates, plant seedlings through black plastic and use row covers. Keep the soil evenly moist. Apply liquid fertilizer every two weeks.

Allow peppers to turn completely red before harvesting. Snip them off the plant and hang them to dry out of direct sun, or use a dehydrator (remove stem and seeds first), until pods turn very brittle.

Store peppers in zip-lock plastic bags in the freezer. Grind them as needed with a blender or coffee grinder. We found that a blender gives the finest grind. For a superfine powder, sift after grinding.

NORMAN A. PLATE (2)

Grow gardens anywhere in pots, baskets, and window boxes (for details, see the article beginning on page 98). For more information on the handsome butterfly havens shown here, see page 101

April

gardenguide

Natural rock garden in Reno

■ Perched at 5,000 feet, Linda Good's backyard provides a grand view of the Reno skyline and the Sierra Nevada, framed by a volcanic outcropping—a perfect foundation for a rock garden. "When I first saw the outcropping, I knew I wanted to keep the planting there as natural and wild as possible," says Good. So, instead of defying nature, she decided to work with it.

Good knew that for plants to survive among the rocks, they must be tough, like the horehound and rabbitbrush that grew wild. So she began planting cold-hardy, drought-tolerant, low-maintenance plants (including 20 perennials) anywhere she could dig a pocket and amend the clay soil with compost. "I started by digging tiny holes and planting tiny [4-inch] plants," she says.

At first "the rabbits ate everything" she planted. They were especially fond of tansy, so Good set out extra plants. That seemed to content the cottontails,

A zinnia of a different stripe

■ I never met a zinnia I didn't like (with the possible exception of that pea-soup-green one called 'Envy'). But 'Candy Cane Mix' (pictured at left), a cheerful little hybrid from W. Atlee Burpee Co., is an especially endearing member of the clan. Its swirls of pink, rose, or red stripes on white look as refreshing in the summer garden as peppermint ice cream, and its pattern is a welcome contrast to zinnia's usual bright solids. Flowers are double and 4 inches across on a plant 17 inches tall.

Like all zinnias, 'Candy Cane Mix' is easy to grow. Sow seed directly in the garden where you want the flowers to come up. They germinate quickly—seedlings emerge 7 to 10 days later. Water regularly but avoid overhead sprinkling, which tends to promote mildew. Feed occasionally. And cut often to encourage more bloom. To order, call (800) 888-1447. — *Sharon Cohoon*

CONNIE COLEMAN

who left the rest of the garden alone.

In the foreground of the photo above (taken in July) are purple catmint, red and white gaura, 'Munstead' lavender, Missouri primrose (*Oenothera missourensis*), and yarrow (*Achillea kellereri*). Behind them, maroon gaillardia and gold woadwaxen (*Genista tinctoria*) provide colorful punctuation.

— *Suzanne Touchette Kelso*

Catch our pumpkin mania

■ Last October in *Sunset's* test garden, Bud Stuckey harvested three behemoth pumpkins: 347-pound "Steve," 400-pound "Tony," and 175-pound "Rosalie" ("smaller but very cute," says Bud)—all from one 'Atlantic Giant' vine. Since Steve ripened first (October 13, to be exact), Bud entered him in the Half Moon Bay, California, giant pumpkin contest.

Sorry, Steve, the winner sent the arrow spinning to 867 pounds. But what Steve lacked in heft he made up for in silver-screen looks. Bud started seeds indoors in paper cups (one seed per cup) in late May, then transplanted the most vigorous seedling about two weeks later in rich soil well amended with compost. He allowed the vine plenty of room to grow—at least 25 square feet—and mulched the soil with straw. To keep the pumpkin skins from sunburning, he covered the ripening fruits with white sheets. And he slipped a 4- by 4-foot piece of 1-inch-thick polystyrene foam under each growing fruit to keep the undersides clean and free of rot and scarring.

Want to see whether you can beat Bud's record? If so, order seeds now and get growing. Mail-order sources for 'Atlantic Giant' include Ferry Morse Seeds (800/283-6400) and Territorial Seed Company (541/942-9547).

In *Sunset's* October issue, we'll reveal some of Bud's harvest tips and have more fun with pumpkins. We'd love to hear how your big bruisers turn out, too. Send your growing tips to Giant-Pumpkin Editor, *Sunset Magazine*, 80 Willow Rd., Menlo Park, CA 94025.

— *Kathleen N. Brenzel*

NORMAN A. PLATE (3)

MICHAEL S. THOMPSON

NEW PLANT REPORT
A pretty tough rhododendron for cold country

■ Rhododendrons are among the showiest of broad-leafed evergreens. But their susceptibility to cold has consigned most of them to the mild coastal-influenced climates of the West. Now 'Northern Starburst', a genetically improved version of the hardy 'PJM' variety, has been bred to tolerate temperatures as low as –30°, making it tough enough to survive most winters in mountain and intermountain communities.

'Northern Starburst' has red buds that open into 4-inch trusses of pink blossoms in early spring. The trusses rise above 2-inch oval leaves that develop a bronze tint in autumn. This rhododendron reaches about 3 feet tall in 10 years.

Put the plant in a spot that gets filtered sunlight and protection against cold winds. If your garden soil is alkaline, dig a 4-inch layer of peat moss into the soil at planting time. Planted now, 'Northern Starburst' will have plenty of time to become established before next winter; it should bloom the following spring. You can order by mail from Whitney Gardens & Nursery (800/952-2404; 3-gallon plants cost $25 each) or Wayside Gardens (800/845-1124; 1-gallon plants cost $30 each).

— *Jim McCausland*

TREE TRAINING
Prunus thrives on prudence

■ Growing side by side, a pair of 'Mt. Fuji' Japanese flowering cherry trees (*Prunus serrulata* 'Shirotae') forms a seamless cloud of blossoms in Georgia Penfield's Seattle garden each spring. These trees are probably a half-century old, and through the years they've been carefully shaped to follow this variety's natural form: 'Mt. Fuji' has a horizontal branching habit, growing wider than it does tall (it reaches a height of 20 feet).

If you want your trees to look like these, you've got to start encouraging their form from day one. If you put in a young plant ('Mt. Fuji' is sold in full bloom this month), allow it to lean a bit when you plant it. If multiple trunks sprout, let them develop and fan out in several directions. When the plant gets well above head height, begin training it. Light regular pruning will do the trick. In April, May, and June, when suckers emerge along the trunks and major branches, snap them off. If an errant shoot appears, snip it off while it is still young.

Winter, when the tree is leafless, is the best time to observe its structure and a good time to prune out unwanted growth. But next spring, keep an eye on the pruning cuts: when aggressive new shoots emerge around each cut, snap them off.

— *Steven R. Lorton*

BRIAN HUNTOON

A pool swims in a desert paradise

When Helen and Rob Harrigan bought their house in Paradise Valley, Arizona, they gained a yard with mature desert trees and cactus, and a pool with a big problem. "Every time it rained," Helen recalls, "runoff from the slope behind the house, the driveway, and the roof would end up in the pool, which was in the lowest part of the yard."

Solving the problem involved bringing in loads of fill soil to raise the level of the new pool, and forming a drainage swale to channel runoff around the area. The renovated pool has softly curving edges punctuated by granite boulders. A raised spa and water feature were installed at one end.

The surrounding landscape, designed by Michael Rockwell and Peter Curé of Phoenix-based Arterra, combines native plants and drought-tolerant introductions to provide year-round interest. Abundant color comes not only from flowers but also from fo-

liage that ranges from chartreuse to olive and blue to silver, with bronze and gold tones from the cactus spines. Cactus aren't usually thought of as good choices for poolside landscaping, but they work in this case because a minimum of 18 inches separates the spines from the edge of the patio.

The skeleton of a saguaro cactus found on the property is the centerpiece of a bed planted with red hesperaloe (*H. parviflora; Sunset* climate zones 10–13) and desert marigold (*Baileya multiradiata;* all zones). The old saguaro's skeletonic beauty is reflected in the pool's surface. — *Judy Mielke*

BACK TO BASICS

Pinch those tips

■ Many annuals and some perennials benefit from being pinched back early in the season: chrysanthemums, euryops, fuchsias, geraniums, impatiens, petunias, snapdragons, and zinnias, for instance. Pinch the tender new growth between the nails of your thumb and forefinger, nipping off one to three sets of leaves. Take just-forming buds, too. With proper water and fertilizer, plants will soon put out bushy new growth.

NORMAN A. PLATE

STEVEN GUNTHER

A jungle in suburbia

■ Like the jungles of Guatemala, this patio in the Point Loma neighborhood of San Diego is leafy, green, and shaded—thanks to a single vine that drapes the stucco wall and dangles from the ceiling. That's just the effect owners Ruth and Schuyler Hoffman wanted. "Make our patio look like the jungle is running into the house," Ruth told me.

I remembered the jungles I'd seen in Guatemala, and knew just the vine to duplicate that look: evergreen mock orange (*Philadelphus mexicanus*), a native of Mexico and Guatemala. I planted the vine from a 1-gallon nursery can in a garden bed adjacent to the Hoffmans' patio, and in just three years, it sprawled and climbed for 30 feet, easily covering the wall and, with a little help, the ceiling as well. (I attached the vine to the stucco by squeezing dollops of clear silicon caulking onto the stucco, embedding ties of plastic-wrapped wire in them, and letting them dry, then wrapping the ties around the vine's supple green branches.)

In spite of its vigor, this espaliered mock orange is graceful and airy. The weeping stems of apple-green leaves contrast nicely with the warm tan of thatch. And during spring and late summer, the plant blooms on new wood. Its flowers are not as spectacular as those of other mock orange species, but they're pretty, and their perfume—an intense honey-citrus scent—is delightful.

I prune the vine lightly after each bloom cycle to keep it shapely, but save the deepest cuts for late winter.

P. mexicanus is sold in well-stocked nurseries such as Buena Creek Gardens in San Marcos and Walter Andersen Nursery in San Diego.

— *Damon Hedgepeth*

Circular garden solves a puzzle

■ Stephanie and Robert Brasher loved the view from their corner lot in Laguna Niguel, but not its odd shape. The large side yard, once a parking lot for the tract's model homes, was a disorientingly irregular triangle, with an apex out there somewhere that didn't line up with the living room's French doors, or anything else. There was no focal point, and the Brashers couldn't figure out how to turn the space into a garden.

Fortunately, landscape architect Mark Scioneaux had a simple solution. "When you're faced with an odd-shaped space, try cutting a circle in it," he suggests. "The eye is drawn to the circle and lingers there. It rides around the rim rather than resting at any one point." So Scioneaux situated a circular planting bed opposite the French doors, crossed it with steppingstones, and placed a sundial in the middle. Now, from inside and out, there are clear axis lines, which give the space strong definition.

To emphasize the circle, the planter-seat wall behind it echoes its curves, ignoring the straight lines of the original wall that delineated the triangle. Now garden viewers do the same. "Your eye perceives the planter walls as the edges of the garden," says Scioneaux. — *S. C.*

VEGETABLE BEDS
Sure bet in Las Vegas

STEVEN GUNTHER

■ Tom and Cindy Kapp wanted to grow vegetables organically in their Las Vegas garden. But they faced an immediate barrier: the native soil was so bad that there was no point in even trying to improve it. The combination of hardpan and poor soil chemistry (mostly high pH and excessive salt) is a common problem around Las Vegas, according to Bob Morris at Clark County Cooperative Extension. One sure way to overcome this problem is with raised beds.

The Kapps made their beds with treated Douglas fir and filled them with imported soil. Altogether, they built eight beds with 18-inch-tall sides, in different dimensions. Originally, they filled the beds with silt that had organic components. Since then, Cindy says, they've improved the soil so much "that it's not the same stuff any more." To refresh the soil each season, she adds chicken manure, seaweed compost, garden compost, peat, and worms.

Although she grows a few cool-season crops, like broccoli and kohlrabi, she concentrates on the warm-season vegetables. "Last season we did great with tomatoes. My favorites were 'White Beauty' (fruit ripens creamy white) and 'Green Zebra' (yellow fruit with green stripes)." She also grows Armenian cucumbers, beans, peppers, squash, and tomatillos. "I plant corn on the west side so it shades everything else when the afternoon temperature hits 120°." She devotes one bed to herbs.

Watering is critical to their garden's success. At first the Kapps used an overhead sprinkler system, but they've gradually replaced this with spaghetti tubing and other drip emitters that direct water to the root zones. —*J.M.*

NURSERY SHOPPING
Perennials galore in Mendocino

■ Most visitors to the scenic Mendocino, California, coast head for hiking trails, great restaurants, and relaxing B & Bs. But gardeners in the know head for Heritage House Nursery in Little River and Digging Dog Nursery in Albion for outstanding selections of new and unusual perennials.

Heritage House Nursery opened its doors unofficially in 1987, when head gardener Peggy Quaid was propagating the plants she needed to relandscape the 37-acre grounds around Heritage House Inn. Periodically, she would sell 4-inch plants to interested visitors. To meet the growing demand for her plants, the inn officially opened the nursery in 1989, then moved it to a much larger site (pictured at right) in 1993.

Today, the plants that grow on the property are for sale at the nursery, as are many others—including natives from Australia, New Zealand, the Mediterranean, South Africa, and California.

Heritage House Nursery is open from 9 to 5 Thursdays through Tuesdays. For information, call (707) 937-1427.

Digging Dog Nursery, a family-run mail-order and retail business just down the road in Albion, specializes in easy-care grasses, perennials, and shrubs with year-round interest. Owners Deborah Whigham and Gary Ratway sell intriguing plants that they've gathered and propagated from trips overseas. The nursery is open by appointment only; call (707) 937-1235.

— *Lauren Bonar Swezey*

NORMAN A. PLATE

Pacific Northwest Garden Notebook

BY STEVEN R. LORTON

Of all the wildflowers I've come to know, one stirs my memory most: the 'Flanders Field' poppy (*Papaver rhoeas*), whose bright red blooms dot the landscapes of northwestern Europe. I first saw these poppies while touring France and Belgium. Then two summers ago, I got a better look. I was visiting my friend Rosemary Verey, garden designer and writer, at Barnsley House in Gloucestershire, England. Verey had helped design the garden at Highgrove, Prince Charles's country estate, which isn't far from her place. One morning Rosemary surprised me by announcing, "We're going to Highgrove." When we got there—to my amazement—the prince himself came bounding out of his house and spent the next half-hour strolling around the gardens with us. I was impressed at how well he knew his plants. He led us around a hedge to a stunning sight: sweeping meadows of the greenest grass I've ever seen, peppered with red poppies and dotted with black sheep. The poppies had naturalized from seed sown by the prince.

When I got back home, I couldn't resist ordering a pound o poppy seed ($25)—enough to sow half an acre—from Wild seed Farms (Box 3000, Fredericksburg, TX 78624; 800/848 0078 or 830/990-8080), a good source for bulk seeds of man wildflowers. 'Flanders Field' poppy bears single flowers inches across on wispy stems that reach 2 feet high. In April, freely sowed the poppies in a meadow at my place in Washing ton's Upper Skagit Valley. They bloomed in late June, self sowed, and put on a stronger show the next season. I don have any black sheep yet, but my poppies are fit for a prince.

that's a good question ...

Q: What wildflowers will grow in the deep shade under cedar and other tall conifers? — *Marin Landis, Brier, Washington*

A: There aren't many candidates, but one of my favorites Solomon's seal (*Polygonatum biflorum*). In spring, its cream white bell-like flowers dangle along feathery, 3-foot-tall stems. In au tumn, the stalks turn bright yellow, then drop. This deciduous perennia spreads slowly by underground rhizomes. To create the cool, even moist medium the rhizomes love, let a thick layer of humus, includin fallen needles, accumulate under cedar trees.

Northern California Garden Notebook

BY LAUREN BONAR SWEZEY

*L*andscaping with native plants, particularly in hillside and woodland areas, has always seemed so sensible to me. Choose the right ones and they adapt superbly to your climate and terrain.

On April 26, during Park Day School's Secret Gardens of the East Bay tour, one of the Bay Area's oldest and best native plant gardens is open for viewing. The ½-acre garden in the Berkeley hills is owned by Jenny and Scott Fleming, founding members of the California Native Plant Society. It contains multiple plant communities—meadow, bog, woodland, and chaparral gardens (great ideas here for combining plants)—as well as a waterfall and stream system.

To see this and nine other gardens on the tour, order tickets ($35 each) by calling (510) 653-6250.

SPEAKING OF NATIVE PLANT GARDENS ...

The California Native Plant Society has just published *California's Wild Gardens: A Living Legacy,* edited by Phyllis M. Faber (California Native Plant Society for the California Department of Fish and Game, Sacramento, 1997; $29.95 paperback, $42.95 hardbound). It's one of the most fascinating books I've seen in years—like an armchair ride through the state's many plant communities. The 236-page volume divides the state into 10 ecological re-

gions, within which are 80 "hot spots"—areas where conditions favor a proliferation of rare or endemic plants. More than 500 exquisite color photographs show these areas and the plants that make them special. Environmental threats to the areas, and conservation efforts, are also described.

The book is available from the publisher; (916) 447-2677.

that's a good question ...

Q: Where can I order seeds or seedlings of Joshua trees (*Yucca brevifolia*) and coast redwood trees (*Sequoia sempervirens*)?

A: Seedlings of Joshua trees (*Sunset* climate zones 8–24), native to the deserts of Arizona, Nevada, Southern California, and Utah, can be purchased by mail from Las Pilitas, 3232 Las Pilitas Rd., Santa Margarita, CA 93453; (805) 438-5992. The nursery's incredibly comprehensive catalog of California native plants is now on the Web at www.laspilitas.com. Redwood trees are available at most retail nurseries.

MARINA THOMPSON

Southern California Garden Notebook

BY SHARON COHOON

*L*ast summer, the airspace above my African blue basil was as congested as that over LAX. Scores of bees, hover flies, and skippers buzzed in daily. So intent on siphoning nectar were they, the winged set barely budged when I elbowed in to deadhead. If you've had trouble with poor fruit set with tomatoes or other summer crops due to a scarcity of bees, try planting the basil (a cross between *Ocimum kilimanscharium* and *O. basilicum purpurescens*) this spring. Pollinators, apparently, can't resist it. And if its nectar tastes as spicy-sweet as its flowers smell, no wonder.

Enjoy African blue basil as an ornamental; there are better culinary basils. It has a long bloom period—the plant doesn't set seed but keeps trying, producing flowers well into winter—and its purplish leaves darken handsomely with the onset of colder weather. It's a perennial, but it's tender. Wonderful plant.

SPEAKING OF PLANTS ...

Many excellent plant sales take place this month. Here's one I'm looking forward to: Landscapes Southern California Style, at the Western Municipal Water District's water conservation demonstration garden. Hundreds of perennials, shrubs, and herbs will be available at this parking lot sale from 8 to 3 on April 4. Visit the idea-inspiring garden while you're there, and pick up the free 30-page booklet. The garden is at 450 Alessandro Blvd. in Riverside. For more details call (909) 780-4177.

that's a good question ...

Q: I'm sick of spraying my hibiscus with water to fight giant whitefly, many readers have complained. Isn't there something else I can do?

A. Not really. A strong stream of water directed at the underside of infested leaves (syringing) works as well as or better than chemicals in combating giant whitefly (*Aleurodicus dugesii*), according to the University of California Cooperative Extension. If water hasn't worked for you, maybe you're not using a forceful enough stream. Buy a nozzle that adjusts down to a needle-thin jet so you can really blast away. Continue treatment once a week until the problem disappears. your leaves are already heavily bearded with wax and covered with black sooty mold, use insecticidal soap or a foliage cleanser to eliminate the honeydew residue.

Mountain Garden Notebook

BY JIM McCAUSLAND

While traveling around Colorado last summer, I was wowed by an herb garden I saw at Fox Acres Country Club in Red Feather Lakes (elevation 8,200 feet). The 300-square-foot garden supplies the club's restaurant with fresh herbs and edible flowers from June through October—a harvest two to three months longer than many mountain gardeners enjoy. The secret that makes this possible was designed into the garden by Marla Hawkins of Hawkeye Landscape Design in Livermore. She buried heating blankets under about 10 inches of soil. The blankets are actually thermostatically controlled propagation mats. At Fox Acres, the blankets are set at 65° to 70° about a week before planting in late April, then turned off when the weather warms up in summer. They're turned back on again when the autumn nights drop below freezing, allowing harvest to extend to the end of October.

For a similar effect, you could try looping heating cables beneath the soil. A 48-foot heating cable (which can warm 12 square feet of soil) costs $28.75, plus shipping, from A. M. Leonard (800/543-8955).

THE ENGLISH HAVE IT IN SPADES

I'm a gopher at heart: I love to dig. When I carve a new flower bed out of my ever-shrinking lawn, I dig down 2 to 3 feet, stripping off the sod. I do most of my digging with English garden spades: a long-handled one because I'm tall and it gives me great leverage, and a short-handled spade when I'm working in tight quarters—among shrubs, for example, where a long handle gets in the way. The blade of an English spade has only a slight curve to its back and edge (like a parenthesis on its side), so it cuts fairly straight edges and slices easily under the sod. By comparison, American shovels have rounder blades that cut scalloped edges—not the look I want for my beds.

that's a good question ...

Q: When should I feed tulips?

A. On a recent visit to Holland, I learned that Dutch growers feed tulips with 12-10-18 fertilizer right after flowering. They also allow leaves to grow for about three months after bloom. The foliage and fertilizer nourish new bulbs that will produce flowers the next year. The old bulbs, by the way, are completely expended at flowering time.

MARINA THOMPSON

Southwest Garden Notebook

BY JIM McCAUSLAND

i'm a gopher at heart: I love to dig. When I carve a new flower bed out of my ever-shrinking lawn, I dig down 2 or 3 feet, stripping off the sod and burying it at the bottom of the bed, where the grass decomposes. I do most of my digging with English garden spades. I like a long-handled one because I'm tall and it gives me great leverage. I use a short-handled spade only when I'm working in tight quarters—among shrubs, for example, where a long handle would get in the way. The blade of an English spade has only a slight curve to its back and edge (like a parenthesis on its side), so it cuts fairly straight edges and slices easily under the sod. By comparison, American shovels have rounder blades that cut scalloped edges—not the look I want for my beds.

PREPARING FOR THE SOUTHWEST'S SCARIEST SEASON

When I was 10, my father and I walked up our street one night and watched as thousands of acres of chaparral burned in the hills behind our house. As I remember it, the fire had followed abundant spring rains that made the grass grow tall and thick before it dried out and became perfect tinder. Our place was spared when a Zuni firefighter bulldozed a firebreak between the flames and the line of houses along our street.

April marks the start of wildfire season in the Southwest— and there are steps you can take to safeguard your property. Start by clearing leaves, brush, dry grass, and other combustibles back 30 feet from your house. Keep trees at least 10 feet from the house and from each other; limb them up at least 6 feet so fire can't climb into their canopies from the ground. Finally, clear leaves from your roof and gutters and regularly treat wood shakes and shingles with a fire retardant such as phosphate salt—or replace them with fire-resistant materials.

that's a good question ...

Q. What's the difference between a mandarin and a tangerine?

A. Nothing. However, there are four kinds of mandarins: the 'Mediterranean' (*Citrus deliciosa*) and 'King' (*C. nobilis*), which are not grown much in the West, and the common mandarin (*C. reticulata*) and seedless, relatively hardy Satsuma (*C. unshiu*) from Japan, both of which are more widely grown here.

Pacific Northwest Checklist

PLANTING

☑ **BARE-ROOT STOCK.** Zones 1–3: Get going pronto if you want to plant bare-root fruits, roses, and ornamental trees. Keep the roots moist until you can get them in the ground.

☑ **BERRIES.** Zones 1–7: Plant blackberries, blueberries, raspberries, and strawberries.

☑ **BEDDING PLANTS.** Zones 4–7: Nurseries offer a huge selection, including celosia, geraniums, impatiens, and sweet alyssum. Set them out as soon as danger of frost is past (normally sometime in the last half of the month). Frost-tolerant plants like lobelia and dusty miller can go out immediately. Seedling snapdragons and petunias are hardy enough to handle anything but a deep freeze. In zones 1–3, wait until May.

☑ **DAHLIA TUBERS.** Gardeners in zones 4–7 often leave dahlia tubers in the ground year-round. But if you dig and store tubers, get them back in the ground this month. In zones 1–3, where digging is a necessity, wait until next month to set tubers out.

☑ **TREES.** Deciduous and evergreen trees can be planted throughout the Northwest this month.

☑ **VEGETABLES.** Zones 1–7: Cabbage, carrots, lettuce, parsnips, peas, potatoes, radishes, spinach, and Swiss chard can all be planted now.

MAINTENANCE

☑ **AMEND SOIL.** Once the soil has thawed and is dry, dig organic matter into beds. Peat moss, compost, leaf mold, and well-rotted manure are all good amendments. After you dig them in, rake the ground smooth and let it settle for a week before planting.

☑ **COMPOST.** As you accumulate garden debris, speed up decomposition by mixing new material with old compost and high-nitrogen fertilizer. Turn the compost pile regularly and keep it damp but not soggy.

☑ **GROOM RHODODENDRONS.** As flower trusses fade, snap them off. Most will come off with a tweak of the thumb and index finger. Just below the flower heads, new growth buds emerge; be careful not to break them.

☑ **MOVE TENDER PLANTS OUT-DOORS.** Zones 4–7: Cymbidiums can go out early in the month. Begonias, fuchsias, and geraniums should go out mid- to late month.

☑ **MOW LAWNS.** For the next two to three months, you may have to mow grass weekly.

PEST AND WEED CONTROL

☑ **SLUGS.** Zones 4–7: It's impossible to overstate the importance of staying on top of the slug battle. Bait, beer traps, handpicking—whatever your method, stick with it. The more you get now, the fewer you'll have nibbling through the growing season.

☑ **WEEDS.** Get them while they're young and easy to pull or they'll mature and scatter their seeds. ◆

Northern California Checklist

PLANTING

☑ **PLANT BARE-ROOT.** Zones 1–2: Deciduous plants, such as cane berries, flowering shrubs, flowering vines, fruit and nut trees, grapes, rhubarb, roses, and strawberries, can go in the ground now. Bare-root planting is the best and least expensive way to start these plants.

☑ **PLANT HERBS.** Zones 7–9, 14–17: Nurseries should have a good selection of common herbs this month, including basil, chives, mint, oregano, parsley, and thyme. For a huge selection of both unusual and traditional herbs, order the plants by mail from Mountain Valley Growers, 38325 Pepperweed Rd., Squaw Valley, CA 93675; (209) 338-2775 or www.mountainvalleygrowers.com.

☑ **PLANT TOMATOES.** Zones 7–9, 14–17: 'Brandywine' (3 to 4 inches wide) is a winner for flavor. 'Stupice' (2 inches wide) and 'Early Girl' can't be beat for flavor and production in cooler climates. To obtain a comprehensive list of heirloom tomato seeds that you can order by mail, write to Grandview Farms Seeds, 12942 Dupont Rd., Sebastopol, CA 95472. Most seed packets cost $2.50 (shipping included).

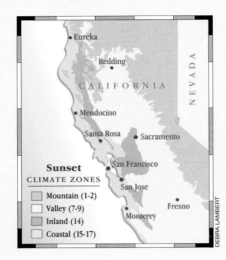

Sunset
CLIMATE ZONES
☐ Mountain (1-2)
☐ Valley (7-9)
☐ Inland (14)
☐ Coastal (15-17)

DEBRA LAMBERT

☑ **START A WATER GARDEN.** Zones 7–9, 14–17: Choose a glazed ceramic container with no drainage hole. Fill with water and add a pump, if desired (drill a hole under the lip of the pot for the cord to exit, or drape it over the pot edge and hide it with plants). Add plants, such as blue spike rush, dwarf umbrella plant, floating heart, Japanese iris, primrose creeper, water poppy, and water snowflake (a good source for plants is Lilypons Water Gardens; 800/999-5459). Support the pots on bricks or other, upside-down pots. Add mosquito fish.

MAINTENANCE

☑ **DIG OR HOE WEEDS.** Zones 7–9, 14–17: Dig out deep-rooted weeds such as dandelions with a hand weeder or trowel (water first to loosen soil). To make sure you get the entire root, slip the tool into the soil and pry up the taproot. You can also hoe out all types of weeds when they're small by cutting just below the soil surface with a sharp hoe or cultivator. To prevent them from surviving on surface moisture, hoe in the morning so the sun bakes the weeds during the day.

☑ **FEED ACID LOVERS.** Zones 7–9, 14–17: After azaleas, camellias, and rhododendrons finish blooming, feed them with an acid fertilizer (purchase bags or boxes of dry fertilizer for acid-loving plants). Also, pinch or snap off spent blooms; be careful not to damage emerging growth.

PEST CONTROL

☑ **APPLY ANT CONTROL.** Zones 7–9, 14–17: Ants feed on honeydew secreted by aphids, scale, and other pests. They also protect the pests from natural predators. To keep ants off trees and shrubs, such as camellias, citrus, and roses, wrap the trunks with a 1- to 2-inch-wide strip of masking tape and coat with a sticky barrier like Tanglefoot. Reapply when the barrier gets dirty and becomes ineffective.

☑ **CORRECT CHLOROSIS.** Zones 7–9, 14–17: If plants such as camellias, citrus, grapes, and gardenias are chlorotic (yellow mottling between green leaf veins), spray leaves with a foliar fertilizer containing iron and zinc. For more long-term results, apply chelated iron or an acid-forming fertilizer containing chelated iron. ◆

Southern California Checklist

PLANTING

☑ **PLANT SUBTROPICALS.** In Southern California's mildest coastal and inland climates, this is the month to plant bougainvillea, gardenia, ginger, hibiscus, passion vine, and subtropical fruits and nuts such as avocado, citrus, macadamia, and white sapote. Ornamental trees such as Hong Kong orchid tree (zones 13, 19, 21, and 23) and tabebuia (zones 20–24) can also go into the ground now. Subtropicals planted in midspring will have a long warm season in which to get established before hardening off for winter.

☑ **PLANT VEGETABLES.** If you live within sight of the ocean, plant last crops of quick-maturing, cool-season vegetables such as beets, carrots, chard, leaf lettuce, radishes, and spinach. Inland (zones 18–21), shift attention to warm-season crops such as basil, beans, corn, cucumber, eggplant, peppers, melons, okra, pumpkins, summer and winter squash, and tomatoes. High-desert (zone 11) gardeners should delay summer planting for two to four weeks; frost is still a possibility until midmonth.

Sunset CLIMATE ZONES
1-3 7-9 11 13 14-24
DEBRA LAMBERT

☑ **SHOP FOR CONTAINER-GROWN ROSES.** Though bare-root roses are less expensive, blooming roses in containers allow you to judge flower color and form. Nurseries are well stocked with flowering plants this month. Choose a plant that has at least four strong canes, and make sure the swollen bud joint at the base of the plant is at least an inch above soil level.

☑ **REPLACE ANNUALS.** When spring annuals poop out, pop in summer bedding plants. For sunny areas, choices include ageratum, amaranth, bedding dahlias, marigolds, nasturtiums, nicotiana, petunia, portulaca, sanvitalia, summer phlox, verbena, and zinnias. For shade, consider bedding begonias, caladium, coleus, impatiens, and lobelia. Gardeners in the high desert (zone 11) can still plant pansies, snapdragons, stock, sweet alyssum, and violas.

MAINTENANCE

☑ **TREAT PLANTS FOR IRON DEFICIENCY.** If bottlebrush, camellias, citrus, gardenias, hibiscus, pyracantha, roses, or other ornamentals have yellowing leaves with green veins, feed them with iron chelate.

PEST AND WEED CONTROL

☑ **COMBAT POWDERY MILDEW.** Warm days and cool nights—typical in April—are ideal conditions for powdery mildew on susceptible plants like roses. Prevent this fungus by hosing off foliage every morning to wash off spores. Or spray with 1 tablespoon *each* baking soda and summer oil diluted in a gallon of water. (Don't spray when temperatures exceed 85°.) Or try neem oil.

☑ **CONTROL APHIDS.** Tender new plant growth attracts these pests. Dislodge with a strong blast of water from a hose, mist plants with insecticidal soap (if blossoms are delicate), or strip aphids from plants by hand.

☑ **CONTROL WEEDS.** Dig out deep-rooted weeds such as dandelions with a hand weeder. (Water first to loosen soil.) Slip weeder into soil and pry against taproot to make sure you get its entire length. Use a sharp hoe to scrape out shallow-rooted weeds, cutting just below the soil surface.

☑ **CONTROL WHITEFLIES.** Hang yellow sticky cards (available in most nurseries) around fuchsias and other susceptible plants to trap these pests. ◆

Mountain Checklist

PLANTING

☑ **BARE-ROOT STOCK.** Set out bare-root berries, grapes, roses, and both fruit and ornamental trees this month. Bare-root plants are less expensive than container-grown stock, and they adapt to garden soil more easily.

☑ **FLOWERS.** Nurseries are full of cool-season annual seedlings. You can set out annuals like calendulas, English daisies, pansies, primroses, snapdragons, stock, and violas and a host of flowering perennials, including bergenia, bleeding hearts, and forget-me-nots.

☑ **HARDY VEGETABLES.** Early in the month, plant bare-root asparagus, horseradish, and rhubarb. As soon as you can work the soil, sow beets, carrots, endive, kohlrabi, lettuce, onion, parsley, parsnips, peas, radishes, spinach, Swiss chard, and turnips. Set out transplants of broccoli, brussels sprouts, cabbage, cauliflower, and green onions. Plant seed potatoes. Use floating row covers or hot caps to protect seedlings from late frosts and to hold warmth around plants so they get off to a fast start.

☑ **SPRING-BLOOMING TREES AND SHRUBS.** You can buy and plant flowering shrubs in containers, including flowering quinces, forsythias, magnolias, and redbuds.

Sunset
CLIMATE ZONES

1-3   10-11

DEBRA LAMBERT

MAINTENANCE

☑ **FEED LAWNS.** Apply 1 to 2 pounds of high-nitrogen fertilizer per 1,000 square feet of turf (put more on heavily used lawns and those growing in poor soil). Spread the fertilizer evenly over the lawn, then water it in thoroughly.

☑ **MULCH.** A 2- to 3-inch layer of organic mulch suppresses weeds, holds in moisture, and—when the weather heats up—keeps roots cool. Spread mulch around annuals, perennials, trees, and shrubs. But keep mulch a few inches away from warm-season vegetables since their roots need the warmest soil possible until hot weather sets in.

☑ **PRUNE.** Early in the month, before new growth emerges, finish pruning grapes, roses, vines, and deciduous fruit and ornamental trees. Wait until after flowering to prune spring-blooming trees and shrubs such as forsythia and spiraea; or prune them lightly after buds swell, and bring the cuttings indoors to display in vases.

PEST & WEED CONTROL

☑ **APPLY DORMANT SPRAY.** After pruning but before leaves and flowers appear, spray fruit trees with a mixture of dormant oil and lime sulfur or oil and copper. If rain washes it off within 48 hours, reapply. If you use oil and copper, keep spray off walls, fences, and walks that might become stained.

☑ **DIG OR HOE WEEDS.** When weeds are small, wait until soil is dry, then hoe early in the day. Sun and dryness will kill tiny roots by day's end. For larger weeds, water thoroughly, then pop them out with a hand weeder, roots and all. Let whole weeds dry in the sun before you compost them.

☑ **ROTATE VEGETABLE BEDS.** To avoid soil-borne diseases, never plant the same kinds of crops in the same beds two years in a row. For example, if you planted cabbage family members in a bed last year, switch to a completely different crop (such as tomatoes) this year. ◆

Southwest Checklist

PLANTING

☑ **ANNUALS.** Zones 10–13: Try ageratum, calliopsis, celosia, cosmos, four o'clock, globe amaranth, gloriosa daisies, kochia, lisianthus, marigolds, Mexican sunflowers, portulaca, strawflowers, vinca rosea, and zinnias.

☑ **CITRUS.** Zones 12–13: Plant 5- to 7-gallon citrus trees in full sun in holes dug as deep as the rootballs and two to three times as wide. Water two or three times per week at first; by summer's end you'll need to water only every five to seven days. Wrap trunks in white cloth or paint with white latex to prevent sunburn.

☑ **LAWNS.** Zones 1–2, 10 (Albuquerque and El Paso): Sow or reseed cool-season lawns with bluegrass, fine or tall fescue, and perennial ryegrass. Zone 11 (Las Vegas): You can grow hybrid or common Bermuda, but tall fescue and perennial ryegrass are the lawns of choice. Sow them this month. Zones 12–13: When average nighttime temperatures top 70°, plant hybrid Bermuda grass.

☑ **PERENNIALS.** Start chrysanthemums, columbine, coreopsis, gaillardia, gazania, geraniums, gerbera, hollyhock, salvia, and Shasta daisies.

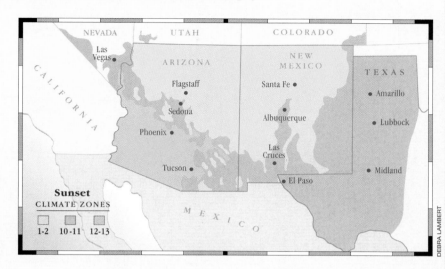

Sunset
CLIMATE ZONES
☐ 1-2 ☐ 10-11 ☐ 12-13

DEBRA LAMBERT

☑ **SUMMER BULBS.** After danger of frost is past, plant caladium, canna, crinum, dahlias, daylilies, gladiolus, irises, and montbretia. You can also buy container-grown agapanthus, society garlic (*Tulbaghia*), and zephyranthes.

☑ **VEGETABLES.** Zones 10–11: Sow cucumbers, melons, okra, pumpkins, soybeans, squash, and watermelons; set out eggplant, peppers, sweet potatoes, and tomatoes. Zones 12–13: Sow beans and cucumbers by mid-April; set out eggplant, okra, peanuts, squash, and sweet potatoes any time this month.

☑ **VINES.** Zones 12–13: Plant tender vines like bougainvillea, cape honeysuckle, and pink trumpet vine. Put them in a warm spot that gets good winter protection.

MAINTENANCE

☑ **FEED GARDEN PLANTS.** Almost everything in the garden can use a dose of fertilizer now. Apply about 1 pound of a complete fertilizer (10-10-10) per 100 square feet. Water the day before you spread the fertilizer and immediately afterward.

☑ **FEED LAWNS.** To give Bermuda grass a push for the summer, apply 3 to 4 pounds of high-nitrogen fertilizer per 1,000 square feet about two weeks after the grass greens up. Water thoroughly.

☑ **MULCH SOIL.** A 2- to 3-inch layer of organic mulch suppresses weeds, holds in moisture, and keeps roots cool. Spread it around all annuals, perennials, trees, shrubs, and vegetables, especially where summers are hot and dry. ◆

Hummingbird pot brims with nectar-bearing perennial flowers. Clockwise from bottom left are red 'Firebird' penstemon, deep red *Salvia greggii,* dark purple *Salvia guaranitica,* light purple Mexican sage, and *Phygelius capensis* 'Scarlet' with dangling bell-shaped blooms. Glazed ceramic pot is 23 inches across. Design: Jean Manocchio.

YOU CAN

GROW

GARDENS

ANYWHERE

IN POTS,

HANGING

BASKETS,

AND

WINDOW

BOXES

Twenty-five years ago, *Sunset* published its first big story on container gardening. It began with color baskets—moss-lined hanging baskets filled from top to bottom with colorful annuals. At that time, Western nurseries—led by Roger's Gardens in Corona del Mar, California—were starting to specialize in these seasonal baskets, and gardeners just couldn't hang them fast enough. Soon afterward, bowls brimful with seasonal flowers began appearing in nurseries. Container gardening had taken root. • Today, it's hard to find a Western home without at least one container—a colorful basket, pot, or window box—sprouting from a patio, on a porch, or right out of the house itself. • Lew Whitney, chairman of Roger's Gardens, attributes the ever-increasing popularity of containers to both the growing passion for gardening and the diminishing size of yards. "Gardening is

Small space, big show

the number-one pastime, yet lots keep getting smaller," says Whitney. "You fit a patio and Jacuzzi into a garden and there's not much space left for planting." With containers, you can grow plants anywhere. • Container gardening has evolved dramatically since those first hanging baskets caught our eye. Plantings now are more diverse, often including long-lasting perennials and shrubs for an extended show. The containers themselves have become more sophisticated, with new basketmaking materials and a flood of imported pots expanding the range of designs, colors, and textures. • On the following pages, we report on the West's continuing love affair with container gardening. Use the designs on these pages to inspire your own creations.

BY LAUREN BONAR SWEZEY

NORMAN A. PLATE (2)

Cascading begonias in salmon and pink shades mingle with variegated ivy and 'Beacon Silver' lamium, while a mother fern arches above. A sturdy bracket attached to a wood post supports the moss-lined 24-inch-wide wire basket. Design: Bud Stuckey.

Exotic theme pots

■ Jean Manocchio of Belli Fiori in Redwood City, California, specializes in container gardens. Sometimes her designs are spontaneous, developed while she's shopping at the nursery. But more often, she starts with a theme. "Themes keep you focused, and they help unify the look," she explains.

Using permanent landscape plants, Manocchio chose different themes for the pots shown here and for the one on page 98. Then she selected the color palettes for the plants. Finally, she looked for appropriate containers to complement the themes. "I always choose unusual pots—ones with interesting shapes and colors," she says.

NORMAN A. PLATE (3)

Billowing grasses: Purple fountain grass _es over gold Carex buchananii_ in a moss-_d_ 20-inch-wide wire basket. The tall _sses_ are skirted by, from left, rushlike _es of Chondropetalum tectorum,_ reddish _wn_ 'Tom Thumb' flax, white-striped _Acorus mineus_ 'Variegatus', 'Yellow Wave' flax, _, below it, Carex hachioensis_ 'Evergold'.

outhwest accents: A stone iguana pot from _xico_ wears pearls (_Senecio rowleyanus_), _te-striped Agave americana_ 'Medio-picta', _k Sedum spectabile_ 'Carmen', rusty red _um telephium_ 'Autumn Joy', and a leafy _wn of Euphorbia characias wulfenii._

utterfly havens: Three glazed pots are _nted_ with flowers that provide nectar and _al_ food for butterflies. **1.** Purple Mexican _h_ sage is underplanted with pale yellow _ana,_ gold _Coreopsis verticillata_ 'Zagreb', _pale_ purple aster. **2.** Purple heliotrope _'s_ off yellow 'Early Sunrise' coreopsis and _w_ lantana. **3.** Orange lion's tail (_Leonotis urus_) waves above red and orange _lepias curassavica_ and yellow lantana.

Jean Manocchio's **tips:**

•_Consider the effect._ Before you shop for plants, think about the look you want to achieve. Plants can be bold, soft, or sculptural.

•_Choose plants wisely._ Select plant colors to coordinate with the container and elements around your garden and home. You can change plants from season to season (spring and fall) or choose more permanent plants (perennials, shrubs) that last two years or longer. But make sure plants are compatible; don't mix sun and shade plants together.

•_Use an ample container._ Suit the pot to the number of plants and their ultimate size. "Larger is always better."

•_Coordinate containers._ Choose a color that works with the house, patio, or landscape. The pot can blend in or stand out. Some choices include bowls, urns, and pots with handles or decorated with reliefs.

•_Amend the potting mix._ "I always add controlled-release fertilizer and composted chicken manure (⅓ manure to ⅔ potting mix)."

•_Seal clay pots._ To prolong their life, apply a terra-cotta sealer or roofing compound inside pots. "I use a two-part epoxy sealer."

•_Plant on the spot._ Pots are heavy when filled with soil. Plant up the pot where it will be displayed. Plant your focal point first (1- to 15-gallon plants), then fill in with others (sixpack-size to 5-gallon plants).

•_Raise the pot._ Set the pot on rubber bumpers or use pot feet to improve air circulation and avoid staining decks and patios.

•_Keep pots spiffy._ Remove faded plants when necessary, and fill in the blanks with new ones.

Bouquets on high

■ "A hanging basket is like a bouquet in the air," says Toni Parsons. As the production manager at Roger's Gardens, Parsons makes hundreds of aerial bouquets every year. Parsons has found that hanging baskets are perfect for decorating an entry, displaying in front of a window, or embellishing a patio structure.

Of course, color baskets have changed a lot since Roger's Gardens and *Sunset* popularized them. The ones shown here make use of new materials that allow quick, easy assembly—and you won't find an annual among the plants in them. All the color comes from perennials selected for their long-lasting blooms and cascading habits. Once planted, the perennials take from four to eight weeks to grow out and give the basket a full look. Bud Stuckey, *Sunset* test garden coordinator, designed the baskets shown at right, using wire baskets with preformed, moss-covered foam liners (MossCraft by Mapco, 800/598-9084).

ABOVE: A heavenly sphere is formed by red-and-blue-flowered bat-faced cuphea (*C. llavea*) underplanted with purple 'Petite Wonder' scaevola and 'Lavender' Tapien verbena in an 18-inch-wide basket.

BELOW: A cloud of 'Mauve Mist' bacopa is accented by 'Pink' Tapien verbena (top left) and white-on-green variegated creeping Charlie (*Plectranthus coleoides*). The 14-inch-wide wire basket has a moss-covered foam liner.

Toni Parsons's
tips:

• *Choose the right container.* The most attractive hanging containers are made of wire, wood, or clay. Large containers won't dry out as quickly as small ones.

• *Hang in a sturdy location.* Planted baskets are often heavy. Hang them from strong eaves or patio covers, or wall-mount them with special brackets for hanging pots.

• *Use a swivel hook.* This allows you to rotate the plants so they get light on all sides.

• *Try this foolproof planting scheme:* Line a shallow, bowl-shaped 18-inch basket with moss (or use a preformed liner), fill with a good-quality potting mix, plant a 1-gallon *Liriope* in the center, add three 1-gallon mother ferns, and fill in around the ferns with five 4-inch impatiens and three 4-inch trailers (ground ivy, moneywort, variegated *Vinca major*).

• *Water, groom, and feed plants.* Watering with drip irrigation is ideal (run ¼-inch drip tubing down from the eaves to irrigate hanging baskets). Remove dead flowers and pinch back growth to shape plants. "I feed plants every two weeks with a water-soluble fertilizer."

ABOVE: A puff of white 'Snowflake' bacopa is fringed by 'Pink' Tapien verbena (left) and dotted with 'Cherry Pink' Million Bells (*Calibracoa*), a perennial whose blooms resemble miniature petunias.

RIGHT: Flush with flowers and greenery, this moss basket is packed from top to bottom with deep pink stock, purple and burgundy pansies, white sweet alyssum, and English ivy. Design: Roger's Gardens.

Bloom boxes

■ "The beauty of window boxes is that you can easily change their look and, at the same time, change the look of your house," says landscape architect Jonathan Plant of St. Helena, California. In addition to wood, the boxes can be made of a variety of materials, including fiberglass, plastic, and sheet metal. Since window boxes are quite heavy when they're filled with soil, sturdy brackets should be used to secure them to exterior surfaces.

"The best window-box flowers have a long bloom period, like geraniums and impatiens, and mingle well with other plants," says Plant. Root space in boxes is limited (often only 8 to 12 inches deep), so overly vigorous plants aren't the best choice. And the more heat and wind the plants are exposed to, the tougher they have to be.

Shade-loving plants flourish in this wood-framed copper box. From far left are pink *Begonia* 'Richmondensis', white nicotiana, bronze coleus, and pink-and-white fuchsia, underplanted with variegated ivy, pale pink impatiens, and chartreuse-magenta coleus.

Jonathan Plant's
tips:

•*Consider the location.* Window boxes viewed from a distance don't have to be as perfectly manicured as boxes viewed close up or from indoors. Less accessible boxes should be planted with low-maintenance plants, such as impatiens, ivy geraniums, alyssum, and ivy.

•*Protect the structure.* Make sure water from the window box does not drain down the wall, particularly a wood wall. Drain holes should direct runoff toward the outside edge of the box. To prevent leakage, wood boxes can be lined with rubber or rigid plastic inserts (with holes for drainage).

•*Amend the potting mix.* Adding 20 percent loam to a potting mix keeps it from drying out too quickly. Adding a soil polymer (such as Broadleaf P4) can improve water retention and prevent wet-dry cycles.

•*Feed plants regularly.* Work a controlled-release fertilizer into the soil mix at planting time or make more frequent applications of a liquid fertilizer (15-30-15, for example).

•*Prime plants before you go on vacation.* Cut back overgrown plants and give them extra food. By the time you return, they'll come running out of the gate and look good.

•*Rejuvenate the soil.* When replanting, add fresh potting mix to the box.

•*Keep a record.* Write down what worked and what didn't. Learn from experience.

NORMAN A. PLATE

W I N D O W   D R E S S I N G

Visitors to the Far Niente winery in California's Napa Valley admire the Old World look of the stone structures built in 1885. Yet when Gil Nickel bought the property in 1979, the buildings had been abandoned for 60 years. To regain the winery's historic charm, he embarked on a major remodeling effort, which included decorating the façade with window boxes.

The Boston ivy–covered walls accent windows framed in handsome cut stone. Custom-made fiberglass boxes, painted to match the stonework, are mounted with barely visible brackets and planted heavily so visitors see only billowing flowers. The boxes are filled with three to five colors of impatiens, lobelia, and sweet alyssum. "The impatiens give the building a sophisticated appearance," says Nickel.

Multicolored impatiens and white sweet alyssum elegantly underscore the stone-framed windows of Far Niente winery in Oakville, California. Design: Jonathan Plant.

Cotoneaster, trained
as an informal
espalier, spreads
gracefully curving
branches against a
stucco wall in a
Northern California
garden.

Living sculptures

Shrub espaliers beautify blank walls. And they're surprisingly easy to train

BY SHARON COHOON
AND STEVEN R. LORTON

■ For year-round beauty, it's tough to beat big, beautiful shrubs like camellias and rhododendrons. They soften the garden with their handsome foliage and provide leafy backdrops for other, less steadfast plantings. The trouble is, billowy shrubs take up a lot of room. And as gardens get smaller, so do the options for plants that will grow in them.

What's the answer to this space dilemma? In a word, espaliers—shrubs trained to grow flat against trellises, in geometric or sculptural shapes. They're perfect for narrow side yards and for walls around tiny patios. Best of all, growers are training an ever-widening spectrum of ornamental plants as espaliers, so you can buy, plant, and enjoy a candelabra or gridwork of foliage, and perhaps flowers or fruit, immediately.

As the plant grows, gently train it along a fence or wall, cutting off errant shoots. (See training tips on page 108.) Then the starter trellis—like training wheels on a bike—can be removed.

GETTING STARTED

Choose plants that will thrive against the wall you have in mind for them, whether a sunny, south-facing wall or a shadier, north-facing wall.

Remove the plant from the can and massage the rootball to loosen its roots, or pull roots free so they grow out into surrounding soil.

During the growing season, check an espaliered plant at least weekly. Prune regularly (the expression *nip it in the bud* has never been truer). If a new shoot is heading in the wrong direction, snip it off. Better you get it when it's young and tender than wait until it's an established branch that will leave a gap or scar if removed.

18 great shrub espaliers

Blue hibiscus (*Alyogyne huegelii*)	Juniper
	Loropetalum
Bougainvillea	*Lycianthes rantonnei*
Camellia	
Citrus	Magnolia
Cotoneaster	Photinia
Elaeagnus	*Pieris japonica*
Euonymus	Pyracantha
Gardenia	Rhaphiolepis
Hibiscus	Roses (many varieties)

TRAINING TIPS FROM ESPALIER PRO GARY JONES

To many, the terms *espalier* and *IRS audit* have similarly chilling effects. Facing either prospect makes us freeze up like a vapor-locked engine. In the case of an audit, the terror may be justified. "But there's nothing scary about espaliering," insists Gary Jones of Hortus nursery in Pasadena. Jones eliminates the fear factor through seminars on espaliers.

Espaliering is simply a practical way to squeeze a shrub or tree into a space where you thought only a vine would fit, says Jones. You do this by allowing branches that grow in the same plane as the wall (or other support) to remain—and cutting away everything else. In other words, what can be trained to grow flat stays, and what can't goes. That's it, he says. All the fancy espalier patterns that have evolved over the centuries are just variations on this principle. "Now what's so terrifying about that?" he asks.

Still, Jones concedes, it might not be a good idea to try a Belgian fence or candelabra your first time out. Start with an informal fan, the easiest form of espalier, to build up your confidence before attempting something more intricate.

Use a plant with a loose, open habit. Abutilon is an excellent choice, as is a plant that develops a horizontal branch pattern naturally, such as cotoneaster. Let the plant's natural growth dictate its eventual shape. Once you've achieved a pattern that pleases you, simply prune to maintain it.

Provide support. Grow espaliers against a chain-link fence, redwood lattice, or wire trellis. Or glue dime-size plastic disks with ties through their centers (available in nurseries) directly to a wall, and tie the branches to th[e] disks. "The disks pop off eventuall[y] but by then the plant has usually deve[l]oped enough wood to support itself[,] says Jones.

Give woodier plants extra sup[port]. Train branches of shrubs tha[t] need more discipline on horizont[al] wires. These can be attached direct[ly] to brick, stone, or concrete walls a[s]

shown at left. Fo[r] each wire, drill [a] series of holes [3] to 4 inches apar[t,] insert expansio[n] shields (preferabl[y] lead) into th[e] holes, and scre[w] 5- to 7-inch eye bolts into the shields[.] (Make sure the bolts project at leas[t] 4 inches from the wall to perm[it] good air circulation.) String the wir[e] through the eye bolts and twist t[o] secure. Jones generally starts his low[-] est wire about 18 inches from th[e] ground, and positions the wires 16 t[o] 20 inches apart.

Use a post-and-wire framewor[k] for a freestanding espalier. Place 4[-] by-4 posts 8 to 10 feet apart. Long, ver[-] tical bamboo stakes can be used as tem[-] porary support for branches as the[y]

Espalier pro Gary Jones shows off a gardenia (left) at Hortus nursery in Pasadena. These plants thrive in containers for a few years (above).

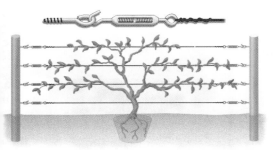

grow from tier to tier. When the tree or shrub reaches the top wire, remove the bamboo stakes.

Invest in narrow-nosed pruning shears. "They prevent a lot of scraped knuckles when you're working in tight spaces," says Jones.

Don't fertilize as much as you normally would. Nitrogen just encourages growth. And that means you're creating work for yourself.

A post-and-wire structure (left) holds a freestanding espalier. Put lowest wire (#14 galvanized) 18 inches off the ground, and those above it 1 to 2 feet apart. Secure wires to posts with 5- to 7-inch-long eye bolts or lag screws; incorporate turnbuckles into both ends of each wire to tighten as espaliers mature.

Feel free to cheat. "The more old espaliers you look at," says Jones, "the more you see how often gardeners have fudged." If a branch didn't grow on the side of the trunk that a gardener wanted it to, for instance, he or she might bend over a stem from the left. "Sometimes plants just refuse to cooperate, and you have to improvise." Don't worry about it, he suggests. "Flaws give espaliers character." ◆

Lycianthes rantonnei.

An espalier for all seasons

■ In spring, the pyracantha espaliered against Eric Holdeman's front wall in Puyallup, Washington, erupts with tiny white flowers that shimmer in sunlight. In summer, this living candelabra relaxes a bit—embellishing a blank wall with its neat, green leaves and geometric shape—before red-orange berries set it ablaze in fall. In winter, this ever-changing plant is dressed in glory of a less natural sort: hundreds of tiny white lights set it aglow, welcoming guests and delighting passersby.

Holdeman built the trellis as a grid of 1-by-2s mounted to 1-by-2 spacers against the wall. Then he planted pyracantha from a 1-gallon can at its base. The plant completely covered the 7- by 9-foot trellis in four years. — *Kathleen N. Brenzel*

Spring

Fall

Winter

Nursery-hopping around Puget Sound

BY STEVEN R. LORTON

long with great views, fresh seafood, and copious amounts of rain, the Puget Sound area is well supplied with excellent nurseries. More than anything else, what drives the nursery trade here are people who have turned their passion for plants into successful businesses.

We've selected nine of our favorite places to shop for plants. With the help of the map on the facing page, it's easy to string several of these nurseries together for a day's outing.

1. *Christianson's Nursery, Mount Vernon.* Anyone who's been to the Northwest Flower & Garden Show has probably fallen in love with the English cottage gardens designed by John and Toni Christianson. The couple specializes in roses (more than 750 varieties), long-blooming perennials, and uncommon trees and shrubs. If you have chil-

dren, they'll enjoy seeing the llamas and goats that prance and bleat around the 7-acre nursery. The gardens surrounding the 1888 schoolhouse on the grounds are open for strolling this month. The nursery is in the middle of the Skagit Valley tulip fields, which erupt into bloom in April. *9–6 daily. 1578 Best Rd.; (360) 466-3821.*

2. *Wells Nurseries, Mount Vernon.* Founded by Harold Wells 60 years ago, this family business is now headed by his son-in-law, Neil Hall. If you're lucky, Neil will be on hand when you ask about a conifer like *Pinus aristata* 'Sherwood Compact'. Everything is a specialty in this nursery: as family members find plants they love, they propagate them at their nearby growing grounds. *8–5 Mon-Sat. 424 E. Section St.; (360) 336-6544.*

3. *Emery's Garden, Lynnwood.* Owner Emery Rhodes has surrounded

himself with a savvy staff who believe that real gardening is more than decorating with plants. The emphasis of this handsome, two-year-old nursery is not seasonal color but plants with four-season interest, such as great Northwest natives, from vine maple (*Acer circinatum*) to camas (*Zigadenus elegans*). *10–6 daily. 2829 164th St. S.W.; (425) 743-4555.*

4. *Molbak's, Woodinville.* Danish-born Egon and Laina Molbak opened for business in 1956. Now, with 15 acres devoted to retail sales (100,000 square feet under cover) and 42 acres of growing fields, their nursery is known for quality, selection, and volume. Grab a caffe latte at the coffee stand and start strolling. The place bulges with garden accessories, ornaments, furniture, and tools, as well as fresh floral arrangements and indoor plants. This month, check out the pots of daffodils, hyacinths, tulips, and other bulbs. *9–8 Mon-Thu, 9–9 Fri, 8–8 Sat, 9–6 Sun. 13625 N.E. 175th St.; (425) 483-5000.*

5. *Valley Nursery, Poulsbo.* More than anything, Brad Watts wants the plants he sells to thrive. With that in mind, he chooses everything from ap-

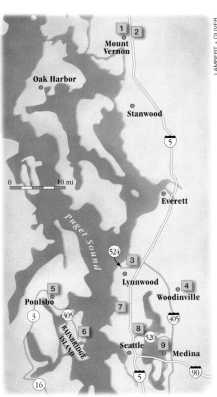

ABOVE: At Swanson's, the pink blooms of angel's trumpet (far right) dangle over a garden sculpture and ornamental grass. RIGHT: In Molbak's greenhouse, a visiting painter renders a floral scene.

ples to roses for their adaptability to Puget Sound gardens. Check out the superb stock of dwarf conifers; before you're done, you'll probably walk out with a *Cedrus deodara* 'Snowsprite' or perhaps a *Pinus thunbergii* 'Thunderhead'. *9–6 Mon-Fri, 9–5 Sat-Sun. 20882 Bond Rd. N.E.; (360) 779-3806.*

6. Bainbridge Gardens, Bainbridge Island. Scampering around his father's nursery before World War II, Junkoh Harui picked up an extravagant love of plants—one that cuts across every category from flowers to trees, vegetables to ornamental grasses. When you visit this 7-acre nursery, wander along the nature path, poke around nursery beds in search of the unusual, and stop at the espresso

bar for a snack and a loaf of fresh-baked bread. *9–5:30 Mon-Thu & Sat, 9–8 Fri, 10–5:30 Sun. 9415 Miller Rd. N.E.; (206) 842-5888.*

7. Swanson's Nursery, Seattle. This nursery has been an institution since 1924. Twenty years ago, Wally Kerwin bought the business, and now the large and varied stock of plants is complemented by fine garden accessories, including imported containers. The excellent cafe, Festivities, serves light luncheon fare; the quiches,

salmon cakes, chicken salads, soups, and desserts are all scrumptious. Linger over lunch as fountains splash, birds twitter, and the fragrances of exotic plants waft through the air. *9–6 daily. 9701 15th Ave. N.W.; (206) 782-2543.*

8. City People's Garden Store, Seattle. Cluttered with the elegant, the whimsical, and the stylishly practical, this inner-city nursery is the kind of garden shop you'd expect to find in Paris. Owners Judith Gille and Steve Magley ferret out unusual and well-grown plants as well as garden tools, accessories, and ornaments. *9–6 Mon-Sat, 10–6 Sun. 2939 E. Madison St.; (206) 324-0737.*

9. Wells Medina Nursery, Medina. Ned Wells started this nursery 27 years ago; since then he's been joined by all four of his children. If a plant is the best of its genus or a rising star of the horticultural world, you'll find it here. Take a look at the sensational new *Daphne burkwoodii* 'Moonlight' (creamy white leaves thinly edged in green) and the 'Caerhays Belle' deciduous magnolia (huge, peonylike salmon-pink flowers). *9–6 Mon-Sat, 10–5 Sun. 8300 N.E. 24th St.; (425) 454-1853.* ◆

Nursery-hopping in Santa Cruz County

From begonias to lavenders, a wealth of plants
awaits you at specialty nurseries

BY LAUREN BONAR SWEZEY

Famed for its sandy beaches and challenging surf, the Santa Cruz County coast attracts visitors year-round. But a short distance inland, garden treasures await discovery at the many specialty nurseries dotting the landscape. The area's benign climate makes it possible for commercial growers to propagate everything from abutilon to zygocactus.

We can't think of a better way to spend a spring day than nursery-hopping from Santa Cruz to Watsonville. We've selected five of our favorite places to shop for plants. With the help of the map on the facing page, it's easy to string several together in a day's outing. More than likely, you'll go home with a carful of plants.

1. Antonelli Brothers Begonia Gardens, Santa Cruz. Begun in 1935 by four brothers, this business has blossomed into a nationally known mail-order supplier of large-flowered hanging and upright tuberous begonias. In the retail store are 100 varieties of begonias (all are the family's own hybrids), along with 50 species of fibrous begonias and Rex and Rieger hybrid begonias. You'll find the best selection of young begonias in spring, but showtime is in late summer, when the plants are in full bloom. Another specialty is fuchsias—more than 400 cultivars. *9–5 daily. 2545 Capitola Rd.; (408) 475-5222.*

2. Florabunda, Santa Cruz. Owned by Richard and Reta Bray, this backyard nursery is packed with more than 250 herbs, including 30 scented geraniums, 20 mints, and 20 thymes. It also has flowering perennials, garden

Aptos Gardens is filled to the rafters with garden accessories and plants, including hydrangeas, fuchsias, and impatiens, which thrive in its lath house.

accessories, and sculpture. Mature specimens of plants are displayed in a charming little demonstration garden. Inside the former home is a floral and gift shop. *9:30–5:30 Mon-Fri, 9:30–5*

ABOVE: Antonelli Brothers Begonia Gardens, shown here at peak bloom in late summer, offers many of its own hybrids, like the two-tone ruffled picotee at far left.

RIGHT: The demonstration area at Sierra Azul Nursery & Gardens is awash in plants that flourish in mild California climates, like the boldly colored phormium at bottom right. Informal tours start at 10 A.M. on the first Saturday of each month.

Sat, 11–4:30 Sun. 1030 41st Ave.; (408) 462-0202.

3. Aptos Gardens, Soquel. Seven years ago, Peter Kiedrowski and Roy Leporini merged their garden shop with Carol Saveria's Wisteria Antiques. Today, the nursery is a shopper's paradise, carrying a wonderful selection of specialty plants, handcrafted garden antiques, containers, and topiaries. Most of the plants—including heirloom roses, geraniums and pelargoniums, and unusual and old-fashioned perennials—are selected from local growers. Many are displayed around furniture and accessories so shoppers can see how to combine them in their own gardens. *10–5 daily. 5870 Soquel Dr.; (408) 462-3859.*

4. Desert Theatre, Watsonville. Kate Jackson began her career as a midwife and delivery nurse, but turned to raising exotic cactus and succulents. She nurtures an extensive collection of plants from all over the world. In the greenhouses, you'll find at least 100 kinds of *Euphorbia,* along with *Echeveria, Haworthia, Mammillaria,* and *Notocactus*—to name a few. Outside, Jackson has what she calls her desert theater—artfully arranged display beds. She also sells pottery and flats of ground covers. *10–4 Tue-Sun. 17 Behler Rd.; (408) 728-5513.*

5. Sierra Azul Nursery & Gardens, Watsonville. Four years ago, Lisa and Jeff Rosendale opened this retail nursery as a companion to their wholesale nursery next door. You'll find a treasure trove of native and exotic perennials, shrubs, and grasses—all suited to Mediterranean climates. Expect fine selections of ceanothus, grevillea, lavender, manzanita, mimulus, penstemon, rosemary, salvia, and yarrow. Stroll through the 2-acre demonstration garden, which features mature specimens of most of the plants they sell. *9–5:30 daily. 2260 E. Lake Ave.; (408) 763-0939.*

Of course, there are many other fine nurseries in Santa Cruz County. If time allows, check out San Lorenzo Lumber Company (408/426-1020), a full-service nursery in Santa Cruz; the Pergola (408/464-2590), a full-service nursery in Soquel; and Dancing Crane Fine Bonsai Nursery (408/479-1343) and Native Revival Nursery (408/684-1811), both in Aptos. ◆

At Summers Past Farms, a footbridge crosses a recirculating stream in a display garden adjoining the nursery, where a shopper (above) eyes 4-inch pots of zinnias and other summer annuals.

Nursery-hopping in San Diego County

Specialty nurseries offer a vast selection of plants, from subtropicals to succulents

BY SHARON COHOON

San Diego County offers gardeners what Las Vegas offers gamblers: optimum opportunities to succumb to temptation. Certainly, there are more seductive nurseries here than anywhere else in Southern California. The county's benign climate attracts scores of wholesale growers, who in turn provide retail nurseries with an immense variety of plant materials. As if that weren't enough, many retail nurseries propagate additional stock themselves. It all adds up to a range of choices that plant shoppers won't find anywhere else. We've selected nine of our favorite places to shop for plants. It's easy to

visit several in a day's outing (see the map on the facing page). But be forewarned: If you're the type of gardener who can't walk out of a nursery without a plant, your willpower will be sorely tested on the route ahead.

1. Judy's Perennials, San Marcos. Judy Wigand is wild about flowers, as the exuberant blooms in her front yard clearly show. She was among the first to achieve the look of an English cottage garden with Mediterranean plants. She propagates a limited number of plants, but those she offers are proven performers—drought-tolerant, nondemanding, and long-blooming. *10–4*

Wed-Fri and the first and third Saturdays of the month. 436 Buena Creek Rd.; (760) 744-4343.

2. Buena Creek Gardens, San Marcos. Owner Steve Brigham's love affair with plants started with the tough, drought-tolerant species of Australia and South Africa, but his tastes were too eclectic to stop there, so he also stocks his 4-acre nursery with perennials, California natives, subtropicals, and many other temptations. There are acres of daylilies and reblooming irises to explore, too. The demonstration gardens give you ideas for putting it all together. *9–5 Wed-Sat, 11–4 Sun. 418 Buena Creek Rd.; (760) 744-2810.*

3. Weidners' Gardens, Encinitas. If you want showy specimens for hanging baskets or patio pots, this is the place. Owners Evelyn and Mary Weidner have built their reputation on supplying easy-care, long-blooming plants. Many plants that have become container staples, including 'Red Riding Hood' mandevilla and 'Blue Wonder' scaevola, were introduced here. *9:30–5 Wed-Mon (open April–September 15*

At Buena Creek Gardens, well-labeled plants (top left) invite shoppers to read about their virtues. In a demonstration area, 'Red Velvet' cannas play off deep pink shrub roses (above), while succulent rosettes dot a wall (left).

and November–December 22). 695 Normandy Rd.; (760) 436-2194.

4. Samia Rose Topiary, Encinitas. Just around the corner from Weidners', you can shop for finished topiaries and topiary supplies, including frames, moss, and more kinds of ivy than you knew existed. *9–5 Tue-Sat. 1236 Urania Ave.; (760) 436-0460.*

5. Encinitas Gardens, Encinitas. If you want to be ready for the next drought—and you know it's coming—don't pass up this nursery. Owner Jim Duggan's specialty is drought-resistant plants. He has a good eye, especially for foliage plants, and his collection proves that tough can also be beautiful. *9–4 Wed-Sat. 1452 Santa Fe Dr.; (760) 753-2852.*

6. Cedros Gardens, Solana Beach. This boutique nursery has quickly established itself as a regional favorite. Whether you're looking for plants, garden art, books, or gifts, owner Mia McCarville has a way of winnowing out the best and displaying it in attractive vignettes. There are lots of other appealing stores here in the Cedros Design District, and it's a good area to stop for a lunch break. *9–5 Mon-Sat, 10–4 Sun. 330 S. Cedros Ave.; (619) 792-8640.*

7. Solana Succulents, Solana Beach. If you think you don't like succulents, it may be because they're usually displayed in haphazard ways. That's not the case here, however—superb specimens, often growing in hand-crafted pots, compose a gallery of living sculptures. *10–5 Wed-Sat, 12–5 Sun. 355 N. Hwy. 101; (619) 259-4568.*

8. Summers Past Farms, Flinn Springs. Though it's only a half-hour drive from downtown San Diego, this nursery feels like the country. You can stroll through the herb and flower beds and browse for gifts in a big red barn. Bring a picnic and linger over lunch. *8–5 Wed-Sat, 10–5 Sun. 15602 Old Hwy. 80; (619) 390-1523.*

9. Perennial Adventure, La Mesa. In a residential setting, Chris Wotruba's home-based nursery invites you to wander among beautifully planted borders as you decide which combinations would work in your garden. *10–4 Thu-Sat and by appointment. 10548 Anaheim Dr.; (619) 660-9631.*

Of course, there are many other fine places to shop for plants in San Diego County, like Ganter Nursery (760/758-8375) in Vista; Herban Garden (800/407-5268) in Fallbrook; and the granddaddy of them all, Walter Andersen Nursery (619/224-8271) in San Diego. For a brochure listing many more nurseries, send a self-addressed, stamped envelope to North County Nursery Hoppers Association, Box 231208, Encinitas, CA 92023; or call (800) 488-6742. ◆

Mountain and desert nurseries worth a special visit

From Idaho to Arizona, these places offer a vast
selection of plants for mountain and desert gardens

BY JIM McCAUSLAND

Brimful of flowers and other irresistible plants, a well-stocked
nursery can make you feel like
a kid in a candy shop. Temptation sur-
rounds you and it's okay to succumb—
your garden will thank you for it.

We've selected nine of the West's
most tempting nurseries, based on visits by *Sunset* staff members and a poll
of expert horticulturists. All of these
places are well worth a visit. The nurseries are listed north to south, and
most are at their springtime best in
April. Bring your wish list and allow
yourself plenty of browsing time.

Moss Gardens, Ketchum, Idaho.
Famous for tourists and a short growing season, Ketchum might not leap to

mind as a plant-buying destination.
But once you've seen Greg and Jody
Moss's exquisite hanging baskets,
you'll be a believer. In addition to
trees, shrubs, and vines, Moss Gardens
usually stocks about 1,000 varieties of
annuals and perennials, all tested and
hardened-off at the nursery's 6,000-
foot elevation. Indoor plants are sold
year-round; outdoor bedding plants
and baskets go on display the last week
in April. *8:30–6 daily. 420 Second St.
(at East Ave.); (208) 726-0949.*

**Mitchell's Nursery & Gifts, Sandy,
Utah.** Only three years old, Mitchell's
6-acre site is already well known for
annuals and perennials, many of which
are displayed in eight 700-square-foot

Moss Gardens in Ketchum, Idaho,
specializes in annuals and perennials,
color-packed hanging baskets, and
terra-cotta containers.

beds. Mitchell's offers 1,500 kinds of
perennials as well as a full line of
woody plants, including 18-foot weeping sequoias. Visit the 6,000-square-
foot main store and wander through
the three greenhouses filled with
everything from house plants to gifts.
*9–8 Mon-Fri, 8–8 Sat, 10–5 Sun. 1220
E. 7800 South; (801) 561-9380.*

Paulino Gardens, Denver. Now
the biggest nursery in Colorado,
Paulino Gardens carries a huge number of perennials, dwarf conifers, trees

At Paulino Gardens in Denver, gardeners fill a shopping cart (left) with delphiniums and ornamental grasses, which are among the plants featured in the nursery's demonstration beds (below).

shrubs, vegetables, and annual flowers, along with what may be the Rockies' best collection of indoor plants, orchids, cactus and other succulents, and classic terra-cotta containers. Two small display gardens are full of planting ideas. *9–6 Mon-Sat, 9–5 Sun. 6300 N. Broadway; (303) 429-8062.*

Amargosa Farms Garden Center, Las Vegas. When Gerry and Mike Hackney started out, they decided to carry basic nursery stock supplemented with plants that few other nurseries were growing. To gather the latter, they traveled near and far, bringing back sabal palms, palmettos, and perennials from around the United States, and obscure bottlebrushes and eucalyptus from Australia (including *Eucalyptus neglecta,* an evergreen hardy to -20°). They've assembled an intriguing mix of unknown and familiar plants. *7–5 Mon-Fri, 8–5 Sat, 10–4 Sun. 5050 N. Rainbow Blvd.; (702) 645-4070.*

Santa Fe Greenhouses, Santa Fe. As local resident and garden photographer Charles Mann puts it, "Santa Fe Greenhouses is by far the most congenial nursery around. It has the biggest and nicest facilities, a great demonstration garden, and an outstanding mail-order catalog [High Country Gardens; free]. They're always trying out new things, and they're in touch with all the West's best plant people." Besides all that, the nursery offers a full selection of drought-tolerant plants for water-thrifty gardens. *9–5:30 Mon-Sat, 10–5 Sun. 2904 Rufina St.; (505) 473-2700.*

Desert Winds Nursery, Phoenix. This full-service nursery grows much of its own stock and offers a large supply of plants from Arizona and California. Check out the great selection of annuals, which a landscaper we know describes as "fantastic," and don't miss the fine collection of heat-tolerant roses. If you time your visit for Saturday morning, you can sit in on a seminar; topics range from citrus care to vegetable gardening. *6:30–6 daily. 17826 N. Tatum Blvd.; (602) 867-8140.*

Baker Nursery, Phoenix. When Jim Baker bought this nursery 30 years ago, he knew what he wanted to do: sell a vast range of extraordinary plants inexpensively. To do that, he pays cash for everything and chooses the most interesting and unusual stock he can find from suppliers throughout the Southwest. The demonstration garden is also his home garden, and his reputation (sterling among garden designers) is his only advertising. *7:30–5:30 daily. 3414 N. 40th St.; (602) 955-4500.*

Harlow's Landscape Center & Nursery, Tucson. Mature trees and shaded walkways give Harlow's a well-established feel; after all, this full-line nursery has been in Tucson since 1939. Always strong on colorful annuals and perennials, Harlow's fairly bursts with flowers this month. Trees, shrubs, pottery, and a gift shop round out the selections. *9–5 Mon-Sat, 10–5 Sun. 5620 E. Pima St.; (520) 886-5475.*

Mesquite Valley Growers, Tucson. Spread over 17 acres and growing almost 90 percent of what it sells, Mesquite is a living catalog of what grows in Tucson, from seasonal annuals to specimen trees in boxes. Expect to find natives, desert-adapted exotics, tropicals, subtropicals, fruits, and vegetables—the works. *8–5 daily. 8005 E. Speedway Blvd.; (520) 721-8600.* ◆

ROBERTO SONCIN-GEROMETTA

Grevillea 'Poorinda Blondie' bears flower clusters that resemble toothbrushes.

The showiest grevilleas

This clan includes trees, shrubs, and ground covers

BY LAUREN BONAR SWEZEY

Like the mythical Proteus, the Greek "old man of the sea" who could assume many different shapes at will, the genus *Grevillea* seems to reinvent itself from one plant to the next. A member of the Protea family, this group of strikingly handsome plants from Australia—one of the oldest groups of flowering plants on earth—is incredibly diverse.

Grevilleas range from towering trop-ical trees and broad, spreading shrubs to alpine ground covers that crawl along the soil. The leaves—just as vari-able—may be needlelike, stiff and oak-like, or so deeply cut that they appear lacy. They range from silvery gray to bright green to bronzy. The flower clus-ters are shaped like spiders or tooth-brushes. "They're unlike anything else in the gardening world," says Steve Mc-Cabe of the University of California at Santa Cruz Arboretum. Their colors span much of the color wheel, but the most common tones are orange, pink, red, and yellow. Most types bloom over a long period, often starting in winter; some bloom much of the year.

And best of all, "most have flowers that are absolutely irresistible to hum-mingbirds," says Luen Miller of Mon-terey Bay Nursery in Watsonville, Cali-fornia. This is especially true of 'Long John' and 'Robyn Gordon'. "A garden of grevilleas and salvias will have hum-mingbird wars all year," he says. And deer don't touch most of the plants.

"There's been an explosion of inter-est in grevilleas," says Miller. "What you find in the trade now are far showier than well-known old-time grevilleas such as *G.* 'Noellii'."

HOW TO USE GREVILLEAS

As striking as these plants are, grevilleas aren't for everyone. The ones Western-ers use for landscaping look most at home in gardens with native, Mediter-ranean, and Australian plants, as well as durable shrubs such as escallonia and rhaphiolepis; grevilleas don't mix well with thirstier cottage garden plants. They're also somewhat tender (al-though hardiness varies), so planting is restricted to mild-winter climates with lows between 15° and 25°.

With some notable exceptions, grevil-leas generally grow to a substantial size, which makes them unsuitable for small gardens (although pruning can restrain some of them). And with only a few ex-ceptions, they prefer good drainage. Most grevilleas do not grow well in alka-line, clay soil.

HOW TO CARE FOR THEM

Unless otherwise noted, plant grevil-leas in full sun and well-drained soil that's low in organic matter. Don't plant them in low spots where water collects. Irrigate plants weekly the first year to get them established, then cut back watering to about once every three to four weeks in summer. Heavy wet soil will kill them.

Grevilleas grow best in soils that are low in nutrients. They don't need phos-phorus. In fact, "most grevilleas won't tolerate high levels of phosphorus and alkalinity," says Steve Brigham of Buena Creek Gardens in San Marcos, Califor-nia. "In my decomposed-granite soil (about pH 7), they grow like gang-busters." If the foliage turns yellowish, apply iron and magnesium.

To restrain the size of grevilleas, prune after flowering. You can also prune the large ones into trees.

If you can't find the variety you want, have your nursery order it from Mon-terey Bay Nursery or Rosendale Nurs-ery in Watsonville (both are wholesale only). In Southern California, Buena Creek Gardens (retail; 760/744-2810) and San Marcos Growers in Santa Bar-bara (wholesale) sell them.

Growers' picks: Nine showy grevilleas

Small flower clusters cover the branches of *G. lavandulacea* 'Penola' (near right). *G. rosmarinifolia* 'Scarlet Sprite' (far right) bears spidery blooms on branch tips.

GROUND COVERS

Grevillea gaudichaudii. Extremely low-growing ground cover (1 foot tall by 10 feet wide) with green-and-burgundy oaklike leaves. Magenta toothbrush-flower clusters bloom much of the year. Needs good drainage (thrives in sandy soil). Takes some shade. Hardy to 15° to 20°.

G. lanigera (low form). Medium-height ground cover (or low shrub). Grows 2 feet tall by 4 feet wide with soft, 1-inch-long gray-green leaves. Pinkish red-and-cream spiderlike flower clusters appear in profusion from winter to spring. Grows in most soils. Takes some shade. Hardy to 15° to 20°.

MEDIUM TO LARGE SHRUBS

G. lavandulacea **'Billywing'.** Low-growing shrub or tall ground cover. Grows 2½ feet tall by 5 feet wide (denser with pruning). Gray, ½-inch-long needlelike leaves are a handsome foil for red-and-cream spiderlike flower clusters (shown at far left) from winter through spring. Does best with good drainage. Hardy to 15° to 20°.

***G. l.* 'Penola'.** Much larger shrub than 'Billywing', with a heavier show of deep rose red spiderlike flower clusters set off by soft, 1-inch-long dark gray leaves. Grows 4 to 5 feet tall by 8 to 12 feet or more wide, but can be kept smaller with light pruning. Tolerates heavier soil. Hardy to 15° to 20°.

***G.* 'Robyn Gordon'.** Said to be the most popular plant in Australia. Six-inch-long toothbrush clusters of coral flowers appear much of the year. Green leaves are deeply cut and lacy-looking. Grows 5 feet tall by 10 feet wide. Needs good drainage; does not do well in clay soil. More tender than some; hardy to 25° to 30°. Deer sometimes eat this one.

G. rosmarinifolia **'Scarlet Sprite'.** Compact shrub grows 3 to 6 feet tall by 5 to 10 feet wide (prune to restrain) with soft, needlelike dark green leaves. Spiderlike clusters of rose red flowers (shown at left) appear in late winter and spring. Hardy to 15° to 20°. ***G.* 'Pink Pearl'** (also sold as 'Canberra Gem') is similar, with deep pink flowers; rugged choice for Southern California and the Central Valley. Hardy to 15°.

LARGE SHRUBS

***G.* 'Long John'.** Large, upright shrub grows 8 to 10 feet tall by 12 feet wide with 12-inch-long leaves deeply cut into wispy, narrow, and linear leaflets. Big, terminal clusters of large, dark pink-and-white spiderlike flower clusters. Blooms from spring through fall or longer. To keep in bounds, cut back severely after a few years of growth, then trim foliage periodically (excellent in flower arrangements). Hardy to the mid-20s.

***G.* 'Poorinda Blondie'.** Vigorous, spreading shrub grows 8 to 10 feet tall by 15 feet wide with green herringbone-patterned leaves and bronzy new growth. Masses of yellow-and-rose-pink flower clusters (shown on page 77) appear from late winter into summer. Can be pruned into a small tree. Tolerant of clay soil. Hardy to 15° to 20°. ◆

Roses brought West by pioneers—such as this hybrid China 'Paul Ricault' (1845)—are still thriving, thanks to the efforts of dedicated rosarians. Their story begins on page 136.

May

garden guide 25

WESTERN CONTRIBUTIONS TO HORTICULTURE • BY KATHLEEN N. BRENZEL

COURTESY OF BODGER'S SEEDS

Bodger's
SENSATIONAL *New* NASTURTIUMS
DOUBLE FLOWERING
SWEET SCENTED
FEATURING OUR LATEST SEASON NOVELTIES
GOLDEN GLEAM and GLORIOUS GLEAM
SCARLET GLEAM HYBRIDS

4

TOP SEEDS. During the first half of the century, Southern California nurseries such as Bodger's Seeds became the world's leading producers of bulk flower seed. Among the new varieties they introduced: 'American Beauty' aster, 'Early Klondyke Orange Flare' cosmos, dwarf marigolds, scarlet petunias, and 'Golden Gleam' nasturtium—winner of the first All-America Selections Award, in 1931.

1 | RELIABLE RAIN. Orton Englehardt, a farmer in Glendora, California, patented impact sprinklers in 1933 to improve irrigation of citrus and avocado groves. Later, he developed lawn sprinklers with Mary and Clem La Fetra, founders of Rain Bird Sprinkler Company.

2 | "SOIL" IN A BAG. In 1957, the University of California at Los Angeles introduced UC mix—a lightweight blend of inorganic matter (fine sand and perlite) and organic materials (ground bark, peat moss, and redwood sawdust). It set the standard for potting mixes.

3 | COMPOST COOK-OFF. Seattle Tilth, a nonprofit group that specializes in urban organic gardening, started the first citywide composting program (Seattle; 1989).

NORMAN A. PLATE

5

HIT PARADE. Western hybrids took the plant world by storm. Among them: 'Elephant' garlic (Santa Rosa, California; 1919). 'Hass' avocado (La Habra Heights, California; 1926). Low-chill lilacs (La Cañada, California; 1942). Dwarf citrus (Carmel, California; 1949). 'Early Girl' tomato (Reno, Nevada; 1973).

6 OUT OF THE ASHES. Postwar subdivisions that encroached on wild land began to burn in the 1960s, prompting new studies to identify flammable plants. Klaus Radtke, a wildland resource scientist, introduced the concept of landscaping against fire in the 1970s.

7 X-RATED GARDENING. Denver introduced the world to water conservation through xeriscaping (from *xeros*, meaning *dry*) with an X-Rated Garden Party in 1982.

8 SOD BUT TRUE. Gene Milstein unrolled Wildflower Carpets—sod sown exclusively with wildflowers—in Denver in 1983. You buy the sod, roll it out, water, and watch the flowers grow. For a supplier near you, call (800) 247-6945.

9 GOING TO POT. Growing plants in cans, a practice first used by Southern California growers, revolutionized the wholesale growing of plants in the 1930s. Boxed trees followed.

1971: THOMAS CHURCH returned to *Sunset* for his fifth stint as a juror in the Western Home Awards program.

12 CHURCH YARDS. In the 1930s, legendary landscape architect Thomas Church and his contemporaries introduced "outdoor living"—the concept of living all over the lot. In 1951, Church designed the 7-acre, oak-studded garden at *Sunset's* headquarters in Menlo Park, California. Its shrub border celebrates plant communities of the Pacific Coast.

13 INDOOR ANTICS. After seeing totem poles in Alaska in 1928, the West's largest grower of decorative indoor plants—Roy Wilcox of Montebello, California—devised the idea of training philodendrons on moss poles he called "totems." Wilcox also introduced the idea of combining several house plants in a single pot.

10 AIRBORNE BLOSSOMS.

The first shipment of California-grown cut flowers was sent by air from San Diego to the eastern United States in 1944.

11 ORE-GONERS. Northwest trees ruined by poor pruning led Seattleite Cass Turnbull to found PlantAmnesty in 1987. Its newsletter—"for people who don't beat around the bush"—now has readers all over. For pruning info, send a self-addressed, stamped envelope to PlantAmnesty, 906 N.W. 87th St., Seattle, WA 98117.

14 NATIVES COME HOME. Theodore Payne issued the first seed catalog for native plants in Southern California in 1906. Payne cultivated Matilija poppies and other beauties now grown the world over. For a catalog ($3.25), contact the Theodore Payne Foundation, 10459 Tuxford St., Sun Valley, CA 91352; (818) 768-1802.

15 HEAVENLY BASKETS. Herb Warren, city parks administrator in Victoria, British Columbia, hung baskets spilling with flowers from downtown lampposts to commemorate the city's 75th birthday in 1937. The idea was later copied in cities around the world.

16

ECKE'S ACRES. The poinsettia got its start as the world's favorite Christmas plant in 1906 when Paul Ecke discovered the Mexican native growing in the Hollywood Hills and began propagating and hybridizing it. Eventually, the Ecke family moved the nursery to Encinitas, California, where it continues as the world's leading grower of potted poinsettias.

17 | SEEDS OF YESTERDAY. Native Seeds/SEARCH was formed in Tucson in 1983 to perpetuate the seed of ancient crops of the Southwest. For a copy of *Seedlisting* ($1), call (520) 622-5561.

18 | STRATEGY FOR TODAY. Integrated pest management (IPM), a strategy for controlling garden pests using low-toxic methods, was introduced by the University of California in the 1970s.

19 | CALL OF THE WILD. Lawrence Halprin designed a "rolling meadow" garden to blend with the wild landscape around it (*Sunset,* March 1955), adding momentum to a 1940s idea of "natural" gardening. Later, Halprin designed the landscaping for Sea Ranch (*Sunset,* October 1971) to harmonize with a windswept stretch of Northern California coast.

20 | MASTER GARDENERS. This program began in Washington in 1972, training volunteers to help cooperative extension agents answer garden questions.

21 DEATH OF DDT. *Sunset* published "It's Time to Blow the Whistle on DDT" in August 1969. The article, written by then–garden editor Joseph F. Williamson, alerted the public to the dangers of this toxic chemical and helped lead to its ban in 1972.

22 BROAD JUMP FOR DEER. An outriggerlike deer fence, designed and built by the California Department of Fish and Game and the California Forest and Range Experiment Stations in the 1950s, proved that our rose-eating ruminant friends are better at high jumping than broad jumping.

23 | THE "S" ZONE. *Sunset* published its first *Western Garden Book* in 1932. Subsequent editions helped solidify the book's reputation as the "Bible of Western Gardening." In the book's 1967 edition, *Sunset* introduced the first climate zone system created by horticulturists and climatologists specifically for Western gardeners.

24 | HOT ROSES. 'Climbing Cécile Brunner' was introduced in the 1890s in Riverside, California. Between the '30s and the '50s, Southern California hybridizers introduced 'Charlotte Armstrong', 'Chrysler Imperial', 'High Noon', 'Mojave', 'Queen Elizabeth', 'Sutter's Gold', and 'Tiffany'.

25

COOL TOOL. Ralph Henningsen of Sebastopol, California, introduced his Henningsen Circle Hoe, for weeding in tight places, in May 1997. It's available in three sizes: a 15-inch hand hoe ($18.75, plus $5 shipping) and 60- and 66-inch standard hoes ($28.95, plus $5.50 shipping) from Index Manufacturing; (800) 735-4815.

100 WESTERN CONTRIBUTIONS

Pacific Northwest Checklist

PLANTING

☑ **ANNUAL FLOWERS.** Zones 4–7: Set out ageratum, globe amaranth, impatiens, lobelia, marigolds, nicotiana, petunias, salvia, sunflowers, sweet alyssum, and zinnias. Zones 1–3: Plant these warm-season annuals after the last frost. Cold-hardy calendula, pansies, and sweet peas can go into the ground immediately.

☑ **DAHLIAS AND TUBEROUS BEGONIAS.** Planted now, both will reward you with blooms from summer into fall. Stake or cage tall dahlias at planting time to avoid puncturing tubers later in the season.

☑ **FUCHSIAS AND GERANIUMS.** Zones 4–7: Early in the month, plants can go into the ground or in outdoor containers. Put plants in rich, loose soil and water well. Begin a feeding program two weeks after you set them out. In zones 1–3, wait until month's end to set plants out.

☑ **HERBS AND VEGETABLES.** Zones 4–7: When the soil warms up, plant herbs (basil, dill, fennel, rosemary, sage, and thyme) and vegetables (beans, corn, eggplant, melons, okra, peppers, pumpkins, squash, and tomatoes). In zones 1–3, choose short-season varieties and plant through black plastic. Use hot caps, row covers, or even old tires to hold warmth around plants.

MAINTENANCE

☑ **FERTILIZE.** As soon as annuals get established, start feeding them. Liquid plant food such as fish emulsion works well because the nutrients go directly to the roots. For perennials, use liquid or granular fertilizer. For shrubs, scatter a granular fertilizer around the base of each plant. For lawns, apply a high-nitrogen fertilizer evenly over the grass to keep it growing thick and green.

☑ **PRUNE SHRUBS.** If you prune spring-flowering shrubs such as lilacs and rhododendrons while they are in bloom, you can use cut blossoms for indoor bouquets. Remove damaged and crossing branches first, then prune for shape, working up from the bottom of the plant and from the inside out.

☑ **TRIM HEDGES.** If you prune hedges twice each year, shear or clip them between now and early June, then again in mid- to late summer. Otherwise, prune them just once, in early July. A good rule of thumb is to shear coniferous hedges and clip broad-leafed ones. Trim hedges so that the bottom is wider than the top; this allows sunlight and rain to reach the foliage.

PEST CONTROL

☑ **SLUGS.** Newly set-out flower and vegetable seedlings are sitting ducks for hungry slugs. Spread a defensive circle of poison bait around plants or set out beer traps. ◆

Northern California Checklist

PLANTING

☑ **ANNUALS AND PERENNIALS.** Zones 7–9, 14–17: Set out ageratum, coreopsis, dahlias, gaillardia, globe amaranth, impatiens, lobelia, Madagascar periwinkle (vinca), marigolds, nicotiana, penstemon, perennial statice, petunias, phlox, portulaca, salvia, sanvitalia, sunflowers, sweet alyssum, torenia, verbena, and zinnias. Zones 1–2: Wait to plant warm-season annuals until after the last frost. You can still plant cold-hardy calendula, pansies, and sweet peas.

☑ **DAHLIAS AND BEGONIAS.** Planted now, both will reward you with blooms from summer into fall. Among dahlias, choices run from dwarf varieties to ones that grow 6 feet tall and bear plate-size flowers. Stake or cage tall dahlias at planting time to avoid puncturing tubers later in the season. Among tuberous begonias, choose upright types for beds or cascading types for hanging baskets.

☑ **HERBS AND VEGETABLES.** It's prime time to plant heat-loving herbs and vegetables, including basil, beans, corn, eggplant, melons, okra, peppers, pumpkins, squash, and tomatoes (see next item). In zones 1–2 and 17, choose short-season varieties and plant through black plastic. Use row covers or hot caps to hold warmth around plants and protect them from late spring frosts.

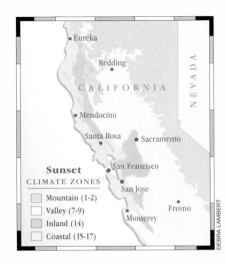

Sunset
CLIMATE ZONES
☐ Mountain (1-2)
☐ Valley (7-9)
☐ Inland (14)
☐ Coastal (15-17)

DEBRA LAMBERT

☑ **TOMATOES.** It's late to start plants from seed, so buy nursery-grown seedlings. Select stocky, not leggy, plants with a rich green color. At transplanting time, pull off the lowest leaves and plant up to the next leaf set; roots will form along the buried stem.

MAINTENANCE

☑ **AERATE LAWNS.** To improve air and water circulation in the soil around roots, aerate the lawn. You can rent an aerator from an equipment supply store (look in the yellow pages under Rental Service Stores & Yards). Rake up the cores and topdress with mulch. If you haven't fed the grass lately, apply a lawn fertilizer and water it in well.

☑ **HARDEN OFF SEEDLINGS.** Zones 1–2: Move seedlings of warm-season flowers and vegetables outdoors to a coldframe or other protected spot and gradually expose them to longer periods of stronger sunlight. As planting time draws near, cut back on water and fertilizer to ease transplant shock.

☑ **MAKE COMPOST.** A well-tended compost pile can break down an amazing amount of garden debris and kitchen waste: annual weeds, coffee grounds, eggshells, evergreen needles, fruit and peels, grass clippings, leaves, prunings, sawdust, small wood chips, and tea leaves. (Do not add any animal or fish residues or pet manure.) Keep the pile evenly moist and occasionally add a handful of nitrogen fertilizer or manure. Turn the pile frequently with a spading fork. When the compost is crumbly and develops an earthy brown color, use it as a soil amendment or as a water-conserving mulch.◆

Southern California Checklist

PLANTING

☑ **PLANT SUMMER ANNUALS.** Nurseries carry a huge selection this month. Sturdy standbys like petunias and vinca are available in refreshing pastel shades. There are rudbeckias compact enough for containers. And some coleus now thrive in the sun. Other options include alyssum, candytuft, bedding dahlias, dianthus, geraniums, lobelia, marigolds, nicotiana, phlox, portulaca, and verbena. Start cleome, cosmos, nasturtiums, sunflowers, and zinnias from seed. They're all easy and rewarding.

☑ **PLANT CULINARY HERBS.** Nurseries are well stocked with herbs, and it's a good time to plant. Try basil, chervil, chives, lemon grass, marjoram, mint, oregano, parsley, rosemary, sage, savory, tarragon, and thyme. Cilantro and dill are best started from seed.

☑ **PLANT SUMMER VEGETABLES.** Set out plants of cucumber, eggplant, melon, pepper, squash, and tomato. Sow seeds of corn, cucumbers, lima and snap beans, melon, okra, pumpkin, and summer and winter squash. In the low desert (zone 13), plant Jerusalem artichoke, okra, peppers, and sweet peppers.

☑ **START LAWNS.** This is a good month to plant subtropical grasses like St. Augustine, Bermuda, and zoysia. You can lay sod (the simplest method) or plant plugs.

Sunset
CLIMATE ZONES
1-3 7-9 11 13 14-24

DEBRA LAMBERT

MAINTENANCE

☑ **STEP UP WATERING.** As temperatures warm, plants need to be watered more often. Check new plantings regularly. Seedlings and transplants need frequent shallow watering for a few weeks to establish new roots. Water established plants—including lawns—less often but more deeply to encourage deep root growth. Use a soil probe to test moisture content, and irrigate as needed. Adjust or override automatic sprinklers to meet water needs.

☑ **REPLENISH MULCH.** A 3- to 6-inch layer of mulch around trees, shrubs, and established perennials keeps roots cool and moist and discourages weeds. To prevent diseases, leave a clear area around the base of trunks.

☑ **PREVENT BLOSSOM-END ROT IN TOMATOES.** Overfertilizing and heat waves in late spring and early summer trigger this frustrating disease. To prevent it, be stingy with feeding, mulch deeply around plants, and maintain even soil moisture.

☑ **THIN FRUIT.** On apple, peach, and other deciduous fruit trees, thin fruit so it's spaced about 6 inches apart.

PEST CONTROL

☑ **WATCH FOR TOMATO HORNWORMS.** The green worms will be easier to spot if you sprinkle the tomato foliage lightly with water first. Then shake off the water to make worms more visible. Handpick them.

☑ **COMBAT POWDERY MILDEW.** Warm days and cool nights are ideal conditions for powdery mildew in susceptible plants like roses. Frequently hose off foliage in the early mornings to wash off spores. Or spray with 1 tablespoon *each* baking soda and summer oil diluted in a gallon of water. (Don't spray when temperatures exceed 85°.) Or try neem oil. ◆

Mountain Checklist

Sunset
CLIMATE ZONES

☐ 1-3 ☐ 10-11

DEBRA LAMBERT

PLANTING

☑ **ANNUALS.** Early in the month, set out hardy bachelor's buttons, lobelia, pansies, and violas. At month's end, set out warm-season annuals (marigolds, petunias, sunflowers, and zinnias), but if frost is predicted, cover them with hot caps or row covers.

☑ **LAWNS.** New plantings should go into tilled, raked, fertilized, and relatively rock-free soil. Sow bluegrass, fescue, rye, or—better yet—a mix of those grasses. Denver Water recommends these low-water turf grasses: blue grama grass (*Bouteloua gracilis*), buffalo grass (*Buchloe dactyloides*), and tall fescue (*Festuca arundinacea*).

☑ **PERENNIALS.** Plant bleeding heart, bluebells, blue flax, campanula, columbine, delphiniums, gaillardia, geraniums, hellebore, *Heuchera,* Iceland and Oriental poppies, lady's-mantle, lupines, Maltese cross, penstemon, phlox, primroses, purple coneflower, Russian sage, Shasta daisies, sweet woodruff, veronica, and yarrow.

☑ **PERMANENT PLANTS.** Set out container-grown shrubs, trees, vines, and hardy ground covers such as *Lamium maculatum* and woolly thyme.

☑ **VEGETABLES.** Plant seedlings of cool-season crops such as beets, carrots, lettuce, peas, and Swiss chard. Early in the month, sow seeds indoors for warm-season crops (basil, corn, cucumbers, eggplant, melons, peppers, squash, and tomatoes) to transplant after danger of frost is past. If there's no danger of frost, sow these, and beans, directly into well-prepared soil.

MAINTENANCE

☑ **CARE FOR TOMATOES.** Indeterminate types, which keep growing all season, need to be staked or caged early or they'll sprawl all over.

☑ **FERTILIZE.** Before planting beds of flowers or vegetables, amend the soil by digging in 1 to 2 pounds of a complete fertilizer per 100 square feet. Start a monthly fertilizing program for annuals, long-blooming perennials, and container plants (especially the last). If you live where hyacinths rebloom, fertilize them this month with superphosphate to build up bulbs for next year's bloom.

☑ **HARDEN OFF TRANSPLANTS.** Before transplanting, move seedlings to a partially shaded patio or coldframe, gradually exposing them to more sun and nighttime cold. After 7 to 10 days, they ought to be tough enough to go into the ground.

☑ **MAKE COMPOST.** Alternate 4-inch-thick layers of green matter, such as grass clippings, with brown matter, such as dead leaves and straw. Keep the pile as moist as a wrung-out sponge and turn it weekly.

☑ **MOVE HOUSE PLANTS OUTDOORS.** After the last frost, take house plants outside to a shady place for the summer. Prune them for shape, then fertilize and water well. They'll fill out and grow strong before you bring them back inside next fall.

☑ **MULCH.** Spread organic mulch around annuals, perennials, and vegetables. Ground bark, compost, grass clippings, and rotted leaves all do a good job of suppressing weeds and conserving soil moisture.

☑ **PRUNE FLOWERING SHRUBS.** After spring bloom, prune plants such as lilacs, mock orange, and spiraea. ◆

Southwest Checklist

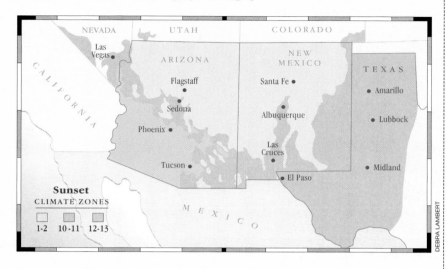

PLANTING

☑ **COLOR IN THE SUN.** Zones 10–13: Set out ageratum, celosia, coreopsis, cosmos, firebush (*Hamelia patens*), four o'clock, gaillardia, globe amaranth, gloriosa daisies, kochia, lantana, lisianthus, nicotiana, portulaca, salvia, strawflowers, tithonia, vinca rosea (*Catharanthus roseus*), and zinnias. Zones 1–2: Plant any of the above after danger of frost is past.

☑ **COLOR IN THE SHADE.** Good choices include begonias, caladium, chocolate plant (*Pseuderanthemum alatum*), coleus, gerbera, impatiens, lobelia, oxalis, pentas (*P. lanceolata*), spider plant, and *Tradescantia fluminensis*.

☑ **LAWNS.** Zones 12–13: Plant Bermuda or improved buffalo grass when nighttime temperatures rise above 70°. Zones 1–2, 10–11: Plant or overseed with bluegrass, fescue, rye, or a combination of these early in the month.

☑ **PERMANENT PLANTS.** Zones 1–2, 10–11: Plant container-grown trees, shrubs, vines, and ground covers.

☑ **SUMMER BULBS.** Plant acidanthera (*Gladiolus callianthus*), cannas, dahlias, daylilies, gladiolus, montbretia, tiger flower (*Tigridia*), and zephyranthes (except in zones 10–11). Zones 12–13: Also plant agapanthus, caladium, and crinum. Zone 13 only: Plant society garlic (*Tulbaghia violacea*).

☑ **VEGETABLES.** Zones 12–13: Plant eggplant, Jerusalem artichoke, okra, peanuts, peppers, soybeans, summer squash, and sweet potatoes. Zones 10–11: Plant all the above, plus beans, corn, cucumbers, melons, pumpkins, radishes, Southern peas, and tomatoes. (Put most in early in the month; okra, Southern peas, and sweet potatoes can be planted through midmonth.) Zones 1–2: Plant cool-season crops outside and start seeds indoors for warm-season crops (corn, cucumbers, eggplant, melons, peppers, squash, and tomatoes) to transplant into the garden after danger of frost is past.

MAINTENANCE

☑ **CARE FOR ROSES.** Zones 12–13: When heat starts to take its toll on May's flush of bloom, water plants deeply, mulch, and fertilize. In the Phoenix area, try to give plants afternoon shade.

☑ **FERTILIZE.** Feed flowering shrubs after bloom. Start monthly feedings of annuals, long-blooming perennials, and container plants. For citrus trees, water first, then feed with 1 cup ammonium sulfate per inch of trunk diameter; water again. If citrus foliage still looks yellow, apply chelated iron, magnesium, and zinc. ◆

New plant pioneers

Ten globe-trotting **adventurers**
are **discovering** plants
in the **West** and abroad
that you can **grow**

BY JOHN R. DUNMIRE
AND
LAUREN BONAR SWEZ

PHOTOGRAPHS BY
FRANCE RUFFENACH

■ First came figs, olives, and oleanders. Padres brought these "exotics" west from Spain to plant in their missions. Then came cuttings of such garden treasures as Harison's yellow rose; pioneers brought them west in their wagons as reminders of homes left behind. And gradually, with each new settler, the Western plant palette began to expand beyond existing vegetation and crops grown by Native Americans. But deliberate plant pioneering—the systematic search of the world for unfamiliar plants to enhance our gardens—began in earnest in the 1850s. • To feed the West's growing nursery business, plant fanciers started traveling the globe in search of horticultural surprises. By 1860, William Walker of San Francisco was offering seeds of Australian plants. Acacias and eucalyptus soon became familiar sights in Western gardens. • Today the search continues. Devoted nurserymen, collectors from arboretums and botanic gardens, and amateurs with time and resources are venturing into wild places seeking new species, new flower colors. • Of the many plant pioneers traveling the globe, we introduce you to 10 who have helped expand the selection of garden plants in our nurseries.

GARY HAMMER

DESERT TO JUNGLE NURSERY
MONTEBELLO, CALIFORNIA

Gary Hammer grew up in Southern California surrounded by plant lovers. His grandfather and uncle owned nurseries, so it was only fitting that he would follow them into the profession. After graduating with a horti-culture degree, he was temporarily sidetracked by a job installing commercial landscapes.

At the time, though, he was living on a property that was partially zoned for commercial trade, so he opened up a small retail business called Glendale Paradise Nursery. Here he sold unusual cactus, succulents, palms, and perennials. "I would scour nurseries for oddball plants," he says. "But I was never

satisfied, because there weren't enough unusual plants out there."

That's when Hammer turned to plant collecting. In the mid-1970s he and his father searched in Baja California. "Baja is so well explored, we didn't bring anything new back," he admits. So he turned his attention to mainland Mexico, which has a wealth of undocumented plants. Since then, Hammer has traveled all over the world, including Australia, Belize, Ecuador, New Zealand, Peru, Swaziland, and Thailand.

He opened Desert to Jungle Nursery in the mid-1980s, and World Wide Exotics (at another site) in 1991. "I had plenty of room to grow plants, so Desert to Jungle Nursery gave me the opportunity to expand my selection," says Hammer. And even more reason to go plant collecting. His two favorite countries—for the diversity of plant material they offer—remain South Africa and Mexico.

Often Hammer goes out into the wild to collect plants, but sometimes he finds them right in town. On a trip to Mexico in the late 1980s, he visited a small village outside San Cristóbal in Chiapas. There he discovered a beautiful *Chamaedorea* palm, which he thought was just an attractive new variety of *C. glaucifolia*, growing in a yard. When he got home, he found it was a completely new species, *C. plumosa*.

Hammer finds plant exploring exciting, not only because of the plants he discovers, but also because of the interesting places he sees and people he meets. "I now have friends all over the world," says Hammer. "I can go anywhere and have a good time."

Hammer's favorite finds

Canna 'Durban' and 'Transvaal Beauty'. Multicolored foliage and flowers. All *Sunset* climate zones.
Westringia 'Wynyabbie Gem'. A rosemary look-alike with gray-green leaves and light purplish flowers much of the year. Zones 8–9, 12–24.

Desert to Jungle Nursery (3211 W. Beverly Blvd., Montebello, CA; 213/722-3976) is open 10–4 Wed-Sat. World Wide Exotics (11156 Orcas Ave., Lake View Terrace, CA; 818/890-1915) is open 10–4 Sat.

M. NEVIN SMITH

SUNCREST NURSERIES
WATSONVILLE, CALIFORNIA

M. Nevin Smith was destined to work with plants; he grew up weeding and watering in his father's Northern California nursery. During his free time, he and his brother Tim explored the Hood Mountain Range in Sonoma County, shimmying through dense chaparral. "The area is botanically very diverse," says Smith. "I made my first selections of native plants there in the early 1970s. We're still growing a natural hybrid [manzanita] we discovered there called *Arctostaphylos* 'Hood Mountain'."

After earning degrees in political science and doing a brief teaching stint, he returned to the nursery business, eventually managing Leonard Coates Nurseries. From 1978 to 1991, he and his brother operated Wintergreen Nursery, a small, wholesale nursery.

Now, as horticultural director of Suncrest Nurseries, Smith continues his search for native plants, traveling throughout northern and eastern California. "The Yolla Bolly Mountains of Lake and Mendocino counties are particularly rich in native plants," he says. He's especially excited by the beautiful forms of toyon (*Heteromeles arbutifolia*) and redbuds (*Cercis occidentalis*).

Smith has introduced many of his own selections of exotic plants, like the nerines pictured below and California natives such as *Penstemon heterophyllus* 'Walker Ridge'. "Several years ago, I took part in a plant salvage effort at Vandenberg Air Force Base, where a mile-wide swath was being cleared for a space shuttle landing strip," he says. "*Arctostaphylos rudis* 'Vandenberg' remains one of the most promising plant selections we made there."

Smith's favorite finds
Lewisia 'Dark Cloud', 'Pink Cloud', and orange selections. Native perennials, with clusters of 1-inch-wide flowers. Zones 1–7, 14–17.

Suncrest Nurseries is not open for retail business, but Smith's discoveries can be found at retail nurseries throughout California.

UC SANTA CRUZ ARBORETUM
SANTA CRUZ, CALIFORNIA

Ray Collett and the University of California at Santa Cruz met each other at a happy time. The university, freshly founded (in 1965) and devoted to undergraduate educational adventure in the most liberal sense, was open to new ideas.

Collett suggested that an arboretum be planted on a splendid site at the southwest edge of the campus—high enough to escape most of the sea fogs but near enough to the Pacific to share its humidity and tempering influence. The site's south-facing slope provided maximum sunshine and protection from north winds; it also furnished good air drainage to minimize frost. That made it just about perfect for growing plants from places like Australia and New Zealand.

Collett was named the arboretum's founding director (his qualifications included having learned from his pioneer grandmother how to grow plants from cuttings), and before long the arboretum had acquired the best collection of Southern Hemisphere plants north of the equator. These included South African plants such as huge-flowered proteas and many ornamentals from Australia.

And Collett hit the road to find more plants. On one memorable trip, he drove 7,000 miles across Australia and back in a rental car ("never let a rental car agency tell you it's impossible to do," he says). "Australians are aware of their plant wealth," he adds. "Even the smallest towns have several nurseries offering native plants."

Many of the arboretum's plants have made their way into nurseries.

Collett's favorite finds

Australian fuchsia (*Correa harrisii*). Evergreen shrub; red flowers. Zones 14–24.
Blue hibiscus (*Alyogyne huegelii*) 'Santa Cruz'. Shrub, with lavender to deep blue flowers. Zones 15, 17, 21–24.
Geraldton waxflower (*Chamelaucium uncinatum* 'University'). Shrub, with needlelike leaves and small, waxy, reddish-purple flowers. Zones 8–9, 12–24.

The arboretum is at the southwest corner of the UC Santa Cruz campus (enter from Empire Grade, a continuation of High St.). Open 9–5 daily. Admission free; (408) 427-2998.

HERONSWOOD NURSERY
KINGSTON, WASHINGTON

Dan Hinkley may just be the Northwest's own Indiana Jones. His all-consuming passion for trekking around the world in search of new plants began 10 years ago when he was teaching horticulture at the community college in Edmonds, Washington. Lecturing, for him, had lost its luster; he wanted to show the students what the plants looked like in the wild. "It also thrilled me to think that there might be plants growing in the wild that we'd never grown here," says Hinkley.

Today, Hinkley makes two or three major expeditions a year to exotic destinations around the world, including China, Japan, Korea, and Nepal. The rest of the time, he joins his partner, Robert Jones, in running Heronswood Nursery, a world-class mail-order and retail business. The two sell all of the amazing new plants that Hinkley finds overseas.

Among his most memorable trips was a trek through the Himalayas three years ago in search of species of plants such as *Arisaema, Cardiocrinum, Diosporopsis,* and *Sorbus.* For the four-week trip, 24 porters accompanied five plant explorers. They camped at 16,000 feet. "There's no place to buy food and supplies, so you have to bring it all with you," says Hinkley. "It was incredible to see this group of people marching through the mountains." Many of the plants from this trip are just appearing in his catalog.

Before Hinkley starts out on his

journeys, he prepares a want list of plants. Plant collecting is "like shopping at the grocery store," he explains. "You may not find what you came for, but you might find 10 other plants that are intriguing."

Although plant exploring may sound romantic, "it's plain hard work," says Hinkley. "We collect from sunup to sundown, go back to our cold tent or hotel room with one lightbulb and spend half the night making records and cleaning seeds (to meet all USDA guidelines). But every plant I collect is another piece in an amazing puzzle."

Hinkley's favorite find

Polygonatum franchetianum. Large clusters of white, bell-shaped flowers on a 17-foot-tall plant. Found in the Szechwan region of China. Possibly zones 4–9, 14–23 (the plant won't be available for several years).

Heronswood Nursery is open by appointment only (7530 N.E. 288th St., Kingston, WA 98346; 360/297-4172). The nursery's 264-page mail-order catalog costs $5.

A word about collecting in the wild

TO PRESERVE native plant populations, pioneers such as the Starrs and Gasses gather *only* seeds or cuttings, never plants. "You can collect 10,000 seeds off of one yucca plant in the wild and preserve the plant," says Starr. "But if you dig up the plant, it will never produce seed again (it needs a special moth to pollinate the flower, and this moth doesn't exist around cultivated plants)." Collecting seeds preserves plant communities for future generations to enjoy.

And collecting any plant material in the wild is best left to professionals. But if you're considering bringing plant material into the United States from another country, call the Permit Unit of the U.S. Department of Agriculture's Animal and Plant Health Inspection Unit for guidelines (301/734-8896).

THE GASS-STARR TEAM

In the mid-'80s Ron Gass was a pioneering nurseryman in Phoenix, having collected plants in the Southwest and Mexico since the late '60s. With his wife, Maureen, he owned Mountain States Wholesale Nursery.

He met Greg Starr when Starr visited the nursery looking for new and unusual plants while working on a master's degree in horticulture (Starr later opened a retail nursery in Tucson). They made their first trip together in 1986, to the Chihuahuan desert in northeastern Mexico. Since then, they've combed the deserts together.

"Every time we get out of the car in Mexico, we stumble onto something interesting," says Gass. "One of our favorite discoveries was made while we were being followed by a policeman," says Starr. Gass pulled over, and they both hurriedly jumped out of the car. Starr started snapping pictures with his camera so he would look like a tourist, and Gass wandered around taking plant cuttings off some scraggly plants. Fortunately, the policeman passed them by. But some of those cuttings Gass brought back turned out to be *Dalea capitata,* an attractive ground cover with yellow, pea-shaped flowers, which Gass and Starr now refer to as policeman's dalea.

By 1988, Greg and Carol Starr and the Gasses were a team, heading off into the canyonlands south of Monter-

rey in the Eastern Sierra Madre mountain range of Mexico. On that trip, they collected seeds of *Leucophyllum langmaniae, Vauquelinia corymbosa, Yucca rostrata,* and eight colors of *Salvia greggii.* "It helps to have four pairs of eyes looking out both sides of the car," says Gass.

The Starrs and Gasses have collected close to 20 plants that have made it into the trade and been successful—about 10 to 15 percent of what they've actually brought back from their trips.

Favorite finds

The Gasses': *Leucophyllums* (*L. laevigatum griseum, L. langmaniae, L. pruinosum, L. revolutum, and L. zygophyllum* 'Cimarron'). All are 3- to 6-foot-tall shrubs, with lavender to purple flowers. Zones 7–24.
The Starrs': *Dasylirion longissimum.* Grasslike plant, with narrow, dark green leaves; grows to 6 feet tall. Zones 12–24.

Mountain States Wholesale Nursery is not open for retail business, but its plants are available at retail nurseries in Arizona, New Mexico, southern Utah, Las Vegas, El Paso, and the desert regions of California.
Starr Nursery (3340 W. Ruthann Rd., Tucson; 520/743-7052) is open by appointment only.

BILL EVANS:
A LEGACY OF FANTASY
LANDSCAPES

MORGAN "BILL" EVANS is interna- tionally known as the landscape genius behind the Disney con- stellation of theme parks. For nearly 44 years, he has helped clothe the fantasies of Disney's talented designers with ap- propriate landscapes, be they simulated mangrove swamps for a jungle river, storm-battered conifers for the Matter- horn, or municipal cannas and gerani- ums for Main Street. Along the way he has learned how to create or move en- tire forests to meet the parks' changing needs. But to those who know him best, he is above all a dedicated plantsman, eager to seek out the newest and best and just as eager to maintain in cultiva- tion choice plants that are in danger of being forgotten. "It's not only necessary to find new plants; you have to preserve the older ones," says Evans. "If they're not written up, they're not grown, and they disappear from the nursery trade."

In the early 1920s, Bill's father, Hugh, established a remarkable garden on 3½ acres in Santa Monica, California. The variety of plants he grew was so im- mense (and the volume of visitors so great) that Evans senior—with the help of sons Bill and Jack—established a nursery, moved it to Brentwood, and took in a partner, Jack Reeves of the Beverly Hills Nursery. Thus was born the Evans and Reeves Nurseries, a treasure house of new and rare plants.

A big break came when Walt Disney engaged Jack Evans to design his Bel Air garden in 1951. Pleased with his

work, Disney sought both brothers out in 1954 to do the landscaping for Disney- land. (At the same time, Bill began his as- sociation with *Sunset* as an adviser to the garden writers.)

Bill has worked with the Disney enter- prises on three continents ever since— as lead landscape architect for the first 20 years, and as consultant for the past 24 years. A new project is Disney's Ani- mal Kingdom Park in Florida. With Paul Comstock, Disney's chief landscape ar- chitect for this project, Bill is growing some African veld acacias to re-create an authentic feeling, but if these prove too tender, Southwestern trees such as mesquite will be substituted.

Of the dozens of plants Bill has intro- duced to the nursery trade, one of his favorites is *Schefflera pueckleri* (known as *Tupidanthus calyptratus* until re- cently), a large evergreen shrub or tree. He secured seeds from a British forestry official in Assam, India, and grew them. The plant is now widely grown.

Recent introductions are the ever- green Shogun trees, which Bill brought back from Japan. Among the 10 new species are Japanese blueberry tree (*Elaeocarpus decipiens*), a dense, nar- row, upright tree with bronze new growth and small sprays of white flowers fol- lowed by blue berries; and Japanese sil- ver tree (*Neolitsea sericea*), which is nar- row and dense, and shows a heavy coating of brown fur on the young leaves. Six species are now distributed by Monrovia Nursery, a wholesale grower.

PANAYOTI KELAIDIS

DENVER BOTANIC GARDENS
DENVER, COLORADO

Panayoti Kelaidis grew up in Boulder, Colorado, loving plants. When he was 8 years old, he and his older brother-in-law used to find plants for their home garden (back then, collect- ing plants was legal, explains Kelaidis). "I thought it was the coolest thing."

When Kelaidis was in his 20s, Univer- sity of Colorado professor Paul Maslin took him all over the West collecting seeds and plants. "Paul had a plants- man's garden, with beautiful foliage and flowers," says Kelaidis. It sparked Ke- laidis's interest in plants with year- round good looks. Since 1980, as cura- tor of Denver Botanic Gardens's Rock Alpine Garden, Kelaidis has been on col- lecting trips to South Africa, Greece, and Turkey, looking for colorful, hardy spec- imens suited to Rocky Mountain gardens.

He has introduced hundreds of plants to the nursery trade, including *Delosperma floribundum* 'Starburst' and a hardy gazania, *G. linearis* 'Col- orado Gold', both from South Africa.

But Kelaidis is most excited by the numbers of plants awaiting discovery. "I think the best is yet to come," he says.

Kelaidis's favorite find
Chihuahuan phlox (*Phlox mesoleuca*). Grows 6 inches tall by 1½ feet wide. Yel- lowish flowers. Zones 2–24.

Denver Botanic Gardens (1005 York St.) is open daily. (303) 311-4000. ◆

'MONSIEUR TILLIER'
(1891) has sumptuous
pink blooms.

Heritage roses

Many of the plants brought West by pioneers are still thriving, thanks to efforts by dedicated rosarians

BY LAUREN BONAR SWEZEY

■ Before the turn of the century, Mendocino, California, was an isolated community, connected to the rest of the world only by ships that plied the Pacific. But that didn't stop Daisy Mac-Callum—daughter of one of the area's original settlers, William Kelley—from obtaining roses. Many of them arrived on her father's supply ships to adorn her gardens in Mendocino and Glen Blair, east of Fort Bragg. MacCallum was a generous woman, and as the years went by, she gave cuttings of her roses to anyone who wanted them. Now, more than 100 years later, only 6 of her original 140 roses still live in the MacCallum House garden in Mendocino. But many descendants of those first plants thrive around old homes and in abandoned gardens.

Stories like MacCallum's abound in the West. When pioneer families came

here by wagon on the Oregon and California trails, or by ship around Cape Horn, many carried their favorite roses with them. They protected the plants as lovingly as their other prized possessions—sometimes even sacrificing their drinking water to keep the roses alive.

Heritage roses—old roses that have survived since those times—can still be found growing in communities from Arizona to Oregon. Dedicated rosarians like Miriam Wilkins and Erica Calkins (see page 138) have made it their mission to save and perpetuate this diverse group of plants with names that run from the humble 'Adam' to the exotic 'Duchesse de Brabant'.

Organizations such as the Heritage Roses Group, founded by Wilkins, document the plants and work to locate, identify, tend, and renew them. At the

HYBRID CHINA 'PAUL RICAULT' (1845) grows in Mendocino, California.

WHERE TO SEE OLD ROSES

California
EL CERRITO. *Celebration of Old Roses.* One of the most outstanding rose events runs 11–4:30 May 17 at El Cerrito Community Center, 7007 Moeser Lane (at Ashbury St.). Free. (510) 526-6960.

FORT BRAGG. *Heritage Rose Garden,* Mendocino Coast Botanical Gardens, 18220 N. Hwy. 1. Open 9–5 daily. (707) 964-4352.

GRASS VALLEY. *Empire Mine Historic Park Rose Garden,* 10791 E. Empire St. About 950 roses dating before 1929. (530) 273-8522.

MENDOCINO. *A Walking Tour of Mendocino Heritage Roses.* Self-guided tour brochures are available at the Mendocino Ceramic Studio, corner of Kasten and Ukiah streets.

SACRAMENTO. *Sacramento Historic Rose Garden,* Sacramento City Cemetery, 1000 Broadway (at 10th St.). More than 300 roses, mostly from the 1800s. (916) 443-2146.

SAN JOSE. *San Jose Heritage Rose Garden,* Guadalupe River Park & Gardens, Taylor St. (at Spring St.). (408) 298-7657.

Colorado
DENVER. *Fairmount Cemetery,* 430 S. Quebec St. (at Alameda Ave.). About 1,500 old roses. (303) 399-0692.

Oregon
OREGON CITY. *Heritage Gardens at the End of the Oregon Trail National Historic Site,* 1726 Washington St. (503) 557-1151.

SALEM. *Tartar Old Rose Collection at Bush's Pasture Park,* 600 Mission St. S.E. (High St. entry). Over 150 pioneer roses. (503) 588-6336.

WILKINS with 'Jacques Cartier'.

ROSARIANS' GRANDE DAME

Mᴵᴿᴵᴬᴹ WILKINS'S love affair began in 1950 when she saw an ad for an old rose catalog in a women's magazine. Since then, she has collected almost 1,000 old roses—in fact, she ran out of space in her own garden in El Cerrito, California, and now has hundreds growing in her neighbor's garden. "I just got carried away," she explains.

In 1974, she placed a notice in the American Rose Society (ARS) bulletin inviting people interested in old roses to write her. "I was overwhelmed by the response," Wilkins says. In 1975, she started the Heritage Roses Group, a society dedicated to old roses. Today, the organization has 2,000 members in the United States, as well as groups in Australia and New Zealand. Similar groups exist in England and France.

To join the Heritage Roses Group in your region, write to Beverly Dobson, 1034 Taylor Ave., Alameda, CA 94501.

• WILKINS'S FAVORITES: 'Charles de Mills' (gallica; crimson aging to purple), 'Félicité Parmentier' (alba; pink), 'Jacques Cartier' (Portland; pink), 'Lady Hillingdon' (tea; apricot), 'Mme. Alfred Carrière' (climbing noisette; white), 'Mme. Hardy' (damask; white), *Rosa roxburghii* (species; double pale pink to cerise).

same time, more growers are offering heritage roses (see sources on the facing page), making it easy for gardeners to plant some living history.

Rescuing old roses in California

"I FELL IN LOVE with old roses 35 years ago when I bought my first home," says Joyce Demits. "I discovered they were the roses that survive in deer country." For more than three decades, she and her sister, Virginia Hopper, have been finding and preserving heritage roses.

The sisters have traveled up and down the Mendocino coast, scouting for plants and gathering cuttings at abandoned homesteads. "Sometimes we would happen upon a row of rose bushes in full bloom partially covered by brush," says Demits. "Suddenly, we could 'see' a fence line. Of course, there was nothing left of the fence they bordered, or the home."

Demits and Hopper have documented nearly 400 varieties of heritage roses growing in Northern California. In the mid-1980s, they established the Heritage Rose Garden at the Mendocino Coast Botanical Gardens, where visitors can view almost 50 varieties. The sisters also started a local chapter of the Heritage Roses Group.

Alice Flores, another aficionado, joined in local preservation efforts about 12 years ago. "I became fascinated with Mendocino's heritage roses because they're so beautiful and have wonderful fragrance," she says. "These tried-and-true roses are disease- and drought-resistant." Flores started identifying and mapping plants, locating about 50 sites in town where at least one historic rose grows.

Sadly, not everyone appreciates the value of these roses. "People see an old plant in their yard that hasn't been cared for and they rip it out," says Flores. She

has helped persuade some homeowners to rejuvenate their old roses instead.

Thanks to the work of these women, Mendocino's historic roses are sure to live on. The three rosarians propagate and sell the plants through their mail-order nurseries. An endowment established by Hopper and Demits funds the Heritage Rose Garden, which also receives support from the Mendocino County Heritage Roses Group.

ERICA CALKINS nips a cluster of blooms from an old white alba rose at the End of the Oregon Trail National Historic Site.

Tracking pioneer plants in Oregon

APPRECIATING ROSES must be in her genes, figures Erica Calkins of Oregon City, Oregon, since her grandparents were rose lovers too. But it wasn't until six years ago, when Calkins began studying pioneer history and the Oregon Trail, that her fondness for old garden roses really blossomed.

As Calkins delved into the past, she

Demits's favorite old roses: 'Blush Noisette' (noisette; blush lilac-pink), 'Duchesse de Brabant' (tea; light pink and yellow), 'Lamarque' (noisette; white with yellow center), 'Marie Van Houtte' (tea; cream with pink wash), 'Souvenir de Mme. Léonie Viennot' (climbing tea; cream, gold, and pink).

Flores's favorites: 'Mme. Gabriel Luizet' (hybrid perpetual; light pink), 'Paul Ricault' (hybrid China; medium pink), *Rosa nutkana* (species; medium pink), *R. rugosa* (species; mauve pink or white).

saw that roses played an important role in the lives of pioneer women. "I discovered stories about real people and their roses," she says. What impressed her most about the women was their determination to bring a touch of beauty to unfamiliar, often hostile surroundings.

During her research, Calkins discovered a manuscript by Mary Drain Albro that documented firsthand accounts of 23 roses and their journeys West. Like Albro, Calkins scoured the countryside, searching abandoned cemeteries, old homesteads, and roadsides. "I need a license-plate frame that says 'I brake for old roses,'" she jokes. Calkins has located 18 of the 23 roses on Albro's list. These survivors are now growing in the Heritage Gardens, which Calkins designed for the End of the Oregon Trail National Historic Site in Oregon City.

Yet several plants have eluded her. So at bloom time every spring she searches along backroads, hoping she'll glimpse a promising rose bush.

Calkins's favorites: 'Lady Penzance' (*Rosa eglanteria* or sweetbriar hybrid; salmon), 'Mme. Plantier' (alba; white), moss roses (red, pink, or white), 'Mutabilis' (China rose; honey yellow, pink, and chestnut blooms on same plant), *R. centifolia* (cabbage rose; pink shades), 'Rosa Mundi' (gallica; crimson with white and pink stripes).

'LADY PENZANCE' (TOP), 'ROSA MUNDI'

Plant sources

Antique Rose Emporium, 9300 Lueckmeyer Rd., Brenham, TX 77833; (800) 441-0002. Catalog $5.

Heirloom Old Garden Roses, 24062 N.E. Riverside Dr., St. Paul, OR 97137; (503) 538-1576. Catalog $5.

Heritage Roses at Tanglewood Farms, 16831 Mitchell Creek Dr., Fort Bragg, CA 95437; (707) 964-3748. Catalog $1.

High Country Roses, Box 148, Jensen, UT 84035; (435) 789-5512 or easilink.com/~smf. Catalog $2.

Michael's Premier Roses, 9759 Elder Creek Rd., Sacramento, CA 95829; (916) 369-7673 or www. michaelsrose.com. Free catalog.

Petaluma Rose Company, Box 750953, Petaluma, CA 94975; (707) 769-8862. Free catalog.

Rose Acres, 6641 Crystal Blvd., El Dorado, CA 95623; (530) 626-1722. Send a self-addressed, stamped envelope for catalog.

Ros-Equus, 40350 Wilderness Rd., Branscomb, CA 95417. Catalog $1.50.

Rose Ranch, Box 326, La Grange, CA 95329; (209) 852-9220. Catalog $3; free list.

Vintage Gardens, 2833 Old Gravenstein Hwy. S., Sebastopol, CA 95472; (707) 829-2035 or www. vintagegardens.com. Catalog $5.

White Rabbit Roses, Box 191, Elk, CA 95432; www.mcn.org/b/roses. Free catalog. ◆

THE TOMBSTONE LADY AS TOUGH AS WYATT EARP

THE WORLD'S LARGEST ROSE, according to the *Guinness Book of World Records,* is—at age 114—one tough lady. She resides in Tombstone, Arizona. A Lady Banks' rose (*Rosa banksiae banksiae* 'Alba Plena'), she has a branch system that covers 8,000 square feet and a trunk measuring 150 inches in circumference.

The rose came to Tombstone in 1884, sent to a young bride named Mary Gee from her family back in Scotland. Gee gave a rooted cutting to Amelia Adamson, proprietor of Cochise House (now the Rose Tree Museum), who planted it on the patio. By 1937, the rose had grown so large that Robert Ripley noted it in his column, *Ripley's Believe It or Not.*

Today, Burt and Dorothy Devere own the rose and museum. The 9-foot-tall evergreen climber's fragrant white blossoms appear in March and April.

Admission to tour the historic home (at Fourth and Toughnut streets) and see the rose costs $2. For details, call (520) 457-3326.

Along the walkway of this Albuquerque courtyard, drought-tolerant and native plants form a dense tapestry of foliage and flowers. For details, see page 148.

June

garden guide

FLOWER GARDENING

Long live lisianthus

■ Lisianthus (*Eustoma grandiflorum*) appears to have everything going for it. Its striking flowers last well over a week in water-filled vases if their stems are trimmed every few days. So why isn't it more widely grown in home gardens?

This short-lived perennial, grown as an annual, needs warm weather to thrive. And it's slow-growing. But according to Kevin Neely of Riverside Landscaping and Nursery Supplies in Fresno, it performs superbly in inland gardens if given protection from direct afternoon sun and planted in well-drained soil.

Near the coast where summer fogs are frequent, plant seedlings in the warmest spot in your garden—against a wall or along a walk where they'll get reflected heat.

If you're not inclined to baby lisianthus along, you can buy cut flowers. A new series called Mariachi, from Sakata Seed in Morgan Hill, bears large, quadruple flowers, which come in six colors, pictured at left. It's sold at many florist shops (or ask to have it ordered for you).

— *Lauren Bonar Swezey*

pots

Finding a genuine 18th-century English stone trough to use as a planter is about as likely as winning the lottery, which works out fine since it would take lottery winnings to pay for one. Until recently there was only one other option—making your own vessel out of the lightweight concrete mixture called hypertufa. Now there's a third choice. Stonesmith Garden Vessels in Cambria, California, sells hypertufa containers ready to plant. In addition to the ball and cube shapes shown here (that's ornamental oregano in the ball, *Sedum spectabile* 'Carmen' in the cube), they come in bowls, troughs, and other shapes. Stonesmith Garden Vessels are sold in nurseries, but if you can't find a source, call the firm at (805) 927-0827. — *Sharon Cohoon*

NORMAN A. PLATE (2)

CONNIE COLEMAN

A great estate garden in Seattle

■ In 1915, businessman Arthur G. Dunn commissioned Fredrick Law Olmstead's famous landscape design firm to help develop the grounds of his estate at the north end of Seattle. His son, E. B. Dunn, a dedicated gardener, capitalized on the Olmstead plan. The estate garden he and his father created now contains some of the oldest exotic trees and shrubs to be found in the Pacific Northwest.

Thanks to his family, which established the E. B. Dunn Historic Garden Trust in 1993, 7 acres of the estate were spared from development. These grounds are open for tours by appointment. Paths lead past grand old rhododendrons, along perennial borders, and down into woodland plantings.

Tours are conducted on Thursdays, Fridays, and Saturdays; $7, $5 students and ages 65 and over; under 12 not admitted. To make a reservation, call (206) 362-0933.

— *Steven R. Lorton*

ROSES GROW in formal beds against a backdrop of Italian cypresses.

Classic roses for a Fallbrook garden

■ Marilyn Herlihy's rose garden is a classic. Within its formal framework of gravel paths and clipped hedges, symmetrical beds contain old-fashioned roses and billowy lavender. "The rolling hills in the distance and the rock outcroppings spoke Italy to me," says Herlihy. "And a Mediterranean garden honored the architecture of the house."

Reading *The Gardens of Russell Page* gave her the idea, she says—especially Page's note about letting "the genius of the place" be your inspiration.

After much trial and error, she found the right roses for her hot inland loca-

tion. "Teas and hybrid musks are all foolproof," she says. Most rugosas fare well, too. She particularly likes 'Blanc Double de Coubert', 'Hansa', and 'Roseraie de l'Hay'. After that, she says, it gets trickier. There are lots of disease-prone roses among the hybrid perpetuals, for instance, but the category also includes the stalwart matriarch 'Reine des Violettes'.

She combines many of her roses with perennials. Geraniums are one of her favorite rose companions. The scented ones, some of which get to be shrubsize, provide sturdy shoulders for her floppier roses to lean against, she says.

And some of the Martha Washington geraniums pick up the shades of her roses so well they look dyed-to-match.

But nothing looks more Mediterranean than gray foliage, and Herlihy uses lots of it. In addition to lavender, she likes 'Powis Castle' artemisia, Jerusalem sage (*Phlomis*), and lychnis.

Herlihy opens her Fallbrook garden for tours on Tuesdays, Thursdays, and Saturdays through June 13; $13 per person (includes a lecture and the opportunity to buy roses). Reservations required. Call (760) 728-9799 after 6 P.M.

— S. C.

Nearly ever-blooming vine

■ *Thunbergia mysorensis* makes *T. grandiflora,* the better-known *Thunbergia* vine, look like a slacker. Though *T. grandiflora* is certainly no slouch (it cranks out sky blue flowers steadily from fall through spring), it does slow down during summer. Its exotic, yellow-flowered cousin *T. mysorensis,* on the other hand, never seems to take a break. The flower cluster shown at right is on a plant that has been blooming nonstop for nearly three years at San Marcos Growers in Santa Barbara.

Considering the vine's heroic efforts, its demands are few—just average soil, watering, and feeding. It has no significant pest or disease problems, and despite its tropical Indian origins, it will even handle light frost (28° to 25°). It'll grow in *Sunset* climate zones 16 and 21–24.

For best effect, train *T. mysorensis* to an overhead pergola or tall trellis where its long, dangling yellow and reddish-brown flower clusters will hang unimpeded and can best be appreciated.

Your nursery can obtain plants from San Marcos Growers. Kartuz Greenhouses in Vista sells plants on-site and by mail; (760) 941-3613. — *S. C.*

FIERY 2-INCH BLOOMS open gradually along a dangling, 18-inch stem.

Going native in Calabasas

■ "A native-plant garden in the most exacting sense." That's what landscape architect Rick Fisher of Toyon Design in Altadena calls the John and Julianna Gensley Demonstration Garden on the grounds of Soka University in Calabasas. The 125 species grown here aren't just any old natives, but were propagated from seeds, bulbs, and cuttings collected from the campus, making them direct descendants of the area's endemic plants. A native garden doesn't get any purer, says Fisher, who designed the garden.

But authenticity wasn't his only concern. Since the university wanted the project to inspire visitors to adapt a similar aesthetic in their gardens, visual appeal was equally critical. Simply mirroring the plant communities in the surrounding chaparral and woodlands wasn't enough. The natives had to look as at home surrounding a Spanish-style cottage as they do in the Santa Monica Mountains. The garden, in other words, had to look like a real residential garden. And it does, as the photograph at left shows.

The Gensley Demonstration Garden is open 9 to 5 daily. Docent-led tours are conducted at 10 the first Tuesday of the month or by appointment; (818) 878-3703. To reach the university, exit U.S. Highway 101 at Las Virgenes/Malibu Canyon. Go south about 3 miles and turn left (east) on Mulholland Highway. At the first driveway, turn right into the campus and stop at the Information Center. — *S. C.*

MARION BRENNER

A better phlox

■ Summer phlox (*P. paniculata*) can be a heartbreaker: just when this perennial hits peak bloom, mildew moves in and ruins the show. That scenario may be a thing of the past. Dutch flower breeder Bartels Stek obtained a mildew-resistant strain of phlox in what was then the Soviet Union and used it to breed disease resistance into a new group of large-flowered phloxes. These include 'Ice Cap' (white), 'Miss Marple' (white with reddish pink eye), 'Miss Candy' (hot pink), 'Miss Pepper' (pink with red eye), 'Red Eyes' (shown at left), and 'Miss Violet'. Properly pinched, these plants develop 1-inch blooms in 4-inch clusters.

In *Sunset's* test garden last year, they performed beautifully, without a trace of the powdery mildew that showed up on nearby vegetables.

If you can't find plants locally, ask your nursery to order from the wholesaler, Here & Now Garden, in Gale Creek, Oregon.

Set plants out in full sun, water well, and apply a complete fertilizer in about two weeks. Pinch young plants back to the sixth pair of leaves; they'll branch and grow to about 3 feet.

— *Jim McCausland*

Beds full of Alaska's bounty

■ Gardeners who visit Alaska are astounded by the size of the plants and the zeal with which fellow gardeners practice their craft in the far north. Many perennials, shrubs, and trees thrive here despite temperatures that regularly plunge well below freezing.

You'll see many of these at the Mat Valley Agricultural Showcase, a demonstration and experimental garden in the Matanuska Valley about 45 miles northeast of Anchorage. This isn't a huge place (only about half an acre), but every bed is crammed with edible and ornamental plants.

Most of the beds are raised or gently mounded so the soil warms up quickly in spring. Raspberries, red and black currants, and rhubarb grow lush and large here. Perennials tower and sprawl. If your attention is riveted by a white iris, you're likely looking at *I. setosa* 'Alba', an Alaska native.

The garden is in the town of Palmer, next to the visitor center on South Colony Way. It's open daily; admission is free. For more information, call (907) 745-2880. — *S. R. L.*

Fragrance at hand

■ Some plants grow splendidly together. Take this marriage, for instance. Madagascar jasmine (*Stephanotis floribunda*) and 'Sombreuil' antique rose are entwined along an exterior stairwell, offering visitors arm-level flowers and fragrance.

Stephanotis is a vigorous climber near the San Diego coast, but to flower well and look its best, it needs a protected location and regular feedings.

PERFUME APLENTY comes from 'Sombreuil' rose and stephanotis.

The vine's top can take full sun, but its roots prefer shade. In this garden, a nearby queen palm (*Syagrus romanzoffianum*) lightly shades the south facing stairwell and the lower third of the vine (as well as the rose's lower canes) from afternoon sun.

The 'Sombreuil' rose grows in the same bed as the stephanotis. It blooms most heavily in April, while the stephanotis blooms May through September.

Both vines were planted in April three years ago from 5-gallon cans. The stephanotis, purchased as a pole-trained rather than trellis-trained plant, has covered the 20-foot-long wall in that time (it's attached with silicone and ties). The rose is still twining its way there. — *Damon Hedgepeth*

CHARLES MANN

LANDSCAPING WITH WATER

A garden made for meditating

■ When Jackie and Richard Wolber of Lakewood, Colorado, decided to transform a tennis court into a garden, they told landscape architect Martin Mosko, "We want a place for meditation." Mosko created a landscape boldly accented by sculptural stones and softened by a tapestry of flowering plants woven among dwarf aspens, hawthorns, maples, junipers, and spruces.

Using water as a unifying theme, Mosko laced the landscape with a recirculating stream that flows to a sunken garden, where a waterfall and pond contribute to a meditative mood. 'Tiny Rubies' dianthus and rose pink thrift (*Armeria maritima*) brighten sunny parts of the garden. Bursts of color come from irises, daylilies, and yarrow.

Mosko's design won a merit award for Marpa & Associates of Boulder in a competition sponsored by the Associated Landscape Contractors of Colorado. — *J. M.*

BACK TO BASICS

Supporting perennials

■ Many flowering perennials look and grow better if you stake them at planting time. To determine which type of stake is best, take a cue from the plant's growth habit. To support tall, spiky plants such as delphiniums, tie stalks to tall, slender bamboo stakes or use metal Y-shaped stakes. For tall, bushy plants like dahlias and *Salvia azurea grandiflora,* use wire cylinders or tomato cages. For sprawlers such as penstemon, use metal hoops like the one shown. These 12- to 18-inch-diameter hoops sit on three legs and have crossbars in the center to support stems.

NORMAN A. PLATE

Mirror, mirror on the "wall"

■ A folly, according to *Webster's Tenth,* is "a foolish act or idea" or an "extravagant picturesque building erected to suit a fanciful taste." But Sarah Forseter's wood folly in Fort Bragg, California, is neither foolish nor extravagant. It's a practical solution: the fanciful screen masks a view of a motel that borders the property.

Forseter created a 12-foot-tall structure, complete with windows and a gate that appears to lead to another garden. The "walls" are made of lattice backed with wood and black weed cloth (to keep light from shining through). Forseter attached mirrors to the door and windows. The mirrors reflect the main garden across the driveway. A vine of fiveleaf akebia covers the structure's face. — *L. B. S.*

A flowerful courtyard in Albuquerque

■ The first time Dan Caudillo saw his new home in Albuquerque, the yard was knee-high in tumbleweeds that had moved in soon after the house was built. But Caudillo, a landscape designer, saw the potential for a courtyard garden in the long, narrow beds bordering a nearly 100-foot driveway. To enclose the area, he built a stucco wall and installed a gate. A few piñon trees planted by the contractor had taken hold in the gravelly soil, so Caudillo used them to form the evergreen anchors of his garden.

Then he began selecting plant materials suited to the high desert climate (*Sunset* climate zone 10) and the garden's 6,300-foot elevation. Caudillo laced the beds with drought-tolerant and native plants such as perennial blue flax (*Linum perenne*), gaillardia, and Mexican hat (*Ratibida columnifera*). Along the walkway (shown on page 140), he planted sweeps of red valerian (*Centranthus ruber*), *Erysimum* 'Bowles Mauve', pink Mexican evening primrose (*Oenothera berlandieri*), and snow-in-summer (*Cerastium tomentosum*).

The plants form such a dense tapestry of foliage and flowers that there's no room for tumbleweeds anymore.

— *Judith Phillips*

A Mediterranean garden in Las Vegas

■ When Tom and Cindy Kapp were landscaping their Las Vegas home, they wanted a lush Mediterranean look. Two broadleaf evergreens helped them achieve this effect: a multi-trunked Mediterranean fan palm (*Chamaerops humilis*) and a variegated tobira (*Pittosporum tobira*). Both can take splashing from the pool, a fair amount of heat and cold, and partial shade from a nearby tree.

The fan palm was a single tree when it was planted, but over time, it has spread out nearly as much as it's grown upward, sending out new offshoots from the main trunk. This palm will probably stay less than 20 feet tall.

The pittosporum grows slowly and will probably top out at less than 6 feet. —*J. M.*

Pacific Northwest Garden Notebook

BY STEVEN R. LORTON

My garden in Washington's Skagit Valley sits at the base of a hill where a stream trickles by. When I had a pond dug to collect water for—heaven forbid—fire-fighting purposes, the flow seemed to increase. So I started tinkering around with swamp and water plants. I haven't put in any water lilies yet, but I've made some interesting discoveries.

I started off with culinary watercress (*Nasturtium officinale*) because I love its crunchy texture and peppery taste in salads and on sandwiches. I really can't pick this rambunctious grower fast enough. About twice each summer, I go along the stream picking out sprigs to share with my neighbors and pulling out the rest to toss on the compost pile.

My next find was marsh marigold (*Caltha palustris*), a shade lover that produces clumps of waxy green leaves and bursts of rich, sunset yellow flowers with a daisylike form.

The slugs persuaded me to relocate my *Lobelia* 'Queen Victoria', a perennial with deep burgundy leaves and regal spikes of scarlet flowers. I got tired of watching them graze on it like cows on grass, so I planted clumps of the plant in the middle of the stream. To my amazement, the lobelia sprouted from beneath as much as 6 inches of water. My slugs haven't learned to swim yet, so 'Queen Victoria' is flourishing.

On the stream's sunny side, I put *Silphium perfoliatum,* a striking perennial that stretches to about 4½ feet tall, with square stems and big, pointed leaves that stand up, making shallow cups that catch rainwater. In midsummer it bears clusters of yellow flowers, not unlike those of *Ligularia dentata* 'Desdemona'—another plant that's growing well in the soggy soil at stream's edge.

I love cattails, too, despite their reputation for being highly invasive. Randy Raburn of Hughes Water Gardens in Tualatin, Oregon, talked me into planting the dwarf cattail *Typha minima*. Its clumps of tiny spears erupt with velvety brown heads the size of acorns. I grow this plant in a water-filled ceramic pot set atop a flat rock in full sun. Before the seed heads can ripen and spread their reproductive fuzz, I cut the cattails and take them indoors.

If you'd like to experiment with water plants, visit Hughes Water Gardens; this is a great place to pick up plants and ideas. It's at 25289 S.W. Stafford Rd.; hours are 9 to 5 Mondays through Saturdays, 10 to 4 Sundays. For more information or to request a free catalog, call (503) 638-1709.

that's a good question ...

Q: How do you fertilize plants growing in water?

A: I use Aquatic-Tabs, which contain controlled-release fertilizer (10-15-10). I push one or two tablets down into the mud close to the root mass of the plants. This fertilizer doesn't seem to increase the algae in my pond.

MARINA THOMPSON

Northern California Garden Notebook

BY LAUREN BONAR SWEZEY

$\mathcal{M}$y garden is at one of those frustrating stages right now where nothing seems quite right. I suppose I didn't help its appearance earlier in the year when I yanked out two tired buddleias, which left a gaping hole behind the flax. And what am I supposed to do when my dog, Jet, keeps piddling on my (formerly) beautiful leather leaf sedge?

Whenever I'm feeling at a loss about what to plant next, I head to the nearest nursery for inspiration. Last weekend, I discovered the perfect solution for the spot where my buddleias once grew—*Lavatera maritima*. Its maple-like gray-green foliage will look outstanding behind the flax's strappy, bronze leaves. I haven't figured out what to do about the dog problem yet. I wonder if I could train Jet to use a litter box?

ARTISTS AND THEIR GARDENS IN MENDOCINO

If it's inspiration you're looking for, don't miss the sixth annual Mendocino Coast Garden Tour, from 10 to 5 on June 20. This year's circuit includes the outstanding gardens of 10 widely acclaimed artists.

Landscape artist E. John Robinson's Monet-inspired cottage garden features a stone bridge, beautiful plantings of perennials, and dozens of roses covering walls and climbing handmade trellises. And cement sculptress Sue Brown's exuberant country garden overflows with unusual plants.

The garden tour costs $25, $35 with lunch. A walking tour of Mendocino Village Gardens on June 21 costs an additional $10. For information and reservations, call (800) 653-3328. And don't forget to make reservations at Little River Inn (888/466-5683), the Lodge at Noyo River (800/628-1126), or one of the many great B & Bs in the area.

SYMPOSIUM IN SAN FRANCISCO

If the Italianate gardens featured in "Tuscany Along the Pacific" (page 96) piqued your interest, you can learn more about this landscaping style at a symposium titled "Gardening Under Mediterranean Skies." The event, cosponsored by *Pacific Horticulture* magazine and Strybing Arboretum Botanical Gardens, takes place September 25 and 26 in the San Francisco County Fair Building in Golden Gate Park. Speakers include experts from southern Europe and California. Advance registration (before September 1) is $175 for members and $200 for nonmembers. For details, call (415) 661-1316, ext. 354.

(Editor's note: dates and times in this article were valid for 1998; events and schedules will vary from year to year.

that's a good question ...

$\mathcal{Q}$: A recent issue of *Sunset* made mention of "summer oil." Is this the same as horticultural oil?

— *Brian Leonard, Pleasanton*

$\mathcal{A}$. Summer oil is a type of horticultural oil. Before the 1970s most horticultural oils were heavy or "dormant" oils that could be used only during the dormant season or they would clog leaf pores and burn leaves. Now most oils sold in nurseries are highly refined, making them lighter, and can be used year-round. These lighter oils are often referred to as summer oils, but most products still sold as dormant oils are also light. But always check the label first to see what you're getting.

Southern California Garden Notebook

BY SHARON COHOON

dump a few preconceptions, make room for some radical notions, and you'll have a more exciting garden. That's what Jim Duggan learned from Robert Irwin. Duggan is the owner of Encinitas Gardens nursery. He is also the chief horticulturist for the Central Garden at the Getty Center near Westwood. Irwin, as anyone who picked up a newspaper last year knows, is the artist behind the controversial Central Garden.

Duggan took me on a tour recently and pointed out instances where Irwin broke the rules beautifully. Take a grouping of plants on the lower slope of the canyon. Cannas, New Zealand flaxes, yuccas, and copros-

mas, all sharing the same yellow-green variegation, sit side by side—a flagrant violation of the general assumption that variegated plants should be reserved for accents. But being a nongardener, Irwin didn't have this preconception, says Duggan. As an artist, Irwin just knew he wanted a wash of lime green here, and he assembled plants that would collectively read that way. If you love variegated plants, as Duggan clearly does, this is liberating. It means you don't have to thin out your collection. You just need to plant compatible patterns together.

Another overturned assumption: perennial partnerships have to be permanent. Irwin loved the patterns of zonal geranium leaves and put the geraniums with dozens of other plants when trying out plant combinations. "Budworms will be a problem," Duggan warned. "Zonals can get pretty ratty-looking." "Can't we just replace them when they do?" Irwin countered innocently. Another "aha" moment, says Duggan. Why *not* enjoy something inexpensive like zonal geraniums when they look good and yank them when they falter? Especially after you've seen gold-leafed zonals and purple heliotrope together.

There are dozens more fresh ideas in the Central Garden you can apply to your own. Be sure to bring a camera and notebook with you when you visit, to record it all.

that's a good question ...

Q. "How do I treat powdery mildew on squash, melons, and cucumbers?"

A. Try to catch the problem early, says Gary Matsuoka at Laguna Hills Nursery. To keep mildew spores from spreading, pick off leaves that are covered with the fuzzy white mold as soon as you see them. (Bag the leaves and discard; don't compost.) Washing off foliage frequently also helps. Spray only early in the day, though; moisture on foliage in the evening compounds the problem. If additional control is needed, apply a baking soda/horticultural oil spray. Matsuoka uses 1 tablespoon baking soda and 5 tablespoons SunSpray Ultrafine Oil to 1 gallon of water. Apply to both upper and lower leaves, treating up to once a week as long as the problem persists.

MARINA THOMPSON

Westerner's Garden Notebook

BY JIM McCAUSLAND

*N*orth American natives one and all, the horsemints (*Monarda* species) rank high on my list of multipurpose perennials. Their roundish, pink to purple flower clusters are spaced along their stalks like so many pompoms. The tubular flowers are full of nourishment for bees, butterflies, and hummingbirds. And pioneers brewed Oswego tea from the minty leaves of bee balm, *M. didyma*.

Many of the best bee balms are hybrids, but until now, they've had a disfiguring flaw: as they come into their flowering glory, powdery mildew knocks them down. But there's good news. Canadian researchers have come up with a new mildew-resistant form of *Monarda* called 'Petite Delight'. It grows just over a foot tall and almost 2 feet wide, and is covered with lavender-rose flowers in summer. Hummingbirds love the blossoms, which rise over a mound of dark green leaves. The perfectly hardy plant perennializes well but isn't invasive.

Look for 'Petite Delight' in retail nurseries, or order by mail from Wayside Gardens (800/845-1124). Grow it in rich, well-drained soil in full sun and deadhead flowers as they fade. In fall, cut it back almost to the ground. Feed lightly in spring.

A DEADLY RUB FOR INVASIVE GRASSES

Every gardener has a list of most-hated weeds, and mine starts with the grasses. They send runners through my perennial bed, where they're nearly impossible to extract. This year, I've tried a different approach to grass control that shows great promise. I slip on a rubber glove, then a cotton glove over that. I dip the fingertips of the cotton glove in a bowl of glyphosate (Roundup or Kleenup, for example) and gently rub the herbicide onto the leaves of the grasses. Applied manually like this, the chemical kills only the grasses and doesn't touch the surrounding perennials as a spray would.

I picked up this tip from a wonderful new book, *The Well-Tended Perennial Garden*, by Tracy DiSabato-Aust (Timber Press, Portland, 1998; $29.95; 800/327-5680). It's a great read and an indispensable guide to perennial plant care, from pruning to disease control.

that's a good question ...

Q: My tomato sets fruit well through late spring, but in early summer, the blossoms just fall off and no new fruit appears. What's going on?

A: When daytime temperatures top 90° and nights remain above 75°, it's just too hot for tomatoes to set fruit. If you keep the plants well watered and fed, they'll start to set fruit again once the weather cools down in fall.

Q: What's the difference between Scotch and Irish moss?

A: Scotch moss is golden green, while Irish moss is more grass green. Both are actually perennials, not mosses, and the confusion doesn't end there: Irish moss refers to either *Arenaria verna* or *Sagina subulata*, while Scotch moss is either *A. v.* 'Aurea' or *S. s.* 'Aurea'. Only *Sagina* will grow in the coldest mountain areas (*Sunset* climate zone 1) or the intermediate or high deserts (zones 10–11). *Arenaria* can be grown only in zones 2–3.

Pacific Northwest Checklist

PLANTING

☑ **ANNUALS.** Zones 1–7: All annuals, from ageratum to zinnias, can go into the garden now.

☑ **DAHLIAS.** Zones 1–7: Get tubers into the ground pronto for bloom from summer to early autumn.

☑ **FUCHSIAS.** Zones 1–7: Set out newly bought fuchsias in pots or hanging baskets; repot overwintered plants in rich, quick-draining soil. Pinch back growth to encourage bushier plants.

☑ **PERENNIALS.** Zones 1–7: Blooming plants are available in 1-gallon cans. Soak overnight before planting to reduce transplant shock. Don't fertilize newly set out plants until flowers fade.

☑ **VEGETABLES.** Zones 1–7: Sow bush beans, rutabagas, and turnips. Set out seedlings of basil, cucumber, eggplant, peppers, and squash.

MAINTENANCE

☑ **CARE FOR ROSES.** To ensure new growth, cut just above a leaflet with five, not three, leaves. New growth will emerge just below the cut.

☑ **DIVIDE PERENNIALS.** Dig and divide plants right after blooms fade, to cause as little disruption as possible in their flowering cycle. Circle each overgrown plant, slicing down with a sharp spade or shovel. Pop the plant out of the ground and cut it into chunks; a dinner plate–size clump will make four

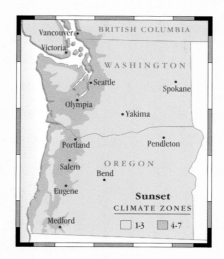

new plants. Remove hard, old roots and any pieces of the crown that have died out. Replant the divisions immediately in rich soil amended with organic matter; water thoroughly. Do not fertilize them until early next spring.

☑ **THIN FRUITS.** Once trees have dropped their immature fruit naturally, thin clusters so the remaining fruit develops to full size. On trees with heavy crops, thin doubles and triples to one or two, respectively, then thin remaining fruit to 6-inch intervals along the branch. You'll get fewer, but larger, fruits, and you'll ease the strain on tree limbs.

☑ **TRIM HEDGES.** Twice-a-year hedge trimmers should get busy early this month, then again in late summer or early fall. Once-a-year trimmers can do the work in early to mid-July. Trim

so that the hedge is slightly wider at the base than at the top, allowing sunlight and rain to reach the entire foliage surface.

PEST AND WEED CONTROL

☑ **BEFRIEND GARTER SNAKES.** These docile, nonvenomous snakes serve as pest police in the vegetable patch. On the west side of the Cascades, encourage them by putting a pile of rocks or a 4- by 8-foot piece of plywood at the sunny end of the garden. From this hideout, they'll slither out to gobble up bothersome bugs and slugs. (Warning: If you try this on the east side of the Cascades, you'll attract rattlesnakes as well.)

☑ **FIGHT SLUGS.** Gardeners, choose your weapons: beer traps, handpicking, poison bait.

☑ **WEED.** Hoe or pull weeds young, before they can set seed.

Northern California Checklist

PLANTING

☑ **PLANT SUMMER BLOOMERS.** For annuals try garden verbena, gentian sage, globe amaranth, Madagascar periwinkle (vinca), portulaca, scarlet sage, sunflower, 'Victoria' mealy-cup sage, and zinnias. For perennials look for coreopsis, gaillardia, 'Homestead Purple' verbena, penstemon, rudbeckia, Russian sage, salvia, statice, and summer phlox. Good foliage plants for fillers are low-growing artemisia, dusty miller, and golden or purple sage.

☑ **PLANT VEGETABLES.** June is prime planting time for warm-season vegetables. Start beans, carrots, and corn from seed. You can also plant cucumber, pumpkins, and squash from seed, but be sure to get them in the ground as soon as possible. Two new Northern California mail-order seed companies to try are **Natural Gardening Company** in San Anselmo (707/766-9303), which sells 250 kinds of untreated seeds, and **Seed Dreams** in Santa Cruz (Box 476, Santa Cruz, CA 95061; 408/458-9252), which sells 100 varieties of organically grown rare and endangered heirloom vegetable and grain seeds. Also look for seeds from **Renee's Garden**—a new company in Felton, California, that supplies gourmet vegetable, herb, and cottage garden flower seeds to local nurseries; call (888) 880-7228 for a nursery near you.

Sunset
CLIMATE ZONES

☐ Mountain (1-2)
☐ Valley (7-9)
☐ Inland (14)
☐ Coastal (15-17)

DEBRA LAMBERT

☑ **SOW HERBS.** To make sure you have plenty of basil and cilantro for cooking through the summer and fall, plant successive crops of seeds every six to eight weeks. For basil try 'Anise', purple 'Red Rubin', Thai lemon, or one of the Italian types, such as 'Genova Profumatissima'. Grow a slow-bolting variety of cilantro. All are available from Shepherd's Garden Seeds; (860) 482-3638.

MAINTENANCE

☑ **FEED AND GROOM ROSES.** To encourage growth and new flowers on repeat bloomers, remove faded flowers and feed plants with a complete fertilizer and, if necessary, iron chelate. Mulch to conserve soil moisture. On hybrid teas and grandifloras, snip off faded blooms ¼ inch above the first (top) leaf with five leaflets.

PEST CONTROL

☑ **CHECK ROSES FOR RUST.** Cool, moist springs promote rust—a fungus that causes rust-colored pustules on the undersides of leaves. Handpick and dispose of diseased leaves. Spray with a sulfur-based fungicide. Water early in the morning and avoid wetting foliage.

☑ **CONTROL BUDWORMS.** If your geraniums, nicotiana, penstemons, and petunias appear healthy but have no flowers, budworms are probably eating the flower buds before they open (look for holes in the buds). Spray every 7 to 10 days with *Bacillus thuringiensis* (BT).

☑ **CONTROL LAWN MOTHS.** Sod webworm moths appear in late spring or early summer to lay eggs in lawns. The adults fly at night just above the grass, dropping their eggs, and then hide during the day. Damage is caused by the worms, which hatch from the eggs and feed on grass blades. Saucer-size brown patches appear on the lawn surface. You may also find areas of lawn ripped up by raccoons scavenging for the worms. Control the worms with microscopic environmentally safe nematodes (available at nurseries). Do not spray lawns with pesticides afterward or they will kill the nematodes. Getting rid of the worms should also control raccoons.

Southern California Checklist

PLANTING

☑ **PLANT SUBTROPICALS.** They're widely available in nurseries now and grow quickly in warm weather. Many will provide garden color well into winter. Choices include banana, bird of paradise, cestrum, ginger, hibiscus, palms, philodendron, and tree ferns. And don't forget flowering vines. Look for bougainvillea, bower vine (*Pandorea jasminoides*), mandevilla, stephanotis, thunbergia, and trumpet vine (*Distictis*).

☑ **PLANT IN SHADY SPOTS.** The soil in northern and eastern exposures near walls is finally warming up. It's a good time to add ornamentals to these cool spots. Good choices include abutilon, *Brunfelsia pauciflora* 'Floribunda' (yesterday-today-and-tomorrow), clivia, coral bells, hydrangea, Japanese anemone, and shrubby fuchsias.

☑ **PLANT SUMMER VEGETABLES.** Set out transplants of cucumbers, eggplant, melons, peppers, and tomatoes. Sow seeds of beans, corn, cucumbers, New Zealand spinach, okra, pumpkins, and summer and winter squash. Coastal gardeners can squeeze in another harvest of leaf lettuce. High-desert gardeners (zone 11) can plant short-season varieties of beans, corn, cucumbers, melons, pumpkins, squash, and tomatoes.

☑ **PLANT SUMMER ANNUALS.** Fill empty spots in the garden with heat lovers like ageratum, portulaca, verbena, vinca, and zinnias.

Sunset
CLIMATE ZONES
1-3 7-9 11 13 14-24

DEBRA LAMBERT

MAINTENANCE

☑ **FEED ACTIVELY GROWING PLANTS.** Roses, lawns, annual flowers and vegetables, container plants, and just about anything actively growing in the garden will benefit from fertilizing now. Don't feed natives or drought-tolerant Mediterraneans, though.

☑ **TREAT IRON DEFICIENCIES.** If gardenias, citrus, and other susceptible plants exhibit yellowish leaves with green veins, they may not be getting enough iron. To correct, apply iron chelate as a soil drench or foliar spray, following package directions.

☑ **DIVIDE IRISES.** Crowded or poorly performing clumps of bearded irises can be divided now. Discard woody centers, rotted portions, and rhizomes without leaves and divide remainder. Each division should have one fan of leaves, a young rhizome,

and developed roots. Shorten leaves with scissors to compensate for root loss before replanting. If you garden in the high or low desert (zones 11 and 13, respectively), wait until October to divide.

☑ **RESET LAWN MOWER HEIGHTS.** Let tall fescues grow taller to shade roots and conserve soil moisture. Set blades to cut at 2 to 3 inches. Bermuda, on the other hand, should be cut shorter. Set blades to trim at 1 inch. Zoysia, St. Augustine, and kikuyu grass can be cut even shorter.

PEST CONTROL

☑ **COMBAT ROSE PESTS.** Along the coast, "June gloom" creates ideal conditions for powdery mildew. Combat by hosing off foliage frequently in the early morning to wash off spores. Or spray with 1 tablespoon *each* baking soda and fine-grade horticultural oil diluted in a gallon of water. Avoid spraying when temperatures exceed 85°. Inland, start watching for spider mites.

☑ **WASH AWAY PESTS.** Aphids, mites, thrips, whiteflies, and other small insect pests can be kept to manageable levels with water. Use a strong jet to dislodge from plant leaves. Avoid pesticides; they kill beneficial insects, too.

Mountain Checklist

PLANTING

☑ **ANNUALS.** Sow seeds of cosmos, marigold, portulaca, sunflower, and zinnia. Or set out seedlings of any of the above, plus African daisies, bachelor's button, calendula, clarkia, forget-me-nots, globe amaranth, lobelia, pansies, snapdragons, spider flowers, sweet alyssum, sweet William, and violas. After last frost, set out coleus, geraniums, impatiens, Madagascar periwinkle, marigolds, nasturtiums, and petunias.

☑ **BULBS.** For late summer color, plant canna, dahlias, gladiolus, montbretia, tigridia, and tuberous begonias. Stake tall varieties of dahlias and glads at planting time.

☑ **LANDSCAPE PLANTS.** Plant trees, shrubs, ground covers, and vines now. After planting, check soil moisture frequently; water as needed.

☑ **PERENNIALS.** Sow seeds of aster, basket-of-gold, campanula, columbine, delphinium, erigeron, gaillardia, gilia, heuchera, penstemon, perennial sweet pea, potentilla, and purple coneflower. Or set out seedlings of all of the above, plus coreopsis and salvia. For foliage fillers, plug in artemisia, dusty miller, and golden or purple sage.

☑ **STRAWBERRIES.** Plant strawberries from nursery sixpacks or pots. Choose a sunny place and provide a coarse soil mix amended with lots of organic matter.

Sunset
CLIMATE ZONES

☐ 1-3   ☐ 10-11

DEBRA LAMBERT

☑ **VEGETABLES.** Sow seeds of cucumber and squash, plus successive crops of beets, bush beans, carrots, chard, lettuce, onions, parsnips, peas, radishes, spinach, Swiss chard, and turnips. If the season is long and warm enough in your area, sow corn, melons, and pumpkins, and set out nursery seedlings of eggplant, peppers, and tomatoes.

MAINTENANCE

☑ **CARE FOR ROSES.** Cut off faded flowers, fertilize, then build a basin around each plant to concentrate water around the root zone.

☑ **FERTILIZE.** Feed lawns now with nitrogen fertilizer; repeat in four to six weeks. If you haven't already done so, apply fertilizer to flower beds and vegetable gardens.

☑ **PRUNE SPRING-FLOWERING SHRUBS.** After forsythia, flowering quince, lilac, spiraea, *Rosa hugonis,* and weigela have bloomed, remove dead, injured, diseased, crossing, and closely parallel branches. Remove stems at base; cut out about a third of the old growth.

☑ **THIN FRUITS.** For larger fruit, thin apples, apricots, peaches, pears, and plums. Space apricots, peaches, and most plums 4 to 5 inches apart, apples and pears 6 to 8 inches apart.

☑ **TREAT CHLOROSIS.** When leaves turn yellow while veins remain green, they're showing the telltale sign of chlorosis, a condition caused by a lack of iron. Correct it by applying an iron chelate compound to the soil over the root zone.

☑ **WATER.** Beyond periodic deep watering for permanent plants, focus your watering efforts on seedbeds, new plantings, containerized plants, and anything sheltered from the rain.

PEST AND WEED CONTROL

☑ **PROTECT FRUIT CROPS.** Cover strawberries and ripening cherries with bird netting or row covers until fruit is ready to pick.

☑ **WEED.** Remove weeds now, while they're small and haven't set seeds.

Southwest Checklist

PLANTING

☑ **PALMS.** Plant or transplant them into a hole that's the same depth as the rootball and twice as wide. Tie the fronds up over the center "bud" or heart to protect it. After new growth begins, cut the twine.

☑ **SUMMER COLOR.** Zones 10–12: Plant cockscomb, globe amaranth, Madagascar periwinkle, portulaca, purslane, salvia, and zinnia early in the month in a place that gets only filtered sun in the hottest part of the day.

☑ **SUMMER CROPS.** Zones 12–13: You can still plant black-eyed peas, corn, melons, okra, peanuts, sweet potatoes, and yard-long beans. Zones 10–11: Plant cucumbers, melons, and summer squash by midmonth, and corn early in the month.

☑ **FALL CROPS.** Zones 1–2, 10: Sow brussels sprouts, cabbages, and carrots anytime this month. Wait until midmonth to sow broccoli and cauliflower. Zones 12–13: Sow tomato seeds indoors for transplanting into the garden in late July. Some good varieties include 'Champion', 'Early Girl', 'Heatwave', 'Solar Set', and 'Sunmaster'.

MAINTENANCE

☑ **CARE FOR ROSES.** Cut off faded flowers, then build a basin around each plant to concentrate water around the root zone. Mulch each plant well. Finally, wet the soil, fertilize, and immediately water again.

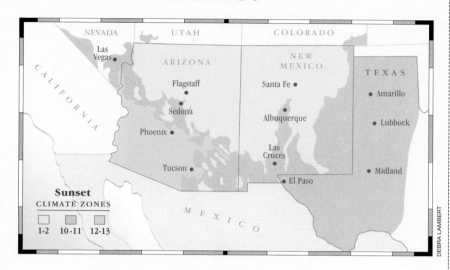

☑ **MOW.** Cut Bermuda, St. Augustine, and zoysia grass 1 to 1½ inches high. Keep hybrid Bermuda at about 1 inch.

☑ **MULCH TREES AND SHRUBS.** Zones 10–13: Spread a 2- to 4-inch layer of organic or gravel mulch over the root zones of trees, shrubs, vines, flowers, and vegetables.

☑ **TREAT CHLOROSIS.** When leaves turn yellow while veins remain green, they're showing a sign of iron deficiency (chlorosis). Apply iron chelate.

☑ **WATER.** Deep-water by flooding or drip irrigation; if you use a drip system, flood-irrigate monthly to wash salts down out of the root zone.

PEST CONTROL

☑ **BEET LEAFHOPPERS.** The greenish yellow, 1-inch-long insects spread curly top virus to cucumber, melon, and tomato plants. Protect crops by covering them with shadecloth. Remove infested plants.

☑ **SPIDER MITES.** If you see stippled leaves and fine webs, blast mites off with a strong jet from the hose, or treat with a miticide.

☑ **SQUASH VINE BORERS.** Look for tiny eggs on squash vines. Rub them off before borers hatch out, drill into the vine, and weaken the plant.

☑ **PROTECT GRAPES.** Cover ripening grapes with bird netting.

ABOVE: A peacock poses atop a garden wall at Villa Narcissa.

RIGHT: The pendant flowers of *Phygelius* 'Tommy Knockers' nod above an ornate clay urn in Thomas Hobbs's garden. Sedums and sempervivums are tucked in small terra-cotta pots.

■ Elin Vanderlip and Thomas Hobbs live at very different latitudes on the Pacific Coast, yet their gardens are related: both are strongly influenced by the horticultural style of Tuscany. • Villa Narcissa, Vanderlip's Italianate house, looks as if it has been plucked from the hills of northern Italy and transplanted onto the Palos Verdes Peninsula south of Los Angeles. That wasn't always the case with her garden. "Initially, it was a little bit of this and a little bit of that, because I wanted everything," she explains. But when she spent a year in Italy, visiting every great garden, her taste changed. Vanderlip learned to love the pared-down simplicity of the gardens she saw, especially those of Tuscany. Geometry and foliage are the essence of great Italian gardens, she says. "Just a few flawless evergreens: olive trees, cypress, agaves—green, gray, blue. And the very selective use of hot colors." By the time she returned to California, Vanderlip was a convert. Now her garden is as Mediterranean as its climate (*Sunset* zone 24). • The house and garden of Thomas Hobbs and Brent Beattie look out over Vancouver, British Columbia, and the mountains beyond. Though the view is pure Pacific Northwest, the stucco-clad house echoes the Old World and the garden clings Tuscan-style to a hill. The home's owners stripped away its English border garden and set about creating one that was more like the gardens they'd seen on travels for their terra-cotta-pot import business. Because of the relatively mild winters in Vancouver (zone 4), they were able to use some classic plants, including edible fig and windmill palm, and they supplemented these with appropriate but frost-tolerant substitutes: yucca for agave, akebia for jasmine, and climbing rose for bougainvillea. The resulting garden is "more of a hybrid Pacific Northwest–Mediterranean," says Hobbs, but "my Italian friend says it looks just like Tuscany."

Italian landscapes and Mediterranean plant inspire gardeners in Southern California and Vancouver, B.C.

BY SHARON COHOON AND STEVEN R. LORTON

Tuscany along the

Pacific

AROUND A POOLSIDE TERRACE at Villa Narcissa, vines, potted plants, and hanging baskets provide splashes of color and soften the hardscape. A creeping fig skims across a wall and gate (top left), while wisteria twines over an arch. Potted plants include variegated lemon (left), rose, and begonia (center). Baskets of *Kalanchoe pumila* hang from the eaves.

TUSCANY IN L.A., BY WAY OF NORWAY

The red ocher walls and mustard yellow trim of Elin Vanderlip's Villa Narcissa seem as Italian as chianti and spaghetti. Actually, the colors were inspired by the folk art of Vanderlip's native Norway. Though the blue-green of the garden gates echoes the Mediterranean Sea, the gates themselves are Norwegian. But when it comes to the garden, there is no ambiguity: the style is pure Tuscany.

The plants are the same ones you'd find in the great gardens of Italy, and

the disciplined way they are marshaled into line is classically Italian too. For instance, one area of Vanderlip's garden has been pared down to a neat rectangle of clipped boxwood framing blue ice plant (*Malephora*) backed by acanthus. "Nothing but foliage," she says. "Green, blue, darker green. That's it."

In another case, Vanderlip edged a wide brick terrace facing the Pacific with olive trees and matching rows of potted hydrangeas. The look is lean,

but it makes the terrace a wonderful space to spend time.

Maybe it takes someone like Vanderlip, who grew up around icy fjords, to recognize the opportunities of gardening in the West's mildest climate and make the most of its long season of sun.

Each year during April, Villa Narcissa is open for tours. Proceeds from the tours benefit Friends of French Art, a foundation that funds art restoration projects. For more information, call (310) 377-4444.

mediterranean style

- **MORE HARDSCAPE THAN LAWNS.** Gardeners use labor- and water-intensive lawns sparingly, preferring to cover flat, open areas with flagstone pavers set in sand, brick, or decomposed granite to create outdoor living areas—courtyards, patios, and terraces.
- **STRONG HORIZONTAL AND VERTICAL LINES.** Terraces and retaining walls perform necessary functions on rocky hillsides by keeping water and topsoil—both precious commodities—from washing away. But the strong lines these features create, balanced by intersecting pathways, are also important design elements. Clipped hedges and the exclamation points formed by cypress trees repeat this geometry.
- **POTS.** Exquisite ceramic pottery has been a fixture in Italy since the Etruscan era more than 2,400 years ago. Modern Italian gardeners always seem to find the perfect spot for a pot bursting with pelargoniums or the swordlike leaves of dracaena. Plants in pots have the added benefit of softening expanses of hardscape without greatly taxing the water supply.
- **NATIVE PLANTS.** European gardeners often use the word native to describe any plant that comes from a region with a similar climate. This includes plants from coastal California, Chile, South Africa, and Australia. Once established, these plants can survive with minimum supplemental irrigation.
- **FOLIAGE INTEREST.** Most plants are evergreen: Since gardeners see the foliage daily, not just for a season, they pick plants that look good year-round. Fortunately, the same natural traits that help these plants tolerate drought (fuzzy or waxy leaf surfaces, for example) also make their foliage appealing to the eye.
- **LIMITED BUT BOLD USE OF COLOR.** Color is used primarily as an accent, but when it is used, the effect is rarely timid. Bougainvillea, hibiscus, and jacaranda are vivid examples.
- **SHELTER FROM THE SUN.** In southern Europe, the light is beautiful but intense. People escape the sun under vine-covered pergolas or other shady shelters. Plants that like full sun in colder areas (roses, for example) often prefer dappled shade in Mediterranean climates.

BOUGAINVILLEA (right) is a flamboyant counterpoint to a wrought-iron gate. An entry walk made of recycled roof tiles leads to a formal garden with clipped boxwood hedges in geometric shapes and pots of white roses trained as standards. A terra-cotta goddess imported from Italy serves as the focal point of the garden.

Thomas Hobbs and Brent Beattie's house in Vancouver is 1930s mission revival style and looks, as Hobbs puts it, "like Norma Desmond's place in *Sunset Boulevard*."

The house is framed by tall, narrow spires of arborvitae (*Thuja occidentalis*) and flamboyant fans of hardy windmill palm (*Trachycarpus fortunei*). On the south side of the house, a path curves through a collection of old, tree-size rhododendrons (remnants of the original garden). Resembling Tuscan pittosporum, these rhodies were pruned to expose their lower trunks, creating a canopy for shade-loving plants, including evergreen gingers and hellebores.

At the rear of the house, a stone terrace with a fountain is where most of the outdoor entertaining is done. The terrace is surrounded by a lush tangle of perennials, shrubs, and vines, with annuals tucked in for summer color. On the terrace, big baroque pots contain a huge assortment of echeverias—succulents prized for their bluish and gray foliage (these plants spend the coldest months, November to April, in the greenhouse).

Primed by generous doses of fertilizer, pampered by the pinching off of faded blooms and foliage, and primped by having its errant shoots and tendrils redirected or snipped off, this garden could confidently say, on any given day, "I'm ready for my close-up, Mr. DeMille." ◆

LEFT: Sunlight streams into the rear garden, where windmill palms brush against stucco walls. A small pool is filled with yellow flag (*Iris pseudacorus*) and assorted water lilies. In a stone urn, succulent rosettes of echeveria encircle dwarf New Zealand flax (*Phormium tenax* 'Jack Spratt').

RIGHT: In the front garden, flowers and foliage create a rich procession of blue, silver, and green. Along the right edge of the entry walk, an ornamental ball nestles in a clump of Johnny-jump-ups backed by the silver lace of *Artemisia* 'Valerie Finnis' and the fernlike foliage of *Melianthus major*. Woolly thyme fills the gaps between the paving stones.

classic plants

- **ACACIA.** The wind- and salt-tolerant golden mimosa (*A. baileyana*) that graces the French Riviera is a typical Mediterranean shade tree. Its airy canopy buffers intense light but doesn't block it out—just what the region's sun-loving plants like. Eucalyptus works in a similar way.
- **ACANTHUS.** The oak leaf–like foliage of *A. mollis,* which was once used as a model for the leaves that decorate the capitals of Corinthian columns, adds sculptural interest to modern landscapes. *A. mollis* grows in zones 4–24. Artichokes, cardoon, and *Melianthus major* provide similarly bold foliage in gray-green shades.
- **AGAVE AMERICANA.** Century plant grows in zones 10 and 12–24. In colder areas, plant yucca instead: *Y. filamentosa* and *Y. baccata* grow in all zones.
- **BOUGAINVILLEA AND PASSION VINE.** These superbly showy climbers can be grown in the ground in frost-free areas; some kinds of passion vine (*Passiflora*) are hardy enough to take mild freezes of short duration. In colder climates, grow them in containers and move plants to sheltered areas during winter, or use hardier climbers like roses.
- **ITALIAN CYPRESS.** Tall, narrow columns of *Cupressus sempervirens* 'Fastigiata' counterbalance the strong horizontal lines in Italian landscaping, and they provide shelter from the mistral and sirocco, seasonal winds that plague the region. This cypress grows in zones 4–24.
- **MYRTLE.** Precisely clipped hedges are another hallmark of the classic villa garden, where boxleaf and dwarf myrtle (*Myrtus communis* 'Buxifolia' and 'Compacta'; zones 8–24) are frequently used. In colder climates, substitute English or Korean boxwood or other small-leafed shrubs.
- **OLIVE TREES.** Gnarled trunks of ancient olive trees add poetry to the austere formality of Italian gardens, and their soft, gray-green foliage is an asset too. *Olea europaea* grows in zones 8–9 and 11–24.
- **PALMS.** The magnificent Canary Island date palms we associate with Mediterranean landscaping are not tropical: *Phoenix canariensis,* which grows best in zones 9 and 12–24, is actually hardy to 20°. The smaller Mediterranean fan palm (*Chamaerops humilis*) can be grown in zones 4–24 and will even tolerate snow.
- **ROSEMARY, LAVENDER, AND THYME.** These three herbs provide the aromatic essence of the Mediterranean. Their hardiness varies, but all require good drainage.

CONNIE COLEMAN (2)

Two Western **growers** share **secrets** for raising and using these fragrant **plants**

BY LAUREN BONAR SWEZEY
PHOTOGRAPHS BY CONNIE COLEMAN

Lovely Lavender

On a warm summer morning outside Victoria, British Columbia, Lynda Dowling strolls between rows of lavender at her farm, Happy Valley Herbs. A wonderfully sweet scent fills the air, and bees buzz from flower to flower. It's harvesttime—a moment Dowling has anticipated for months. "Harvest day is a day out of time," she says. "You stand in the middle of a purple field, inhale the intoxicating fragrance, and listen to the bees sing. No faxes or phones nearby." • For Dowling, lavender has become a way of life. She breathes it, eats it, and bathes in it. She's not alone in her passion—in Oregon, Margaret Sansone and her guests gather bunches of lavender from her fields to weave into "wands" (see page 167). • Both of these aficionados have learned a lot about this beautiful herb that carpets whole hillsides in southern France. On the following pages, they share some of their tips, such as which varieties are the most heavily scented, and ways to use the fragrant flowers in cooking and crafts. • It's not too late to plant your own lavender. (The plants listed on pages 166 and 167 grow well in *Sunset* climate zones 4 to 24.) One whiff of your own homegrown flowers and you'll understand why Dowling and Sansone look forward to harvesttime with such gusto.

Shades of lavender—from deep purple to violet—fill Lynda Dowling's fields (left) in early summer. Dowling grows as many as 20 varieties. They're harvested into bunches (above) to use in crafts and cooking.

Lynda Dowling's Lavender Lemonade

PREP AND COOK TIME: **45 minutes**

NOTES: 'Hidcote' lavender turns lemonade rosy pink. Other varieties turn it a paler color. Avoid piney-smelling lavenders, such as spike.

MAKES: 6 cups; about 6 servings

- 1 cup **sugar**
- ¼ cup (a generous handful) **fresh** or 1 tablespoon dried **lavender blooms** stripped from stems
- 1 cup **freshly squeezed lemon juice**, strained
- **Ice cubes**
- **Lavender sprigs** for garnish

1. Combine sugar with 2½ cups water in a medium pan. Bring to a boil over medium heat, stirring to dissolve the sugar.

2. Add the lavender blooms to the sugar water, cover, and remove from heat. Let stand at least 20 minutes (and up to several hours).

3. Strain mixture and discard lavender. Pour infusion into a glass pitcher. Add lemon juice and another 2½ cups water. Stir well and watch lemonade change color.

4. Pour into tall glasses half-filled with ice or refrigerate until ready to use. Garnish lemonade with fresh lavender sprigs.

Per serving: 139 cal., 0% (0 cal.) from fat; 0.2 g protein; 0 g fat; 37 g carbo (0.2 g fiber); 0.7 mg sodium; 0 mg chol.

fresh herb. "In aromatherapy, lavender is used for harmony and balance," says Dowling. "It keeps me sane."

DOWLING'S FAVORITE PLANTS

L. angustifolia **'Hidcote'.** "The intense purple flowers color jellies, lemonade, and vinegars beautifully. Grows 1 to 2 feet tall.

Spike lavender (*L. latifolia*). "It's a great big tall bush—very endearing. Grows 3 feet tall. Violet flowers.

Happy Valley Herbs, 3505 Happy Valley Rd., Victoria, B.C. V9C 2Y2; (250) 474-5767. Open 10–5 during lavender season, July 1–15. August-December, farm tours, lectures, and workshops are offered by reservation, and dried lavender is available by mail.

CRAFTING A TRADITION IN OREGON

Margaret Sansone has always grown and cooked with fresh herbs. With the purchase of a 5-acre farm in Beaver Creek, Oregon, in 1980, her passion became a business—Phoenix Garden.

Her adventure into lavender began in 1981 when she met Adgie Hulse, then known as the Lavender Lady in Portland herb circles. Hulse had been growing lavender for the cut flower industry since the 1950s and taught classes on the medicinal and floral uses of herbs.

When Sansone visited Hulse's ½-acre lavender field, she was stunned by the sight. "I had never seen that much lavender growing at one time," says Sansone. She was smitten.

Over the years, Hulse and Sansone became close friends and shared many lavender tips. "I got the idea for our lavender potluck from Adgie," says Sansone.

Since Hulse passed away 11 years ago, Sansone has been gathering her friends together for the summer lavender harvest in mid-July, "just when the bees start working the lower flowers," she explains. Each guest brings a dish (which usually has an herbal emphasis). The friends swap stories as they make wands (shown at right) using long-stemmed spike lavender. They've gotten very creative with the wands, explains Sansone—"particularly the way they weave in special ribbons."

Though she does sell her organically grown herbs, Sansone doesn't sell

LAVENDER PASSION IN VICTORIA

Lynda Dowling's love of lavender began 12 years ago when an elderly friend brought her an old, woody 'Munstead' lavender plant she'd just dug up because she was moving to a condominium. Her friend "believed in my vision to farm my grandmother's land, which has been in the family since 1910," says Dowling.

Bucking all recommended gardening advice for her climate in January, Dowling clipped the old plant into 500 cuttings and stuck the cuttings into a coldframe. "Fortunately, it was a mild winter and they all survived," she says.

Three years later, the plants had matured and were blooming profusely. Suddenly, Dowling had bundles of

lavender on her hands. "That's when I went gung ho," she says. She approached nearby Butchart Gardens to find out who supplied the lavender for their sachets. "I told them I could do better, and they said, 'The contract is yours if you can give it to us for the same price.'" Now she supplies Butchart Gardens with 45 pounds of lavender per year.

Friends brought Dowling seeds from all over the world, including France, England, and Tasmania. Today her fields are striped with 1,200 lavender plants in multiple colors. Florists and chefs flock to her farm for her hand-harvested organically grown lavender.

Lavender has become the signature plant of Dowling's farm. It has also inspired her to create recipes using the uch of her lavender. She grows it just or its beauty and in honor of a special woman she once knew.

ANSONE'S FAVORITE PLANTS

ansone grows 20 kinds of lavender in er garden, but three are particularly pecial to her.

L. intermedia **'Provence'**: "The eautiful blooms are very, very fragrant," ays Sansone. Violet flowers. Grows 2 to feet tall.

L. angustifolia **'Baby Blue'**: Compact; dark purple flowers in summer. rows 12 to 14 inches tall.

Spike lavender *(L. latifolia)*: Sturdy, 12- to 18-inch-long flower stems are superior for wands.

Phoenix Garden, Box 38, Beaver Creek, OR 97004; (503) 632-7865. Sells fresh herbs by appointment only.

LAVENDER PLANTS BY MAIL

Goodwin Creek Gardens, Box 83, Williams, OR 97544; (541) 846-7357. Catalog: $1. Sells 38 kinds.
Woodside Gardens, 1191 Egg & I Rd., Chimacum, WA 98325; (360) 732-4754. Catalog: $2. Sells more than 30 kinds.

GROWING TIPS

•Plant lavender in full sun and well-drained soil. Sansone plants her lavender in raised beds to ensure good drainage during wet winters.
•Water plants deeply, but infrequently, when the soil is almost dry.
•Spread compost over roots once a year, in spring.
•Prune in early spring or at harvesttime. For low-growing varieties, trim back foliage 1 to 2 inches. Tall (3 to 4 foot) lavenders should be cut back by about ⅓ to keep plants from getting overly woody (start the second year). ◆

HOW TO MAKE A LAVENDER WAND

TIME
About 30 minutes

WHAT YOU NEED
About 18 (or more) stems of lavender, at least 12 inches tall

3 yards satin or other ribbon, ⅛ to ¼ inches wide

Use fresh lavender with unopened flowers. (To store stems for a day, wrap them in moist paper towels.) Harvest in the morning after dew has dried.
1. For a fat wand, use 50 stalks (25 double stems), weaving two at a time. For a slimmer wand (best for first-time weavers), try 18 stalks (9 double stems).
2. Strip off leaves. Line up flower heads

so the bases of the heads are even.
3. Starting at one end of the ribbon, tie ribbon tightly around the base of the flower heads **(a)**.
4. Turn stalks upside down and gently bend two stems at a time evenly over the blooms to surround the flower heads **(b)**.
5. Weave the ribbon under and over the double stems **(c)**, pulling it very tight as you go (the lavender shrinks as it dries). Continue weaving until you reach the tips of the lavender blooms (you can also weave to the stem ends).
6. Wind the ribbon around the wand a couple of times, tie a slip knot, and cut the end. Using another piece of ribbon, tie a bow around the wand over the first knot.
7. Rub off any buds that stick out of the wand. Trim stem ends to the same length.

NORMAN A. PLATE (3)

FRIENDS AND FAMILY of Margaret Sansone (seated, in red dress) weave wands from freshly harvested spike lavender. Behind, lavender bushes are at peak bloom, and rows of organically grown herbs thrive in the fields.

Tuscan beauties

Old World–style pottery can bring classic elegance to your garden

BY SHARON COHOON AND JIM McCAUSLAND

■ The rosy clay pots and weathered stone urns that grace Mediterranean gardens have a timeless appeal. And it's no wonder. Gardeners have been using them to decorate the landscape for millennia.

Wealthy Romans used clay olive oil jars, called *dolia,* as containers for trees and shrubs in the first century A.D.; Pliny the Younger (circa A.D. 61–113) described these containers in his letters. When Pompeii and Herculaneum were excavated, perfectly preserved dolia were found among the ruins. But Romans hardly invented garden vessels, says Glorianna Pionati, a Los Angeles–based archaeologist, antiquities instructor, and Italian garden ornament importer. Ancient Egyptians—as we know from their hieroglyphs—used terra-cotta containers as planters. And they probably swiped the idea from the Mesopotamians.

DOUG PLUMMER

Stone urns and vases are, by comparison, relative newcomers. They became popular garden ornaments among wealthy landowners during the Italian Renaissance. Many classical antiquities were unearthed during this period, says Pionati, and Tuscan stonecutters copied and reinterpreted the designs in quarried stone.

During the 19th century, mechanization made it feasible to produce artificial stone (precursor to concrete) in mass quantities for the first time, bringing garden ornaments within the price range of the middle class.

Today you can buy containers embellished with the very same designs used in Renaissance Italy, but with an important difference: now most pots are made from materials that stand up better to time and the elements than those made centuries ago.

Terra-cotta (Italian for *baked earth*) is made from clay. When high-fired, terra-cotta can withstand some abuse and frost without chipping or cracking. It is usually lighter and thinner-walled than concrete, but high-fired terra-cotta is more expensive. Before you buy a pot, ask if it's high-fired terra-cotta (some catalogs spell it out). Low-quality terra-cotta won't last as long.

Cast concrete is usually cheaper and more durable than terra-cotta. Much of it is gray, but manufacturers commonly stain it in a variety of long-lasting earth tones. Antique copper, brown, whitewashed terra-cotta, ochre, and black are commonly used, as are near-perfect terra-cotta tints. With some concrete pieces, you'll have to ask: Is it terra-cotta or concrete? Aerospace materials like fiberglass and polystyrene are now sometimes added to cement to increase

HEAVY AND HANDSOME terra-cotta pots come in a wide range of shapes and styles. At Lucca Statuary in Seattle (left), owners Peter Riches and Francine Katz show off their wares.

CONNIE COLEMAN

JIM McCAUSLAND (7)

The meaning of the motifs

LOOK AT A FEW DOZEN Italian containers and you'll notice the same motifs recurring. Some, like the basket-weave pattern, were developed in this century, but most go much further back in history. It's safe to say that they've stood the test of time.

LIONS AND RAMS once represented royalty and virility, respectively.

ACANTHUS LEAVES may have been copied by Renaissance potters from the capitals of Corinthian columns.

FRUITS (olives, lemons) represent the harvest, and sometimes hint at what the container was designed to grow or hold.

GARGOYLE'S face is supposed to ward off evil. Similar (but hornless) Green Man, with leaves on his face, exists to protect the garden.

CHERUBS have meanings associated with what they're holding: wheat for summer, grapes for autumn, flame for winter, flowers for spring.

strength and reduce weight.

Most of the Italian-style containers pictured on these pages are made in the West, often by families with roots in Bagni di Lucca, an ancient pottery-making town in Tuscany. You can find their work (and pieces from other factories) at statuary shops and garden centers.

HOW TO DISPLAY TUSCAN POTTERY

To use ornamental pots the way the Italians do, treat them as statues. That's the advice of Ron Bracci, co-owner of Al's Garden Art in Colton, California, a major player in what he describes as the "small, incestuous family of garden statuary."

"Europeans don't distinguish between these pots and statuary," says Bracci. "They use pots interchangeably to frame vistas, mark the crossing of intersecting paths, or complement the horizontal lines of a balustrade or terrace. That's why the containers are left unplanted as often as not." If you do decide to plant, keep it simple—a single architectural agave or cordyline, a small tree like a bay or kumquat, a shrub with a naturally neat habit like boxwood, or geraniums in a single color.

However you use them, keep in mind that most of these containers are heavy. Filled with well-watered soil and plants, the largest ones can weigh hundreds of pounds. Think about where you want them before you plant. If you anticipate moving heavy containers much, put them on permanent wheeled platforms.

Also, any drainless container is death to live plants. Nest already-potted plants inside them, and fill the gap between the inside pot and the rim of the Italian pot with moss.

WHERE TO BUY TUSCAN POTTERY

These sources have large stocks.
Seattle
Herban Pottery sells choice Italian pieces from Vietri and Impruneta, in northern Italy. These handmade pieces aren't cheap,

but only Paul Newman weathers as well. A 15-inch Impruneta lemon pot costs $390; a Chinese copy runs $42. Visit the store or order by mail. 250 N.E. 45th St.; (800) 618-4742. Free catalog.

Lucca Statuary offers the Northwest's largest selection of Italian pottery, all made from poured concrete. Prices range from around $20 for a 5- by 7-inch garland pot to about $900 for a 32-by 42-inch round garland container. 7716 15th Ave. N.W.; (206) 789-8444 or www.luccastatuary.com.

Price Ragen Co. has a good selection of very large Italian terra-cotta pots (to 72 inches in diameter), all made in Florence or Impruneta, as well as small containers ($75 for a 12-inch pot). A 26-inch pot costs $328; 36-inch, $1,225. Will ship. 517 E. Pike St.; (206) 329-8155.
San Francisco
A. Silvestri Company Garden Ornaments manufactures a large share of the Italian-style pottery sold in the West, with many designs coming from Bagni di Lucca. Prices are comparable to those at Lucca Statuary in Seattle. The showroom is at 2635 Bay Shore Blvd.; (415) 239-5990.
Greater Los Angeles
Al's Garden Art, owned by the Bracci family, is another major Italian-style pottery manufacturer. Prices are comparable to those at Lucca and Silvestri. The showroom is at 2110 Tyler Ave., South El Monte; (626) 448-8880.

Cloverleaf Stone Guild in Ventura produces classic Italian-style pots and urns out of fiber-reinforced concrete. It manufactures for dozens of high-end showrooms in the Los Angeles and San Francisco area, but you can also order directly by catalog. Prices tend toward triple figures. A 26-inch-wide garland pot runs $275. (805) 648-4514.

Glorianna Pionati Import-Export represents several Italian terra-cotta factories in Siena. You order by catalog and the pots are shipped from Italy directly to you. Prices start in the single digits—a simple, rolled-rim 12-inch pot costs $9—and move up with size and level of detail. (818) 766-7210.

Marina del Rey Garden Center has one of the largest selections of concrete and terra-cotta pots in Southern California. Mail order. 13198 Mindanao Way, Marina del Rey; (310) 823-5956. ◆

PLUMED CELOSIA
n three fiery
shades sets a
ed aflame.

NORMAN A. PLATE

Paint your garden with the vibrance of van Gogh

Hot-colored flowers are back in style.
Here's how to use them in your summer garden

BY STEVEN R. LORTON

In 1888, the Dutch painter Vincent van Gogh left Paris for southern France in search of inspiration. He found it in Provence—under the Mediterranean sun. Dazzled by the scenery, van Gogh wrote to his brother Theo: "What intensity of color, what pure air, what vibrant serenity." His paintings of flowers and fields from that period are rendered in intense shades of yellow, orange, and red. These warm hues that so inspired van Gogh are the flower colors that are once again brightening our gardens.

That's a refreshing change, since for the last decade, horticultural fashion has leaned toward cooler pastels such as lavender and mauve. Admittedly, the warmer shades are not as easy to work into the landscape; unless you combine them thoughtfully in just the right places, they can turn a garden into a kaleidoscopic jumble. But use them right and you'll have beds that shimmer like van Gogh's swirling brush strokes.

All the plants you need to paint a summer bed or border are only a nursery stop away. You can't miss such vivid beauties as cannas, celosias, and dahlias; the palette on page 173 offers many more choices of annuals, perennials, and bulbs and tubers, including some of the most reliable named varieties. Follow the design guidelines on page 172 to blend them on your canvas.

How to paint with hot colors

PAIR SHADES OF A SINGLE COLOR. Fire-engine red dahlias paired with a matching skirt of red pelargoniums, for example, might spill into a mound of silver *Artemisia* 'Powis Castle'. A similar scene could be composed of yellow daylilies or yarrow and one of the yellow forms of poker plant.

PLAY WARM COLORS OFF EACH OTHER. Try red against yellow, for instance—or be daring and try hot pinks against oranges. Celosias, cannas, and dahlias lend themselves to this approach.

FOLLOW THE COLOR WHEEL. Start planting with one color, then go to the next shade on the color wheel. For example, plant yellow (maybe *Potentilla fruticosa* 'Jackman's Variety') at one end of a bed, changing to orange (*Kniphofia ritualis*), then burnt orange, perhaps with a hint of yellow (gloriosa daisies), and finish off with red (cannas).

CONTRAST COOL AND HOT. Choose a cool color—blue, purple, or white—and use it sparingly to lower the temperature in a feverish bed. A puff of white baby's breath, impatiens, or petunias is great for this. Blues, from tall delphiniums to low-growing lobelias, can take the jitters out of a pulsating combination of reds, oranges, or yellows. Orange lion's tail (*Leonotis leonurus*) sizzles by itself, but when it's placed near deep blue globe thistle (*Echinops exaltatus*) or purple salvia, the heat goes down.

UNIFY AND FRAME WITH FOLIAGE. Silver or gray foliage is great for visually unifying a bed and separating hot colors. Try dusty miller between two shades of red, for example. Green foliage is equally useful in framing a composition of colorful flowers.

TOP: Brilliant dwarf cannas include 'Pfitzer Salmon' (far left), 'Picasso' (yellow petals with red flecks), and 'Lucifer' (red petals with yellow edges). ABOVE: *Crocosmia* 'Lucifer'. RIGHT: *Tithonia* 'Goldfinger'.

NORMAN A. PLATE

MARION BRENNER (2)

Flaming reds

Pulsating pinks

Scorching oranges

Sunny yellows

Vibrant flower palette for Western gardens

Annuals

CELOSIA ● ● ● ●

CLEOME HASSLERANA ●
(spider flower)

COSMOS ● ● ● ●

GAILLARDIA ● ●
G. pulchella

IMPATIENS ● ●
I. balsamina, New
Guinea hybrids

MARIGOLD ● ●

MEXICAN SUNFLOWER ●
Tithonia rotundifolia
'Goldfinger', 'Torch'

PETUNIA ● ● ●

SUNFLOWER ● ●
Helianthus annuus 'Big
Smile', 'Sunrich Orange',
'Orange Sun'

ZINNIA ● ● ● ●

Perennials

ALSTROEMERIA ● ● ● ●
'Lutea' (yellow), 'Orange
King', 'Florist's Red'

ASTER NOVAE-ANGLIAE ●
'Honeysong Pink'

COREOPSIS ●
'Early Sunrise', 'Robin',
'Sunray'

DAYLILY ● ●
'Pardon Me' (dwarf red)

GAILLARDIA ● ● ●
G. grandiflora 'Golden
Goblin' (yellow)

GERANIUM ●
(some species) *G. mad-
erense, G. psilostemon*

GERBERA ● ● ● ●
(Transvaal daisy)

GLORIOSA DAISY ●
Rudbeckia hirta
'Indian Summer'

LIATRIS SPICATA ●
'Kobold'

LION'S TAIL ●
(*Leonotis leonurus*)

LOBELIA ●
'Queen Victoria'

MALTESE CROSS ●
(*Lychnis chalcedonica*)

ORIENTAL POPPY ●

PELARGONIUM ● ●

PENSTEMON ● ●
'Firebird' (red), 'Apple
Blossom' (pink),
'Huntington Pink'

POKER PLANT ● ● ●
Kniphofia uvaria 'Shining
Sceptre' (yellow-gold),
K. ritualis (orange),
K. northiae (red-orange)

POTENTILLA ● ● ●
P. fruticosa 'Jackman's
Variety' (yellow),
'Klondike' (yellow),
'Sutter's Gold', 'Tangerine',
'Red Ace'

SALVIA (species) ●
S. coccinea 'Lady in Red',
S. elegans, S. splendens

SUMMER PHLOX ● ●
P. paniculata
'Miss Candy' (hot pink),
'Miss Pepper' (pink with
red eye)

SUNFLOWER ●
Helianthus multiflorus
'Loddon Gold' (double
flowers)

YARROW ● ●
Achillea filipendulina
'Coronation Gold', 'Gold
Plate'; *A. millefolium*
'Cerise Queen', 'Fire King'

Bulbs, Tubers, and Corms

ASIATIC LILY ● ● ●
'Yellow Gold', 'Juanita'
(orange), 'Hello
Dolly' (red)

BEGONIA ● ● ●
(tuberous types)

CANNA ● ● ● ●
'Phasion' (orange)

CROCOSMIA ● ● ●
'Citronella' (yellow),
'Solfatare' (golden
yellow), 'Queen
Alexandra' (orange),
'Lucifer' (red)

DAHLIA ● ● ● ●

ORIENTAL LILY ●
'Acapulco', 'Pink Icicles'

Shrub

HELIANTHEMUM ● ●
'Henfield Brilliant' (or-
ange), 'Supreme' (red)

Garden competitions are sprouting up in cities around the world. For details on this colorful garden—the 1997 winner of Edmonds in Bloom—see page 180.

July

gardenguide

Master beds in Montana

■ As one of the Rocky Mountains' pre-eminent landscape architects, Chris Moritz had many of his projects published in *Sunset* when he lived in Colorado. Then he moved to Bigfork, Montana, where he took on a major landscaping project for his harshest critic—himself.

The site faced wooded hills on all sides, giving Moritz a natural background. He left a semicircle of native trees around his new home, then planted great drifts of flowering peren-nials in the foreground.

The perennial beds completely surround a bluegrass and fescue lawn. Trees—some native, some planted—give the beds depth and provide varying amounts of shade, while ornamental grasses create movement as they blow in the wind. In the bed shown above, blue oat grass (*Helictrotrichon sempervirens*) is underplanted with purple violas, with tall red sweet William (*Dianthus barbatus*) be-

BLUE OAT GRASS fountains above a purple carpet of violas.

hind. The grass leaves an seed heads keep their beaut well into winter.

Because the site's nativ soil is very sandy, Morit amended it with compost before plant ing. This improved the soil's nutrient and water-holding capacity, though th beds still need regular overhead water ing and one or two doses of con trolled-release fertilizer every summe to make things thrive.

—*Jim McCauslane*

A **narrow** escape in **Denver**

CORAL BELLS and blue campanula dot the path.

■ When she moved into a two-story house, interior designer Karen Forey knew she needed some exterior design help to improve the view, create a sense of privacy, and provide summer shade. So she called on landscape architect Charles Randolph of Lifescape Associates in Denver. He accomplished all of these things by transforming a long, narrow space into the planted colonnade shown at right.

The colonnade supports a wrought-iron arbor for part of its length. 'Concord' grapevines scramble up the columns and over the pergola, growing about 5 feet per year. A year after planting, the vines started bearing fruit, producing enough grapes for a batch of jelly. The vines growing over the arbor will be pruned as they fill in to al-low filtered sunlight to reach the plants dotting the path below. Boston ivy (*Parthenocissus tricuspidata*) also runs up some of the colonnade. Near the house, a star magnolia (*M. stellata*) is covered with star-shaped white flowers in spring, and its dark green leaves cast shade in summer.

The path, made from sandstone slabs embedded in a 3-inch layer of crushed rhyolite gravel, supports a patchwork of perennials, including red-orange *Penstemon pinifolius,* creeping veronica, coral bells, *Campanula elatines garganica,* coreopsis, and lamb's ears.

The design earned Randolph a Grand Award in a contest sponsored by the Associated Landscape Contractors of Colorado.

— *J. M.*

LEFT: TERRENCE MOORE   RIGHT: CHARLES MANN   BELOW: CURTIS ANDERSON

tool

Here's a new pruning tool that's just made to tuck into a pocket. The Pocket Pruner from Fiskars is about the size of a Swiss Army Knife. It has pruning shears and a knife blade, both of which fold into the handle. Keep this versatile little tool in your back pocket, ready to use whenever you need to do a bit of harvesting, deadheading, or nipping. Pocket Pruner is available by mail from Gardener's Supply Company. $34.95; (800) 444-6417.

— *Lauren Bonar Swezey*

A river of hen and chickens

■ Succulents, especially the *Sempervivum* species, lend themselves to pattern plantings. Gardeners at Minter Gardens in Chilliwack, British Columbia, created the streamlike pattern shown here using two colors of hen and chickens: gray-green *Sempervivum tectorum* and its bronze-green sister, *S. t. calcareum*. They planted the two kinds in a bed of sand, and carefully placed river rocks in the "stream" and along the edges to enhance the flowing illusion.

You could try a planting like this anywhere: hen and chickens are tough (they'll grow in the crack of a rock), but they need good drainage. When they flower, the "hen" dies and the chickens fill in around her. You can divide and transplant the chicks, but discard the hen after bloom. — *J. M.*

JIM McCAUSLAND

Orchids on high

■ The dendrobium orchid pictured above adds eye-level interest, and all the magic of a real jungle, to the coastal San Diego garden it calls home. That's because it grows in a basket that's attached to the trunk of a queen palm *(Syagrus romanzoffianum)*.

The queen palm faces south and gets reflected heat from hot stone steps, stucco walls, and a stairway. That puts the dendrobium in full sun year-round, though it also gets a cooldown from coastal breezes, and a greenbelt of protection from the *Carissa edulis* 'Tomentosa' planted at the palm's base. This thorny climber runs up the tree and provides more visual interest behind the flowers. It also provides leaves and flowers that rain down all year to become organic mulch for the orchid.

The six-year-old dendrobium grows in medium-size bark in a moss-lined wire basket that's concealed by the carissa. It typically sets three bloom stalks in April, four or five in June, and two or three in September.

Dendrobiums are available at well-stocked nurseries throughout Southern California.   — *Damon Hedgepeth*

Patching a lawn

■ If you need to repair parts of the lawn that are dead or worn out, start by preparing the soil. Rake out dead grass, then rough up the top inch of soil with a bow rake or a cultivator. Scatter a light dose of lawn fertilizer over the area, then sow seeds to match the existing grass, as shown. Lightly rake the seeds into the soil, and cover with a thin layer (¼ inch) of organic mulch such as peat moss. Keep the seeded area well watered (perhaps twice a day in hot weather) until the grass is tall enough to mow.◆

Seamless bloom on a steep slope

Flowering perennials cloak the sun-bathed slope at right in such a seamless fashion that it's hard to imagine the site once "looked like a bomb had gone off." At least that's how Greta Mestre of Reno describes the challenge she and her husband, Steve, faced when they bought the property. The former owners had gouged a virtual crater out of the slope, removing the soil to level another part of the yard.

The Mestres set out to revive the hillside. First, they filled the depression with 30 yards of composted manure. Then, to halt soil erosion on the 30° slope, they built dry-stack stone retaining walls, terraces, and steps.

Once the stonework was in place, Greta planted the slope with tough perennial flowers and grasses, many of them native to the area. In this photo, golden black-eyed Susan and red hawkweed spring from the rocks at the base of the steps. Above them, pink Mexican evening primrose creeps up the wall toward scarlet *Verbena hybrida*.

— *Suzanne Touchette Kelso*

BLACK-EYED SUSAN pops from stones at foot of steps.

Wild and tame flora at Alaska Botanical Garden in Anchorage

Among the rugged wonders of Alaska, a botanical garden seems beside the point. But any gardener who wanders the trails of the Alaska Botanical Garden in Anchorage will be glad to have taken an afternoon away from glaciers and grizzlies to step into this living laboratory of frontier horticulture.

Opened in 1993, the garden is funded by memberships and donations. Only 11 of the 110 acres are devoted to formal plantings. The rest have been left in wild, native Alaskan flora, including dwarf dogwood (*Cornus canadensis*) and high bush cranberry (*Viburnum edule*). Trails mulched with wood chips wind along the lush forest floor.

There are three formal gardens: the upper perennial garden (shown at right), the lower perennial garden, and the herb garden. In the upper garden, cement core samples (salvaged from construction sites) are used to edge beds filled with warm-colored flowers—coreopsis, lilies, gaillardias, rudbeckias. In the lower garden, delphiniums tower up to 7 feet tall, and in the herb garden, raised beds brim with annuals and perennials used for culinary, medicinal, and ornamental purposes.

Alaska Botanical Garden is in Far North Bicentennial Park on the east side of Anchorage. Hours are 9 to 9. Admission is free, though donations are appreciated. For an in-depth look at the Alaska gardening scene, see the article starting on page 192. — *Steven R. Lorton*

Fireworks in a vase

■ When outdoor parties call for flowers in festive colors, try this "summer sparkler" bouquet designed by *Sunset* test garden coordinator Bud Stuckey. The arrangement uses blooms that you might find growing in your own garden this month.

Deep pink lace cap hydrangea billows over the rim of the vase. Above it, blue agapanthus and pink and white dahlias unfurl their pastel petals. Myers asparagus and purple butterfly bush fan out behind them.

To set off the show, spikes of tiny white gaura flowers and the grassy flower heads of *Miscanthus transmorrisonensis* burst forth like fireworks glittering against the night sky.

— *L. B. S.*

FLORAL DISPLAY

Edmonds in full bloom

■ To beautify their bombed-out cities after World War II, the British developed a program called Keep Britain Tidy. It eventually turned into a garden competition and took on local names like London in Bloom. Since then, the program has been adopted by cities around the world, including Edmonds, Washington, where it took root three years ago.

This is the month to see the results of Edmonds in Bloom. All of the 100-or-so participating gardens are visible from the street, so they're easy to appreciate. Just pick up a city map and a list of entries at the Edmonds Parks & Recreation Department in the Frances Anderson Center (700 Main St.; 8 A.M. to 10 P.M. Mon-Fri, 9 to 5 Sat).

Last year, we saw everything from window boxes bursting with blossoms to a fire hydrant ringed with nicotiana, petunias, and lobelia. We especially liked the mixed flower beds of Katie and Roger Niva's 1997 winner (shown on page 174). For more information on Edmonds in Bloom, call (425) 77. 2631.

While you're in town, don't miss Edmonds's wealth of garden-related shops. Check out the Haws watering cans at Garden Gear (102 Fifth Ave. N. or the moss- and flower-laden bicycle at the Weed Lady and Other Wondrous Wares (122 Fourth Ave. S.). If you get hungry, stop by Café Pinceau (610 Fifth Ave. S.; 425/775-0199) for lunch or dinner on the deck overlooking the gardens, where owner-chef Henry Arc grows herbs and edible flowers to garnish his salads. — *J. M.*

LANDSCAPING SOLUTIONS

A creek bed to collect rain

■ Las Vegas doesn't get much rain: only about 4 inches fall in an average year. To tap this sporadic water supply, Las Vegas landscape architect Jack Zunino designed a dry creek bed that harvests rain for the plants in Vance and Anita MacDonald's garden.

A backhoe was used to dig the creek bed into a flat lot. Lined with river rock, it looks like a natural arroyo. When rain falls, the water drains off the roof of the house and makes its way into the channel, where it slakes the thirst of desert spoon, mesquite, ocotillo, saguaro, grasses, and ground covers like *Acacia redolens* 'Desert Carpet'. Since rainfall is spotty, most of these plants receive supplementary water from drip emitters. — *J. M.*

WHIPLIKE OCOTILLO and mesquite trees grow in the creek bed.

Control those avocado persea mites

If the foliage on your avocado trees looks like it has the measles, persea mite (*Oligonychus persea*) is probably the culprit.

This mite crossed the border into coastal San Diego in 1990, and it has been working its way north and east ever since. It feeds on avocado tree foliage, leaving small yellow and brown dead spots on the leaves. If the infestation becomes severe, the tree drops leaves in defense, exposing fruit to sunburn. 'Hass', 'Gwen', and 'Reed' avocados have proved particularly susceptible.

The best solution is a biological control. Commercial growers have been releasing two insectary-reared predatory mites, *Galendromus helveolus* and *G. anectens,* to control the persea mite, and they have had satisfactory results. *G. helveolus* has the advantage of reproducing more quickly, but *G. annectens* overwinters better. Homeowners can buy either one of the predators or a combination of both from American Insectaries in Escondido, CA (760/751-1436) or Rincon-Vitova Insectaries in Ventura, CA (805/643-5407). A minimum order of 1,000 mites, which is enough to treat four trees (or to share with a neighbor), costs about $30, including shipping. Providing plenty of water and fertilizer during leaf flush also helps mite-stressed trees recover. — *Sharon Cohoon*

HANDSOME PRIVACY

Diamonds forever

■ For years, the front entry of Adele Proom's Berkeley home was open to the road, which offered her little privacy. Then Proom mentioned her dilemma to Oakland mason Ronnie Hansson, who had just finished installing her new brick driveway.

Hansson offered to build a wall to blend with the style of the house. The handsome stucco wall spans the length of the driveway, and at 5½ feet tall, it provides plenty of privacy. Lights in the posts are covered with green-flecked glass that "looks like leaves" when the lights are on. An ivy espalier trained on wire adds textural interest to the wall.

"We crisscrossed wire between bolts at the top and bottom to create a diamond pattern," says Proom. English ivy was planted at the base of the wall below each bolt, and the stems were entwined on the wire.

By year's end, the ivy had mostly filled in. To keep it perfectly shaped, she lightly shears the stems every few weeks. — *Lauren Bonar Swezey*

TECHNIQUE

Build a watering moat

■ To get established, young trees and shrubs such as roses need extra water in summer during their first growing season. One way to ensure that water reaches their root zones efficiently is to build a moat around the

plants. Mound a berm of soil 3 to 4 inches high just outside the perimeter of the plant's rootball, and another one 2 to 3 inches from the plant's trunk. When you irrigate with the hose, let the water trickle slowly enough to fill the moat yet keep the trunk base dry. This method works on level ground or gentle slopes.

Pacific Northwest Garden Notebook

BY STEVEN R. LORTON

Ornamental grasses shine in July. With the early-blooming perennials finished for the season and the late bloomers still forming buds, these grasses really stand out. If you're dying to plant in the heat of summer, ornamental grasses are among the toughest candidates. They don't require much, if any, extra summer water. Three deciduous grasses in particular are stellar performers in my garden.

I have several established clumps of eulalia grass (*Miscanthus sinensis*). The silvery green leaves reach 5 to 6 feet tall, and the blooms stand well above that. Its seed heads look like tawny ostrich feathers waving in the breeze. Of all the named varieties, *M. s.* 'Gracillimus', or maiden grass, is my favorite. I let the seed heads stand through much of the winter, cutting the plants back to within 6 inches of the ground in late February.

Northern sea oats (*Chasmanthium latifolium*), another clumping grass, grows 2 to 3 feet tall and has bamboolike foliage. It bears large, drooping seed heads that look like tiny lanterns. Late in the summer, I cut the seed stalks off and take them indoors to display; otherwise, this self-sowing grass would fill my garden with its offspring.

I recently planted giant feather grass (*Stipa gigantea*). Its tufts of fine leaves can reach 2 feet, and the big wands of bloom stretch up 6 feet or taller. It will be in full flower this month. When the wind blows in late afternoon and early evening, the swaying blooms put on a show that reminds me of samba dancers in Rio de Janeiro.

Every three years or so, between November and mid-February, I dig up the clumps, divide each into three or four sections, and replant. You'd be surprised at how quickly you can create a grassy savanna by dividing plants this way.

that's a good question ...

Q: I love the look of pampas grass, but it's too big for my garden. Is there any good substitute?

A: Try dwarf pampas grass (*Cortaderia selloana* 'Pumila'), a noninvasive cultivar. I grow this plant in the ground and in a big pot. It produces dense, 4- to 6-foot-tall clumps of gray-green leaves, which are topped in summer by silky plumes of creamy white flowers that look great through the winter.

Northern California Garden Notebook

BY LAUREN BONAR SWEZEY

*e*very now and then, I'm asked to judge gardens at local garden shows. The shows are all different, so I never know what to expect. Take the display gardens at the Sonoma County Fair, for instance. I judged those last year. I had never been to the Sonoma County Fair before, but when I entered the Hall of Flowers to view the gardens, I entered a veritable fantasy world.

The display gardens were not small, like so many others. They were huge—650 to 1,000 square feet—with waterfalls, garden pavilions, and an unbelievable show of flowers in every possible color and form. I later found out that show designer Greg Duncan, who has designed most of the show areas at Marine World Themepark, decides on a theme and builds the sets for the gardens. Individual designers then interpret the idea by creating gardens within the sets.

The theme at this year's fair, which runs July 28 to August 10, is Adventure in Paradise. Among the displays you'll see: a 35-foot volcano; a rain forest; aviaries filled with tropical birds, waterfalls, and water features; and gardens that look like they're from Bali, the Caribbean, Hawaii, and Tahiti. "It takes us over three months

to build the sets," says Duncan of Scenic Designs in Santa Rosa.

The fairgrounds are at 1350 Bennett Valley Road in Santa Rosa. Fair admission costs $5, $2 ages 7 through 12. For more information, call (707) 545-4200.

EUROPE'S BEST OPEN GARDENS
Many Westerners travel to Europe for culture and history. But plant lovers often go for the many fascinating private and public gardens. If you're planning on garden-hopping through Europe this summer or fall, you might want to pick up one or all four of the new color guidebooks to Britain, France, Germany, and Italy in *The Garden Lover's Guide* series (Princeton Architectural Press, New York, 1998; $19.95, 800/722-6657). The guides are written by renowned garden experts Patrick Taylor, Charles Quest-Ritson, and Penelope Hobhouse. Each guide contains more than 100 entries, all of which include a color photograph, commentary on the garden, and touring information.

(Editor's note: dates and times in this article were valid for 1998; events and schedules will vary from year to year.

that's a good question ...

Q: I don't have room to grow gourds in my garden, but like to use them for craft projects. Where can I order them by mail?

A. Welburn Gourd Farm (40787 De Luz Murrieta Rd., Fallbrook, CA 92028; 760/728-4271) offers thousands of gourds in many different shapes and sizes, ranging in cost from 50 cents (plus shipping) for a 2- to 4-inch gourd to $10 for a 13-inch gourd. Write or call for a price list.

MARINA THOMPSON

Southern California Garden Notebook

BY SHARON COHOON

*P*lumeria, frangipani, lei flower, perfume of the Hawaiian Islands—who could be indifferent to your seductive charms? Me, once, that's who. I used to think plumeria was rather homely. (Maybe that's because I'd mostly seen it in a dormant stage, when it is leafless as well as flowerless and looks a lot like a planted rubber pole.) Maybe that's why I assumed it was difficult to grow—another misconception. In any case, my prejudice against this sweet tree was pretty firmly entrenched. Then two men came along and uprooted it.

When I was on Oahu last, Andy Butler took me to Koko Crater Botanical Garden. Near the crater is an old plumeria grove, which visitors often walk by without noticing. We didn't, though. Andy started handing me blossoms, and we played the game of identifying fragrances. We came up with tuberose and gardenia, as you might expect. But also peach and carnation. And some real surprises, like cherry Kool-Aid and menthol. By the time we left, I was floating on a cloud of perfume, and my resistance was weakening.

Back on the mainland, I met plumeria fancier Bud Guillot of Huntington Beach. Guillot bought his first plumeria ("just a stick with some wax on the end") about 45 years ago. Instructions were vague—something like "plant in the ground." But plumeria culture proved so easy, he says, that just planting it was enough. Today, cuttings from that same plumeria grace many of his neighbors' yards, and form a grove at a city park. The plumeria didn't have a cultivar name when Guillot bought it, but it does now. The Plumeria Society of America registered it as 'Guillot's Sunset' last year. By the time you read this, Guillot will have shared more cuttings with potential plumeria converts. I'll be one of them.

For a brochure on Koko Crater Botanical Garden, write to Honolulu Botanical Gardens (50 N. Vineyard Blvd., Honolulu, HI 96817).

that's a good question ...

Q: "What are the spiny black insects crawling over my white potato vine?" writes a reader. "And what should I do about them?"

A: They're the adolescent form of a sucking insect called the keel-backed treehopper (*Antianthe expansa*). The adult insect is harder to spot. It looks like a green thorn attached to a stem—until you touch it and it jumps. Tomatoes, peppers, cestrum, and other members of the *Solanaceae* (nightshade) family may also host *A. expansa* colonies. Frequently examining susceptible plants during the summer and crushing the treehoppers you find with your fingers are usually sufficient to keep the population in check. (Wear gloves—both young and adult insects are unpleasantly scratchy.) Spraying horticultural oil on the twigs and stems, where the eggs are deposited, is another option.

Mountain Garden Notebook

BY JIM McCAUSLAND

*j*ust when I think my garden is under control, a new pest arrives to test my plants and me. One recent intruder was the Cooley spruce gall aphid, which has afflicted my trees horribly. This insect attacks many kinds of spruces, causing ugly bulbous galls to form at branch tips. To find a treatment, I turned to a new CD-ROM: *Put Knowledge to Work CD97* (Colorado State University Cooperative Extension, Fort Collins, 1997; $45.50, 970/491-6198). It contains the combined horticultural wisdom of 16 American universities. For example, the entry I found for Cooley spruce gall aphid was written by CSU Cooperative Extension's Whitney Cranshaw, one of the foremost experts on insect problems in the Rockies. To control this pest, he recommends spraying trees with dormant oil in winter. Early next year, I'll give it a try.

CELEBRATING HERBS IN MONTANA

Those of us who grow herbs in gardens on glacial till know the challenge of planting in rocky soil. That's why I have a special place in my heart for Shady Side Herb Farm, just outside Montana's Glacier National Park. To overcome the rocky soil, owner Amy Hinman-Shade used stones from her property to build more than 200 raised beds, all planted with herbs and flowers. You can buy plants here (either potted or field-grown) take classes (subjects range from aromatherapy to soap making), or just kick back and enjoy one of the prettiest spots in Montana.

Shady Side Herb Farm is 6 miles southwest of West Glacier. For more information, call (406) 387-4184 or visit www. montanaweb.com/gardens.

GELDING THE LILY

Whenever I sniff the sublime fragrance of an Oriental lily, I keep a keen eye on the flower's anthers, which are powdered with saffron-colored pollen. They can paint your nose so gently that you won't know it until your friends laugh and point.

I have a lily-growing friend who doesn't like wearing pollen blush, so she strips the pollen-bearing anthers off her lilies before she harvests the flowers. With filaments and pistils intact, the flowers still look complete and smell like heaven. Nobody but a botanist would notice that the flowers

that's a good question ...

Q: One of my Asiatic hybrid lilies grew a stalk about three times as thick as normal, and the flowers bloomed practically on top of each other. It made a whopper of a bouquet. Can I grow more like it?

A: In growers' parlance, your lily was fasciated. This kind of chance mutation is wonderful to behold, but it rarely reappears on the same plant the following year and can't be reproduced (on lilies) by propagation.

Southwest Garden Notebook

BY JIM McCAUSLAND

driving east through the long, rolling desert between Los Angeles and Phoenix, I'm always heartened when I finally cross the Colorado River. In a few miles, I spot the first saguaro cactus (*Carnegiea gigantea*), marking the edge of the Sonoran Desert. Many of the saguaros have only one arm here, while in the northeastern part of their range, these giant cactus commonly have several. During this blistering time of year, saguaros often sport a crown of red, ripe fruit atop each arm.

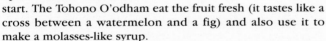

Coyotes, birds, javelinas, and rodents love to eat the fruit, as do people: for centuries, the Tohono O'odham people have harvested saguaro fruit with picking poles made from saguaro wood. Picking season runs from the time the fruits ripen and split open until the monsoons start. The Tohono O'odham eat the fruit fresh (it tastes like a cross between a watermelon and a fig) and also use it to make a molasses-like syrup.

Even saguaros grown in suburban gardens will bear fruit, but it's a long wait between planting and eating: the first flowers come after about 65 years on plants that have reached 7 feet tall. You can easily find plants up to 1 foot tall for less than $20, but taller ones are very hard to find.

To learn more about this classic desert plant, pick up a copy of *The Great Saguaro Book,* by Susan Hazen-Hammond (Ten Speed Press, Berkeley, 1997; $16.95, 800/841-2665). The photos are compelling, the information solid, and the reading enjoyable.

GELDING THE LILY

Whenever I sniff the sublime fragrance of an Oriental lily, I keep a keen eye on the flower's anthers, which are powdered with saffron-colored pollen. They can paint your nose so gently that you won't know it until your friends laugh and point.

I have a lily-growing friend who doesn't like wearing pollen blush, so she strips the pollen-bearing anthers off her lilies before harvesting the flowers. With filaments and pistils intact, the flowers still look complete and smell like heaven.

that's a good question ...

Q: Do citrus-scented geraniums (*Pelargonium asperum,* often sold as *P. citrosa*) really repel mosquitoes?

A: Not according to a study done at the University of Guelph's department of environmental biology in Ontario, Canada. Volunteers standing next to potted citrosa plants got the same number of mosquito bites as a control group who weren't near the citrosa. Adding insult to injury, mosquitoes were spotted resting on the plants between forays. On the other hand, the study showed that subjects who used deet (a chemical repellent) had more than 90 percent protection for at least eight hours after application.

Pacific Northwest Checklist

PLANTING

☑ ANNUALS. It's not too late to plant annuals in the ground or pots. Buy plants in sixpacks and 4-inch pots.

☑ HARDWOOD CUTTINGS. Propagate azaleas, fuchsias, hydrangeas, and wisteria by taking tip cuttings and rooting them in a sterile sandy potting mix.

☑ SHRUBS. If you plant a shrub now, be sure to water it well for the next three months. Before planting, soak the rootball overnight in a tub of water. Dig a generous hole, fill it with water, and let it soak down three times so that the soil around the rootball is saturated. Mix organic matter such as compost or peat moss into the backfill soil, plant, and water again.

☑ VEGETABLES. Zones 4–7: Sow seeds of beets, broccoli, bush beans, carrots, chard, Chinese cabbage, kohlrabi, lettuce, radishes, scallions, spinach, sugar pod or snow peas, and turnips for fall and winter harvest.

MAINTENANCE

☑ CARE FOR MUMS. For bigger and more abundant flowers, feed chrysanthemums every three weeks with a liquid plant food (5-10-10 is a good choice) until buds start to show color. When the first blooms open, feed weekly.

☑ FUCHSIAS. As flowers fade, snip them off to keep blooms coming. Feed plants monthly with a complete liquid plant food or twice a month with a half-strength dilution.

☑ GROUND COVERS. After they've bloomed, shear plants back to keep them compact and neat, then feed with a balanced fertilizer and water thoroughly.

☑ HOUSE PLANTS. Make certain that plants summering outdoors have enough water. If normally green leaves take on a bronzy cast, they're getting too much sun; move plants to a shadier spot. Hose off dusty leaves.

☑ MULCH. Conserve soil moisture by spreading a 3- to 4-inch layer of organic mulch around the root zones of shrubs.

☑ STRAWBERRIES. Remove dead leaves and stems. Fertilize and water plants thoroughly.

☑ WATER. Water perennials in the early morning hours so plants can soak up as much moisture as possible but still have the day ahead to dry out, reducing risk of mildew. Lawns can be watered in the evening.

WEED CONTROL

☑ THISTLES. Get them before they set seed. In small gardens, dig thistles out by the roots. If you have big spaces with lots of thistles, cut them back. As flower heads form, cut thistles to the ground.

Northern California Checklist

PLANTING

☑ **MAKE A POND.** Using a preformed pond or flexible liner, build a pond. Or fill a large glazed urn that has no drainage hole with water. Fill the "pond" with water plants, such as Japanese water iris (*Iris ensata*), parrot feather (*Myriophyllum aquaticum*), water lilies, and water poppy (*Hydrocleyes nymphoides*). Add mosquito fish, goldfish, or koi.

☑ **PLANT FALL VEGETABLES.** Zones 1–2: For fall harvest (except in highest altitudes), plant beets, broccoli, bush beans, cabbage, carrots, cauliflower, green onions, peas, spinach, and turnips. Below 5,000 feet, plant winter squash among spinach plants; the spinach will be ready to harvest before the squash takes over.

☑ **START PERENNIALS.** To get ready for fall planting, take cuttings of dianthus, geraniums, salvias, Shasta daisies, verbena, and other herbaceous perennials, dip them in rooting hormone, and plant them in a mixture of one part perlite and one part peat moss. Keep cuttings out of direct sun and cover with plastic to keep the humidity high. Lift the plastic for air circulation every few days. Check for rooting in about two weeks.

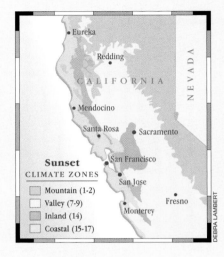

Sunset
CLIMATE ZONES

- ☐ Mountain (1-2)
- ☐ Valley (7-9)
- ☐ Inland (14)
- ☐ Coastal (15-17)

DEBRA LAMBERT

MAINTENANCE

☑ **ADJUST CONTROLLERS.** Depending on where you live, the weather this month can be hot and dry, or cool and foggy. If you water with an automatic controller, make sure the system runs often enough for plants to get the water they need, but not so often that the soil stays overly wet. As a test, check soil moisture just before the system is due to come on by digging down with a trowel or using a soil probe. If the soil seems too dry or too moist, adjust the controller.

☑ **CARE FOR FRUIT TREES.** To prevent breakage, use wood supports to brace limbs of apple, peach, pear, and plum trees that are sagging with fruit. Also, worms, diseases, and other pests may be living in fruit that has fallen to the ground. Pick up and discard these grounders as soon as you notice them.

☑ **TAKE A COMPOSTING CLASS.** Many organizations, such as botanical gardens, Master Gardeners, local nurseries, and community gardens now offer free composting classes. Call one of these organizations near you or look for schedules published in local newspapers.

PEST CONTROL

☑ **CONTROL YELLOW JACKETS.** These stinging wasps are uninvited guests at outdoor picnics and barbecues. One simple way to control them is to use a yellow jacket trap that contains an attractant to lure the wasps. Yellow jacket traps are available at some nurseries (such as Orchard Nursery in Lafayette; 925/284-4474) or by mail from Peaceful Valley Farm Supply (530/272-4769).

Southern California Checklist

PLANTING

☑ **PLANT SUBTROPICALS.** Look for landscaping staples like datura (*Brugmansia*), hibiscus, and princess flower, or consider one of the many gorgeous vines. Other choices include bougainvillea, coral vine (*Antigonon leptopus*), mandevilla, passion flower, stephanotis, thunbergia, and trumpet vines (blood-red, vanilla, or royal).

☑ **PLANT SUMMER ANNUALS.** Fill empty spots in the garden with heat lovers like portulaca, verbena, vinca, and zinnias. Plant bedding begonias, coleus, and impatiens in the shade.

☑ **PLANT SUMMER VEGETABLES.** For a late-summer harvest, continue to plant vegetables in coastal and inland gardens (zones 22–24 and 18–21, respectively). Set out cucumber, eggplant, pepper, squash, and tomato plants. Sow snap beans and corn. Don't forget culinary herbs. Plant basil, chervil, chives, parsley, rosemary, sage, savory, and thyme. Start dill and cilantro from seed. In the low desert (zone 13), plant pumpkins and winter squash.

Sunset
CLIMATE ZONES
1-3 7-9 11 13 14-24

DEBRA LAMBERT

MAINTENANCE

☑ **FERTILIZE PLANTS.** Feed actively growing plants such as annual flowers and vegetables, cymbidium orchids, ferns, fuchsias, roses, tropicals, and warm-season lawns. If not done last month, fertilize avocado and citrus trees. Feed camellias and azaleas with an acidic fertilizer. Feed bromeliads (use an acidic fertilizer, diluted to half-strength or less). Don't neglect hard-working foundation plants like rhaphiolepis and pittosporum. If they weren't fertilized in the spring, feed them now.

☑ **HARVEST CROPS.** For further production, harvest beans, cucumbers, squash, and tomatoes frequently.

☑ **MOVE HOUSE PLANTS OUTDOORS.** House plants grow faster and look healthier if they can spend all or part of the summer outside. Give them a shady spot where they'll be protected from strong winds and harsh sunlight. Spray foliage with water occasionally to wash off dust.

☑ **PRUNE HYDRANGEAS.** After flower clusters fade to brown or green, cut back stalks to two or three buds from the base of the plant. The pruned stems will spring back rapidly, and next year's flowers will come from this new growth. (Don't prune stems that haven't bloomed yet. They'll bear flowers later this year or next.)

PEST CONTROL

☑ **BAKE AWAY FUNGUS AND NEMATODES.** Use the sun to destroy fungus, bacteria, and nematodes. Level the soil in the troublesome area with a rake or hoe, thoroughly moisten it, and cover tightly with a thick, transparent plastic tarp, weighted down around the edges. Leave tarp in place four to six weeks, then replant in fall in a new, healthy bed. Solarization works best in full sun and warm inland locations.

☑ **WASH AWAY PESTS.** Aphids, mites, thrips, whiteflies, and other small pests can be kept to manageable levels with water. Use a sharp stream of water to dislodge the pests from plant foliage. Avoid using pesticides—they kill beneficial insects, too.

Mountain Checklist

PLANTING

☑ **FALL VEGETABLES.** In all but the highest elevations, plant beets, broccoli, bush beans, cabbage, cauliflower, carrots, green onions, peas, spinach, and turnips. Below 5,000 feet, plant winter squash among spinach plants; it will fill in when you harvest the spinach. Above 7,000 feet, plant warm-season vegetables in large pots. If temperatures are predicted to drop below 60°, move pots under cover.

☑ **IRISES.** Dig overcrowded clumps three weeks after flowers fade. Discard dried-out or mushy rhizomes; cut apart healthy ones, trim leaves back to 6 inches, and replant in fast-draining soil in full sun. Plant new rhizomes the same way.

☑ **PERMANENT PLANTS.** Summer is an especially good time to plant ornamental trees and shrubs, ground covers, and vines. Planted now, they have the rest of the season to settle in. Nurseries are selling many new crabapple trees. If you're in the market for shrub roses, consider plants of the Carefree, Explorer, or Morden series, all of which are outstanding performers in cold country.

Sunset
CLIMATE ZONES

☐ 1-3 ☐ 10-11

MAINTENANCE

☑ **FERTILIZE.** Feed annuals and vegetables with high-nitrogen fertilizer, watering it in well.

☑ **CARE FOR BULBS.** In coldest climates, pluck faded flowers and seed heads from daffodils, tulips, and other spring-flowering bulbs. When bloom is finished, feed with high-phosphorus fertilizer. Let leaves remain until they turn brown, then clip them off.

☑ **CARE FOR ROSES.** After each bloom cycle, remove faded flowers, cutting them off just above a leaf node with five leaflets (nodes closest to the flower have three leaflets). Then fertilize and water deeply to encourage the next round of bloom.

☑ **MULCH.** To conserve moisture and reduce weeds, spread organic matter such as compost or straw under and around plants. Use black sheet plastic for heat-loving vegetables like eggplants, peppers, and tomatoes.

☑ **PRUNE CANE BERRIES.** After harvest, remove old raspberry canes when they begin to die. This helps prevent mildew by encouraging air circulation. In coldest climates, wait until August.

☑ **STAKE TALL PLANTS.** If you didn't do so at planting time, stake beans, delphiniums, peas, peonies, and tomatoes. Drive stakes at least 1 foot into the ground and tie plants to them securely.

☑ **THIN FRUIT TREES.** On trees with heavy fruit set, thin plums to 2 inches apart, and apples, nectarines, and peaches to at least 4 inches apart.

☑ **WATER.** Continue a regular deep-watering program for ground covers, lawns, shrubs, and trees.

PEST CONTROL

☑ **SPIDER MITES.** Mottled leaves and fine webs indicate spider mites. Spray with insecticidal soap or a stronger miticide. Keep foliage clean by rinsing with water.

Southwest Checklist

PLANTING AND HARVEST

☑ **HARVEST CROPS, FLOWERS.** As vegetables mature, pick them often to keep new ones coming, and to keep ripe ones from becoming overmature (cucumbers, zucchini) or downright rotten (tomatoes). To encourage continued bloom, pick flowers before they go to seed.

☑ **PLANT VEGETABLES.** Zones 1–2, 10–11: Plant beets, broccoli, cabbage, carrots, cauliflower, green onions, leaf lettuce, peas, spinach, and turnips for fall harvest. Zone 10 (Albuquerque and El Paso): Plant cantaloupe, eggplant, okra, peppers, pumpkins, tomatoes, watermelons, and winter squash. Potatoes can go in at month's end.

MAINTENANCE

☑ **CARE FOR ROSES.** After each bloom cycle, remove faded flowers, cutting them off just above a leaf node with five leaflets (nodes closest to the flower have three leaflets). Then fertilize and water deeply to stimulate the next round of bloom.

☑ **FERTILIZE.** Zones 1–2, 10–11: Feed annuals and vegetables with high-nitrogen fertilizer, and water it in well.

☑ **MULCH.** Apply a 3-inch layer of organic mulch around permanent plants to retain soil moisture, keep down weeds, and give plants a cool root run.

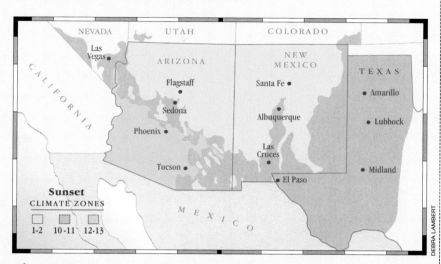

Sunset CLIMATE ZONES
1-2   10-11   12-13

DEBRA LAMBERT

☑ **THIN TREES.** Open up top-heavy trees like acacia, Brazilian pepper, mesquite, and olive to allow wind to pass through. Prune out suckers; dead, diseased, and injured wood; and branches that run closely parallel to each other.

☑ **WATER.** Water annual vegetables and flowers only after the top inch of soil has dried out. Basins and furrows help direct water to the roots.

PEST CONTROL

☑ **BUDWORMS.** These tiny worms eat the flower buds of geraniums, nicotiana, penstemons, and petunias, preventing further bloom. If they attack, spray plants every 7 to 10 days with *Bacillus thuringiensis* (BT), a biological control.

☑ **SPIDER MITES.** Mottled leaves and fine webs indicate spider mites; spray affected plants with insecticidal soap or a stronger miticide. Keep foliage clean by rinsing with water.

☑ **TOMATO HORNWORMS.** If you see chewed tomato leaves spotted with black droppings, look for green worms with white stripes and green horns with black sides. You can control the small ones by spraying BT; handpick the big ones (they can reach the size of a cigar).

Ideas for your garden

Out of Alaska

OOP DREAMS (ABOVE): Strapping delphiniums reach for stardom.

LOWERS GALORE (LEFT): The floral display round Dave and Beth Schroer's house in Homer (on the Kenai Peninsula) causes raffic jams. Every March, Dave starts eeds in his greenhouse for the garden. As soon as the snow melts and the ground haws, he digs in a mix of commercial ertilizer and compost. Then he sets nnuals in beds and pots—celosia, cosmos, narigolds, petunias, snapdragons, and alvias are always in the cast because of heir rich colors and long bloom periods. Regular watering, cool temperatures, nd regular deadheading keep them boking good.

Sourdough gardeners share their great techniques for growing plants beautifully— despite snow, moose, and grizzlies

■ Everything about Alaska is big. Mountains, valleys, rivers, glaciers, moose, and grizzly bears: you name it, it's big. Even Alaskans— latter-day pioneers—are big-spirited people with a can-do attitude. • Last summer I stopped in Willow, 70 miles northwest of Anchorage, to see Joe and Joan Marshall's garden. Joe met me at the door with a rifle under his arm. I'd heard that in some parts of Alaska—where the wild things are—it's every man for himself. Still, the gun-barrel greeting startled me. I held up my hands. "Don't shoot. I'm innocent." Joe laughed. "Naw, don't worry. We've had a grizzly bear out there the last couple of days. This is just to make sure he doesn't bother us." • Despite the rifle, I jumped at every rustle in the bushes as we rounded the bends in the garden paths. • Later, in Wasilla, about 45 miles north of Anchorage, Karin Covey showed me her raised beds, whose irregular shapes were inspired by her seven kids, seven grandchildren, dogs, and moose. "They seemed to follow the same paths. So I made the garden beds where they didn't go," Covey explained. • All over Alaska, novel ideas and great gardening stories drifted my way like snow in an Arctic winter. But the theme of each tale was the same: Alaska gardeners are courageous and inventive. • They're also undaunted by adversities that would send gardeners "Outside" into a tailspin. Winter temperatures regularly plunge to bone-chilling subzero double digits, and heavy snows snap tree branches. In summer, foraging moose dispatch entire vegetable gardens in a night, and grizzlies break off whole trees at the trunk to get to fruit in the top branches. • But nature makes up for these adversities with long summer days that coax plants to incredible sizes—delphiniums that tickle the eaves of a house, for instance. • And Alaskans make up for it with their joyful zest for gardening.

Y STEVEN R. LORTON • PHOTOGRAPHS BY NORMAN A. PLATE

island beds

Making the most of seasonal color

A SYMPHONY OF silvers, grays, blues, and pinks, with an occasional note of yellow or cream, occupies center stage outside Teena Garay's Homer home. Designed to be viewed from both inside and outside, this planting features tall plants in the rear, medium ones in the middle, and low plants in front. No forest of stakes holds up the tallest plants; Garay plants robust varieties close, so they'll sway rhythmically in the cool winds that blow off nearby Kachemak Bay. Dry-rock walls edge one side of the long bed; billowy plants such as creeping thyme and dianthus grow among the stones.

Between January and March, Garay starts seeds indoors and in a coldframe. In late April, she moves seedlings into pots, then plants them outdoors in June.

a border for all climates

Superstars of the border include creeping thyme (1), *Dianthus barbatus* (2), *Artemisia stellerana* 'Silver Brocade' (3), *Digitalis grandiflora* (4), *Aquilegia alpina* (5), *Nepeta sibirica* (6), 'Dwarf Blue Heaven' delphinium (7), *Filipendula ulmaria* (8), and 'Pacific Giant' delphinium (9). In the West's warmer climates, most of these plants are cool-season growers, best planted in fall for spring bloom.

perennial paradise

English country meets "The Call of the Wild"

CARVED OUT OF DENSE BIRCH and spruce forest, Les Brake's garden in Willow, 70 miles northwest of Anchorage, is packed with perennials growing in free-form island beds. As you wander among the beds, towering delphiniums, some 7 feet tall, block views of the cedar-and-log buildings. Carpets of bloom trail off into stretches of lawn, and all around, the woods seem thicker and more impenetrable than walls of Cotswold stone.

Brake grows mostly perennials. In February, he starts them indoors from seed under grow lights. In late March, he moves the seedlings into his greenhouse for transplanting outdoors in late May or early June.

A serious horticulturist, Brake has selected plants that reliably survive frigid temperatures and heavy snow. Peonies are among his favorites, and experience has taught him that the modern hybrids are less hardy than the old-fashioned offspring of *Paeonia lactiflora*. Other star performers in his garden are *Thalictrum rochebrunianum* (tall stalks of ferny foliage and smoke puffs of bloom), *Meconopsis grandis*

(eye-popping blue flowers that can measure 5 inches across), *Gentiana septemfida* (blue flowers), *Campanula latifolia* (blue-violet or white flowers), and *Digitalis purpurea* (pink, rose, and even creamy white blooms).

To tie the whole color scheme together, Brake uses two plants throughout the garden—*Helictotrichon sempervirens* (tufts of spiky blue foliage) and lamb's ears (*Stachys byzantina;* fuzzy mats of silver foliage). *Rosa glauca* adds splashes of small pink flowers, and Asiatic lilies shoot up here and there, exploding into bloom like little Roman candles.

Twiggy garden furniture provides rustic accents.

SIATIC hybrid ies provide ursts of color hroughout Les rake's garden Willow.
BOVE LEFT: In he cool dusk of n Alaskan ummer, a fire nd bright looms help arm the arden, shown about 2 A.M. EFT: Big island eds and narrow aths give the arden a headowlike ok, with a view f the birch oods beyond.

small-space ideas

ANCHORAGE: A FREESTANDING TRELLIS SCREEN (ABOVE). As ornamental as it is useful, this cedar trellis rises from a raised bed in Mel Monsen's vegetable garden. It's 6 feet tall and 8 feet long; both end posts are topped with finials. The horizontal pieces at the top are 2-by-4s; the inside grid is made of 1-by-1s. Sweet peas stretch up the grid; 'Snow Crystals' alyssum, dusty miller, and campanula grow at the trellis's feet. A pea gravel mulch holds in moisture, reflects heat, and eliminates mud when plants are watered.

WILLOW: COLOR ON HIGH (LEFT). Baskets of tuberous begonias hang all around the porch at Katherine and Stuart Bigler's home. To prevent cold soil from stunting growth, Stuart warms their frigid well water to 70°. He plants the begonia tubers in rich potting mix, applies 20-20-20 liquid plant food every two weeks, and waters plants daily during the growing season.

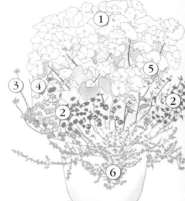

a pot for all climates

HOMER: *Lavatera trimestris* 'Mont Blanc' (1) spreads its cloud of white flowers above purple Swan River daisies (2), bluish marguerites (3), hot pink dianthus (4), and pansies (5) in this pot designed by Teena Garay. Silvery *Helichrysum petiolare* (6) tumbles over the edge. Garay fertilizes the pot twice a month with a liquid solution of 5-10-15 and clips spent blooms frequently.

virtuoso vegetables

Tall-tale cabbages

YOU'RE NOT LIKELY TO SEE 22-pound rutabagas in grocery stores, or for that matter, 24-pound onions, 14-pound beets, or squash that could wrestle a big-chested watermelon to the ground. But by late August in Alaska, such giant vegetables are horticultural heroes at the Alaska State Fair in Palmer. They win big prizes. The biggest winners of all are cabbages—hulking rosettes of green leaves that look like dinosaur food.

And when it comes to cabbages, few can butt heads with the heavyweights produced by Don Dinkel, professor emeritus of horticulture at the University of Alaska, Fairbanks. Dinkel's only competition might be the 89-pounders grown by his son, Gene, and his brother, Gene, and the 98-pound cabbage—the largest ever entered in the state fair—grown by another relative.

What's the Dinkel dynasty's secret? Variety, for one thing. 'O-S. Cross' is the standard "whopper," but Dinkel's not telling which one he grows. He'll say only that his cabbages are slow to mature so they're still fresh-looking by fair time.

Timing is critical, says Dinkel. If planted too early, a cabbage can "turn to mush" by fair time. He sows the seeds in the greenhouse around April 1, then transplants seedlings into well-amended garden soil in early May. He covers the beds with plastic to warm the soil. A drip system feeds and irrigates the plants daily.

Harvesting cabbages is a two-person job that involves cutting the plastic around each head, cutting the cabbage stalk with a handsaw, then lifting the plastic with the cabbage on top.

Dinkel has a few other tricks up his sleeve for growing giant cabbages and other vegetables in his 5-acre garden, despite assaults from moose, grizzlies, and voles, and frenzied digging by Dawg (who can shuck his own corn, thank you). The most important:

RAISE THE SOIL TEMPERATURE. Alaska soil temperatures rarely rise above 60° at root depth. Mulch planting beds with clear plastic to warm them. Covering the soil also helps prevent infestations of root maggots and cutworms, problems in Alaska.

PROVIDE CONSTANT FERTILIZER AND WATER. "Growing a prize-winning cabbage is like milking a cow. Ya gotta tend to it every day," says Dinkel.

CHOOSE THE RIGHT VARIETIES. Alaska's long days cause many crops to bolt prematurely. Annual crops—some squashes, for instance—produce female flowers too late in the season to yield fruit. So the right variety is very important. Cabbages aside, Dinkel's favorites include 'Emperor' and 'Shogun' broccoli, 'Earlivee' yellow sweet corn, 'Nantes' carrots, 'Ithaca' and 'Salinas' lettuce, 'Delira' and 'White Fox' cauliflower, and 'Golden Hubbard' squash.

— *Kathleen N. Brenzel*

Red, white, and bloom

BY SHARON COHOON

Come the Fourth of July, we don our patriotic T-shirts, hang the flag in front of the house, garland the deck with streamers, and decorate our tables in all-American colors. Hooray for the red, white, and blue! Meanwhile, the dominant color in our garden remains ... pastel pink? You can extend the spirit of the holiday in your garden without replanting a single bed. A few pots planted in red, white, and blue will do it.

The patriotic planting pictured above, designed by *Sunset* test garden

coordinator Bud Stuckey, is the floral equivalent of the American flag. Deep blue Chinese delphiniums are combined with red pentas (whose tall, starburst clusters look like fireworks), red verbena, a bit of 'Paprika' yarrow, trailing lobelia, and white sweet alyssum. As the lobelia and sweet alyssum grow, they'll cascade over the pot's edges.

You can copy Stuckey's design, or choose other plants whose flowers fit the patriotic palette. Blue is the tough part. Nature didn't create many flag-

blue flowers. Ageratum, blue lace flower (*Trachymene coerulea*), or blue annual salvia are a few sky-blue possibilities. Or buy the darkest blue petunias you can find.

Red is easy. Instead of pentas, you might prefer to use red begonias, annual salvia, petunias, nicotiana, Gerbera daisies, scarlet bee balm (*Monarda didyma*), or red miniature roses.

For white, you have other options as well, including pentas, verbena, vinca, petunias, and Shasta daisies.

Romancing the whites

White flowers and creamy foliage can make magic in moonlight or dappled shade

BY SHARON COHOON

■ White is such a quiet, unassuming color, never insisting on our attention. Yet it gets it. In fact, the cool beauty of an all-white garden on a warm summer day can freeze us in our tracks. Our knees buckle, our jaw drops, our breath quickens. Our overheated brain slows down. We're rooted in the moment and made mindful of all the small, wonderful details that make up a garden. And after dark it just gets better. Under moonlight, white flowers and foliage glow as if illuminated from within. How is it that white gardens create this magic? On the following pages, three gardeners share their theories on white gardens.

Tranquility has its strength, says Honolulu interior designer Mary Philpotts-McGrath. When Philpotts-McGrath moved into her home in historic Nu'uanu Valley, the basic elements of her green-and-white garden (pictured on page 56) were already in place—a taro irrigation stream (*auwai*) weaving through the front yard, a sweeping lawn of Hilo grass, and a swath of white-flowered spathiphyllum forming a low hedge along the drive. The serenity of the scene was immediately appealing to Philpotts-McGrath. "There's a peaceful, restorative, spiritual quality to this garden that I love very much and have been careful to preserve," she says.

The classic green-and-white garden is the horticultural equivalent of the little black dress, suggests Corine de Libran Longanbach, an interior designer in Rancho Santa Fe, California. Longanbach had an all-white garden when she lived in Provence, and she created another when she moved to California. A tall oleander hedge (white-flowering, naturally) wraps around her backyard pool, providing a backdrop for cream-colored flowers in containers and small island beds. "White gardens have a timeless elegance," says Longanbach. "They're never out of style, and you never tire of them."

'ICEBERG' ROSE blooms above a carpet of white hellebore, creeping sedum, and star jasmine.

MARION BRENNER

ISLANDS OF WHITE annuals and perennials curve through a Southern California garden. At the rear, a hedge of white oleander forms a backdrop.

Summer whites

These 10 flowering plants are especially fragrant at night.

•ANGEL'S TRUMPET (*Brugmansia candida*). Rangy shrub with large trumpet-shaped flowers in single and double forms. *Sunset* climate zones 16–24.

•GARDENIA (*G. jasminoides*). Evergreen shrub with very fragrant, double flowers. Zones 7–9, 12–16, 18–23.

•NICOTIANA. Tender perennials usually grown as summer annuals. Unimproved white species (*N. alata* and *N. sylvestris*) more fragrant than hybrids. All zones.

•NIGHT JESSAMINE (*Cestrum nocturnum*). Evergreen shrub with clusters of cream-colored flowers in summer. Zones 13, 16–24.

•STAR JASMINE (*Trachelospermum jasminoides*). Evergreen vine, ground cover, or sprawling shrub. Profuse clusters of sweet-scented flowers. Zones 8–24.

•STEPHANOTIS (*S. floribunda*). Tropical, evergreen vine with waxy, funnel-shaped flowers. Zones 23–24; elsewhere a house plant.

•SWEET MOCK ORANGE (*Philadelphus coronarius*). Deciduous shrub with small, oval leaves and perfumed flowers in summer. Zones 1–17.

•TUBEROSE (*Polianthes tuberosa*). Tuberous-rooted perennial with tubular flowers in spikelike clusters on 3-foot stems. Zones 15–17, 22–24.

•WHITE EVENING PRIMROSE (*Oenothera caespitosa*). Short, clump-forming perennial with narrow leaves and cup-shaped flowers that open at sunset. Zones 1–3, 7–14, 18–21.

•WHITE GINGER LILY (*Hedychium coronarium*). Broad-leafed, tender perennial with terminal clusters (as big as 12 inches) of richly fragrant flowers. Zones 17, 22–24, or in a greenhouse.

Though the Carolee Shields White Flower Garden at the University of California at Davis Arboretum (pictured on page 203) is the most romantic spot on the campus, superintendent Warren Roberts, one of its creators, appreciates it for more practical reasons. "White gardens look their best when you most want to see them," he says. Summers are blazing hot in California's Central Valley, making early evening the most enjoyable time to be in the garden. White remains visible long after other colors have faded into the shadows, says Roberts, so white flowers make great sense in a garden enjoyed mostly by moonlight. White flowers are often their most fragrant after dusk, which is another plus.

They are quiet gardens, these cool, white ones. But their silence speaks volumes.

DEIDRA WALPOLE

ABOVE: Sweet mock orange perfumes the air. RIGHT: A white-flowered form of *Centranthus ruber* complements the silvery white–edged leaves of *Miscanthus sinensis* 'Morning Light'. BELOW RIGHT: Drifts of white impatiens edge an irrigation stream in Honolulu.

Designing in white

Successful white gardens take planning. Here are a few guidelines.

• Provide a dark background for contrast. Yew, the traditional English choice for this role, is too formal for the more casual Western style. But euonymus, Italian cypress, myrtle, natal plum, oleander, pittosporum, viburnum, and many other common Western shrubs can play the same roles.

• Cluster white plants in dappled shade. Western light is strong compared to foggy old England's. White flowers can look washed-out in full sun here, but they always look inviting in dappled shade. (A massive monkeypod tree shades most of Philpotts-McGrath's garden, for instance, and southern magnolias soften the light at the Carolee Shields White Flower Garden.)

• Plant for all seasons. English white gardens need to look good only for the summer, but many Western gardens have no real downtime. So use plants that flower often—modern roses such as 'Iceberg', for instance—and use sufficient foliage with white variegation to make sure part of the garden always reads white.

• Consider lime instead of gray for additional interest. Where the English may use gray foliage to separate icy whites from creamy ones, some Western gardeners prefer to use yellow-green foliage and flowers.

White gardens to visit

If you need inspiration when designing your white garden, plan a visit to one of these public gardens.

Carolee Shields White Flower Garden, Davis Arboretum, on the UC Davis campus. Always open. Occasional special curated moonlight tours (go to www.aes.ucdavis. edu/arboretum/arbhome.html for days and times). For more information call (530) 752-4880.

Descanso Gardens, 1418 Descanso Dr., La Cañada Flintridge, CA. One-quarter acre of the International Rosarium is devoted to white roses and white companion plants. There is also a small silver foliage garden near Descanso's entrance. The gardens are open 9–4:30 daily except Christmas. Call (818) 952-4401 for more information.

William Land Park, 15th Ave., east of Land Park Dr., Sacramento. In the park's WPA Rock Garden section, look for the large white border designed by Daisy Mah (no signage). ◆

Flowers and foliage form a rich tapestry of colors and textures in this end-of-summer garden. For details on the late bloomers and colorful foliage shown here, see page 210.

August

gardenguide

Arizona natural in Tucson

■ A lizard darts across the rocks, then disappears into a crevice. Sheltered by an agave, a rabbit cautiously sniffs the air for predators before hopping to the edge of the pool for a drink.

The animals and plants are real, but the rest of this desert scene is hardly what it seems. The rocks and the pool are artificial creations—centerpieces of an award-winning landscape at the home of Mark and Jan Barmann in Tucson.

When the Barmanns relocated here

from California, they fell in love with the beauty of Arizona's natural attractions. In landscaping their new home, they sought to replicate one of their favorite places—Sabino Canyon just north of Tucson in the Santa Catalina Mountains.

The Barmanns worked closely with John Harlow Jr. of Harlow's Landscape and Nursery Center in Tucson to re-create the canyon environment. The design features a waterfall coursing down "rocks," which are actually fiber-

Best bets in beets

■ Spring-planted beets often have problems with insects and with bolting in summer heat. Beets planted in late summer fare much better.

Started early this month in the coldest *Sunset* climates (zones 1–2), they'll be mature enough to begin harvesting by hard frost; you can mulch them for winter, then harvest again in spring. In the high desert (zones 10–11), plant them late in the month for harvest from November through winter. In the intermediate and low deserts (zones 12–13), plant in September for harvest all winter.

Beets do best when given full sun (filtered sun in the desert), a deep root run in well-amended soil, and regular water. As plants grow, push soil around the beet crowns to keep them from getting that rough, weathered look.

RELIABLE BEETS include, from left, 'Winterkeeper', 'Golden', 'Albina Verduna', and 'Sangria'.

Last August, we planted several varieties in our test garden in Menlo Park, California. During harvest, we tasted boiled samples of each beet. Order seed from the sources listed at right.

'**Albina Verduna**' (TS), a white variety, is earthy, with a sweet aftertaste.

'**Golden**' (WAB) is a gold-fleshed beauty with a flavor that reminded tasters of sweet potatoes.

'**Kleine Bol**' (SG) was the clear favorite. Tasters loved the big, sweet beet flavor of the juicy, deep red meat.

'**Sangria**' (SG) has sweet, crunchy, dark red flesh, but only mild flavor.

'**Winterkeeper**' (TS), another red, scored well, but pick it young—a tough texture may develop when globes get really big.

SG: Shepherd's Garden Seeds (860/482-3638)

TS: Territorial Seed Company (541/942-9547)

WAB: W. Atlee Burpee & Co. (800/888-1447)

— Jim McCausland

RED FRUITS of prickly pear cactus punctuate this planting.

TERRENCE MOORE

reinforced concrete.

number of existing palo verde trees left in place to anchor the land-e. New plantings combine unthirsty e plants with other drought-tolerant ies. In the foreground of the photo e are Engelmann prickly pear (*Op- a engelmannii*), cow's horn agave ve bovicornuta), purple prickly (*Opuntia violacea* 'Santa-Rita'), littleleaf or foothills palo verde (*Cer- m microphyllum*). — *Teri Sivilli*

---

tags

■ In the movie *Green Card,* Gérard Depardieu carefully places a seed packet on a little stake after replanting Andie MacDowell's garden boxes with vegetables. A charming gesture, to be sure, but no doubt that seed packet looked pretty ragged after being exposed to sun and rain. If only Depardieu had used one of Ferry-Morse's attractive new seed packet row markers, maybe MacDowell could have benefited from his efforts. A plastic "envelope" encases each empty seed packet, keeping it looking new indefinitely. A sturdy green stake anchors it in the soil. These row markers are available from Ferry-Morse Seed Company ($1.25 each, $1.89 for two, plus shipping). To order, call (800) 283-6400. — *Lauren Bonar Swezey*

NORMAN A. PLATE (2)

CHARLES MANN

SPECIAL EFFECT

Summer snow in Aspen

■ When landscape designer Phillip Hedrick was asked to plan the gardens for a new house in Aspen, the project started with a hike. The owner took Hedrick for a walk along a mountain trail to show him the effect he wanted. Inspired by the wild daisies they saw, Hedrick decided to re-create the scene on the hillside above the house. You see the results at left: a blizzard of 'Alaska' Shasta daisies threaded by a path.

To prepare the approximately 3,000-square-foot site, Hedrick spread an 8-inch layer of compost and topsoil ove the hillside, then set out 4-inch po of Shasta daisies at 8-inch interval: They are interplanted with snow-ir summer (*Cerastium tomentosum* whose white flowers bloom a mont earlier than the daisies. Columbine and blanket flowers are spotte through the planting to add colc accents.

The path is made from road-ba gravel (no larger than ¼ inch) laid inches deep, then repeatedly damp ened and compacted with a roller. Thi surface is very firm, but maintains th look and feel of a wildland trail.

To keep the flowers thriving, a 1(10-0 formula of liquid fertilizer is ap plied in early June and again in mic August, with a last feeding of liqui 5-10-0 in October. After seed head have ripened at season's end, th flower stalks are cut off 2 inches abov ground level with string trimmers. Th cuttings are left in place as mulch unt spring, when they're raked off. Durin the raking, seeds fall out to add mor daisies to the display. — *J.M.*

LATE SHOW

Grand finale to summer

■ After a big show of blooms, many flowering perennials and shrubs shut down and go on vacation by late summer. But that isn't the case in the garden John Roberts designed for Patrick North's front yard in west Seattle (shown on page 206). Roberts believes that a Pacific Northwest garden should look its best in late summer. "That's when we're outdoors the most," he says. So Roberts filled North's garden with late bloomers and colorful foliage.

Roberts's favorite end-of-summer flowers include silvery blue *Eryngium tripartitum*, crimson *Lychnis coronaria*, coppery rose *Sedum telephium* 'Autumn Joy', and *Verbena bonariensis*, whose spiky purple flowers tower over the garden. To this eclectic mix of perennials, he adds such standards as petunias and Oriental lilies.

The other half of Roberts's late-summer show comes from foliage. Silver and red foliage plays off green-leafed plants and a small lawn. Among the sil-ver-leafed plants, Roberts favors *Artemisia* 'Powis Castle', dusty miller and lamb's ears (*Stachys byzantina*). The silvery foliage contrasts with the burgundy red leaves of *Berberis thun bergii* 'Helmond Pillar', *Dahlia* 'Bec nall Beauty', and *Euphorbia dulci* 'Chameleon'. — *Steven R. Lorto*

BACK TO BASICS

Dividing bearded iris

NORMAN A. PLATE

■ When summer heats up, bearded irises go dormant; that's the best time to dig and divide established plants in all but the hottest desert areas. Dividing irises every three or four years revitalizes crowded clumps. In the low and intermediate deserts, wait to divide irises until the soil cools down in October or November.

First, use a spade to pry each clump out of the ground. Discard old, leafless rhizomes from the center of the clump. Then break or cut the thick, vigorous rhizomes apart at their knucklelike joints into pieces 3 to 4 inches long, as shown above. Trim leaves on each piece back to 6- to 8-inch fans, and clip stringy roots back to about 6 inches. Set rhizomes in dry shade for a day or two to let cuts heal.

Replant the divisions 1 to 2 feet apart in soil amended with compost. Water them well until winter rains take over.

Pacific Northwest Garden Notebook

BY STEVEN R. LORTON

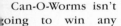

Ah, August! Fuchsias dripping from hanging baskets, lazy afternoons spent swinging in my hammock. So what am I thinking about? Worms. And why not? My worms are working their hardest this month, converting plant waste from the garden and vegetable scraps from the kitchen into organically rich compost. At my home, they perform their recycling wonders inside a contraption called Can-O-Worms. I bought it from Mary Wilcox and George Weiss of Sonoma, California, whom I met at a garden show. They were so wound up about worms that they convinced me I needed their can. I lugged one onto the airplane, along with a box containing 2,000 red wiggler worms (*Eisenia fetida*), and headed back to Seattle.

Can-O-Worms isn't going to win any beauty contests. Imported from Australia, it is made of black recycled plastic and has five parts that, when stacked, form a cylinder 20 inches in diameter and 29 inches tall. At the bottom is a basin with a spigot. Above the basin are three trays with perforated bottoms. You start the vermicomposting process, as it's called, by putting vegetable waste and worms in the first (bottom) tray. Then you begin adding things like carrot tops, limp lettuce, and coffee grounds. This is gourmet fodder for worms, who devour the stuff and transform it into castings. When the first tray is full of scraps, you place the second tray over it; when it fills up, you add the third. The worms wiggle through the perforations, making their way upward from tray to tray. The castings are ready to use as a soil amendment.

The worms also secrete a liquid known as "worm tea," which trickles down through the trays and collects in the basin. You turn the spigot to drain it off, then pour this mild liquid fertilizer directly over the root zones of plants. My fuchsias have never looked better.

You may even find yourself developing a certain affection for the contraption's hardworking inhabitants. Last winter, I put my bin in the basement because I couldn't stand the thought of leaving the worms out in the cold.

If you can't find one in local garden supply centers or nurseries, order from Can-O-Worms, 295 Fifth St. W., Sonoma, CA 95476; (800) 479-3826 or (707) 935-3826. The cost is $119.95 plus shipping. A pound of worms (about 1,000) costs $19.95.

that's a good question ...

Q: My compost pile seems to stop working in late summer every year, then starts up again in fall. What's wrong?

A: Simple: like everything else, it dries out in hot weather. If you apply enough water to keep the pile as moist as a wrung-out sponge and turn it every few days, it ought to make compost as fast as it did in spring.

Northern California Garden Notebook

BY LAUREN BONAR SWEZEY

*a*ugust may be vacation time. But it's gardening time, too. Time to plant fall vegetables: broccoli, cabbage, cauliflower, and peas, for example. Over the years, *Sunset's* test garden coordinator, Bud Stuckey, and I have grown and tested many varieties of cool-season crops both in spring and fall, and we've always had the best success with fall-planted crops. Transplants set out from mid-August to mid-September really get a jump on the season; they develop into big, healthy plants while the soil is still warm and they start producing just when the weather cools. We sow seeds of broccoli, cabbage, and cauliflower in flats or pots in early August so we can get the plants in the ground about six weeks later (although we've bought transplants when pinched for time). Peas do best when sowed directly in the ground in August and September.

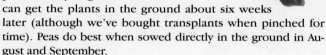

COOL-SEASON FAVORITES

We don't grow just any old pea or broccoli plant, because varieties differ in production and flavor. 'Super Sugar Mel' snap pea is my all-time favorite pea for flavor and dependability.

And for good production and flavor, you can't beat 'Premium Crop' broccoli. Both crops are available through Shepherd's Garden Seeds; (860) 482-3638. 'Snow Crown' cauliflower produces beautiful, large white heads, and 'Stonehead' cabbage develops sweet, firm heads on disease-resistant plants. These two plus 'Premium Crop' broccoli are available from Nichols Garden Nursery; (541) 928-9280.

A WEB SITE FOR BAY AREA GARDENERS

Many gardeners enjoy working in their gardens more than sitting in front of a computer. But computers serve their purposes. Surfing the Internet can turn up a wealth of information on plants, sources, and events. One Web site I often visit for local happenings is the Bay Area Gardener (www.gardens.com). Garden events are listed by date for a two- to four-month period so you can plan outings well in advance. This site also posts stories and columns about gardening with children, gardening sources, classes and talks, and a bulletin board where you can ask questions. Editor Carol Moholt updates the site weekly, so there's always something new to see.

that's a good question ...

Q: I have a large, unsightly brown fence lining the back of my yard and would like to cover it with a climbing vine. I live on sunny Potrero Hill. What do you suggest? — *Melissa, San Francisco*

A. Fortunately, there are a number of vines that will do the trick. Four good evergreen ones are bower vine (*Pandorea jasminoides*), *Hardenbergia violacea*, potato vine (*Solanum jasminoides*), and violet trumpet vine (*Clytostoma callistegioides*).

Southern California Garden Notebook

BY SHARON COHOON

When it comes to deciding which plants to propagate, Michael Kartuz must lead with his nose. The catalog for his nursery, Kartuz Greenhouses, says his specialty is showy plants for indoor and patio gardens—begonias, gesneriads, and that sort of thing. But color is obviously not the only criterion for this Vista nurseryman. His plant descriptions are full of phrases like "honey-scented," "freesia-like," and "spicy-sweet." Clearly, he is a con-

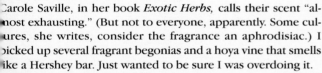

noisseur of fragrance. Just the man, I decided, to help me in my mission—turning my garden into a more "scentual" retreat.

I came home from his nursery with two varieties of Arabian jasmine (*Jasminum sambac*), said to be one of the most powerfully fragrant blossoms on the planet. Garden writer Carole Saville, in her book *Exotic Herbs,* calls their scent "almost exhausting." (But not to everyone, apparently. Some cultures, she writes, consider the fragrance an aphrodisiac.) I picked up several fragrant begonias and a hoya vine that smells like a Hershey bar. Just wanted to be sure I was overdoing it.

Kartuz Greenhouses is primarily a mail-order operation, but visitors are welcome from 9 to 4 Wednesdays through Saturdays (appointments suggested); (760) 941-3613. I recommend sending for a catalog before you go. Walking into a greenhouse full of tiny pots of unfamiliar things is a bit daunting; having in mind a few plants you'd like to see jump-starts conversation.

Speaking of Arabian jasmine, in *Exotic Herbs* Saville says it's the nicest thing you can do for water. Drop a few blossoms in a water-filled jar, refrigerate it 24 hours or more, remove the blossoms, strain the liquid, and enjoy the perfumed water. Or—and I'm looking forward to this—drop a few flowers in your bathwater.

AH, ROMANCE ...

See public gardens in a new light—moonlight. Descanso Gardens in La Cañada Flintridge, Quail Botanical Gardens in Encinitas, and the Arboretum of Los Angeles County in Arcadia undergo a magical transformation after dark. So do other public gardens. Take advantage of this season's evening concerts, plays, and culinary events to experience this fairyland atmosphere. Call Descanso at (818) 952-4400, Quail at (760) 436-3036, and the Arboretum at (626) 821-3222 for information about evening programs. See the weekend listings in your local papers for additional opportunities.

IT'S TIME TO WINDPROOF YOUR POTS

Container plants dry out alarmingly fast in hot summer weather, especially during Santa Ana winds. If you can't monitor them as frequently as you should, take precautions. Group small (4- to 8-inch) potted plants together in a larger pot or other container and fill the empty spaces with sand or soil up to the pots' rims. (The soil acts as an insulator.) Move the pots to a shadier spot. Cluster larger pots together in groups of three or more so they'll shade each other.

Westerner's Garden Notebook

BY JIM McCAUSLAND

*W*hen you think of herbs, you probably think of traditional ones like rosemary and thyme. But Rob Proctor and David Macke, who garden in Denver, don't think of herbs in traditional terms, nor do they confine them to separate pots or knot gardens. That accounts for the surprising plant combinations you'll see in their new book, *Herbs in the Garden: The Art of Intermingling* (Interweave Press, Loveland, CO, 1997; $29.95, 800/272-2193).

Color photos of their mingled plantings reflect the authors' broad definition of herbs: "If you can cook with it; garnish a salad with it; soothe a burn or scratch with it; make a tea from it; soak in the tub with it; perfume your sheets with it; kill a bug with it ... treat a disease with it; weave, dye, or spin something with it ... or cast a spell with it—it's an herb."

You'll even learn which herb to invite to your next garden party. "Every party," they write, "needs a guest like a lady's-mantle, in whose company the catnips glow a little brighter, the sweet Williams look more dapper, the bellflowers shine more radiantly."

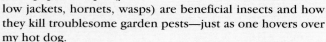

WHEN YELLOW JACKETS COME TO THE PICNIC

My friends know I'm fascinated by insects, so I get occasional questions from them about how to deal with yellow jackets at picnics. Invariably, I launch into a spiel about how paper wasps (yellow jackets, hornets, wasps) are beneficial insects and how they kill troublesome garden pests—just as one hovers over my hot dog.

At picnics keep garbage cans sealed and well away from your table. You can also install a commercial trap at the picnic site, or make your own by suspending a piece of fish or liverwurst an inch above a bucket of soapy water. When they take off from the bait, paper wasps will often drop down slightly and drown in the water.

Don't bother eliminating their papery nests unless they're very close; the wasps may be coming from several nests anywhere within a thousand yards. If you have to zap a nest, do it at night or early on a cool morning by spraying a commercial knock-down pesticide at the nest's entrance from a safe distance (some aerosols can reach 9 feet).

SAVING SEEDS

When I first started trying to save my own vegetable seeds, wiser gardeners advised me not to save hybrid seed: its offspring were always different from the parents, and almost never better. So I tried seed-saving only with nonhybrid (or open-pollinated) vegetables. But my results were mixed. The tomatoes were usually great, but the corn didn't reliably live up to its parents' quality. Why?

After doing some research, I learned that seed-grown plants are most true to type when they're self-pollinated, as beans, peas, and tomatoes are.

Wind-pollinated crops like corn and spinach can cross with plants that are as far as a mile away. If your sweet corn crosses with your neighbor's popcorn, you'll have ears of mixed soft, sweet and hard kernels.

Insect-pollinated plants, which include cucumbers, eggplant, melons, peppers, and squash, can be cross-pollinated by plants up to ¼ mile away. But the closer plants are (in your neighbor's garden, for example), the more likely they are to cross with yours.

The bottom line is that self-pollinated plants grow true from seed most often, wind-pollinated plants least often, and insect-pollinated plants somewhere in between.

To save seeds, shake the dry seed heads or break open the pods over a newspaper. Pour the ripened seeds into a plastic film canister, label and date it, put it in your refrigerator, and plant the seeds next spring or fall.

Pacific Northwest Checklist

PLANTING

☑ **ANNUALS.** Zones 4–7: With a couple of months of warm weather ahead, you can still plant annuals for a good, long show. Impatiens, marigolds, and pelargoniums are all good candidates. For partially shady places, try New Guinea hybrid impatiens, with robust blooms and colorful foliage.

☑ **FALL CROPS.** Zones 4–7: Early in the month, set out beets, Chinese cabbage, mustard, onions, radishes, spinach, and any of the cole crops.

MAINTENANCE

☑ **HARVEST HERBS FOR DRYING.** Pick herbs in the morning just after dew has dried. Place a clean window screen horizontally atop concrete blocks (one under each corner) in a cool, dry spot out of direct sunlight and where dust won't blow on it. Lay the herbs out on the screen, leaving enough room for air to circulate around the plant parts; when herbs are completely dry, store them in jars.

☑ **PROPAGATE SHRUBS.** It's fun to start new plants from cuttings of your favorite shrubs. Evergreen candidates include azaleas, camellias, daphne, euonymus, holly, and rhododendrons. Deciduous plants like hydrangeas and magnolias can also be propagated this way. Take 4- to 6-inch-long cuttings in the morning. Strip off all but the top three or four leaves. Dip the cut ends into rooting hormone, then insert them into 4-inch pots filled with sterile soil, and water well. Place the cuttings in a spot out of direct sunlight and keep them thoroughly moist. Before frost hits, move them into a greenhouse or sunroom. Next spring, you'll have rooted plants to bed or transplant to 1-gallon cans.

☑ **PRUNE CANE BERRIES.** On June-bearing plants, remove all canes that produced fruit this season. On ever-bearing plants, cut back by half any canes that have already borne fruit.

☑ **WATER.** Where water-use ordinances permit, irrigate moisture-loving plants like rhododendrons deeply twice a week. Spray the foliage too; it washes dust off leaves and helps stressed plants absorb water quickly.

PEST CONTROL

☑ **CARPENTER ANTS.** If you use logs or other pieces of dead wood as natural garden sculptures, keep an eye out for carpenter ants. They tend to march along on well-defined trails. If you see them going toward your house, you're likely to have an infestation. Unless you really know what you're doing, call a professional exterminating service.

Northern California Checklist

PLANTING

☑ **PLANT FOR SUMMER-TO-FALL BLOOM.** Some perennials that bloom from now into fall include achillea, asters, begonias, common geraniums, coreopsis, dahlias, daylilies (some), fortnight lilies, lantana, *Limonium perezii,* Mexican bush sage, scabiosa, and verbena. Check hardiness before shopping; a few plants, such as *Limonium perezii* and Mexican bush sage, aren't hardy in all zones.

☑ **PLANT A SHADE TREE.** For optimum cooling effect, plant a tree on the southwest side of the house in a spot where it will shade windows. Use a deciduous tree for shade in summer and sun in winter. In milder climates try Chinese hackberry, Chinese pistache, Japanese pagoda tree, 'Raywood' ash, or red oak. In cold climates try American hornbeam, Eastern redbud, honey locust, or little-leaf linden.

☑ **SOW COOL-SEASON CROPS.** Zones 7–9, 14–17: To start broccoli, cabbage, cauliflower, chard, lettuce, and spinach seeds in containers, choose a well-drained potting mix and fill flats or pots. Moisten the mix thoroughly. Sow seeds according to package directions. Fine seeds are usually planted ½ inch deep. Sow carrots, onions, peas, and radishes directly in the ground: mix compost into the soil, soak it thoroughly, and plant. Sow peas about 1 inch deep. Zones 1–2: Where frosts aren't expected until late October, sow seeds of beets, carrots, spinach, and radishes.

Sunset
CLIMATE ZONES

☐ Mountain (1-2)
☐ Valley (7-9)
☐ Inland (14)
☐ Coastal (15-17)

DEBRA LAMBERT

MAINTENANCE

☑ **CHECK SOIL MOISTURE.** Before watering, always check soil moisture first to see if plants need it. Either dig down with a trowel (an inch or two for shallow-rooted plants, 6 to 18 inches for deep-rooted shrubs and trees) or use a soil probe. For the best watering hose around, look for Flexogen garden hose by Gilmour at building supply stores (also available by mail from Peaceful Valley Farm Supply; a 50-foot hose costs $26.50 plus tax and shipping; 888/784-1722).

☑ **FEED ROSES.** Zones 7–9, 14–17: Now's the time to feed roses to get a big fall flush of blooms. David Lowell of Livermore, California, feeds his prize-winning roses twice a year, once in February and once in August, using this recipe: 1 cup 12-12-12 fertilizer, ½ cup bonemeal, 2 tablespoons Epsom salts (available at pharmacies), and ½ cup sulfur (iron sulfate, ironite, or soil sulfur). Mix together. Apply this amount to each established (well-watered) rose and mix it into the soil. Then sprinkle one shovelful of well-composted chicken manure around each rose and water well.

☑ **HARVEST FRUITS AND VEGETABLES.** Search bean, summer squash, and tomato plants thoroughly so you don't miss ripe ones. If you want to preserve tomatoes by canning them, harvest while they're still firm; soft tomatoes may contain harmful bacteria that can spoil the contents. Harvest corn when the tassels have withered and the kernels are well formed and squirt milky juice when punctured.

Southern California Checklist

PLANTING

✔ **PLANT FINAL SUMMER CROPS.** Coastal gardeners (*Sunset* climate zones 22–24) can set out transplants of eggplant, peppers, squash, and tomatoes. ('Champion', 'Celebrity', and 'Super Sweet 100' cherry tomatoes are good varieties to try for fall harvesting.) Coastal, inland (zones 18–21), and low-desert (zone 13) gardeners can sow a final crop of beans or corn.

✔ **START WINTER CROPS.** Coastal, inland, and high-desert (zone 11) gardeners can start sowing cool-season vegetables in flats midmonth. After six to eight weeks, the seedlings will be ready to transplant to the garden. Good candidates include beets, broccoli, brussels sprouts, cabbage, carrots, cauliflower, collards, kale, kohlrabi, leeks, lettuces, mustard, peas, radishes, spinach, Swiss chard, and turnips.

✔ **START SWEET PEAS.** For sweet peas by December, plant seeds now. To speed germination, soak seeds overnight before planting. Provide a wall or trellis for vines to climb.

✔ **SHOP FOR LATE BLOOMERS.** If blooms are sparse in your garden in late summer, look for perennials that put on a late-season show at local nurseries. Buy now, but hold off planting until weather cools in September or October. Keep plants well watered and in light shade until ready to plant.

MAINTENANCE

✔ **WATER AS NEEDED.** Give mature trees and established shrubs a slow, deep soak once a month. Water avocado, citrus, and stone fruit trees thoroughly and deeply every 7 to 10 days, depending on location. Water tropicals deeply every 5 to 7 days. Water Bermuda grass lawns once or twice a week, tall fescues two or three times. Plants in containers, especially hanging baskets, may have to be watered daily, especially during Santa Ana winds. A good rule of thumb for everything: if the top few inches are dry, water.

✔ **PRUNE WATER SPROUTS AND SUCKERS.** Tall, thin shoots that grow straight up from citrus and stone fruit tree trunks and branches should be removed as soon as they are noticed. They drain the tree's energy away from fruit production. Cut shoots off flush with the bark. Suckers that develop at the base of the plant should be removed, too. Pull them off rather than cutting them away.

✔ **TRIM SPENT BLOOMS.** To promote late flowering, lightly trim coreopsis, dianthus, felicias, foxglove, marguerites, penstemon, yarrow, and other perennials.

PEST CONTROL

✔ **WASH AWAY PESTS.** Aphids, mites, thrips, whiteflies, and other small pests can be kept to manageable numbers with regular syringing. Use a sharp stream of water to dislodge them from plant foliage. Avoid pesticides; they kill beneficial insects too.

Mountain Checklist

PLANTING & HARVEST

☑ **HARVEST CROPS.** Even if you can't use them right away, pick apples, beets, broccoli, bush beans, cauliflower, peaches, potatoes, raspberries, strawberries, summer squash, sweet corn, tomatoes, and zucchini. Never let the crop rot on the plant; it cuts production and spreads disease.

☑ **HARVEST FLOWERS FOR DRYING.** Pick blossoms with long stems, strip off the leaves, bundle flowers together, and hang them upside down in a garage or basement until they're dry.

☑ **HARVEST HERBS.** Pick them after the dew has dried in the morning. Use herbs fresh, or air-dry them on a screen in the shade or hang bundles in a dry, shady place.

☑ **PLANT FALL CROPS.** Where frosts aren't expected until late October, sow seeds of beets, carrots, radishes, and spinach for fall harvest. In mildest climates, set out transplants of broccoli, cabbage, and cauliflower.

☑ **SOW WILDFLOWERS.** Sow seeds of annual and perennial wildflowers now for bloom next spring. Try bachelor's buttons, coreopsis, Mexican hat, perennial blue flax, poppies, prairie asters, Rocky Mountain penstemon, and yellow coneflower.

Sunset
CLIMATE ZONES

☐ 1-3   ☐ 10-11

DEBRA LAMBERT

MAINTENANCE

☑ **CARE FOR ANNUALS.** Shear or pinch off faded flowers, then water and fertilize to encourage bloom through summer's end.

☑ **CHECK FOR CHLOROSIS.** When leaves turn yellowish while veins remain green, plants may be suffering from iron deficiency. Correct the condition (called chlorosis) by applying chelated iron. If leaves are simply yellowish and you can spot no cultural problems, apply a complete fertilizer.

☑ **DIVIDE PERENNIALS.** After delphiniums, irises, Oriental poppies, and Shasta daisies bloom, cut them back, dig, and divide large clumps into sections. Add organic matter to the soil and replant the divisions. (In shortest-season areas, wait until spring to dig and replant.)

☑ **PROTECT VEGETABLES.** In high-elevation gardens, protect vegetables from early cold temperatures by placing cardboard, glass, or row covers over plants by late afternoon. Remove covers before midmorning.

PEST CONTROL

☑ **POWDERY MILDEW.** Dahlias, peas, roses, squash, and zinnias are particularly susceptible to this powdery white fungus. To keep it from spreading, avoid overhead watering and remove and destroy diseased stems and leaves. In severe cases, control with a sulfur-based spray or a fungicide such as benomyl.

☑ **SLUGS.** Beer traps, handpicking, and bait containing metaldehyde or mesurol are all effective in slug-prone plantings. Keep the poison bait away from children and pets.

Southwest Checklist

PLANTING

☑ **COOL-SEASON CROPS.** Zone 10: Sow beans, cabbage family members, collards, corn, cucumbers, potatoes, spinach, squash, and Swiss chard early in the month; put in transplants at month's end. Zone 11: Sow beets, carrots, radishes, and spinach, and put in transplants of broccoli, cabbage, and cauliflower for fall harvest. Zones 12–13: Late in August, sow beans, cabbage family members, carrots, collards, corn, cucumbers, green onions, leeks, lettuce, and squash for a late harvest.

☑ **SOW WILDFLOWERS.** Cultivate soil lightly, broadcast seed, then cover with ¼ to ½ inch of organic mulch such as ground bark. Some flowers to try include Arizona lupine (*Lupinus arizonicus*), blackfoot daisies (*Melampodium leucanthum*), blue flax, chia (*Salvia columbariae*), coreopsis, desert marigolds (*Baileya multiradiata*), firecracker penstemon (*P. eatonii*), firewheel (*Gaillardia pulchella*), goldfields (*Lasthenia chrysotoma*), Mexican gold poppies (*Eschscholzia mexicana*), Parry's penstemon (*P. parryi*), scented verbena (*V. gooddingii*), and sticky asters (*Machaeranthera bigelovii*).

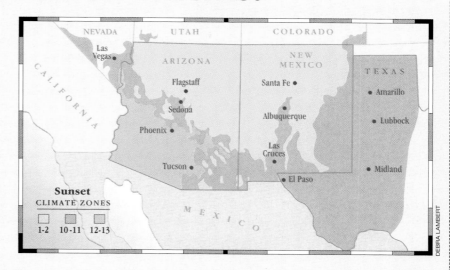

MAINTENANCE

☑ **CARE FOR ROSES.** To help roses get ready for strong fall bloom, acidify the soil with soluble sulfur (Disper-Sul), fortify it with complete fertilizer, and apply iron chelate to correct chlorosis. Water plants thoroughly.

☑ **WATER.** Thoroughly drench the roots of permanent landscape plants.

PEST CONTROL

☑ **LAWN PESTS.** Just as chinch bugs can cause St. Augustine grass to dry out and die back, microscopic Bermuda grass mites can do the same to Bermuda lawns, giving them a classic shaving-brush look. The treatment for both is the same: an application of chlorpyrifos (Dursban) or diazinon.

☑ **SOUTHWESTERN CORN BORERS.** If translucent patches skeletonize leaves of corn plants, corn borer larvae are the likely culprits. They can also kill the plants' growing tips. Spray plants with BT (*Bacillus thuringiensis*), a biological control.

PINK BLOOMS of *Nerine*
bowdenii brighten a bed of aloes,
bromeliads, and hen and chicks.
Behind, tillandsias and orchid
cactus grow in a plum tree.

Tropical dreams

David Feix turned his garden into a
desert-to-jungle sanctuary. His secret?
Tough plants with a lush look

BY LAUREN BONAR SWEZEY
PHOTOGRAPHS BY NORMAN A. PLATE

■ The striking cluster of 5-foot-tall bromeliads growing
next to the front porch is the first hint that David Feix's
garden is different. A step out the back door confirms
it. Tillandsias growing in trees? Yellow gingers blooming in garden beds? Is this Northern California or a
subtropical cloud forest in Brazil's Serra dos Orgãos
(Organ Mountains)? One thing is certain: it's a desert-
to-jungle paradise.

Although many of the plants in Feix's garden come
from the mountains of Central and South America,
they do just as well in Feix's cool, mild, and mostly
shady garden. Of his top 10 favorites (listed on page
222), 5 grow well in desert climates too.

Feix first became interested in bromeliads while on
an extended trip to Brazil. But he really got hooked after he returned home and joined the San Francisco
Bromeliad Society. "I started accumulating free plants,"
says Feix.

Soon his interests expanded to other cloud forest
plants, which he picked up at several Southern California nurseries and at plant sales at UC Berkeley and
Strybing Arboretum and Botanical Gardens in San
Francisco. About 150 species of bromeliads and hundreds of other, mostly subtropical, flowering plants
now grow in his garden.

"Many tropical-style gardens use cannas and other
plants that go dormant in winter," says Feix. "But mine
really looks like it's in the tropics, because the bromeliads always look good." Other plants, such as *Gordonia
axillaris,* tree dahlias, and yellow gingers, give his garden the year-round bloom season typical of the tropics.

Each area of the garden has a slightly different look,
depending partly on the amount of light the area gets,
Feix explains. In the sunniest part of the garden, he
combines bromeliads, aloes, cactus, and kangaroo

IN FOREGROUND, red-and-yellow *Aechmea calyculata* blooms next to blue-gray *Aloe striata* and pink-flowered *Pimelea ferruginea*. Jug behind low pots holds yellow ginger.

Feix's top ten tropicals

•**Asparagus retrofractus.** Erec[t] plant with tufts of green leaves. Grows 8 to 10 feet tall. Zone[s] 12–24. Full sun or part shade.

•**Billbergia sanderiana.** Brome[-] liad with spiny-toothed, leather[y] leaves. Loose 10-inch-long cluster[s] of flowers have blue petals an[d] rose-colored bracts. Grows 1[?] inches wide by 18 inches tal[l]. Zones 12–13, 16–24. Full sun i[n] the fog belt or part shade.

•**Brazilian plume flowers** (*Justici[a] carnea*). Evergreen shrub with sof[t] wooded stems, and clusters of pin[k] flowers midsummer to fall. Grows 4 t[o] 5 feet tall. Zones 8–9, 13–24 (top[s] freeze at 29°). Part shade.

•**Fuchsia boliviana.** Large-leafe[d] fuchsia with pendulous red or pin[k]-and-white flowers. Grows 5 to 1[?] feet tall. Resistant to fuchsia mit[e]. Zones 15–17, 23–24. Part shade.

•**Gordonia axillaris.** Shrub o[r] small tree with glossy green foliag[e] and white camellia-like flowers O[c-] tober through March. Grows 1[?] feet tall or more. Zones 14–1[7], 23–24. Full sun to part shade.

•**Nerine bowdenii.** South Africa[n] bulb produces 12-inch-long gloss[y] green leaves. Pink flowers appea[r] in fall on 2-foot stems. Zones 8–9, 13–24. Sun or part shade.

•**Tillandsia stricta.** Small clum[p] of spiky grayish foliage produce[s] blue flowers with pink bract[s]. Grows 6 inches across. Zone[s] 14–24. Full sun or part shade.

•**Tree dahlia** (*D. imperialis*). Mult[i]-stemmed tree with feathery foliag[e] produces 4- to 8-inch-wide lavende[r] flowers on branch ends in late fal[l]. Frost kills tops back. Grows to 2[?] feet tall. Zones 4–6, 8–9, 14–24. Fu[ll] sun or part shade.

•**Veltheimia bracteata.** South A[f]rican bulb produces clusters of t[u]bular coral pink flowers on 1- to 1½-foot stems from winter into sprin[g]. Foliage grows 1 foot tall. Zones 1[?], 16–24. Thrives in dry shade.

•**Yellow ginger** (*Hedychiu[m] flavum*). Fragrant yellow flowe[rs] appear in late fall to winter on th[e] tops of long stems. Grows 5 to [?] feet tall. Zones 14–24. Full sun o[r] part shade inland. ◆

paws with sun-loving tropicals.

The back of the garden is very shady in winter and brighter in summer, so Feix plants seasonal color there. He also constantly rotates containers of flowering plants in and out of the garden, including the beds. "I just sink 5- and 15-gallon pots into holes and cover the edges with mulch," he says.

In a cloud forest, epiphytes grow in trees, so Feix attached tillandsias to an old Japanese plum tree and hung pots of orchid cactus from the branches. A mist system waters the plants automatically in the dry season. Below the tree is a wood deck scattered with containers of bromeliads, cape primroses, *Iris confusa,* and *Lysionotus montanus.*

Gardeners in low and intermediate deserts may not be able to grow all the plants Feix does, but many tropicals more suited to hot, dry climates can create the same effects: trees like *Acacia abyssinica, A. greggii,* and orchid tree (*Bauhinia*); shrubs including red bird of paradise (*Caesalpinia pulcherrima*); vines such as bougainvillea; cycads; and a variety of palms. The key to a tropical look is a cluster of lush-looking plants of different heights.

Pacific Rim fantasy

How to bring the tropics to your Southern California garden

s there a jungle anywhere on this net where shell ginger, clumping gi- timber bamboo, kangaroo paws, California oaks peacefully coexist? t until now. When Rebecca Kaye ed landscape designer Pat Brodie to nsform her Santa Barbara backyard o the tropical garden shown above d on pages 224–225, a real-looking gle wasn't what she was after. Kaye s seeking her own version of the

tropics—a blend of every exotic locale she and her husband, Chuck, had ever visited or longed to. In short, a fantasy garden with a splash of Hawaii, a dash of Bali, a pinch of Australia, and a trace of Asia. "I wanted a Pacific Rim jungle," Kaye says. "And now I've got one."

Coming up with a plant palette that matched Kaye's fantasy was a challenge, says Brodie, but making sure the exotic cast looked at home in its setting

was even harder. A eucalyptus grove wraps around one side of Kaye's property, a natural stream and oak woodland form the boundary on the other, and chaparral-covered mountains loom in the middle distance. So Southern California could not be excluded from the picture. It had to be incorporated.

The most tropical section of the jungle, close to the house, is focused around a water feature designed by

BY SHARON COHOON • PHOTOGRAPHS BY STEVEN GUNTHER

A TROPICAL LAGOON filled with water lilies
and hyacinths is the focal point of the "wet" garden.
Stone steps on the right lead to a bench (shown on
page 223), which overlooks the "dry" side.

rodie and Bruce Raph of Town and ountry Waterscape. Brodie planted e pond with water lilies, taro, and ther aquatic plants, then surrounded with ornamental bananas, palms, alking irises, and various gingers and nnas. The yellows and oranges of e canna flowers reflecting in the ool echo the colors of the koi swim- ing in it. "I wish I could say I lanned that," says Brodie, "but it was just serendipity."

Upstream the garden changes to a more Asian mood. Korean grass creates a mossy effect underfoot, and an under- story of Mexican and giant clumping timber bamboo obscures the trunks of the eucalyptus trees, visually blending the two plant communities. Another transition occurs near the boulder- strewn midsection against a backdrop of oaks. Here, Brodie planted plenty of billowy grasses and sprawling shrubs. "They suggest seeps and springs even though there aren't any," she says, "and the kangaroo paws are dryland versions of the walking iris."

Kaye isn't losing any sleep over her garden's lack of authenticity. "You can grow practically anything in this pines- to-palms microclimate, and gardeners in Santa Barbara always have," she says. "We're just carrying on the tradition."

acific Rim plants for outhern California

HE TROPIC ZONE

Cannas. Tuberous-rooted perennials ith large green, bronze, or variegated aves. Blooms come in every shade ut blue, including many bicolors. Cul- vars used here are 'Cleopatra' (green aves, yellow flowers with red lotches); 'Black Knight' (burgundy aves, red flowers); and 'Intrigue' lark bronze leaves, orange flowers). iant-size leaves are the most tropical- oking of any foliage in the garden, d when plants are clustered to- ther, they have the strongest impact. Sunset climate zones.

Ginger lily (Hedychium). Large- afed perennials, Indian in origin. hite ginger (*H. coronarium*) grows 3 6 feet tall and has intensely fragrant hite flowers. Kahili ginger (*H. gard- ranum*) grows to 8 feet tall and pro- ces 1½-foot-long spikes of clear yel- w flowers. Zones 17, 22–24.

Red Abyssinian banana (Ensete ntricosum 'Maurelii'). Big, broad, urgundy-tinged leaves grow from unklike vertical stem to 20 feet tall. ergreen in zones 17, 19–24; herba- ous in zones 13, 15–16, 18.

Shell ginger (Alpinia zerumbet). e mother of all gingers, grows 8 to feet tall. Shiny 2-foot-long leaves d waxy white, fragrant flowers with d, purple, or brown markings. Ever- een in zones 22–24; herbaceous in nes 15–17.

Taro (Colocasia esculenta). A berous-rooted perennial with mam- oth, heart-shaped leaves. Fast-grow- g—to 6 feet in one season. A natural

DROUGHT-TOLERANT Mediterranean plants like billowy grasses, purple Mexican sage (behind grass), and bronze-red kangaroo paws cluster near boulders in "dry" garden.

for streamside or bog gardens; it needs plenty of water. Evergreen in zones 23–24; herbaceous in zones 12, 16–22.

THE ASIAN INFLUENCE

No plant suggests Asia like bamboo, and several species of these giant grasses grow in this garden, knitted together by an undulating carpet of Korean grass.
• *Black bamboo (Phyllostachys ni- gra).* A running bamboo that reaches 10 to 15 feet tall, with black culms (stems). Hardy to 0°.
• *Clumping giant timber bamboo (Bambusa oldhamii).* Dense-foliaged bamboo commonly used where tall, dense screening is needed. Potential height 20 to 55 feet. Hardy to 15°.
• *Korean grass (Zoysia tenuifolia).* That mossy Asian look doesn't come eas- ily in a semi-arid climate. This fine-tex- tured grass creates a similar effect with less water. Hardy in zones 8–9, 12–24.
• *Mexican weeping bamboo (Otatea acuminata aztecorum).* Extremely narrow leaves give this clumping bam- boo a lacy appearance; growth habit is willowlike, to 10 to 20 feet. Hardy to 15°.

THE "DOWN UNDER" FACTOR

There's no escaping the ubiquitous eucalyptus in Southern California. At the Kaye garden, for instance, a semicircle of eucalyptus in the back- ground was too prominent a feature to ignore. So Brodie used kangaroo paws (*Anigozanthos flavidus*), which occur naturally in Australia's eucalyp- tus forests, to tie the garden to its Aus- tralian backdrop. ◆

Tropical cool

Gardeners are going bananas over jungly plants.
Here's how to bring the tropics to your garden

PALMLIKE *Cordyline australis* fans out over purple
heliotrope, chartreuse nicotiana, rose-pink pelargoniums,
ivy geraniums, and pale pink schizanthus.

AN EMPRESS TREE
(far left), banana, and
'Little Gem' magnolia
form a leafy canopy. Blue
wheatgrass and Siberian
irises edge the lawn.

■ When designer Ben Hammontree began planning this Seattle garden, he was
merely trying to satisfy his client's desire to wake up a landscape. Like so many gardens in the Pacific Northwest, this one was dominated by finely textured conifers.
Hammontree knew that plants with big, boldly shaped leaves could create dramatic contrasts. Then the jungle drums started pounding in his head. Why not design a tropical garden using hardy plants?

He assembled a collection of plants that looked as if a dinosaur might eat them
for lunch. Then he arranged them in a 15- by 110-foot border so exotic that mon-
keys and mynah birds would look right at home. Lush container plantings on a
deck surrounding the house continue the tropical theme.

Hammontree blazed the trail for a hybrid horticultural style that is sweeping the
region—Northwest tropical. Here's how he brought the tropics to Puget Sound.

BY STEVEN R. LORTON • PHOTOGRAPHS BY BEN WOOLSEY

A designer's tips on achieving tropical style

•*Layer the foliage.* On the "jungle" floor, Hammontree formed a carpet of low-growing plants: *Alchemilla mollis* with lobed, pale green leaves, *Ligularia* in greens and dark reds, and robust hostas, including blue-leafed *Hosta sieboldiana* 'Elegans' and golden *H.* 'Sum and Substance'.

At the middle level, taller broad-leafed gunnera (dinosaur food) contrasts with the spikes of *Iris pseudocorus*.

The tallest plants—empress tree, hardy banana, *Magnolia grandiflora* 'Little Gem', and windmill palm—are woven through the back of the border.

•*Mix leaf forms and colors.* Hammontree plays the gigantic round leaves of *Petasites japonicus* against the spidery, blue-green honey bush (*Melianthus major*).

Spiky plants like New Zealand flax and ornamental grasses help break the monotony of roundish leaf forms.

•*Civilize with containers.* Hammontree scatters big pots filled with plants bearing colorful leaves such as coleus or long-blooming flowers like impatiens.

LACY FLOWER clusters of *Hydrangea aspera sargentiana* play off the starry blooms of 'Coral Bee' Oriental lily and the toothy, gray-green foliage of honey bush.

The pick of the jungle

FOLIAGE PLANTS

•*Alchemilla mollis* (lady's-mantle). Deciduous perennial to 2 feet tall; rounded, pale green leaves 6 inches across. *Sunset* climate zones 2–7.

•**Banana** (*Musa basjoo*). Deciduous perennial to 15 feet tall; papery green leaves 2 by 4½ feet; dies to ground without frost protection. Zones 5–7.

•**Blue wheat grass** (*Agropyron magellanicum*). Evergreen grass; dense clumps (to 1½ feet tall) of metallic blue leaves. Zones 5–7.

•**Cordyline** (*C. australis* and *C.* 'Baueri'). Evergreen shrub or 3- to 15-foot-tall tree; swordlike leaves in shades of bronze to deep purple. Zones 5–7.

•**Dinosaur food** (*Gunnera manicata* and *G. tinctoria*). Perennial to 8 feet tall; lobed green leaves 4 to 8 feet across; spiny stalks. Zones 4–6.

•**Empress tree** (*Paulownia tomentosa*). Deciduous tree 40 to 50 feet tall;

heart-shaped leaves 4 to 7 inches across; young trees need protection. Zones 1–3.

•**Honey bush** (*Melianthus major*). Deciduous perennial 12 to 14 feet tall; marginally hardy. Zones 4–7.

•**Hosta** (*H. sieboldiana* 'Elegans' and *H.* 'Sum and Substance'). Deciduous perennial to 3 feet tall. Zones 1–7.

•*Ligularia dentata* 'Desdemona'. Deciduous perennial 3 to 5 feet tall; roundish green to deep purple leaves 1 foot across. Zones 3–7.

•*Magnolia grandiflora* 'Little Gem'. Evergreen tree to 20 feet tall; glossy, dark green leaves. Zones 4–7.

•**New Zealand flax** (*Phormium tenax*). Evergreen perennial to 9 feet tall; swordlike leaves in shades of yellow to purplish bronze. Zones 5–7.

•*Petasites japonicus*. Deciduous perennial to 2 feet tall; round green leaves to 18 inches across. Zones 4–7.

•**Rhododendron** (*R. fictolacteum, R.*

macabeanum, and *R. sinogrande*). Evergreen trees to 12 feet tall. Zones 5–7.

•**Tasmanian tree fern** (*Dicksonia antarctica*). Evergreen fern to 15 feet tall; finely cut fronds 3 to 6 feet across. Zones 5–7; hardy to 20°.

•**Windmill palm** (*Trachycarpus fortunei*). Evergreen tree to 30 feet tall; fan-shaped leaves 3 feet across. Zones 4–7.

FLOWER ACCENTS

•**Canna.** Tuberous perennial 1½ to feet tall; showy flowers in hot tropical shades; bananalike leaves in rich green to bronzy shades. All zones (lift roots to overwinter indoors in zones 1–3).

•**Daylily** (*Hemerocallis*). Deciduous perennial 1 to 4 feet tall; flowers in sunny colors. All zones.

•**Ginger lily** (*Hedychium coronarium*). Deciduous perennial 3 to 5 feet tall; clusters of fragrant white flowers; root-hardy in mild winters. Zones 5–7.

•*Iris pseudacorus* (yellow flag). Deciduous rhizome to 5 feet tall; yellow flowers and swordlike leaves. Zones 3–7. ◆

A twist of lime

BY SHARON COHOON AND LAUREN BONAR SWEZEY

AN INTERPLAY OF VARIOUS GREENS is the theme of Clarke's shade-garden design.

There are few mixed drinks that don't benefit from a twist of lime. That little jolt of astringency awakens the taste buds and keeps sweetness from being cloying. A visual punch of lime works the same way in the garden.

SOUTHERN CALIFORNIA RECIPE

When you add a dash of lime green foliage or flowers, every other color is intensified, says Christine Wotruba, owner of Perennial Adventure nursery in La Mesa.

A stroll among the beds in Wotruba's demonstration garden illustrates her point. By themselves, the dusky bronze blades of a New Zealand flax might appear overly somber and stiffly aloof. But with a bright mound of chartreuse breath of heaven (*Coleonema* 'Sunset Gold') underfoot, the flax foliage looks tall, dark, and handsome. Ordinarily, the little white daisies of common feverfew look innocently demure, but with a racy skirt of *Helichrysum petiolare* 'Limelight' beneath them, they acquire an air of sophistication. And the violet-blue flowers of *Geranium* 'Magnificum' look even richer when backed by the lime green blooms of *Euphorbia characias*.

Lime also works as a linchpin, pulling together contrasting colors. Thanks to the addition of lime foliage and flowers in Wotruba's garden, yellow coreopsis and blue iris are happily wedded, as are amber roses and purple salvia. "Lime pulls the eye along, uniting everything in the garden," says Wotruba.

Other plants that bring the bite of lime to the garden include golden oregano, lemon thyme, rue, *Stachys byzantina* 'Primrose Heron' (a pale lime version of lamb's ears), chartreuse-colored lady's-mantle, and *Nicotiana* 'Lime Green'.

A NORTHERN CALIFORNIA RECIPE

Take a shady garden. Blend in plants with colorful foliage. Stir in shades of green—soft blue-green to apple green to deep forest green. Mix them well, making sure they include a liberal sprinkling of leaf textures and forms. Add a twist of lime foliage and watch that garden come alive.

That's the recipe Oakland designer Robert Clark created for Diane Taylor's front garden in Piedmont, California. The effect is stunning. And because the plants are easy-care, Taylor got the low-maintenance garden she requested.

Clark used chartreuse and mahogany to spark up the shade, and deep greens to keep the garden from becoming too gaudy. Several of the plants, such as feverfew, bloom for short periods. But their flowers are mostly soft colors—pinks, apricots, and whites.

The feverfew and lime thyme grow between pavers in the handsome slate path. Beside them, low-growing plants such as burgundy ajuga, grayish green lady's-mantle, medium-green *Geranium cantabrigiense* 'Biokovo', and yellow *Acorus gramineus* 'Ogon' make neat mounds. Above them, *Camellia sasanqua* 'Setsugekka', Corsican hellebore, mahogany-colored *Hebe* 'Reevesii', *Helichrysum petiolare* 'Limelight', and *Rhododendron veitchianum* create layers of foliage.

THE CHARTREUSE BLOOMS of euphorbia (foreground) and the gold-green foliage of 'Sunset Gold' breath of heaven (rear) mix well in Wotruba's borders.

NORMAN A. PLATE (2)

FULL-TO-BURSTING bed includes (front row, from left) 'Konserva' kale and 'Dorat' chard; (center row) bok choy; (back row) Red Russian kale and 'Red Giant' mustard.

Winter's tastiest greens

Spinach, bok choy, and chard are tasty, easy to grow, and—yes—good for you

BY LAUREN BONAR SWEZEY

In late fall and winter, when many plants are finished blooming or going dormant, cool-season greens bring a leafy beauty to garden beds. Their leaves are as bold and voluptuous as jungle plants. They combine handsomely in wide beds as shown above.

They're also flavor favorites with cooks around the world. In Portugal, kale or collards mix with potatoes and sausage in the soup *caldo verde*. Italians are fond of spinach or chard pie; the French use chard in a seasonal vegetable soup. Asians add bok choy to stir-fries.

Creative cooks in the West are catching on by blending, braising, and flavoring a wide array of leafy winter greens—among the most healthful vegetables you can grow. As one avid vegetable gardener puts it, "There are plenty of tasty ways to prepare seasonal greens. Cooks just need to be more experimental."

Leafy greens are also fast and easy to grow from seed or seedlings. (You'll have more varieties to choose from if you start plants from seed.) Start seed indoors about six weeks before planting time (do it this month in the Pacific Northwest, September and October in

Northern California, September to November or later in mild areas of Southern California, and October and November in the low desert). Plant in full sun and mix in plenty of compost. Keep the soil moist; greens turn bitter if soil moisture fluctuates between wet and dry.

To harvest, you can either pick one leaf at a time when they're big enough to eat, or pull out the entire plant when it matures. If you're still at a loss for what to do with the greens at harvest time, just sauté them in a little oil with garlic, cover, and cook for a few minutes until tender. Bon appétit.

BOK CHOY (pak choi). This Asian green tastes similar to Swiss chard, but its leaves are thicker and less wrinkled. 'Joi Choi' has wide, white stems and tender, succulent leaves that grow to 15 inches long. 'Mei Qing Choi Hybrid' (baby bok choy) grows only 6 to 8 inches long.

COLLARDS. The mild, cabbage-flavored leaves are high in vitamins A and C and calcium. 'Vates' is nonheading, compact (to 24 inches tall), and slow to bolt. 'Georgia' is vigorous, growing to 36 inches tall.

KALE. Gorgeous heads of succulent green or red leaves, some curled. Plants are hardy to 10°. If you can't find 'Konserva' (pictured on the facing page), try 'Winterboro.'

MUSTARD. Large, green-leafed 'Savannah Hybrid' has a mild flavor; 'Red Giant' and 'Southern Giant Curled' are spicier. Cooking removes some of the spiciness. Most varieties are very fast-growing, maturing in 20 to 45 days.

SPINACH. 'Olympia' has smooth leaves and is productive in spring and fall. 'Tyee' has semi-savoyed (crinkled) leaves and is very vigorous. 'Vienna Hybrid' has fully savoyed leaves and matures very early. All three are resistant to downy mildew (which can limit winter production).

SWISS CHARD. 'Ruby Red' and 'Rhubarb' have dark red leaves and crimson stems that are very ornamental in the garden. 'Dorat' has beautiful light green leaves. 'Bright Lights', a 1998 All-America Selections winner, is actually a mix of chards whose rainbow-colored stems include crimson, orange, pink, white, and yellow. Its leaves range from green to red.

WHERE TO FIND SEED

Natural Gardening Company, 217 San Anselmo Ave., San Anselmo, CA 94960; (707) 766-9303.

Park Seed Company, 1 Parkton Ave., Greenwood, SC 29647; (800) 845-3369.

Territorial Seed Company, Box 157, Cottage Grove, OR 97424; (541) 942-9547.

Those tasty kales

BY RENEE SHEPHERD

ALLAN MANDELL

I've always known that kale is one of the most healthful garden greens, chock-full of vitamins A and C, iron, calcium, and potassium. But I never considered it a delectable vegetable until I discovered Wild Garden Kale mix, a veritable bouquet of shapely, rosy-hued leaves with a crispy-sweet, mild flavor. I have Frank Morton, who grows gourmet salad blends for restaurants, to thank for this discovery. An experienced plantsman, Morton (shown below) is constantly looking for new ingredients to add to his salad mixes. He has recently begun to do his own seed breeding, and developed this superb Wild Garden Kale mix by selecting seeds from the wide and diverse gene pool of heirloom kales.

Morton sent me a packet of Wild Garden Kale mix seed, which I planted in my garden in early fall. Soon, the seeds produced fast-growing plants with 18- to 24-inch leaves in a gorgeous palette of fall hues—deep green, lustrous blue-green, vibrant burgundy, and rich purple-red. The leaves ranged from flat to wavy, tightly curled and softly savoyed to ruffle-edged. As cool weather came on, their colors intensified, so the plants lit up the garden as the days grew shorter.

Now, Wild Garden Kale mix is a staple in my garden. I toss young leaves into salads and stir-fries, and sauté, braise, and steam them. I add the mature leaves to my "simple soup"—a delicious blend of sautéed onions and garlic, chicken stock, rice or potatoes, and chunks of my favorite lean sausage. I've also discovered a few other tasty ways to use wild kale.

WILTED GREENS PASTA. Add clean kale leaves to boiling pasta during the last 30 seconds of cooking, or just before draining the pasta, to set their color and tenderize them slightly. Then drain the pasta and kale and dress with a fruity olive oil, shaved hard cheese, and freshly ground pepper.

BRAISED OR STEAMED GREENS. Cook the kale leaves in a little broth or white wine. To serve, add a little olive oil or butter and sprinkle with fresh lemon juice.

STIR-FRIED KALE. Stir-fry the greens with fresh ginger and garlic. To serve, sprinkle with a little sesame oil and oyster sauce (available in the Asian section of most supermarkets or in Asian grocery stores).

Renee's kale tips

BUY SEEDS of Wild Garden Kale mix by mail from Wild Garden Seed, Box 1509, Philomath, OR 97370 (send a self-addressed, stamped envelope with $2 per packet), or order from Shepherd's Garden Seeds, 30 Irene St., Torrington, CT 06790; (860) 482-3638 (free catalog).

SOW SEEDS ½ inch deep and 1 inch apart in rows 18 inches apart in rich, well-drained garden soil in late summer or early fall. Containers of seed starting mix are fine, too; transplant into garden beds when seedlings have at least one set of true leaves.

KEEP THE SEEDBED evenly moist until seeds germinate (about one week to 10 days).

THIN OR TRANSPLANT SEEDLINGS to 8 to 12 inches apart after plants are established.

START HARVESTING LEAVES after plants have at least eight leaves. My "cut-and-come-again" method: pick the tenderest leaves from the center whorls, leaving the outer leaves to feed the plants. ◆

How do you create the effect of sea spray without water? In this Santa Barbara garden, misty wands of *Muhlenbergia capillaris* wave over *Trachelium caeruleum*. For more on this drought-tolerant "seascape," see page 242.

September

gardenguide

A greenhouse extends the season

■ Thanks to a greenhouse and a pair of pet llamas, Sharon McEntee enjoys a longer, more productive growing season in Sutton, Alaska. Her husband, Pat, built the greenhouse with materials recycled from an old sunroom. The 10-foot-square structure is framed with 2-by-4s and capped by a translucent fiberglass roof that's steeply pitched to prevent snow from building up.

Annual flowers and vegetables are sown in mid-March in bottom-heated coldframes inside the greenhouse.

Later in spring, seedlings of lettuce, peas, and other crops that don't mind cool weather go outside. Meanwhile, warmth-loving tomatoes, peppers, and green beans—all planted in 5-gallon cans of soil—remain inside, producing crops from summer to October.

To keep moose from grazing in the vegetable patch, McEntee surrounded it with a 7½-foot-tall fence. She grows flowers that moose don't seem to like—California and Shirley poppies, candytuft, columbine, nasturtiums, and

HARDY FLOWERS grow around the greenhouse, where tender crops like tomatoes stay all summer.

marigolds—in unfenced areas.

The llamas do their part to enrich the garden. McEntee collects their droppings, and after the first fall freeze, she spreads the aged manure on the ground and leaves it under the snow all winter. When the snow melts in spring, the manure nutrients leach into the soil.

— *Steven R. Lorton*

MAGGIE MacLAREN

NORMAN A. PLATE (2)

Weaving a tapestry

■ It's 110 in the shade garden of Howard Cohen and Brian Coleman of Seattle. Those digits don't refer to temperature, but to the approximate number of plant species that flourish in a space no larger than 20 by 25 feet. Designers Glenn Withey and Charles Price selected the plants and wove them into a luxurious tapestry, but if you look closely, you see that each

SWORDLIKE leaves of New Zealand flax make bold thrusts from a tall urn.

plant is given the space it needs to display its distinctive features. For example, New Zealand flax (*Phormium tenax*) was planted in a tall

cast-iron urn so its swordlike leaves could reach up and catch the light. At the base of the flax, a white-flowered heliotrope reveals its shrubby form, while a vine of *Cissus discolor* dangles its heart-shaped leaves. To the right of the urn, *Hydrangea macrophylla* grows against a lattice where it has room to branch out and show off its lacy flower clusters. Below it, Japanese forest grass (*Hakonechloa macra* 'Aureola') forms a cascade of gold-striped leaves that nearly brush the pea gravel lining the floor of the garden.

When any plant becomes too exuberant, unwanted growth is snipped off or pinched back. — *S. R. L.*

Sheep shears, the kind used to snip wool from sheep, may just be the best shears for cutting back perennials such as campanula, catmint, and diascia after the first bloom flush. Landscape designer Maile Arnold uses them regularly to keep the plants in her garden looking their best. When we tried them, we were hooked. They're very sharp, easy to use, and long-lasting, since there are no moving parts to wear out.

The 6-inch-long blades are also particularly useful for shearing topiaries, edging grass, and cutting other soft-tissued plants. Arnold bought her shears at a farm supply store; you can also order them (ask for item 329) from Kinsman Company, Box 357, Point Pleasant, PA 18950; (800) 733-4146. $35 plus shipping.

— *Lauren Bonar Swezey*

Grand old roses of the Rockies

■ First planted by pioneers, many heritage roses still thrive in the Rocky Mountains. Here are five varieties that have proved themselves in old cemeteries and gardens. They get big—up to 6 feet tall by 6 feet across. Abbreviations refer to the mail-order suppliers which ship potted plants to set out in early fall or spring.

'BALTIMORE BELLE', 1843 (ARE, HCR). This rambler bears clusters of soft pink blooms with an intoxicating perfume.

'COQUETTE DES BLANCHES', 187 (ARE). Clusters of big, cupped white blossoms blushed with pink have spicy fragrance.

'DÉSIRÉE PARMENTIER', circa 1848 (ARE, HCR). This Gallica's blossoms are loaded with petals—pink outer ones, magenta center ones—and fragrance.

'GREAT WESTERN', 1840 (ARE). This hybrid Bourbon bears cupped blooms of deep maroon-magenta with a luscious old rose perfume.

'HENRI MARTIN', 1863 (ARE). Moss rose with fragrant crimson blossoms (pictured at left).

ARE: Antique Rose Emporium, (800) 441-0002; catalog $5.

HCR: High Country Roses, (435) 789-5512; free catalog.

— *John Starnes*

MULLEIN is inspected by Jeff Dawson in the medicinal garden he designed at Kendall-Jackson Winery. Culinary plants grow in adjacent beds.

'HENRI MARTIN' has pine-scented hairs on stems and bases of flowers.

CULINARY DELIGHT

Winery gardens in Santa Rosa

■ Jeff Dawson has done it again. Over the past two years, the highly acclaimed organic gardener (famous for the work he did on the display gardens at Fetzer Winery) has helped to create the 2½-acre Culinary Gardens at Kendall-Jackson Winery's wine center in Santa Rosa.

Chefs at Kendall-Jackson use the gardens' produce for cooking, but hundreds of vegetable varieties are also tested here. You can tour the gardens on your own or with a guide (meet at the wine-tasting room, open 10–5 daily) to gather ideas.

Northbound on U.S. Highway 101, take the River Road exit and turn left at the signal. Turn right on Fulton Road and go ½ mile to the wine-tasting room and gardens on the left. — *L. B. S.*

CHARLES MANN

A mountain meadow at the front door

MISTY WANDS of blue oat grass wave over boulders placed among low-growing perennials.

■ A well-designed garden is one that weds *hardscape* (structural elements) and *softscape* (plant materials). Take this garden, for example, in Edwards, Colorado.

Berms of soil, a rock-lined creek bed, and boulders provide structure, while flowering perennials, ornamental grasses, and aspens provide color, motion, and even sound. By successfully combining these elements, landscape designer Glen Ellison of Avon created

the effect of a wild mountain meadow right outside the clients' front door.

Starting with flat, bare earth, Ellison contoured the site by mounding berms of imported topsoil. Because the berms changed the site's drainage pattern, he formed a dry creek bed to channel runoff water away from the front of the house. The creek bed is outlined with river rock and leads the eye directly to the center of the garden. Carefully placed boulders anchor the design and

provide bold foils for low-growing ice plant and snow-in-summer.

Along the creek bed, Ellison planted long-blooming perennials, including red blanket flower, white Shasta daisies, and orange daylilies. Behind a pair of boulders, the billowing seed heads of blue oat grass sway in the breeze. Closer to the house, aspen trees provide shade and privacy, and their leaves flutter and rattle in the wind.

— *Jim McCausland*

Planting for a party

■ You're giving a party in just a few months, but one of the most visible parts of your front garden looks neglected and bare. What do you do? Faced with this challenge, Tom and Chris Gaspich called in landscape designer Keeyla Meadows to create an inviting space.

Meadows, an artist by training, approached the garden as a blank canvas. First she chose a color scheme: white, yellow, and lime green. Then she designed a patio and added pots and sculptures as focal points.

A stone path leads to a sculptural pot at the far end of the patio; the pot contains a metal trellis painted the color of the nearby crape myrtle flowers. Further enhancing the patio are several other pots and a bench with a back designed to resemble butterfly wings.

Around the patio, flowering annuals and perennials fit the cheerful color scheme: baby's breath, campanula, cleome, coral bells, and foxglove (white); dahlias, daylilies, lilies, and lysimachia (yellow); and nicotiana and zinnias (lime). More permanent plants—'Sunset Gold' coleonema, white roses, and white Sasanqua camellias—anchor the composition. Seven white dogwoods encircle the garden.

The garden was an instant success. "Visitors stand outside it and analyze it like a painting," says Meadows. "That's exactly what I intended." — *L. B. S.*

Dunk your baskets

■ September is one of the hottest, driest, and windiest months in much of the West. The desiccating weather is especially rough on plants in hanging baskets. To keep them from drying out, you can drench them frequently with a hose, but this wastes water and time. Better yet, give them a thorough tub-dunking to saturate the soil and hydrate the whole plant.

Fill a large plastic tub or trash can with water. Immerse the plant, basket and all, completely submerging the soil. Let the plant sit in the water for several minutes until air bubbles no longer rise to the surface. Then lift the basket and let the runoff water drain back into the tub. If you have several hanging plants, suspend a long chain from the eaves over the tub to hold the baskets as they drain.

COSMOS IN WHITE, red, and pink bloom among watsonia (strappy green leaves) and Mexican sage (purple flower spikes).

GARDEN RECLAMATION

Room for a view

Nancy Spiller has a killer view. The home she shares with her husband, Tom Weitzel, in the Adams Hill section of Glendale looks toward the rugged peaks of the San Gabriel Mountains over a sea of rooftops. She isn't the first to enjoy the scenery. Author John Steinbeck lived in the vicinity, as did photographer Edward Weston and Hollywood

actor James Caan. And now a new generation of artists, recognizing a good thing, is moving in.

Though Spiller and Weitzel didn't see it at first, the view is even better from the slope behind the house. When they moved in, their backyard was such a tangle that they rarely ventured into it. Then Pasadena landscape contractor Robert Cornell stepped in. He cleared away tons of ivy and vinca, uncovering several tiers of retaining wall underneath. "Old gardens often

have good bones," he says, "but you have to clear away the undergrowth first to find them."

So the garden would look as old as its walls, Cornell retained a well-established grove of prickly pear cactus. Then—because the steep slope is challenging to work in—he filled out the garden with plants that don't require much maintenance. For annual color, cosmos were sown; they reseed freely and pop up year after year.

— *Sharon Cohoon*

DRY-STACKED stone walls form terraces for beds of vegetables and herbs.

Chef's garden of flavors in Phoenix

■ Chef Jeffrey Beeson always has plenty of fresh arugula for the dishes he serves in Different Pointe of View restaurant in Phoenix. He grows his own salad greens, herbs, and specialty vegetables in hillside gardens near the restaurant at the Point Hilton Resort at Tapatio Cliffs.

Beeson designed terraced planters and filled them with topsoil amended with compost. This month, he'll harvest 23 kinds of chilies, ranging from mild 'Anaheim' to fiery habanero. In early October, he'll plant cool-season crops, including arugula, leeks, 30 kinds of lettuce (he favors 'Lollo Rosso' and 'Red Oak Leaf'), and peas. The leaf crops are fertilized with fish emulsion. All plants are started from seed, mainly from Native Seeds/SEARCH (526 N. Fourth Ave., Tucson, AZ 85705; catalog $1); Shepherd's Garden Seeds (860/482-3638; catalog free); and—for chilies—the Pepper Gal (954/537-5540; catalog free).

— L. B. S.

Paint hard-to-find tools

■ Hand tools with dark blades and handles are hard to see against the soil or among plants. If you set a dark-handled trowel on the ground and go indoors for a while, you may return to your garden only to find that the trowel seems to have disappeared in a tangle of plants.

One easy way to increase a hand tool's visibility is to paint its handle a bright yellow, orange, or red. Oil-base paint works well, though acrylic and epoxy-base paints are also good choices.

First, sand the handle (whether wood, metal, or even sturdy plastic) with light- to medium-grit sandpaper. Then wipe it clean with a cloth. Apply at least two coats of paint; between coats, rub the painted surface lightly with fine sandpaper or steel wool to ensure that each layer of paint bonds to the last.

— *Steven R. Lorton*

EASY WAY TO START PLANTS

Mini-greenhouse with a pair of pots

A great time to propagate many kinds of plants from cuttings is when new growth has started to harden off—usually late summer or early autumn.

Plants commonly grown from cuttings include some perennials (artemisia, cape mallow, felicia, germander, lavender, marguerite, osteospermum, pelargonium, and penstemon), deciduous shrubs and vines (butterfly bush, clematis, fig, fuchsia, and roses), and some evergreens (azalea, camellia, daphne, heather and heath, and rosemary).

You can create an ideal environment for cuttings by using a coldframe, or you can make a portable "greenhouse" with pots as shown in the photos.

TO MAKE CUTTINGS: Take 2- to 6-inch lengths (shorter on fine-leafed plants like heath, longer on larger-leafed plants like daphne) from side branches, including a sliver of heel if you slice the cutting away from an adjoining branch. Each cutting should have at least two leaf nodes (the buds from which leaves grow). Make your cut ⅛ inch below the bottom node (for clematis, cut midway between nodes). Strip leaves off the bottom ⅓ to ½ of each cutting, dip the end into rooting hormone, and plant.

TO ROOT CUTTINGS: **1.** Fill a 10- to 12-inch-diameter clay pot with a mixture of 2 parts sand to 1 part peat moss. Plug the drain hole of an unglazed 4-inch pot with silicone sealer. Nest the smaller pot in the center of the larger one. Dampen the mix. Insert cuttings into the mix 2 to 3 inches apart around the pot, then put six 18-inch bamboo stakes between the cuttings.

2. Fill the small pot with water to keep the mix moist.

3. Cover with a 13-gallon white plastic trash bag to form a moisture-holding tent. Put the pot in filtered sun. Pull the bag off briefly each day to check the water. When cuttings have formed roots (in a few weeks), transplant into individual pots. Protect young plants from hard frosts and set them out in the garden next spring.

— *J. M.*

JIM McCAUSLAND (3)

WATER FEATURES
A lily pond in a pot

■ Want a water garden fast? All you need is a large glazed container—without a drain hole—and a few aquatic plants. Dianne Torgerson, owner of Oasis Water Gardens in Seattle, planted the miniature lily pond shown at right in about five minutes. She chose a pot 23 inches in diameter and 15 inches deep. The pond features the red-flowered, hardy water lily *Nymphaea* 'Gloriosa' and grasslike *Acorus gramineus* 'Ogon'. Both are growing in plastic planters hidden beneath the surface of the water. Floating among the lily pads are the tiny, oval leaves of *Salvinia auriculata* and water hyacinth (*Eichhornia crassipes*), whose circular leaves bob on bulbous stems.

Torgerson places her water gardens in full sun. When the water needs freshening, she slips a hose down to the bottom of the pot and lets it run for a while. — *S. R. L.*

'GLORIOSA' WATER LILY plays off the golden leaves of *Acorus gramineus* 'Ogon' in a Chinese dragon pot.

GREAT COMBINATIONS
Plant a cool seascape

■ How do you create the effect of sea spray without water? In the garden featured on page 232, Santa Barbara garden designer Pat Brodie combines the ornamental grass *Muhlenbergia capillaris* with *Trachelium caeruleum,* a perennial. The violet-blue flowers of this grass are so fine, says Brodie, they look almost like water vapor. And the dome-shaped flower clusters of *T. caeruleum* (just in front of the grass) have a miniature storm cloud look that heightens the cooling illusion. In the background, the purple-and-white flower spikes of Mexican sage (*Salvia leucantha*) fan out, echoing the grass in shape and color. The final touch—the soft gray catmint (*Nepeta faassenii*) in the foreground—could almost be sea foam lapping up onshore.

Despite the cooling effect these plants create, they all stand up to the demands of late summer. All four plants are drought-tolerant and perfectly at home in a dry creek bed situations like the one shown. — *S. C.*

CHARLES MANN

SPIKY AGAVES and cactus in a variety of colors and sizes line the pathway to the front door of Carrie Nimmer's home.

CLIMATE-FRIENDLY GARDEN
Celebrating succulents

■ The garden in front of Carrie Nimmer's home couldn't exist in soggy Seattle or frosty Flagstaff. It takes a climate where warm, sunny days are the norm for subtropical succulents like agaves to thrive. Phoenix provides the perfect conditions. "We live in one of the few places in the world where you can build a garden around succulents. So why not celebrate the fact?" asks Nimmer.

Her garden clearly does. Agaves, rather than shrubs, are the foundation plants. "They start small and build to a crescendo as you reach the door," says Nimmer, a landscape designer. In this photo, you see an *Agave victoriae reginae* on the left, then white-striped *A. americana* 'Mediopicta', yellow-striped *A. americana* 'Variegata', and finally, the imposing *A. weberi*. To provide the best conditions for her prized agaves, Nimmer added mesquite trees for light shade and put in a permeable pathway designed to harvest rainfall and direct it toward the plants.

Instead of using ground covers and woody shrubs to fill in the landscape, Nimmer added more succulents, aloes, prickly pear and barrel cactus, and purple-leafed *Setcreasea pallida*. And each spring, self-sowing wildflowers such as arroyo lupines, Mexican poppies, owl's clover, and verbena pop up to soften the spiky severity of the succulents. — *S. C.*

Pacific Northwest Checklist

PLANTING

☑ **COOL-SEASON CROPS.** It's your last chance to sow seeds for fall and winter salad crops, including arugula, leaf lettuce, mustard greens, radishes, and spinach.

☑ **LANDSCAPE PLANTS.** Zones 1–3: Now through October is the best time to set out trees, shrubs, ground covers, and many perennial plants. Zones 4–7: Do this through November.

☑ **LAWNS.** Start or overseed lawns this month. For guidance in selecting a grass, see the story on page 254.

☑ **SPRING-BLOOMING BULBS.** Bins of bulbs will begin appearing in nurseries around Labor Day: anemones, crocus, daffodils, freesias, hyacinths, and tulips. Select plump and firm bulbs; plant immediately.

MAINTENANCE

☑ **CARE FOR ROSES.** Allow a few flowers to fade on the plants and form hips late this month. This encourages plants to head into dormancy. Hips are handsome in fall and winter, and many birds like to feed on them.

☑ **CLEAN GREENHOUSES.** Before cold winter weather arrives, empty old soil from flats and seedbeds, hose down the greenhouse, replace broken glass and cracked weather-stripping, and check heating and watering systems.

☑ **DIG AND DIVIDE PERENNIALS.** Plants that have finished their bloom cycle can be dug and divided. Use a spade or sharp knife to cut clumps into quarters. Replant divisions in weed-free, well-amended soil.

☑ **MAKE COMPOST.** Start a new pile or bin with grass clippings, spent annuals, prunings, and vegetable scraps. Keep both piles well soaked to speed up decomposition during hot weather.

☑ **MULCH.** Zones 1–3: Before freezing weather hits, weed around plants thoroughly, then spread a 2- to 3-inch layer of organic mulch (compost or pine needles work well) to insulate roots and reduce soil erosion.

☑ **PRIMP ANNUALS.** To coax another round or two of bloom, keep snipping off faded blossoms and feed plants with a liquid fertilizer.

☑ **TEND FUCHSIAS.** Continue your feeding program. Keep spent flowers pinched off. Water regularly.

Northern California Checklist

PLANTING

☑ **HELP YOUR KIDS START A VEG-GIE GARDEN.** Zones 7–9, 14–17: Select a small, sunny garden bed or plant in containers. Choose carrots (try small, round 'Thumbelina' from Park Seed; 800/845-3369), onion sets (easy to handle), sugar snap peas (kids love to pick them off the vine and might even eat them), and radishes (try red, purple, and white 'Easter Egg II', also from Park Seed; they're fun to harvest, though kids might not eat them).

☑ **PLANT COOL-SEASON GREENS.** Zones 7–9, 14–17: Mesclun, a colorful selection of salad greens, is easy to grow at home. Try Ornamental Edibles's Mesclun Magic, a mix that contains 11 varieties of lettuce as well as arugula, kale, and other greens. Or try its Elegant Braising Greens—a combination of chards, kales, and Asian greens. To order these mixes ($12.95 each, plus shipping), call (408) 946-7333.

Sunset
CLIMATE ZONES
☐ Mountain (1-2)
☐ Valley (7-9)
☐ Inland (14)
☐ Coastal (15-17)

DEBRA LAMBERT

☑ **PLANT COOL-SEASON LAWNS.** For guidance in choosing a lawn grass, see the story on page 254.

☑ **PLANT A NATIVE GARDEN.** Zones 7–9, 14–17: You don't have to have a big garden to grow native plants. Any small bed away from heavily irrigated plants can make an attractive native border. Try *Arctostaphylos,* blue-eyed grass, bush anemone, fremontodendron, lyme grass, mahonia, monkey flowers, Pacific Coast irises, *Penstemon heterophyllus purdyi,* and *Salvia clevelandii.* For sources, try Baylands Nursery in East Palo Alto (650/323-1645), Intermountain Nursery in Prather (209/855-3113), Larner Seeds in Bolinas (415/868-9407), Mostly Natives in Tomales (707/878-2009), and Yerba Buena Nursery in Woodside (650/851-1668).

☑ **PLANT VEGETABLES.** Zones 7–9, 14–17: Set out seedlings of broccoli, brussels sprouts, cabbage, cauliflower, and spinach. Plant seeds of beets, carrots, leeks, onions, peas, radishes, and turnips.

☑ **REPLANT FLOWERPOTS.** Zones 7–9, 14–17: After the heat of summer, flowerpots may look bedraggled. To carry the pots through the remainder of the warm season, replant with late-summer annuals, such as marigolds, salvias, and zinnias.

MAINTENANCE

☑ **CARE FOR CITRUS.** Zones 7–9, 14–17: To prevent citrus fruit from drying out as it matures, give trees regular deep soakings during warm fall weather. Irrigate the entire root zone of the tree.

☑ **DIVIDE PERENNIALS.** Dig, divide, and replant overcrowded perennials that have finished blooming. Use a spading fork to lift and loosen clumps of agapanthus, coreopsis, daylily, and penstemon. With a spade or a sharp knife, cut clumps into sections. Before replanting divisions, weed and amend beds.

Southern California Checklist

PLANTING

☑ **BUY BULBS.** Spring-flowering bulbs begin arriving in nurseries this month. Shop early for the best selection. Bulbs that naturalize easily in our climate include babiana, daffodil, Dutch iris, freesia, homeria, ixia, leucojum, narcissus, oxalis, sparaxis, Star of Bethlehem (*ornithogalum*), tritonia, and watsonia. They can be planted immediately. For a long season of cut flowers, plant groupings of anemone and ranunculus bulbs at two-week intervals starting now.

☑ **CHILL BULBS.** Buy crocus, hyacinth, and tulip bulbs now but chill for six to eight weeks before planting. Store in a paper bag (away from ethylene-producing fruit like apples) in the crisper section of your refrigerator. Plant after Thanksgiving. High-desert gardeners (zone 11) don't need to prechill these bulbs.

☑ **PLANT BULB COVERS.** Planted directly over bulbs, forget-me-nots, johnny-jump-ups, lobelia, and sweet alyssum provide color until the bulbs flower (bulbs push through them with ease) and hide bulbs' yellowing foliage after they stop blooming.

☑ **START COOL-WEATHER CROPS.** From midmonth on, coastal (zones 22–24) and inland (zones 18–21) gardeners can begin planting winter crops. Sow seeds for arugula, beets, carrots, chard, collards, endive, kale, lettuces, bok choy, peas, radishes, spinach, and turnips. Set out broccoli, brussels sprouts, cabbage, cauliflower, and celery seedlings. Plant sets of garlic, onions, and shallots. In the high desert, plant lettuce, radishes, and spinach.

MAINTENANCE

☑ **REPLENISH MULCH.** A thick (3- to 4-inch) layer of organic mulch around permanent plants helps protect them from Santa Ana winds by conserving moisture and insulating roots. Renew mulch around shrubs, trees, rose bushes, and woody perennials. But keep mulch off the crowns, stems, and trunks of plants.

☑ **PROTECT AGAINST BRUSHFIRES.** Dead vegetation adds fuel to flames. In fire-prone areas—before the onset of Santa Ana winds—cut and remove all dead branches and leaves from trees and shrubs, especially those that grow near the house. Clear leaves from gutters and remove woody vegetation growing against structures.

☑ **FEED PERMANENT PLANTS.** Fertilize established trees, shrubs, ground covers, and warm-season grasses such as Bermuda. Repeat in a month. Coastal gardeners should feed tropical plants one last time if needed. Don't feed California natives or drought-tolerant Mediterranean plants.

WEED CONTROL

☑ **FORCE WEED SEEDS.** When preparing a new bed for planting, water to start weeds growing. As soon as weeds germinate, pull them out or remove with a hoe.

Mountain Checklist

PLANTING

☑ **BULBS.** Set out bulbs of daffodil, crocus, hyacinth, *Iris reticulata,* scilla, and tulip in loose, well-amended soil. To protect them from soil temperature fluctuations, plant daffodils and tulips 10 to 12 inches deep and small bulbs 5 inches deep. Also, pot up amaryllis and narcissus bulbs by month's end to force blooms for indoor display between Thanksgiving and Christmas.

☑ **LAWNS.** Early fall is ideal for seeding a lawn or laying sod. For help in choosing a lawn grass, see the story on page 254.

☑ **PANSIES.** This is probably the best time of year to plant pansies. They start with fall color, bloom during winter's mild spells, then come on strong again in spring. Plant where they won't be buried in snow for more than a few days at a time.

☑ **PERENNIALS.** Set out campanula, candytuft, catmint, coreopsis, delphinium, dianthus, foxglove, gaillardia, geum, penstemon, phlox, salvia, and yarrow. If you live in a place where the ground freezes hard every winter, mulch plants well to keep them from being heaved out of the ground.

Sunset
CLIMATE ZONES

☐ 1-3   ☐ 10-11

DEBRA LAMBERT

MAINTENANCE

☑ **DIVIDE PERENNIALS.** In all but the highest elevations, lift and divide crowded clumps of bleeding heart, daylilies, hostas, peonies, Shasta daisies, and Siberian irises. Use a spade or sharp knife to cut clumps into quarters. Replant divisions in weed-free, well-amended soil; spread mulch around them.

☑ **MAKE COMPOST.** Compost the weeds, vegetable remains, bean vines, grass clippings, and leaves that come out of your garden this month. If you keep the pile turned and well watered, you should have finished compost in time to dig into beds before winter.

☑ **STORE SUMMER BULBS.** When foliage dies down, lift cannas, dahlias, and gladiolus. Let them dry for a few days, then store at 35° to 50° in a well-ventilated space. Store cannas and dahlias in sand, peat moss, or vermiculite. Leave tuberous begonias in pots, also in a frost-free place.

PEST CONTROL

☑ **PREVENT SNOW MOLD ON LAWNS.** To discourage snow mold from forming, rake the dead thatch out of the lawn, then spray with a fungicide, such as benomyl.

☑ **SOLARIZE FIREWOOD.** Green firewood (less than a year old) can harbor bark beetles, which pose a risk to garden trees. Eliminate them by separating wood into stacks that are no more than 4 feet high, wide, and deep. Cover the stacks with clear plastic. Bury the edges of the plastic and tape the seams, and sunlight will do the rest, cooking the beetles inside within a few weeks.

Southwest Checklist

PLANTING

☑ **ANNUALS.** Zone 12 (Tucson): Plant calendula, larkspur, lobelia, pansies, snapdragons, stock, sweet alyssum, and violas.

☑ **BULBS.** Zones 1–2, 10–11: Plant spring-flowering bulbs, including crocus, daffodils, grape hyacinth, hyacinth (*Muscari*) irises, and tulips. In zones 12–13, prechill bulbs (except irises) by placing them in paper bags and storing them in the refrigerator. Plant the chilled bulbs after the soil has cooled down, around Thanksgiving. In all zones, pot up amaryllis and narcissus bulbs by month's end to force blooms for indoor display between Thanksgiving and Christmas.

☑ **COOL-SEASON VEGETABLES.** Zones 10–13: As soon as temperatures drop below 100°, sow beets, carrots, celery, chard, endive, green onions, kale, kohlrabi, leeks, parsley, parsnips, peas, potatoes, radishes, spinach, and turnips. Sow lettuce and cabbage-family members (like broccoli and cauliflower) in flats now for transplanting in October.

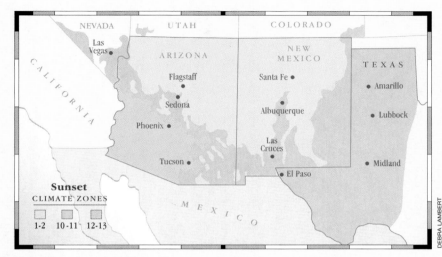

☑ **LAWNS.** Zones 1–2, 10–11: Early fall is ideal for seeding a lawn or laying sod. For help in choosing a lawn grass, see the story on page 254.

☑ **PERENNIALS.** Zones 1–2, 10–11: Plant campanula, candytuft, catmint, coreopsis, delphiniums, dianthus, diascia, foxglove, gaillardia, geum, penstemon, phlox, salvia, and yarrow. Zones 10–13: Start seed of carnations, columbine, coreopsis, feverfew, gaillardia, hardy asters, hollyhock, lupine, penstemon, phlox, Shasta daisies, statice, and yarrow. They'll be ready for transplanting in about eight weeks.

☑ **WARM-SEASON CROPS.** Zones 12–13: Plant beans and corn right away for a harvest by Thanksgiving.

MAINTENANCE

☑ **DIVIDE PERENNIALS.** Zones 1–2, 10: Lift and divide crowded clumps of daylilies, peonies, and Shasta daisies. Use a spade or sharp knife to cut clumps into quarters. Replant divisions in well-amended soil.

☑ **FEED ROSES.** Water deeply, apply a complete fertilizer with chelated iron, water again, and apply a 3-inch layer of organic mulch.

YOUR FOOLPROOF GUIDE TO Fall Planting

BY SHARON COHOON AND LAUREN BONAR SWEZEY

PRETEND IT'S SPRING. We know that's when the urge to dig in the garden strikes, because the weather is warming then and nurseries are filled to the rafters with blooming plants. • But early fall is a much better time to plant, especially if you're tackling major projects like putting in a new flower bed or border. Transplanted now, plants ease into the garden naturally. The soil is still warm enough for their roots to burrow in and take hold, yet the air's beginning to cool, which means you don't have to be out in the garden every 10 minutes watering.

FOLLOW THESE EASY STEPS TO CREATE SPECTACULAR BEDS AND BORDERS

Soon winter rains will kick in. • Nurseries are well stocked now with many perennials, bulbs, and shrubs. But how do you combine all those young green plants (or brown bulbs) so they'll mature into stunning beauties come spring? • Creating handsome beds and borders takes vision and planning. We've taken the guesswork out of it. You can plant one of the four gardens pictured on these pages, or design your own plan using our guidelines for texture, color, and height. To start, check out the nine steps to planting on page 252. • Now is the time to dig in.

Two large English-style borders flank a lawn path in Daniel Sparler and Jeff Schouten's Seattle garden. Both are filled with flowering perennials and foliage plants with interesting leaf shapes and textures. The garden is pictured in its second year.

In the left border: Potted Mediterranean fan palm (*Chamaerops humilis*), nestled among plants in foreground, and eulalia grass (*Miscanthus sinensis* 'Cosmopolitan') are among the many plants that add interesting leaf shapes and textures. Flower color comes from Corsican hellebore (*Helleborus argutifolius*), *Fuchsia magellanica* 'Hawkshead', daylilies, yellow Welsh poppy (*Meconopsis cambrica*), geum, and 'Altissimo' climbing rose.

Stars of the border on the right include the following spring bloomers: African daisy (*Osteospermum*), *Clematis* 'Etoile Violette', climbing 'Frühlingsmorgen' rose, columbines (pink and purple), common calla (white), foxgloves, variegated gladwin iris (*I. foetidissima* 'Variegata'), meadow rue (*Thalictrum flavum glaucum*), snapdragon (*Antirrhinum majus* 'Black Prince'), and 'Zéphirine Drouhin' rose.

Basic elements of a good border

1

Color

Mixing and matching colors is like painting with plants. These strategies can help you compose your own work of art.

USE SHADES OF A SINGLE COLOR. When you stick with one basic color everything automatically goes together. Take purple, for instance. You can mix lavender, violet, and mauve flowers and plum-colored foliage with impunity. Or pastel, rose, and cerise pinks. Like adding a scarf to a basic black dress, you can add accent colors later if you decide the look is too sedate. Some suggestions:

- A pink-flowered spiraea with 'Apple Blossom' penstemon and pink coral bells
- Yellow iris and 'Coronation Gold' yarrow with yellow and cream columbine
- Burnished orange lion's tail (*Leonotis leonurus*) with bronze rudbeckia and a brown sedge like *Carex buchananii*
- Dark pink azaleas with pink Lenten rose and pink primroses.

USE COMPLEMENTARY COLORS. Colors directly opposite each other on the color wheel—red and green, orange and blue, yellow and violet—are always complementary partners. Muting one or both colors makes these combinations subtler. Apricot and lavender are easier to live with for the long haul than citrus orange and grape juice purple, for instance. Following are some possibilities:

- Blue catmint with golden yarrow and buttery yellow Jerusalem sage

Lime blooms of *Euphorbia* 'Palustris' with purple Siberian irises.

ABOVE LEFT: Pinkish *Sedum telephium* 'Autumn Joy' with gray *Artemisia* 'Powis Castle'. RIGHT: Creamy yellow *Hypericum inodorum* 'Elstead' and violet *Veronica longifolia subsessilis*.

Apricot foxglove and diascia with blue salvia and iris

The deep reddish-blue leaves of *Loropetalum* 'Plum Delight' with the chartreuse green ones of 'Sunset Gold' diosma

Bright gold Japanese forest grass with 'Blue Panda' corydalis and a chartreuse and blue hosta.

USE COLOR ECHOES. This is the Mother-Nature-makes-no-mistake approach. Choose a focal plant and then build on its colors.

Variegated 'Norah Leigh' phlox: Repeat the cream in the foliage with cream-colored foxglove and the pink in the flowers with 'Evelyn' pentemon. Back the whole vignette with cream-colored roses.

Aster frikartii: Back the lavender-blue of the flowers with the mauve haze of purple muhly grass, then pick up the aster's yellow centers with golden coreopsis.

Texture

2

Foliage is the heart of a good planting. Putting together plants with different leaf shapes and surfaces is the object. Balance big and small leaves, smooth and fuzzy, strappy and feathery. All are instant texturizers.

ARTEMISIA. Perennials grown for lacy, silver-gray foliage. Handsome as foils for spring pastels.

Use: Try billowy 'Powis Castle' with pink roses and blue delphiniums. Or plant common wormwood (*A. absinthium*) between white marguerites and green santolina. Or (along the coast) try dusty miller (*A. stellerana*) between sea lavender and variegated society garlic.

EUPHORBIA. The dome-shaped bushes of fleshy blue-green leaves and chartreuse flowers (*E. characias, E. amygdaloides,* and *E. martinii*) add instant architectural interest to gardens.

Use: Combine the species listed above with rosemary and santolina; basket-of-gold (*Aurinia saxatilis*) and blue and yellow bearded irises; or sword ferns and green-flowered Corsican hellebore.

HOSTA. Gorgeous heart-shaped leaves with prominent veins. (All forms are deciduous in winter.) Many green, blue, gold, and mixed colors to choose from. Great for woodland gardens.

Use: Try blue-leafed types with the fall gold of laceleaf Japanese maple (*Acer palmatum* 'Dissectum') and lady's-mantle; gold ones with 'The Rocket' ligularia and ferns; and green varieties with Japanese barberry and astilbe.

NEW ZEALAND FLAX (*Phormium*). Its upright, swordlike leaves always create dramatic tension. Flax adapts to most soils and exposures (Sunset climate zones 7 through 24).

Use: Combine apricot-tinged *P.* 'Maori Queen' with orange African daisy (*Arctotis*) and purple Mexican bush sage; reddish brown *P.* 'Bronze Baby' with 'Siskiyou Pink' gaura and Santa Barbara daisy (*Erigeron karvinskianus*); or *P. hookeri* 'Cream Delight' with a cream-and green-striped agave and brittle-bush (*Encelia farinosa*).

ORNAMENTAL GRASSES. They are unparalleled for their ability to add movement to the garden.

Purple fountain grass—which, unlike other pennisetums, won't reseed and make a pest of itself—is one of our favorites. Try it with lavatera and lavender.

Use: In a large garden, grow tall, urn-shaped *Miscanthus sinensis* with asters and veronica. In a smaller one, pair Mexican feather grass with ornamental oreganos and small salvias like *S. greggii* and 'East Friesland'.

OTHER GOOD TEXTURIZERS. *Acanthus mollis,* aloes, barberry, breath of heaven (*Diosma ericoides*), ferns, heavenly bamboo, helichrysum, hellebores, lamb's ears, *Leptospermum,* and rosemary.

Exclamation Points

3

If you plot out the shrubs and perennials you're considering on a piece of paper, or in your head, you'll see that they all occupy oval or circular spaces. Don't let the empty spots between them go to waste. Tuck in some virtually vertical plants—flowers that bloom along tall, leafless stalks.

Biennial foxglove, with its cluster of tubular flowers at eye level, is a perfect example. Tall flowering bulbs and many kinds of irises fit into this category. These plants may put on only a brief performance, but they make up for it in showmanship. Consider these:

• Lavender foxglove with pink roses and lamb's ears
• Pale blue delphiniums with dark blue salvia and *Iris pallida*
• Pale yellow *Verbascum bombyciferum* 'Arctic Summer' with yellow and pink alstroemeria and a pink true geranium like 'Ballerina'
• Rose-pink watsonia with pink rock-rose and artemisia
• *Verbena bonariensis* with yellow roses and French lavender.

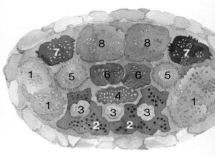

Perennials provide color from sprin to fall in this 6-foot-wide oval raise bed. Design: Bud Stuckey.
1. Catmint (*Nepeta faassenii*) **2.** *Ve bena canadensis* 'Homestead Purpl **3.** *Diascia vigilis* **4.** Santa Barba daisy (*Erigeron karvinskianus*) **5.** Spai ish lavender (*Lavandula stoecha* **6.** *Salvia greggii* (pink) **7.** Border pe stemon (*P. gloxinioides* 'Midnigh **8.** Mexican bush sage (*Salvia leucantha*

NORMAN A. PLATE (2)

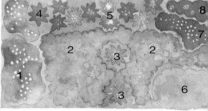

Tulips and lettuce make a surprisir combination in this spring borde Design: Robert Clark, Oakland.
1. 'White Flower Carpet' rose **2.** 'Re Oak Leaf' lettuce **3.** 'Mount Tacom tulip **4.** 'Twinkle' tulip **5.** 'Mauree tulip **6.** Lime thyme **7.** Pans **8.** *Chrysanthemum paludosum.*

9 steps to building a border

1. MAKE A PLAN

Determine the size of your bed or border, then sketch out a plan on paper. Mix together annuals, bulbs, perennials, and shrubs, arranging them according to height (low edgers in front, tall plants in the rear). Choose spiky-leafed plants for accents amid horizontal drifts and rounded clumps of annuals and perennials. Avoid a hodgepodge look by planting at least three of each plant.

For a succession of blossoms, choose spring-, summer-, and fall-blooming plants.

2. DESIGN A WATERING SYSTEM

Drip irrigation is the most efficient way to wa-

ter. And since there's no spray to dampen fe liage, plants are less prone to disease ar taller perennials aren't knocked over. You ca seek professional help to design ar install a system or do it yourself.

Install the valve and connect the ma water line first, then lay the final drip tubir and install emitters after plants are in th ground.

3. PREPARE THE SOIL

A successful border begins with healthy so First test the soil's drainage: Dig a 12-inc deep hole and fill it with water. If the wat doesn't drain away in 12 to 24 hours, install

Two lush borders edge a mossy path in this spring-summer garden. Plant the perennials, roses, and flowering maple in fall, the feverfew and dahlias in spring. Design: Robert Clark.

1. *Oxalis rubra* **2.** *Verbena tapien* 'Pink' **3.** Feverfew **4.** 'Newport' rose **5.** *Liriope muscari* 'Silvery Midget' **6.** 'First Light' rose **7.** White-flowering maple (*Abutilon hybridum*) **8.** New Zealand flax **9.** Magic Fountains blue delphinium (*D. elatum*) **10.** 'Park Princess' cactus dahlia **11.** *Phygelius capensis* 'Moonraker' **12.** Penstemon 'Midnight' **13.** 'Bonica' rose **14.** 'Lucky Number' dahlia **15.** Penstemon 'Elizabeth Cozzens' **16.** 'Eden' climbing rose **17.** Pink-flowering maple **18.** 'Mary Rose' standard rose **19.** 'Dream Weaver' climbing rose **20.** 'Lavender Beauty' yarrow **21.** Scotch moss (*Sagina subulata*) **22.** Lobelia **23.** *Acorus gramineus* **24.** 'Shirley' dahlia

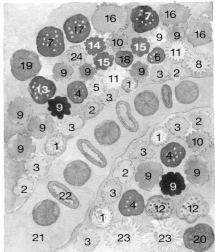

drain, plant in a raised bed, or choose a w site.

Using a shovel or rotary tiller, turn the soil a depth of about 12 inches. Mix in 2 to 4 ches of organic matter such as garden mpost or well-composted manure.

SHOP FOR PLANTS

ke your plan to the nursery. Choose small nts (sixpack-size annuals, sixpack or nch perennials, and 1-gallon shrubs); ey're more cost effective, and they get es-olished faster than larger plants.

ARRANGE PERENNIALS AND SHRUBS

t the pots of perennials and shrubs out on the prepared soil. Make minor adjustments and rearrange plants if some colors or tex-tures don't work well together.

6. SET PLANTS IN THE GROUND

Remove plants from the nursery containers. Loosen their rootballs with your fingers or, if the roots are circling, make several scores down the sides of each rootball with a knife. Dig holes and place the plants in the ground, setting the top of the rootballs even with the top of the soil. Fill in the holes; firm the soil.

7. PLANT ANNUALS AND BULBS

Interplant bulbs among the perennials and shrubs. Overplant with cool-season annuals, so when spring comes, the bulb flowers pop up through them.

8. MULCH THE SOIL

Cover soil with a 2-inch layer of mulch to con-serve moisture and help control weeds.

9. WATER REGULARLY

To get plants established, water two to four times a week to keep the small rootballs moist but not soggy. When winter rains arrive, water only if there are extended dry spells be-tween rains. Once plants are established the following spring, water often enough to keep the soil moist. ◆

A NEW-MOWED LAWN of tall fescue grass makes a lush carpet.

How to select, plant, and care for the best lawn
you'll ever have

BY JIM McCAUSLAND

A lawn you can love

■ We love our lawns. We play on them, buy furniture for them, and surround them with beautiful plants. Many of us devote more time to caring for our lawns (or hire a professional service to do it for us) than we do any other part of the garden. We spend hundreds of dollars on mowers to trim them, fertilizer to feed them, chemicals to weed them, and water to keep them green.

Is a lawn worth all the money and time we put into it? The answer is a resounding "yes"—if it's the right lawn and it's maintained in the right way.

We're demanding more of t[he] grasses that make up our lawns. Co[m]mercial breeders have responded [by] developing improved kinds of nati[ve] and non-native grasses that require le[ss] water and maintenance. They have al[so] bred insect- and disease-tolerance in[to] common lawn grasses. And now yo[u] can choose grasses that have the wea[r] resistance of a football field or on[es] that grow in shade.

This guide can help you find a gra[ss]

NORMAN A. PLATE

Feeding your lawn

■ A lawn needs nitrogen for healthy growth and to outcompete weeds. The amount of nitrogen depends on your climate and which grass you're growing (see the feeding column in the chart on pages 258 and 259).

"Fertilize as little as you can to achieve the quality you want," advises Tom Cook, an associate professor of horticulture at Oregon State University in Corvallis. You don't need to apply excessive amounts of nitrogen to keep a lawn green.

WHICH FERTILIZER? Bagged lawn fertilizers take the guesswork out of feeding; recommended application rates are shown on the labels. Most contain nitrogen in both fast- and slow-acting forms as well as phosphorus, potassium, and micronutrients such as iron. Fast-acting nitrogen gives the lawn an instant boost; the slow-acting form is released over a period of time. Always spread fertilizer evenly and water immed-

iately to prevent burning.

Organic lawn foods are now readily available. Organic nitrogen is released slowly so there's no danger of it burning the grass. It isn't readily leached out of the soil, which makes it environmentally friendly. But organic nitrogen sources break down into usable forms only during mild weather. Organic lawn food is expensive, and you need to apply more of it to get the same amount of nitrogen.

WHEN TO FEED? It depends on whether you have cool- or warm-season grass. Cool-season grasses grow vigorously in spring and fall, so that's when they need fertilizer. Make two applications in spring and two in fall. Warm-season grasses such as Bermuda grow actively in the warm months, so apply fertilizer from March to October. Feed Bermuda lightly in summer to restrain aggressive growth.

— Lauren Bonar Swezey

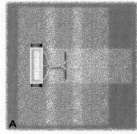
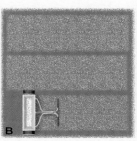
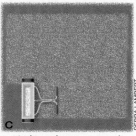

DEBRA LAMBERT

USING A DROP SPREADER. A: Don't go over the same area twice when you apply lawn fertilizer. Double doses burn or kill grass. **B:** Don't include wheels when you calculate width of swath; unfertilized wheel tracks will appear later as light green stripes. **C:** Do overlap wheel tracks so that swaths just touch. The result will be an evenly green lawn.

at fits your needs. The chart on pages 58 and 259 describes the West's best wn grasses and divides them into two oups: cool- and warm-season grasses.

Cool-season grasses thrive in areas at experience cool summers or mild inters; they go dormant in very hot or ry cold weather. You can plant or verseed any cool-season grass this onth. In the coldest climates (*Sunset* nes 1–3), plant right away so that e grass can become established by inter. In warmer climates, wait until

Seed

Unhulled Bermuda
grass seed

Fescue seed
coated with
fungicide

Hulled Bermuda
grass seed

Uncoated tall
fescue grass seed

GRASS SEED is sold uncoated, or coated with fungicide or fertilizer. Bermuda grass seed is sold hulled or unhulled; hulled seed has a higher germination rate. After preparing the site, scatter seed (photo 1) and lawn fertilizer if uncoated; lightly rake seed into soil (2); spread ¼ inch of mulch (3); then roll with an empty roller to press seed into soil.

NORMAN A. PLATE (4)

the end of the month to plant.

Warm-season grasses flourish in hot-summer areas; they go dormant in cold winter weather. Make your selection now for planting early next summer.

MATCH THE GRASS TO YOUR CLIMATE
Your garden's climate is the key factor in choosing a cool- or warm-season grass.

Cool-season grasses, including bent, bluegrass, fescue, and ryegrass, grow best when temperatures are between 60° and 75°. When it gets warmer, most of them go into summer dormancy, turning a straw color and even dying if they don't get water. Late summer or early fall are the best times to plant these.

Warm-season grasses, including Bermuda, blue grama, buffalo, St. Augustine, and zoysia, thrive in hot weather (80° to 95° is optimal) but turn brown in winter. These are best planted in late spring.

Wherever you live, you'll want a grass with a reliable record of performance.

In the coastal Pacific Northwest, blends of perennial ryegrass, fescue, and bent or Kentucky bluegrass are the lawns of choice. Although tall fescue is available, it has trouble competing with the other grasses during wet, chilly winters.

In the intermountain West, Kentucky bluegrass is a favorite, though buffalo grass (sometimes blended with blue

grama) is making inroads with garden ers who want to save water. Tall fescu is another good choice: it needs less wa ter than Kentucky bluegrass and i greener than buffalo grass (but not a cold-tolerant).

In mild areas of California, dwarf ta fescue has become popular because i needs less water and tolerates summe heat better than most other cool-seaso grasses. New, slower-growing varietie stay acceptably green all year.

In hot-summer areas of Californi and the Southwest's low and intermedi ate deserts, Bermuda grass is still the fa vorite. It makes a fine-textured turf tha tolerates drought and wears well. In au tumn, common Bermuda grass can b overseeded with perennial ryegrass for good-looking winter lawn. Zoysia is als coming into its own. This cold-hard grass takes some shade and doesn't de mand much water or fertilizer.

Along the Southern California coas, St. Augustine grass is popular. It hold its color in winter if you give it a poun of fertilizer per 1,000 square feet of tur every six weeks. St. Augustine als grows well in the low desert, where needs plenty of water.

SEED, SOD, SPRIGS, OR PLUGS?
Lawn grass is sold in several forms. A except sod require diligent weed con trol after planting. Seed is widely avai able at garden centers and nurserie Sod, sprigs, and plugs can all be o dered from sod farms, usually throug nurseries or landscape designers.

SEED is the cheapest way to start lawn. Before you buy, read the see package label as much for what doesn't say as for what it does. Look fo names on the bag: for instance, yo want a named variety such as 'Bons 2000', 'Finelawn', or 'Jaguar II', not generic tall fescue. Also, if the labe bears the notation VNS (variety no stated) or UCT (uncertified), the seed may be from old or inferior stock; the might be cheaper but not as good Look for current seed test and expira tion dates; plant within a year of th test date for best germination.

Seed rates run from 1½ pounds (fo Kentucky bluegrass) to cover 1,00 square feet up to 10 pounds (for ta fescue) to cover the same area.

SOD is the most expensive way to g but gives you instant coverage wit

Sod

TO INSTALL SOD, moisten prepared soil, then unroll strips (photo 1) and lay them in brick-bond fashion, pressing the edges together firmly. Use a knife to trim sod (2) to fit snugly around paving and obstacles. Roll the lawn (3) with a roller half-filled with water to press roots firmly into the soil. Water every day (more often in hot weather) for six weeks.

most no weed problems. When you der, try to time delivery for a dry day you stack sod during rainy weather, e grass can develop mildew and die). ke sure the soil is moist before you t the sod down.

Ask your sod supplier for the names d proportions of the grass varieties ur sod contains so that when you ar holes in the sod, you can reseed th the same grass.

UGS give spreading grasses a well-oted start on life. Plant 2- by 2-inch ugs at 8- to 16-inch intervals and wa- well.

RIGS, or shredded stolons, of spread-warm-season grasses give faster cov-age than seeds. Plant sprigs 2 to 3 inches deep at 4-inch intervals in rows 6 to 12 inches apart. One end of each sprig should barely poke out of the ground.

Another way to plant sprigs is called stolonizing: Spread 5 to 10 bushels of sprigs over 1,000 square feet of ground, then barely cover them with topsoil. Do this in 1-yard-square patches, watering each patch as you go. Don't let the sprigs dry out or they'll be history.

SITE PREPARATION

When you plant a new lawn, whether from seed, sod, sprigs, or plugs, it's best to start with a clean slate. Remove existing sod with a lawn stripper (available from rental yards) or kill it with an herbicide like glyphosate.

When the old grass is gone or dead, till the site to a depth of about 8 inches. (If the soil contains too much clay or sand, spread 3 to 4 inches of organic amendment such as mushroom compost, sludge-based compost, or well-rotted manure before you till.) Pick out rocks and roots, level the site, water well, and wait a couple of days for the soil to settle. Then rake seed, lay sod, or plant sprigs or plugs.

To keep seeds or sprigs from drying out, cover them with a $1/4$-inch layer of mulch such as peat moss or aged sawdust. Water often enough to keep the top $1/2$ inch of soil (or sod) moist until the grass takes hold and winter rains take over. ◆

Plugs and sprigs

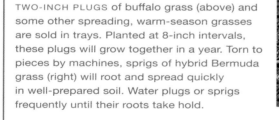

Bermuda grass sprig

TWO-INCH PLUGS of buffalo grass (above) and some other spreading, warm-season grasses are sold in trays. Planted at 8-inch intervals, these plugs will grow together in a year. Torn to pieces by machines, sprigs of hybrid Bermuda grass (right) will root and spread quickly in well-prepared soil. Water plugs or sprigs frequently until their roots take hold.

Buffalo grass plug

GARDEN
Grass Guide

Select a lawn grass suited for your region

Cool-season grasses

Type	Regions	Habit	Light	When to plant	How sold	Feeding	Mowing height	Comments
BENT GRASSES								
Colonial bent grass *Agrostis tenuis*	Northern CA, western OR and WA	Bunching or slowly spreading	Sun, light shade	Seed in spring or late summer; sod in growing season	Seed, sod	1–6 lbs. actual nitrogen* per 1,000 sq. ft. yearly	⅓–¾ in.	Prefers well-drained, slightly acid soil, re... water. Doesn't like dry weather. Highla... strain has better dr... recovery than Asto...
Creeping bent grass *A. palustris*	Northern CA, mountains, western OR and WA	Spreading	Sun, light shade	Seed in spring or late summer; sod in growing season	Seed, sod	4–8 lbs. actual nitrogen per 1,000 sq. ft. yearly	⅕–½ in.	Classic putting gre... grass. Needs mois... tile, acid soil and pl... of water. Susceptib... many diseases.
BLUEGRASS								
Kentucky bluegrass *Poa pratensis*	Mountains as lawn; CA, OR, and WA in blends	Spreading	Sun, light shade	Seed in spring or late summer; sod in growing season	Seed, sod	2–6 lbs. actual nitrogen per 1,000 sq. ft. yearly	1–2½ in.	Classic grass for hi... elevations. Needs r... lar water. Goes dor... in drought but com... back from rhizome... casional pest probl...
COARSE FESCUE								
Tall fescue *Festuca arundinacea*	Westwide except deserts and western OR and WA	Bunching	Sun, shade	Seed in spring or late summer; sod in growing season	Seed, sod	2–4 lbs. actual nitrogen per 1,000 sq. ft. yearly	2–3 in.	Good tolerance of drought and shade... Best heat toleranc... cool-season grasse... but freezes out in c... climates. Looks go... winter in Southern ... fornia, thin and we... cooler places. Take... medium traffic.
FINE FESCUES								
Chewings fescue *F. rubra commutata*	Westwide	Bunching	Sun, shade	Spring or late summer	Seed	1–2 lbs. actual nitrogen per 1,000 sq. ft. yearly	1½–2 in.	Likes well-drained,... shaded sites with i... tile, slightly acid so... Hates wet soil. Son... times mixed with K... tucky blue or peren... ryegrass, or used a... to overseed warm-... son grasses.
Creeping red fescue *F. r. rubra*	Westwide	Slowly spreading	Sun, shade	Spring or late summer	Seed	1–2 lbs. actual nitrogen per 1,000 sq. ft. yearly	1½–2 in.	Soil and shade nee... similar to chewings... cue's (see above). Sometimes mixed... Kentucky bluegras... perennial ryegrass,... used alone to over... warm-season gras...
Hard fescue *F. longifolia*	Westwide	Bunching	Sun, light shade	Spring or late summer	Seed	½ lb. actual nitrogen per 1,000 sq. ft. yearly	Not required	Grows naturally to ... tall meadow grass.... textured than shee... cue (see below). Po... heat tolerance, but... drought if left unmo...
Sheep fescue *F. ovina*	Westwide	Bunching	Sun	Spring or late summer	Seed	½ lb. actual nitrogen per 1,000 sq. ft. yearly	Not required	Grows naturally to ... in.-tall meadow gra... Needs water in the ... summer areas.
RYEGRASS								
Perennial ryegrass *Lolium perenne*	Mountains, western OR and WA as lawn; CA, Southwest as winter cover or in blend	Bunching	Sun	Spring or fall	Seed, sod	2–6 lbs. actual nitrogen per 1,000 sq. ft. yearly	2 in.	Grows fast, wears ... Often blended with... tucky bluegrass. L... color in drought m... slowly then bluegra... but dies faster. Ave... annual ryegrass.

Photo captions (left column):

Creeping bent grass

Kentucky bluegrass

Tall fescue

Hard fescue

Sheep fescue

Perennial ryegrass

Legend:

 Low water use

 Takes some shade

 Takes wear and tear

 Recovers quickly from damage

 Needs overseeding

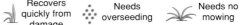 Needs no mowing

 Resista... dog ur...

Buffalo grass

Hybrid Bermuda grass

St. Augustine grass

Zoysia

BLUE GRAMA makes an informal, drought-tolerant lawn in Santa Fe. You can mow this grass or let it grow into a 12-inch-tall meadow.

CHARLES MANN

NORMAN A. PLATE (8)

STEVE GUNTHER (2)

n-season grasses

	Regions	Habit	Light	When to plant	How sold	Feeding	Mowing height	Comments
ma ua	Mountains, Southwest	Bunching	Sun	Early summer	Seed	½–2 lbs. actual nitrogen* per 1,000 sq. ft. yearly	2–3 in.	Tolerates drought, temperature extremes, and wide range of soils, even alkaline ones. Goes brown in winter. Low-quality turf when it's used alone; better when blended with buffalo grass.
rass des	CA, mountains, Southwest	Spreading	Sun	Early summer	Seed, sod, plugs	½–2 lbs. actual nitrogen per 1,000 sq. ft. yearly	3 in.	Lowest water need of any warm-season grass. Takes drought, heat; doesn't like humidity. Goes brown in winter.
n a	CA, low and intermediate deserts	Spreading	Sun	Early summer when evening temperatures are above 65°	Seed	2–4 lbs. actual nitrogen per 1,000 sq. ft. yearly	1 in.	Great tolerance of wear, drought, and a wide range of soils, but not cold. Goes brown in winter; greens up when soil reaches 60° in spring. No serious pest problems.
	CA, low and intermediate deserts	Spreading	Sun	Early summer when evening temperatures are above 65°	Sod, sprigs, plugs	4–6 lbs. actual nitrogen per 1,000 sq. ft. yearly	½–¾ in.	Similar to common Bermuda grass (see above), but doesn't self-sow.
stine tum	Southern CA, low and intermediate deserts	Spreading	Sun, shade	Early summer	Sod, sprigs, plugs	3–6 lbs. actual nitrogen per 1,000 sq. ft. yearly	¾–3 in.	Widely adapted to soils, but does best along coast. Needs regular water. Poor frost tolerance. Goes brown in winter. Susceptible to chinch bug.
	CA, low and intermediate deserts	Spreading	Sun, shade	When evening temperatures are above 65°	Sod, sprigs, plugs	1½–4 lbs. actual nitrogen per 1,000 sq. ft. yearly	½–1 in.	Excellent tolerance of wear, drought, heat, and cold. Goes brown in winter. Slow to establish. No significant pest problems. DeAnza, El Toro, and Victoria varieties hold winter color best, especially on coast.

*ual nitrogen is the amount of unadulterated nitrogen (N) in a bag of fertilizer. For example, if a 50-
nd bag is labeled with a 20-27-5 N-P-K formula, it contains 20 percent, or 10 pounds, of actual
gen, plus phosphorus (P) and potassium (K).

A hollowed pumpkin is a perfect vessel for showing off fall flowers and foliage. For details on this colorful arrangement, see page 268.

October

gardenguide

SUNSET'S OCTOBER

PERFECT TIMING: Late daffodils and midseason tulips bloom together.

SANDRA LEE REHA · BELOW: CHARLES MANN

Mix bulbs like a pro

■ Daffodils and tulips bloom simultaneously on both sides of the old split-rail fence shown here. This coordinated flower show is a tradition of the Roozen family. Since the 1950s they've grown bulbs commercially in the Skagit Valley of northwest Washington. The Roozens plant their display beds in October for peak bloom in April.

In these beds, late-blooming daffodils and early- to midseason tulips are intermingled. On the left side of the fence are two late daffodils: 'Standard Value' (a solid yellow trumpet type) under the birch trees, and 'Music Hall' (yellow trumpets with creamy white petals) behind. At front right are two tulips: 'Apeldoorn' (solid red) and 'Gudoshnik' (yellow with red flecks).

Before planting, the soil is tilled to a depth of 12 inches, then a balanced granular fertilizer is worked in.

For a free copy of the Roozengaarde catalog, call (800) 732-3266 or visit the firm's Web site at www.roozengaarde. com. — *Dick Bushnell*

NEW PLANT REPORT

Damianita (*Chrysactinia mexicana*) is a nearly perfect plant for Southwest gardens. In spring and fall, it's covered with yellow daisylike flowers (summer bloom is sparser). But with its needle-like evergreen leaves, this low-growing shrub looks good even when not in bloom. The foliage is pleasantly aromatic, too. Damianita grows well in *Sunset* climate zones 10 through 13. It tolerates most soils (even caliche) and near-zero temperatures, is very drought-tolerant, and requires little pruning. Because of its compact form (1 to 2 feet tall and wide), the plant is useful in entry planters and small courtyards. If you can't find it in a nursery, ask the staff to order it from Mountain States Wholesale Nursery (602/247-8509). — *Sharon Cohoon*

ENGLISH STRAIN delphiniums reach 7 feet in Eugene, Oregon.

Sorbets in bloom

Sorbet, a new series of violas, comes in pastel shades with mouth-watering names like 'Lemon Chiffon' (yellow), 'Blueberry Cream' (lavender and yellow), and 'Lavender Ice' (white-throated). The series includes 10 other bicolor and solid shades as well as a mix.

Sorbet flowers are only 1¼ to 1½ inches across. But don't let their pretty little faces fool you. They're hardy sprites: in recent winter trials, the Sorbet series outperformed every other flower tested (including pansies and Iceland poppies) at temperatures down to 10°.

For best results, buy Sorbet violas in 4-inch nursery containers and transplant them in rich, well-amended soil. They grow well in full sun or partial shade (shade is essential in hot climates). You can also grow these violas from seed; start it indoors very early in spring, then transplant seedlings outside as frosts diminish. One source is Thompson & Morgan; (800) 274-7333.
— *Jim McCausland*

English delphiniums: Towers of flowers

When English delphiniums started arriving in the West a couple of years ago, we predicted that they'd give our Pacific strain hybrids—which can reach 8 feet—a run for their money. Indeed, they have. Gardeners who've grown the English strain, including Maleah Spinell of Eugene, Oregon, rave about these robust plants. It took Spinell two years to get hers to grow to the height you see in the photo above (her plants reached 5 feet their first year). Huge, 3-inch blooms cover much of the plant. Besides the blue, magenta, and white flowers shown here, they come in pinks, plum red, bicolors, and a picotee.

Nurseries may stock English delphiniums for fall planting, or order now from Jackson & Perkins (800/292-4769; ask for the free fall rose catalog) for delivery at spring planting time. — *Jim McCausland*

SOUTHWESTERN NATIVES clustered along meandering paths re-create the natural look of a high-desert landscape in this Albuquerque garden.

High-country "prairie"

■ Inspired by their hikes in the foothills of the nearby Sandia and Manzano mountains, Tim Psomas and Daniel Forest planted a corner of their Albuquerque garden to recall those colorful highland slopes.

Since the silty clay soil in their valley garden was more suited to growing chilies than wildflowers, Psomas and Forest brought in truckloads of decomposed granite and shaped it into low, gently rolling mounds. Among the mounds, meandering swales are hard-packed to form narrow paths that invite leisurely strolling.

By contouring the landscape, Psomas and Forest created niches for a variety of plants. The mounds provide the drainage many of the Southwestern native plants need.

Rose-pink Parry's penstemon and red-and-yellow *Gaillardia* grace the slopes, while white yarrow grows at the base of the mounds to take advan-tage of the moister soil there. A fe[w] well-placed boulders hold back the so[il] of the steeper mounds. Thread-le[af] groundsel (*Senecio longilobus*) di[s]plays its silvery foliage texture befor[e] bursting with clusters of showy yello[w] daisies. Blue grama grass (*Boutelou[a] gracilis*), a native bunching grass, fi[lls] the gaps between the flowers, reinfor[c]ing the impression of a high-dese[rt] prairie.

— *Judith Phillip[s]*

FIERY LEAVES of *Fothergilla monticola* stand out against surrounding greenery.

AUTUMN COLOR

Plant a bonfire of *Fothergilla*

To kindle a botanical bonfire in your garden, plant *Fothergilla monticola* this month. In autumn, its foliage blazes in shades of brilliant orange, crimson, and scarlet, often lasting a month or more. A deciduous shrub, *F. monticola* (sometimes sold as *F. major*) grows well in *Sunset* climate zones 3 through 7, reaching 4 to 6 feet tall and spreading to about two-thirds of its height. After the leaves drop, the shrub reveals dark, handsome branches. Then in early spring, it bursts with fragrant, creamy bottlebrush blooms.

Two varieties of the related species *F. gardenii* also have fine fall color: *F. g.* 'Mt. Airy' grows about 4 to 5 feet tall. *F. g.* 'Blue Mist' sports summer foliage with a steely blue tint.

Look for plants in nurseries this month. You can also mail-order *F. monticola* and *F. g.* 'Mt. Airy' from Forest Farm (541/846-7269), and *F. g.* 'Blue Mist' from Heronswood Nursery (360/297-4172).

— *Steven R. Lorton*

BACK TO BASICS

Diamonds are for ground covers

October is prime time to plant evergreen ground covers. And you can't go wrong if you set out plants in the diamond pattern shown here. This design works for any size or shape of bed, giving it a neat, geometrical look. Plants will spread and fill in the gaps in a year or less.

To find the best spacing between specific plants, check the nursery tag or consult the *Sunset Western Garden Book*. For example, 1 foot is the recommended distance for many ground covers, including English ivy and Japanese spurge (pictured). For even spacing, use a ruler or marked stick to measure 12 inches diagonally between plants.

HOW DEEP TO PLANT BULBS

This ruler shows the depth for planting common bulbs that bloom in winter and spring. Clip it out and encase it in plastic sheeting or copy it onto wood. Use it to measure the depth of your planting hole, then adjust the hole as needed. If your soil is very light, plant bulbs slightly deeper; if the soil is very heavy, plant shallower.

6"

Hyacinths
(large)
(4–6 in. apart)

Lilies
(Asiatic, Oriental)
(4–6 in. apart)

5"

Daffodils
(large)
(6–8 in. apart)

Tulips
(4–6 in. apart)

Callas
(1–2 ft. apart)

4"

Dutch irises
(3–4 in. apart)

Watsonia
(6 in. apart)

Baby gladiolus
(3 in. apart)

3"

Grape hyacinths
(*Muscari*)
(3 in. apart)

Dutch crocus
(4 in. apart)

2"

Freesias
(2–3 in. apart)

Ranunculus
(6–8 in. apart)

1"

Anemones
(2–3 in. apart)

A spring border to plant now

A great planting usually has two things going for it: a limited color palette and flowers that vary in height, shape, and texture. In the scheme pictured here, flowers in shades of blue play handsomely against burgundy, deep plum, and maroon. The plants are arranged by height—lowest-growers in front, taller ones behind. They are, from front to back, white sweet alyssum, pansies and violas in shades of blue to deep purple and maroon, forget-me-nots, deep purple or maroon tulips, 'Wedgwood' Dutch irises, and Blue Fountains delphiniums. Most are available at nurseries now—the irises and tulips as bulbs, the rest in 4-inch pots. Delphiniums may still be available in 1-gallon cans.

To plant: Amend the soil and rake it smooth. Plant in waves, from back to front or front to back. Plant the tulip bulbs at the depth recommended at left, cover them with soil, and mark their positions with sticks; then plant forget-me-nots in a checkerboard pattern around them.

Bulb-planting tips

- Plant **ranunculus** tubers in October in desert climates, November where winters are mild, November or mid-February in western Oregon and Washington. Set tubers with their prongs downward.

- In parts of Southern California where soil is heavy clay, you can minimize chances of rot in moisture-sensitive bulbs like **anemones, ranunculus,** and many South African **bulbs** by planting them in between layers of coarse, clean sand. Dig a hole two or three times deeper than the size of the bulbs. In the bottom, add a ½-inch layer of sand. Set the bulbs in the holes, then top them with an additional ½-inch layer of sand. Fill the holes with soil.

- Create a meadow: Small-flowered **daffodils,** such as 'Yellow Cheerfulness', 'Grand Soleil d'Or', and 'Geranium', are great multipliers. Set them 3 to 4 inches deep, 4 to 6 inches apart, and watch them spread.

- When planting **daffodils** in clusters, set the bulbs 8 inches apart and you won't have to divide them for two to three years.

- If you live in gopher country, plant your **bulbs** in wire baskets lined with a 2- to 3-inch layer of soil.

FAST-GROWING *Echium fastuosum* nearly encloses this private Montecito hideaway.

Grow a natural retreat

Pride of Madeira plants make beautiful, billowy walls

A "boulder gazebo." That's what landscape architect Susan Van Atta calls the private hideaway she designed for Gary and Karen Kledzik in Montecito. But now that the *Echium fastuosum*—shrubby perennials that bear dramatic spikes of fluorescent blue flowers in spring and gray-green leaves all year—has nearly surrounded the rocky outcrop, perhaps it's time for a new name. The Pride of Madeira Hidden Terrace, for instance.

This secret garden is at the top of a steep slope behind the Kledziks' house. A path of native stone leads to a small terrace of decomposed granite. Nestled between two huge boulders in one corner is a rough-hewn bench—an open invitation to stay awhile. Much of the vegetation surrounding the terrace, including toyon and *Echium,* is native or naturalized. It's cut back regularly to encourage vigorous new growth.

Pride of Madeira is happiest along coastal slopes like this one but can be grown anyplace in *Sunset* climate zones 14 through 24 as long as there's space: it grows quickly, so it takes only a few plants to create a green retreat like this one.

Pride of Madeira gets leggy quickly. "You might not mind that," Van Atta says. "It gives them character." If you do mind, she suggests replanting *Echium* every few years.

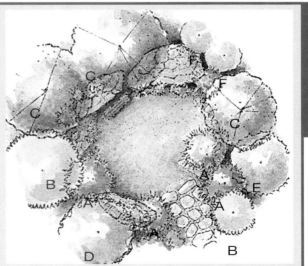

A) *Echium fastuosum* (pride of Madeira) reaches 3 to 6 feet tall and wide. *Sunset* climate zones 14–24 (best on coast).

B) *Sambucus mexicana* (blue elderberry) grows 15 to 30 feet tall. All zones.

C) *Heteromeles arbutifolia* (toyon) grows 15 to 25 feet tall. Zones 5–24.

D) *Rhus laurina* (laurel sumac) grows 6 to 15 feet tall. Zones 20–24.

E) *Ceanothus thyrsiflorus* (blue blossom) grows 6 to 21 feet tall and 8 to 30 feet wide. Zones 6–9, 14–20, 23–24.

F) *Baccharis pilularis* (dwarf coyote bush) grows 8 to 24 inches tall and 6 feet wide. Zones 5–11, 14–24.

A rainbow of bulbs

■ Plant multitudes of tulips and you're almost guaranteed an incredible show of spring flowers—for a short time. But you can extend the show in beds and borders for as long as eight weeks by planting early-, mid-, and late-season varieties together.

Last fall, Oakland landscape designer Robert Clark planned the long bloom show pictured at right in the garden of Charles and Jackie Davis. He chose his favorite tulips—Rainbow Mixture—a blend of Darwin hybrids that includes bright purples, oranges, reds, yellows, and white—from Dutch Gardens (800/818-3861). "I wanted the scene to be cheerful and joyous," says Clark, "something to counteract the sometimes somber weather."

Come spring, the color palette started out cool—pink, purple, and white—then got progressively warmer as subsequent blooms unfurled. (What you see in the photograph is the late-season show in April.)

To help "tone down the bright colors," Clark overplanted the bulbs in fall with forget-me-nots.

First he planted the tulips randomly, 6 inches deep, then he planted the forget-me-nots from sixpacks 8 inches apart

NORMAN A. PLATE

RAINBOW MIXTURE TULIPS in fiery hues set aflame this bed of cool blue forget-me-nots in Piedmont.

above them. Clark attributes his successful shows to the bulbs and the soil. He starts with top-size bulbs and a well-drained planting mix. Regular watering is important, too, if rains don't come. — *Lauren Bonar Swezey*

Splendor in the pumpkin

Flowers and foliage fill a hollowed-out shell

■ When Halloween entertaining calls for special arrangements to greet guests, try a pumpkin bouquet.

Your garden can yield all the fixings for it this month: pumpkins are ripening on the vine, leaves are turning orange and red, and garden mums are blooming in shades of rust to orange and gold. Or substitute flowers and

leaves from the florist or grocery store.

Sunset test garden coordinator Bud Stuckey created the bouquet featured on page 260. First he cut the top off a round, flat-bottomed pumpkin about 16 inches in diameter and hollowed out its center. He lined the inside with a plastic garbage bag and set in two blocks of moist florist's foam. Then he

added foliage and flowers.

To set off the rusts and yellows of the mums, he used snippets of gray-foliaged acacia and red maple, then added accents of red-flowered boronia and branches of orange fruits that florists call "pumpkin trees".

The bouquet stayed fresh-looking for about five days.

Pacific Northwest Checklist

PLANTING

☑ **BULBS.** Nurseries and garden shops will bulge with bulbs this month. Shop early for the best selection, choosing bulbs that are plump and firm. Get them into the ground as soon as possible.

☑ **LANDSCAPE PLANTS.** Shop for trees and shrubs in autumn color now. Plant immediately.

☑ **PERENNIALS.** Throughout the Northwest this is the best perennial-planting time of the year. Plants put into the ground now will have the entire winter to adjust, then shoot into action the instant weather warms in spring. If October is hot and dry, water newly set-out plants.

MAINTENANCE

☑ **ANNUALS.** Zones 4–7: Continue to deadhead, and fertilize one last time early in the month. Zones 1–3: When frost hits, pull plants, shake soil off their roots, and toss them onto the compost pile.

☑ **CARE FOR LAWNS.** If you want to rejuvenate an old lawn, here's how: mow, then rough up bare spots, scatter a generous amount of seed, cover with a thin layer of soil, water well, and keep the seedbed moist until autumn rains begin.

☑ **GROOM ROSES.** Continue to remove faded blooms. As you cut flowers to take indoors, shape plants. Allow a few flowers to form hips. This tells the plant that it's time to head into dormancy.

☑ **MAKE COMPOST.** As you harvest, mow, rake, and prune, pile everything but the diseased stuff onto the compost pile. Turn the pile and keep it moist. By next spring compost should be ready to use.

☑ **MANAGE FUCHSIAS.** Continue to feed until two weeks before the first frost is expected.

☑ **WATER.** Until rains begin, water established plants deeply. Drought-stressed plants are far more likely to be damaged in a hard freeze.

PEST CONTROL

☑ **SET OUT MOUSETRAPS.** As weather cools, mice and rats look for warm spaces to overwinter. The places where you store produce like potatoes and winter squash are especially attractive. Be vigilant about baiting and setting traps.

Northern California Checklist

PLANTING

☑ **NATURALIZE BULBS. Zones 14–17:** To create an informal mass of flowers that look as if they're spreading naturally across the landscape, toss handfuls of a single kind of bulb over the planting area, varying the density. Repeat with a second or third kind, if desired. Plant bulbs where they fall. Choose bulbs that naturalize easily in your climate, soil, and sun exposure; try species daffodils, grape hyacinths (*Muscari*), leucojum, scilla, or species tulips. You can purchase quantities of bulbs at a reasonable cost from Dutch Gardens (800/818-3861) or wholesale from K. Van Bourgondien & Sons (800/552-9996; minimum order $50).

☑ **ORDER GRAPES, FRUIT TREES, BERRIES.** If you plan to purchase special varieties of fruits by mail, get your orders in soon so you're sure to get the types you want, and so they'll arrive in time for dormant-season planting. For a taste treat, try white-flesh 'Arctic Supreme' peach or 'Dapple Dandy' pluot. Check local nurseries, or order by mail from Bay Laurel Nursery (2500 El Camino Real, Atascadero, CA 93422; 805/466-3406).

Sunset
CLIMATE ZONES
☐ Mountain (1-2)
☐ Valley (7-9)
☐ Inland (14)
☐ Coastal (15-17)

☑ **PLANT ANNUALS. Zones 7–9, 14–17:** For bloom from winter through spring, plant cool-season annuals now so they get established and start blooming before the weather turns cold. From containers, choose calendula, Iceland poppies, pansies, primroses, snapdragons, stock, and violas. In zones 15–17, you can also plant calceolaria, cineraria, nemesia, and *Schizanthus pinnatus*. From seed, try baby blue eyes, forget-me-nots, sweet alyssum, sweet peas, and spring wildflowers.

☑ **PLANT FOR PERMANENCE. Zones 7–9, 14–17:** Ground covers, shrubs, trees, and flowers all benefit from fall planting; they get off to a fast start in still-warm soil and then have the long, cool months ahead to develop healthy root systems. For a wide selection of exotic dry-climate plants, try the Dry Garden nursery (510/547-3564).

☑ **SET OUT GARLIC. Zones 7–9, 14–17:** Plant in rich, well-drained soil. Break bulbs apart into individual cloves and plant the scar ends down. Cover regular garlic with 1 to 2 inches of soil, elephant garlic (not a true garlic, but a bulbing leek with mild garlic flavor) with 4 to 6 inches of soil. Press the soil down firmly and water. Irrigate if the weather is dry. For a wide selection of garlic varieties by mail, call or write Filaree Farm, 182 Conconully Hwy., Okanogan, WA 98840; (509) 422-6940 (catalog $2).

MAINTENANCE

☑ **CLEAN UP DEBRIS.** Pull weeds, spent annuals, and vegetables. Clean up all fruit and leaves. Compost only pest-free plant debris. Add other material to your city's compost collection, if it has one.

Southern California Checklist

PLANTING

☑ **CONTINUE PLANTING COOL-SEA-SON CROPS.** In frost-free areas, you can still put in arugula, beets, broccoli, brussels sprouts, cabbage, carrots, cauliflower, chard, chives, collards, endive, kale, leaf lettuces, mustard, parsley, peas, radishes, shallots, spinach, turnips, and white potatoes.

☑ **PLANT COOL-SEASON FLOWERS.** Coastal, inland, and low-desert gardeners (zones 22–24, 18–21, and 13, respectively) can set out transplants of calendula, cyclamen, dianthus, Iceland poppies, nemesia, ornamental kale, pansies, primroses, snapdragons, stock, violas, and other annuals.

☑ **PLANT RANUNCULUS.** Ranunculus have a longer bloom period than most spring bulbs and make great cut flowers, but are susceptible to rot. Water them well after planting, then withhold water until they poke through the ground. (Plant tubers, prong side down, about 6 inches apart.)

Sunset
CLIMATE ZONES
1-3 7-9 11 13 14-24

DEBRA LAMBERT

☑ **SHOP FOR NATIVES.** California natives are excellent for drought-tolerant, low-maintenance, or wildlife-habitat gardens, and fall is the best time to plant them. (They need winter rain and cool temperatures to put down deep roots before summer.) Native-plant sales this month and next at three public gardens in Southern California—Rancho Santa Ana Botanic Garden in Claremont (909/625-8767), Theodore Payne Foundation in Sun Valley (818/768-1802), and Santa Barbara Botanic Garden (805/682-4726)—offer great selections. Call for sale dates.

MAINTENANCE

☑ **PREPARE FOR SANTA ANA WINDS.** Thin top-heavy trees like jacaranda to prevent branch breakage. Give trees, shrubs, and ground covers a deep soaking ahead of time when winds are predicted. Once winds come, mist frequently—especially vulnerable container plants and hanging baskets.

☑ **PROTECT AGAINST BRUSHFIRES.** Dead vegetation adds fuel to flames. In fire-prone areas, before the onset of Santa Ana winds, cut and remove all dead branches and leaves from trees and shrubs, especially those that grow near the house. Clear leaves from gutters and remove woody vegetation growing against structures.

PEST CONTROL

☑ **MANAGE INSECT PESTS.** Aphids and whiteflies multiply when the temperature drops. Dislodge them from plants with blasts of water from a hose or use insecticidal soap.

☑ **PROTECT CABBAGE CROPS.** Those little white butterflies flitting near your broccoli and cabbage lay eggs that turn into leaf-chomping caterpillars. Protect your crops with row covers to keep butterflies away. Or dust with *Bacillus thuringiensis* to kill young larvae.

Mountain Checklist

PLANTING AND HARVEST

☑ **HARVEST TOMATOES.** When frost threatens, protect tomato plants with row covers, or harvest all fruits and bring them indoors to ripen. Compost dark green fruits, but save those with traces of yellow or red; at room temperature they'll eventually ripen.

☑ **PLANT BULBS.** Set out bulbs of daffodils, crocus, hyacinths, *Iris reticulata,* scilla, and tulips. To protect them from soil temperature fluctuations, plant daffodils and tulips 10 to 12 inches deep, smaller bulbs 5 inches deep.

☑ **PLANT PERMANENT PLANTS.** Set out ground covers, trees, shrubs, and perennials.

☑ **SOW WILDFLOWERS.** Early in the month, broadcast seeds over rock gardens, hillsides, and fields. Lightly rake, and cover seeds with a ¼-inch layer of organic matter. If you live in an area that normally gets a light snow cover, wait until spring to sow seeds.

Sunset
CLIMATE ZONES

☐ 1-3   ☐ 10-11

DEBRA LAMBERT

☑ **STORE PRODUCE.** Beets, carrots, turnips, and potatoes keep best at 35° to 45° in barely damp sand. Onions and shallots need cool, dry storage in slotted crates or mesh bags. Leave a 2-inch stem on winter squash and pumpkins; store at 50° to 60°. Store apples and pears indoors in separate containers at around 40°. Carrots, horseradish, kale, parsnips, and turnips can tolerate heavy frost; mulched, they can stay in the ground all winter.

MAINTENANCE

☑ **CUT BACK PERENNIALS.** After the first hard freeze, cut back aster, campanula, daylily, phlox, and veronica to about 2 inches above the ground.

☑ **MULCH FOR WINTER.** Spread 2 to 3 inches of compost, straw, or other organic matter over bulbs, perennial flowers and vegetables, permanent plants, and strawberry beds.

☑ **PREPARE PLANTING BEDS.** Spade planting beds now, working in generous amounts of organic matter. Leave soil rough so it absorbs winter moisture; the freezing-thawing cycle will break apart clods.

☑ **PROTECT YOUNG TREES.** Bright winter sunlight can burn the south-facing side of tender young trunks and cause them to split. Protect them with a coat of white latex paint, tree wrap, or burlap.

☑ **WATER.** After leaves have fallen, water deciduous trees deeply when the temperature is above freezing.

PEST CONTROL

☑ **BARK BEETLES.** Before spring, burn all firewood cut from pines killed by bark beetles. Otherwise, newly hatched beetles may fly into your live pine trees when weather warms.

Southwest Checklist

PLANTING

✔ **BULBS.** Zones 1–2, 10–11: Plant all the spring-blooming kinds outside now, and tender bulbs (like paper whites) indoors for forced winter bloom. Zones 12–13: Plant amaryllis, anemone, calla, crocus, daffodil, grape hyacinth, harlequin flower, hyacinth, iris, oxalis, ranunculus, tulip, and watsonia. (Refrigerate crocus, hyacinths, and tulips for at least six weeks before planting.)

✔ **COOL-SEASON ANNUALS.** Zones 12–13: Plant calendula, dianthus, English daisy, Iceland poppy, lobelia, nemesia, ornamental cabbage and kale, pansy, primrose, schizanthus, snapdragon, stock, and viola this month. In zones 10–11, plant these, plus aubrieta, candytuft, and forget-me-not.

✔ **COOL-SEASON CROPS.** Zones 12–13: Plant beets, broccoli, brussels sprouts, cabbage, carrots, cauliflower, chard, chives, endive, garlic, kale, lettuce, onions, parsley, peas, radishes, and turnips.

DEBRA LAMBERT

✔ **GROUND COVERS.** Zones 12–13: Plant *Acacia redolens,* Baja and Mexican evening primroses, *Dalea greggii,* dwarf rosemary, gazania, lippia, low-growing junipers, snow-in-summer, and verbena.

✔ **LANDSCAPE PLANTS.** Set out all except frost-tender kinds this month, including natives, perennials, trees, and shrubs.

MAINTENANCE

✔ **DIVIDE PERENNIALS.** Zones 10 (Albuquerque), 12–13: Dig and divide daylily and Shasta daisy to revitalize crowded plants.

✔ **TEND ROSES.** Feed and water roses deeply to encourage another round of bloom.

small miracles

BY SHARON COHOON AND LAUREN BONAR SWEZEY

STUCK WITH A TINY YARD? USE THESE TRICKS TO MAKE IT LIVE LARGER

■ The modern tract home is a marvel. Dream kitchens with cabinet space to spare, a full arsenal of appliances, and countertops big enough for the most ambitious meal preparations. Master suites luxurious enough to hide out in all weekend. Bathrooms and closets the size bedrooms used to be. Home offices. • There's a flip side, of course. Such amenities require floor space. To get it, these generously scaled homes hog most of their lots. What's left for the gardener is often minuscule: a mouse pad–size entry, a backyard only marginally bigger, and spaces no wider than hallways on either side of the house. • Older houses often share the small-yard dilemma with tract houses. As their owners remodel them by raising the roof a story or two and pushing out walls as far as municipal codes allow, little space is left over for outdoor living, play, or planting. • Garden designers have become masterful at making the most of such downsized spaces. On these pages are some of their design ideas and advice for making small gardens live large.

NORMAN A. PLATE (2)

RIGHT: Small doesn't mean boring. A stream meanders by boulders and a stone patio, while lush greenery provides a sheltering screen. LEFT: Steppingstones march through baby's tears in the side yard.

BERKELEY, CALIFORNIA
Backyard retreat

The sound of a waterfall gently echoes through the kitchen. Outside a soft breeze rustles a forest of bright green leaves. No, this isn't a country garden in the Sierra foothills; it's Lisa and Tim Goodman's small garden retreat in Berkeley.

The Goodmans, who work together as landscape designers and contractors, created the Japanese inspired garden with a peaceful sounding rock waterfall and stream.

a variety of subtle and interesting foliage plants, and two vine-covered arbors. (Before the remodel, their backyard consisted of a lawn and flowers—no seating, and poor access from the house. "We finally asked ourselves, 'Why have a garden if it doesn't invite you in to linger?'" says Lisa.)

To improve accessibility, the Goodmans installed French doors off the kitchen. They added plenty of seating in the garden, making it function well for entertaining. But the garden has also become an exciting draw for their school-age son, Cole, and his friends. "The rocks and water are an instant magical playground," says Tim.

TIPS AND TRICKS

- **Use slim fences.** Narrow slats make the wood fence visually recede.
- **Create privacy with sound.** The murmur of water masks noises.
- **Grow a screen of green.** Small, narrow landscape plants (azara, Japanese maple, weeping bamboo) and vine-covered arbors block out views of neighboring houses.

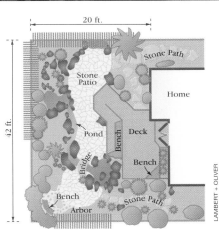

BLUR THE BOUNDARIES

Use trees, vines, and shrubs to obscure the fences and walls that define your property. Imply there is more beyond by constructing a pathway that disappears around a bend.

CHANGE LEVELS

A change in level, even if it's just a few inches, offers a different perspective, which creates the illusion of greater space. Consider raising or lowering patios, or creating gentle berms (mounds) and swales (depressions).

PLANT IN LAYERS

Espalier a first row of plants flat against the wall. That way you can squeeze in two or three layers, making the space appear multidimensional.

EMBELLISH WALLS AND PAVED POCKETS

A pocket garden off the side of the house entered through French doors calls for artistic detailing, even if it encloses only 5 square feet. Consider a small cafe table and pair of chairs. Or a miniature art gallery like the wall pictured above, designed by William Burton of the Del Mar firm Burton Associates; cast-bronze faces peer through a diamond grid made of tubular iron covered with star jasmine. "Smith & Hawken has great garden art," says Burton, "but salvage yards also have interesting things—like old columns and corbels."

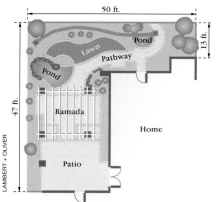

PHOENIX, ARIZONA
Rooms with a view

Divide a backyard into different functional areas and provide lots of eye-arresting details—the way you would for an interior room—and the yard visually expands.

That's what happened when Phoenix landscape architect Greg Trutza relandscaped Jackie Ellis and Kim Williamson's backyard. Before the remodel, their outdoor furnishings filled a narrow porch near the house, making the whole space appear cramped. Trutza added a new, larger patio and a curving path of aged brick, and moved the major seating area into the space that had formerly been the middle of the garden. The columns of a new ramada draw the eye upward, further opening up the space. Most of this garden is located on one side of the house. Still, it provides plenty of space for outdoor dining and entertaining.

TIPS AND TRICKS

•**Grow plants vertically.** Bougainvillea, trailing jasmine, and creeping fig don't use much floor space, but they nearly cover the walls in greenery.

•**Invest in quality materials.** The recycled brick in this patio dates from the turn of the century and is pricier than standard used brick. But it wears better and stands up to the close scrutiny a small garden receives.

SE WATER AS A REFLECTOR

nding space in a small garden for a water ature isn't always easy. But even the tini-st ponds and pools can make a garden ppear larger by adding the illusion of epth, and by reflecting the sky and sur-unding surfaces. Some designers use g troughs to outline architectural details. the Southern California garden pictured oove, water spouts into a long, narrow ool at the base of a wall.

NEWPORT BEACH, CALIFORNIA
A "floating" patio

The modern backyard is too small for soccer or football, yet we persist in car-peting it in sport turf. It may make more sense to devote the space to family din-ing and adult socializing instead, sug-gests Paul Logue Haden, president of the design firm the Collaborative West. That's what his firm did at the property pictured above. "We tried to create a backyard that would say, 'Why don't we eat outside?'" says Haden. The patio was placed in the middle of the yard and surrounded by a water moat. Horsetail (*Equisetum hyemale*), a river-side plant, growing in tall urns re-inforces the aquatic theme. An arbor frames the view (when vines grow up and cover it, the space will feel even more removed from the everyday world). Concrete pads lead to the raft-like patio, where dining out feels like a Huck Finn adventure for adults, says Haden. "But I bet kids would love this space, too."

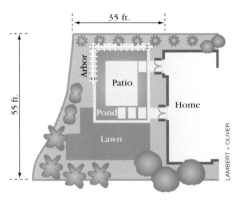

LAMBERT + OLIVER

TIPS AND TRICKS

•**Play with geometry.** To break up the gray concrete slab, white limestone tiles were inset diagonally in the patio above. These "diamonds" lead the eye to the corners of the patio and beyond, making the space seem larger.

•**Heighten the drama.** A freestanding wood arbor rises $8\frac{1}{2}$ feet on two sides of the patio, giving it vertical lift. It acts as a picture frame, defining the space and creating a sense of enclosure. Slen-der urns filled with tall plants comple-ment the classic lines of the arbor. ◆

Perfect peonies

Low-chill kinds thrive in mild or cold climates

BY STEVEN R. LORTON

MAIL-ORDER PLANTS

These growers ship tuberous roots for fall planting. Expect to pay between $15 and $35 for each plant.

• *A & D Nursery,* 6808 180th St. S.E., Snohomish, WA 98296; (360) 668-9690. Catalog costs $2.

• *Caprice Farm Nursery,* 15425 S.W. Pleasant Hill Rd., Sherwood, OR 97140; (503) 625-7241. Catalog costs $2.

• *Marde Ross & Company,* Box 1517, Palo Alto, CA 94302; (650) 328-5109. Catalog costs $1.

■ Some plants possess the power to stimulate our remembrance of good times past. Peonies, with their soft pastel blossoms and light, clean fragrance, may remind you of long-ago springs when your grandmother cut generous bouquets from the garden to fill her favorite cut-crystal vase. As Al Rogers—the dean of Western peony growers in Wilsonville, Oregon—puts it, "When I walk through my beds of peonies in bloom, some of my happiest memories of childhood in New England come flooding back."

But peonies have a highly practical side, too. These herbaceous perennials require minimal care, and they can thrive undivided for decades. And peonies have great three-season value in the landscape. In early spring, their large, strong leaf buds poke up. Then bright flower buds form, bursting into spectacular blossoms. And from spring through autumn, peonies form luxurious clumps of greenery.

Some nurseries sell blooming plants in 1-gallon containers in spring. But there's no need to wait: now is the time to plant peonies from tubers (shown below).

Planted this fall, peonies will produce a few flowers next spring, then a full round of bloom the second year.

Peonies thrive in the Pacific Northwest, where gardeners plant them in massed beds or use

FAR LEFT: 'Mrs. Franklin D. Roosevelt' makes a showy container plant. LEFT: Plant peony tubers with reddish "eyes" pointing up. ABOVE: 'Red Charm' bears double flowers with pompon-like centers.

'CORAL SUPREME' has blossoms up to 7 inches across.

them in mixed plantings with other perennials and shrubs.

In mild-winter areas of Northern California, where temperatures rarely dip below freezing for long, peonies have a reputation for being difficult to grow since many kinds do need a certain amount of winter chill to set buds and flourish. But a dedicated bunch of peony fanciers in California have discovered a number of plants that bloom well even when they don't get much winter chill.

At right, we list 11 peonies that have proved themselves in gardens from the San Francisco Bay Area to Vancouver, B.C. Most are early-blooming (midspring) varieties. These plants will also flourish in cold-winter areas where hard freezes are common. However, some can't tolerate hot summer climates.

Planting tips

Select a spot that gets at least six hours of direct sun a day. Till the beds to a depth of 18 inches, enriching the soil with plenty of organic matter. Plant the tubers with "eyes" (growth buds) pointing up under no more than 1 inch of soil in mild-winter climates, 2 inches in cold climates. Water well.

Pick your peonies
These 11 varieties are proven performers

Note that peonies grown in mild-winter climates tend to be shorter than the maximum heights given here.

'CHARLIE'S WHITE' has creamy white double flowers as wide as 6 inches on stems that reach 4 feet long. Plants, with deep green leaves, grow as tall as 48 inches.

'CLAIRE DE LUNE' bears ivory-yellow, 4-inch-wide single flowers with 11 to 13 petals on 32-inch-long stems. Plants mound as tall as 32 inches.

'CORAL CHARM' bears glowing coral to peach semidouble flowers as large as 8 inches across on 4-foot stems. Plants reach 36 inches tall.

'CORAL SUPREME' has lush pink, almost iridescent semi-double blossoms as wide as 7 inches on stems that can stretch 4 feet or longer. Plants grow 45 inches tall.

'EVENTIDE' bears coral to pink cup-shaped single flowers 6 inches across on 3- to 3½-foot stems. Plants grow 3 feet tall.

'FESTIVA MAXIMA' produces white double flowers with vivid crimson flecks. The 6-inch-wide blooms are borne on 3½-foot stems. Plants, with dark green leaves, reach 36 inches tall. A mid- to late-season bloomer, this one works in coastal climates but has a hard time with inland heat.

'LATE WINDFLOWER' has masses of white, 3½-inch-wide single flowers, each with a tuft of golden stamens in the center. Stems often grow longer than 4 feet. Plants, with finely cut leaves, reach 3 to 3½ feet tall.

'MISS AMERICA' bears white semidouble flowers 4 to 6 inches across on 3-foot stems. Plants form a bush 3 feet tall and as wide as 4 feet.

'MRS. FRANKLIN D. ROOSEVELT' has soft, pale pink double flowers 4 to 5 inches across on 38- to 40-inch stems. Plants stand 28 inches tall. A good choice for coastal California, this midseason variety won't be happy inland.

'RED CHARM' produces dark red, 5- to 6-inch-wide double flowers on 2½-foot stems. Plants grow 3 feet tall.

'ROSELETTE' bears clear pink single flowers, 5 to 6 inches wide, with crinkly petals. Stems can reach 42 inches long. Plants form a dense bush 22 inches tall. ◆

RICHARD SHIELL

'FESTIVA MAXIMA' bears 6-inch-wide double flowers with crimson flecks on some petals.

Playing with fire

Spark up green foliage with a dash of red

BY SHARON COHOON

ABOVE: Tiny tillandsias form a living globe.
BELOW: Red edges aeonium.

NORMAN A. PLATE (2)

IT'S FOLIAGE, NOT FLOWERS, that makes Hawaiian gardens feel like paradise. ˙lm fronds swaying in the ocean breezes, banana leaves backlit by the sun, philo- ˙endron leaves the size of elephant ears, and a cool skirt of lacy ferns beneath it ˙l. Green, green, and more green. Luxurious, soothing, reassuring. And after a ˙hile, maybe a little boring.

That's where red comes to the rescue. Add some crimson, bronze, or plum ˙aves to these scenes for contrast and the chlorophyll chorus sings again. That's ˙hy Hawaiian gardeners tuck fiery-hued bromeliads, bloodroot, and ti plants in ˙ith their philodendrons, cycads, and palms.

Any garden can benefit from a dash of red foliage. Deep purple or plum leaves ˙ld depth and richness to any pastel flower border; purple smoke tree is striking ˙hind pink and peach roses. And bronze and maroon foliage—the swordlike ˙ades of New Zealand flax, for instance—can temper blooms in bright colors like sulfur yellow and pumpkin orange, making them look vibrant rather than garish.

Still, what red leaves do best is comple- ment foliage of other colors, which is the lesson Hawaiian gardens teach us.

˙BOVE: Red-orange ˙omeliads light up Hawaiian ˙eens. RIGHT: Dusky red flax ˙d Sedum 'Vera Jameson' ˙zz up an evergreen garden.

DEIDRA WALPOLE

Fanning the flames
10 red-foliaged plants and ways to use them

ACALYPHA WILKESIANA. This South Pacific island shrub with dramatic mottled leaves combines shades of red, crimson, and bronze. Use it as a contrast with green-leafed subtropicals like hibiscus or to temper strong-hued flowers like yellow-orange *Tagetes lemmonii* and lion's tail (*Leonotis leonurus*). Grows to 6 feet tall. *Sunset* climate zones 21–23.

AEONIUM ARBOREUM 'ZWARTKOP'. Fleshy rosettes are dark bronze. This succulent is good for dry areas of the subtropical garden. Plant it with cactus and other succulents in shades of green, blue-gray, and celadon. Grows to 3 feet tall. Zones 15–17, 20–24.

BROMELIAD. Strappy leaves streaked with firecracker red, carmine, or lime green, depending on the variety. Handsome growing in clusters surrounded by apple-green Pteris fern or attached to tree branches with Spanish moss and epiphythic orchids. Grows to 4 feet tall. Zones 19–24.

CANNA. For a Gauguin-like tropical garden, you need big, exotic leaves. The bold leaves of 'Black Knight', 'Durban', and 'Tropicanna' cannas combine well with the waxy greens of ginger and bird of paradise. Or mix them with fine-textured heavenly bamboo (*Nandina domestica*) and dracaena (*Cordyline autralis*). Grows 3 to 6 feet tall. All zones.

COTINUS COGGYGRIA 'ROYAL PURPLE' AND 'VELVET CLOAK'. Smoke trees planted among dark green–leafed shrubs like natal plum can turn a ho-hum corner into a richly colored tapestry. Next to a *Buddleia davidii* 'Pink Delight', a smoke tree makes the gray-green leaves come to life, but when the buddleia throws its cones of pink blossoms through the deep purple leaves, the whole garden vibrates. Grows to 15 feet tall or more. All zones.

ENSETE VENTRICOSUM. Like a canna, an Abyssinnian banana adds depth and variety to the basically green subtropical garden. Good with palms, bird of paradise, philodendrons, schefflera, *Fatsia japonica,* cycads, and aloes. Grows 6 to 20 feet tall. Zones 13, 15–24.

HOUTTUYNIA CORDATA 'Chameleon'. Looks like an English ivy with red variegation. It's wonderful weaving its way through low-growing, green ground covers or sprawling at the feet of sword-bladed plants like New Zealand flax and iris. Disappears completely in winter. Grows 6 to 24 inches tall. Zones 1–9, 14–24.

IRESINE LINDENII. A low shrub or ground cover. Hawaiian gardeners mix this bloodred-leafed beauty with philodendrons and other green ground covers. Southern Californians could mix it with trailing jasmine and other sun-loving plants that need regular watering. Grows 2 to 3 feet tall. Zones 22–24.

PENNISETUM SETACETUM 'RUBRUM'. This ornamental grass is a stunning focal point, especially when underplanted with a ground cover that has a contrasting leaf color: ground morning glory (*Convolvulus mauritanicus*), lemon thyme (*Thymus citriodorus*), or licorice plant (*Helichrysum petiolare* 'Limelight'). Grows to 4 feet tall. Zones 8–24.

PHORMIUM TENAX. Several varieties of New Zealand flax, including *P. t.* 'Dark Delight' and 'Bronze Baby', have dark red leaves. They look great with dark greens like rosemary, silvery grays like *Artemisia* 'Powis Castle' and lamb's ears (*Stachys byzantina*), or glaucous shades like *Melianthus major* and *Senecio mandraliscae*. The little reds like *P. t.* 'Jack Spratt' are nice poking out of green ground covers—creeping thyme, jewel mint of Corsica (*Mentha requienii*), or even *Vinca minor.* Leaves grow to 9 feet long. Zones 7–24. ◆

— *S. C. with Steven R. Lorton*

DARK RED *Acalypha wilkesiana* is a brilliant foil to marigold yellow *Tagetes lemmonii* and pink clover (*Polygonum capitatum*) in this San Diego garden.

Red splashes
Houttuynia
foliage.

The ultimate
kitchen garden

Sunset's Dream Garden is filled with ideas you can use

BY LAUREN BONAR SWEZEY AND PETER O. WHITELEY

A flower bed and a small lawn are standard fare in most gardens. But today's landscapes can be useful as well as attractive, offering fresh herbs, gourmet vegetables, luscious homegrown fruits, and vibrant flowers all within easy reach of the kitchen.

At *Sunset's* Dream House in Menlo Park, California, a large portion of the sunny side yard has been transformed into a kitchen garden with a layout designed by San Rafael, California, landscape architect Peder Pedersen. Just

outside the kitchen door are four small planting beds, each bursting with herbs, vegetables, and flowers.

"Since the garden is located off the kitchen, it seemed natural to create a formal kitchen parterre," explains Pedersen. Two decomposed granite paths bisect the beds. At the crossroads is a gurgling fountain (from A. Silvestri Company Garden Ornaments, San Francisco).

Pedersen uses all sorts of tricks to make this small garden seem bigger. The path that leads from the kitchen (at

TOP: Flowers and foliage fill four 10- by 10-foot beds. ABOVE: English daisies, cosmos, and red penstemon mingle with lettuce.

eft in photo on page 284) starts out 6
eet wide and narrows to 3 feet toward
he back. "This gives you a greater sense
f depth," says Pedersen.

A single boxwood shrub at the corner
f each bed emphasizes the formality of
he design. Beyond the beds is a sun pa-
io; as the roses and lavender around it
row, they will create a "secret garden,"
ays Pedersen.

Landscape designer Tisa Watts selected
he plantings in each bed with help from
ellow horticulture students at Foothill
College in Los Altos Hills, California. "It's
haos within order," says Watts. But the
olor scheme is daring and intense. Pur-
les, blues, and yellows mix with a smat-
ering of oranges and hot pinks.

Plants are both functional and pretty.
rtichoke was chosen for its bold gray-
reen leaves and purple thistlelike flow-
rs, and 'Bright Lights' Swiss chard for its
olorful ribs. Crookneck squash, egg-
lant, herbs, peppers, strawberries, and
ucchini mingle with colorful flowers
uch as catmint, coreopsis, marigolds,
nd purple coneflowers.

Each bed was planted around a tall fo-
al point—a tepee trellis laced with 'Ken-
ucky Wonder' pole beans in one bed;
omatoes ('Early Girl', 'Yellow Pear', and
Super Sweet 100') staked on aluminum
pirals in another bed, for example.

The beds are watered by automatic
prinklers for about 20 minutes every
ther day. Additional spot watering is
one during hot weather.

---

unset Dream House garden sponsors:
lot Spring Portable Spas; Mervyn's Cal-
ornia (accessories); Ortho & Roundup;
Crane Plastics (TimberTech), and We-
er. Center fountain is from A. Silvestri,
an Francisco.

Other contributors include Monrovia
ursery (plants); Smith & Hawken (fur-
iture and equipment); Toro Company
rrigation and lighting); General Shale
rick; Lyngso Garden Materials; Barbara
utler (playhouse); OneWorld (screen);
elta Bluegrass; and Western Landscap-
ng. For details, visit the Dream House
n-line at www.sunsetmagazine.com.

BEHIND THE SCENES: A THREE-PIECE WORK CENTER

The unsung hero of this garden is the work center, designed by Peder Pedersen, which fits neatly into a triangular area beside the garden gate. Screened from view by its trellis and by 'Tuscan' and 'Obelisk' colonnade apples planted alternately, the center provides space for composting, cutting- and seed-starting, potting, and storage. • Pedersen designed three structures for this area. The largest (below, and at right in photo above) is a 130-inch-long potting center built by Siteworks of Berkeley. From the garden, the 89-inch-tall redwood structure looks like a fence. • The other two structures—a compost bin and a growing table—make effective use of a wood-composite decking material called TimberTech from Crane Plastics (800/307-7780). The product, which is made of sawdust and polyethylene binder, will not rot when in contact with damp soil. The compost area has three bins with removable front panels. • Plans for all three structures are available for $5. Send a check or money order along with a self-addressed, stamped envelope to Dream House Garden Work Center, 80 Willow Rd., Menlo Park, CA 94025. ◆

A garden for all seasons, this Orinda, California, landscape shows off the fiery-hued foliage of maples and liquidambar trees in fall. For a view of the same garden in summer, see page 294.

November

gardenguide

AUTUMN LEAVES settle on boulders and mosses around a pool (above) in one of the pocket gardens along the walkway leading down to the house on the waterfront (below).

JUDITH RYAN (2)

A living tapestry cloaks a slope

■ When Mark and Sharon Bloome bought a house on Puget Sound, they were delighted to live at the water's edge but were initially over-whelmed by the topography. Their house stood at the foot of a 40° slope, 100 feet below the garage and the only access road. The Bloomes' challenge was to turn the slope into a gracious entrance to their home.

It was Mark's vision to form a partnership with nature by retaining the best of the wild plants and supplementing them with cultivated stock. The Bloomes enlisted landscape designer Hendrikus Schraven to help with the project.

All of the established trees were left in place. The couple built retaining walls to shore up the slope, then installed a winding walkway with pocket gardens in niches along the path. Each of these gardens is different. Several incorporate a single specimen plant as a focal point: Japanese maple or a birch-bark cherry, for example.

The Bloomes wove plants into the landscape to form a living tapestry of foliage and branches. The designer chose deciduous plants such as birches, katsuras, locusts, and maples to provide spring and summer green, autumn color, and interesting winter forms. Cedars, hemlocks, redwoods, shore pines, and other evergreens also form part of the landscape. Ground covers, including delicate mosses and ornamental grasses, carpet the slope.

— *Steven R. Lorton*

Fireworks in bloom

■ 'Fourth of July', a velvety red rose with sparkly white stripes, is the first climber in 23 years to win an All-America Rose Society award. Its virtues include large flowers, big clusters (10 to 15 blooms per group), and a habit of producing low, flowering branches—a combination that adds up to an explosion of color.

The plant's canes grow 10 to 14 feet long and cover the whole wall, not just the upper portion as some other varieties do. Its vigor and velvety color come from that classic red climber 'Altissimo'. And from its other parent, 'Roller Coaster', comes its habit of never producing the same stripe twice. 'Fourth of July' has proven to be a consistent performer in all climates and is quite cold-hardy. It's also a strong rebloomer, even in its first season, and sweetly fragrant. Weeks Roses introduced the rose; Tom Carruth was the hybridizer.

Shop for this climber in nurseries starting in December. If you can't find it at your nursery, order it by mail from Edmunds' Roses in Wilsonville, OR (888/481-7673); Regan Nursery in Fremont, CA (510/797-3222); or Spring Hill Nurseries in Tipp City, OH (800/582-8527).

— *Sharon Cohoon*

NEW BOOKLET

Backyard conservation

■ Gardens are for people, it's true, but they're also for birds, ladybugs, bees, salamanders, frogs, fish, and a host of other creatures. When you plant a garden that's attractive to wildlife and that improves the land and water, you've made a place that's better for yourself as well. To this end, an alliance of conservation organizations led by the USDA's Natural Resources Conservation Service (NRCS) has produced "Backyard Conservation," a booklet designed to help make your backyard a sanctuary in every sense of the word.

Besides explaining how to make major garden features—ponds and terraces, for example—and teaching about composting and mulching, the booklet also includes a wildlife habitat section. You can choose wildlife-attracting plants from lists of trees, shrubs, vines, and flowers; find out how to makes nests for bats, birds, and stingless mason bees; and learn how to provide food, cover, and water for just about everything that flies, crawls, or walks.

The NRCS also offers expanded information on most of the subjects covered—composting, for instance; you can request a free four-page brochure covering its fine points.

To get a free copy of "Backyard Conservation," call (888) 526-3227. —*Jim McCausland*

Sunset's new idea garden

Opening November 2

■ Photographs of a handsome garden may inspire, but a walk down a real garden path brings design ideas and plant combinations to life. That's the intent of the Sunset Demonstration Gardens at the Arboretum of Los Angeles County in Arcadia, California. For more than 40 years, our gardens have provided visitors with ideas for everything from paving and fencing to water features.

Now we're starting over. The old gardens have been demolished and new ones are open to the public.

The master plan, designed by landscape architect Ann Christoph, divides the 1½-acre space into eight smaller gardens, each with a theme: a Garden Under the Oaks, Deck Garden, Dining and Entertainment Patio, Formal Courtyard, Nostalgia Garden, Woodland Garden, Native Plant Garden, and Water Retreat. Designed by Southern California landscape architects, the gardens feature some of the latest products for outdoor living: synthetic wood decking, new wall construction forms, manmade boulders, and state-of-the-art barbecues. There's also a demonstration area.

The arboretum, at 301 N. Baldwin Ave., is open 9–4:30 daily. Admission costs $5, $3 for seniors and students, $1 ages 5–12. For details, call (626) 821-3222. — *Peter O. Whiteley*

HOW TO PLANT FROM A NURSERY CAN

Dig a rough-sided, bell-shaped planting hole twice as wide as the original rootball. Fill hole with water to check drainage and amend as needed.

Set the plant container in the hole; lay a shovel handle across the hole to check rootball height. One-gallon plants should be about ½ inch above grade.

Fill the hole with water to soak the surrounding soil, then knock the plant out of its container, loosen tightly knit roots, and set it in the hole.

Fill the hole halfway with backfill, then water. Finish backfilling; water again. Double-check the elevation of the rootball top.

Add a 2-inch layer of mulch over the rootball (don't pile it against the stem). Position drip emitters (optional).

The colors of Mexico

Zingy hues perk up a formerly all-green Pasadena garden

How do you make a dull garden dazzling? By choosing the right plants, as Barry and Pam Meyers discovered when they moved into their Pasadena house. The red-tiled adobe, built in the 1920s, was loaded with character. Not so the garden, which consisted of a few aging junipers and a vast expanse of struggling lawn. "Incredibly boring," complained Barry.

So the Meyerses brought in garden designer Marsha Blackwelder to add some pizzazz. She suggested creating the look of "a tropical Mexican resort nearly engulfed by vegetation." The Meyerses loved the idea. Blackwelder chose red-orange tones to complement the roof tiles. To enhance the tropical motif, she put in lots of bold-leafed cannas and New Zealand flax. Cigar plant (*Cuphea ignea*), a nearly nonstop bloomer, provides bright red-orange flowers year-round. More seasonal performers, like red salvia, add to the dazzle. And a few blues and purples—princess flower, purple fountain grass, and statice—provide a cooling counterbalance.

A wide mixed border now circles the house and is duplicated in the front and side parking strips. This double band of plantings creates a privacy screen welcome on a busy corner lot. It also provides an enormous amount of cutting material for vases. "I give tons away," says Pam. "Hosts and friends love me." And the abundance of tubular flowers means the garden is never without hummingbirds. — *S. C.*

STEVEN GUNTHER

SALVIAS AND CANNAS brighten this rich south-of-the-border planting.

THE PLANTS

PURPLE
•Princess flower (*Tibouchina urvilleana*). Open shrub grows to 5–18 feet, with brilliant royal purple flowers May-January.
•Statice (*Limonium perezii*). A 12- to 18-inch clumping perennial with big clusters of small flowers that dry well. Long bloom season.

RED, BRONZE
•Canna. Tuberous-rooted perennial; big tropical leaves are green to red to bronze. Flowers bloom at end of 3- to 6-foot stalks summer through fall.
•Cigar plant (*Cuphea ignea*). Small, shrubby perennial with bright green leaves and small orange tubular flowers nearly year-round.

•Fountain grass (*Pennisetum setaceum* 'Rubrum'). Perennial grass with reddish bronze leaves and fuzzy burgundy flower spikes. To 4 feet.
•New Zealand flax (*Phormium tenax*). Upright-growing perennial with handsome bladelike leaves. Can reach 7–10 feet. Smaller sizes available. Great color variation.
•Scarlet salvia (*S. splendens*). Perennial often grown as an annual. Scarlet flowers bloom in dense clusters. Grows 1–3 feet tall.

YELLOW
•Daylily (*Hemerocallis*). Evergreen perennial with arching, sword-shaped leaves and lilylike flowers.

A CARPET of pink Mexican evening primrose sweeps through a former brickyard.

Flowers that won't wimp out in Denver weather

■ Freak snowstorms, searing heat, and persistent drought all can wreak havoc during th[e] growing season in Colorado gardens. Janet Raasch and Kevin O'Connor were mindful o[f] Denver's fickle weather when they decided to transform their front yard into a flower ga[r]den using the toughest perennials they could find. They faced another challenge: "Ou[r] house was built on top of an old brickyard," Raasch explains. Every shovelful of the heav[y] clay soil is laced with bits of brick.

Undaunted, the couple killed an existing lawn and planted into the dead sod withou[t] amending the soil. Raasch practices "tough love," allowing only the hardiest plants to re[main]. This photo shows the survivors blooming in June, just two days after a late snowstor[m] dropped 2 inches of snow on the garden. Pink Mexican evening primrose (*Oenother[a] berlandieri*) fills the foreground. Jupiter's beard (*Centranthus ruber*) adds a burst of red a[t] upper left. Scarlet *Penstemon pinifolius* and hybrid penstemons, a tuft of blue oat grass (*H[e]lictotrichon sempervirens*), and purple *Salvia superba* 'Blue Hills' provide more color an[d] texture. Although her west-facing garden really cooks in the summer heat, Raasch wate[rs] only if rain does not fall for several weeks. — *Marcia Tatroe*

A fountain of treasures

■ Lucille Earle collected rocks, bottles, and other objects to decorate her garden. When the garden changed hands, the new owners asked Phoenix craftsman Elijah Walker to design a fountain incorporating some of Earle's treasures. As the base for the fountain, Walker used a recycled 4-foot-diameter mold (a fiberglass satellite dish would also work). He coated the mold with mortar and acrylic admix (you could use premixed mastic instead), then lined it with three different colors of Mexican tile divided by a "river" of rocks. Along the lip, he arranged a row of treasures, including Earle's favorite teapot, which Walker turned into the spout for the water recirculating through the fountain.

— S. C.

N ESCONDIDO

On display this month: Tons of colorful mums

■ The switch from summer to fall is so subtle in Southern California that we need a vivid reminder to recognize the change. That's the idea behind the annual Chrysanthemum Festival at the San Diego Wild Animal Park, now the largest mum show on the West Coast.

Here's what to expect: mums in shades of red, gold, copper, lavender, salmon, and white carpeting planting beds with a blaze of color; thousands more mums cascading from covered walkways and roof beams; a menagerie of topiary animals; and daily demonstrations on chrysanthemum care

The festival usually takes place in November and is included with the price of admission to San Diego Wild Animal Park. The park is at 15500 San Pasqual Valley Rd., Escondido; (619) 234-6541.

— S. C.

STEVEN GUNTHER

A garden for all seasons

Here's what to plant for blooms in spring,
blazing foliage in fall, and good looks all year

IN FALL (shown on page 286), maples and liquidambar trees show off fiery-hued foliage. Summer color (below) comes from perennials and ornamental grasses.

■ Creating a garden that looks as glorious in fall as in spring takes planning. But the effort is worth it.

Take Ann and Glen Christofferson's Orinda garden, for instance. Yellow and green foliage plants—from variegated grasses and gold-leafed plants such as *Acorus calamus* 'Variegatus', *Coleonema pulchrum* 'Sunset Gold', 'Gold Band' pampas grass, and 'Duet' New Zealand flax—provide color all year. These are the garden's mainstays. Among them, perennial blooms come and go, creating a palette of colors that changes from season to season.

The show starts in late winter and early spring with blues, limes, and yellows as daffodils, *Euphorbia dulcis* 'Chameleon', hellebores, and rosemary 'Tuscan Blue' come into bloom. From late spring to summer, purples, reds, and whites dominate as gaura,

penstemon 'Firebird' (red flowers), and penstemon 'Sour Grapes' (purple-and-white flowers) take over. By midsummer (shown above), orange

Phygelius capensis 'African Queen purple coneflower, *Salvia guaranitica, S. pitcheri,* and zebra grass (*Miscanthus sinensis* 'Zebrinus') are i their full glory.

Around late October, the garde suddenly turns brilliant orange-re (see photo on page 286) thanks to th Japanese maples and liquidambar. "Th trees create a backdrop of vibrant colc against the yellow and green foliage, says landscape designer Darcy Hahr "And since some of the maples ar planted downslope, you look right int the canopy, not just the trunks."

A successful garden always begin with good soil preparation. Befor planting, Hahn added cottonsee meal, green sand, and rock dust to th soil. Afterwards, she mulched with fir fir bark.

To keep the garden blooming vigo ously, she fertilizes with an all-purpos organic fertilizer in late winte and sprays the foliage with fish emu sion, iron, and sea kelp in spring an summer.

Design: Darcy Hahn and An Rosseau, Hahn-Rosseau Landscape D sign, Berkeley; (510) 528-8208.

— Lauren Bonar Sweze

BACK TO BASICS

Build a compost pile

Autumn brings an abundance of garden debris, with everything from grass clippings to fallen leaves supplying the basic ingredients for compost. Building a compost pile is a simple matter of layering: alternate 4-inch

layers of green matter (such as grass clippings) and brown matter (such as dead leaves). Green matter supplies the nitrogen that breaks down the brown stuff. If you run low on greens, sprinkle ½ cup of high-nitrogen lawn fertilizer over the brown matter.

Build the pile at least 4 feet across and keep adding material until it reaches 4 feet tall. As you spread each layer, sprinkle water over it to keep the pile as moist as a damp sponge. Once a week, turn the pile with a spading fork to aerate it. When it's done, the compost is crumbly and blackish brown.

Pacific Northwest Checklist

PLANTING

☑ **BULBS.** Set out spring-flowering bulbs now before fall rains stop you.

☑ **CAMELLIAS.** Zones 4–7: Sasanqua camellias are one of the joys of a coastal Northwest winter. Shop nurseries for plants in bloom. Before you put one in the ground, slip it into a decorative pot for display on a porch or patio. These camellias are especially effective espaliered against a wall under a roof overhang where pelting winter rains won't knock the blossoms apart.

☑ **EVERGREENS.** Shop now for conifers and other evergreen trees and shrubs. Plant immediately.

☑ **GARLIC.** Set out single cloves for harvest next summer. The variety 'Inchelium Red' does especially well in the Northwest. One mail-order source for garlic is Filaree Farm, 182 Conconully Hwy., Okanogan, WA 98840 (509/422-6940); catalog $2.

☑ **HARDY ANNUALS.** Sow seeds of candytuft, clarkia, larkspur, linaria, and wildflower mixes.

MAINTENANCE

☑ **CUT BACK MUMS.** Once flowers have faded, cut plants back to within 6 inches of the ground. Next spring, they'll send up vigorous new shoots.

☑ **DIVIDE PERENNIALS.** Zones 4–7: Dig and divide crowded perennials such as daylilies, Shasta daisies, and Siberian irises. Circle clumps with a spade, then lift them out of the ground; cut off and discard knotty old roots. A dinner plate–size clump should divide into three or four parts. Replant the divisions in amended soil. Water well.

☑ **GROOM BORDERS.** Late in the month, cut back frost-downed perennials and rake up leaves and debris. Then spread a 4-inch layer of mulch around plants.

☑ **PRUNE TREES AND SHRUBS.** Remove dead and injured wood and any crossing branches. Then prune for graceful shape.

☑ **TEND LAWNS.** Before winter sets in, get your lawn in shape: rake leaves, mow, and edge. Zones 4–7: There's still time to overseed bare spots; rough up the soil, sow seed, and cover with a thin layer of soil. Water until fall rains take over.

Northern California Checklist

PLANTING

☑ **CHOOSE TREES FOR FALL COLOR.** Trees such as Chinese pistache and maples vary in how well their leaves color up, so this is the time to shop at nurseries while leaves are still on the trees (plant health in the nursery can also affect tree color). Other trees to consider are Chinese tallow tree, crape myrtle, ginkgo, liquidambar, persimmon, Raywood ash, redbud, and sour gum.

☑ **FIGHT EROSION.** If you garden on a slope, make sure you have enough plants there to keep the hillside from eroding if rains are heavy this winter. If the slope is bare or covered with young plants whose roots haven't knit the soil together yet, sow seeds of wildflowers and a perennial grass, such as blue wild rye (*Elymus glaucus*), available by the pound from Peaceful Valley Farm Supply (888/784-1722).

☑ **INSPECT BULBS, CORMS, AND TUBERS.** Zones 7–9, 14–17: As the bulb-buying season comes to a close and bulbs have sat in nursery bins and cartons for a while, make sure to carefully inspect bulbs, corms, and tubers before purchasing them. Bulbs should be firm and not sprouting. Avoid ones with soft spots or any that look dried out.

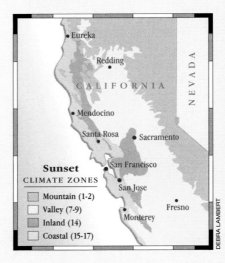

Sunset
CLIMATE ZONES

☐ Mountain (1-2)
☐ Valley (7-9)
☐ Inland (14)
☐ Coastal (15-17)

☑ **SOW WILDFLOWERS.** Zones 7–9, 14–17: For colorful spring bloom, choose a mix that's suited to your climate or buy individual kinds and create your own color combinations. You can also buy mixes for specific purposes, such as wildflowers that attract butterflies or beneficial insects. Three regional seed sources are Larner Seeds, Bolinas (415/868-9407), Wildflower Seed Company, St. Helena (800/456-3359), and Clyde Robin Seed Company, Castro Valley (510/785-0425).

MAINTENANCE

☑ **CUT BACK CHRYSANTHEMUMS.** Zones 7–9, 14–17: As soon as flowers die, cut back plants to within 6 inches of the ground.

☑ **DIVIDE PERENNIALS.** Zones 7–9, 14–17: Dig out and separate overgrown clumps. For delicate roots, use your hands; for tougher roots, use shears, a pruning knife, or a shovel. To divide acanthus, agapanthus, and fortnight lily, you may need to force them apart with a spading fork. Add organic matter to the soil and replant.

PEST CONTROL

☑ **CONTROL SNAILS AND SLUGS.** Zones 7–9, 14–17: Protect newly planted annuals and emerging bulbs from snails and slugs. Handpick pests at night, ring plants or raised beds with copper (available at most nurseries or from Peaceful Valley Farm Supply; 888/784-1722).

Southern California Checklist

PLANTING

☑ **PLANT SHRUBS AND PERENNIALS.** A good place to shop for them is Plants for Dry Places in Menifee Valley. The nursery's selection and demonstration garden prove that drought-tolerant and colorful are not mutually exclusive terms. Its big fall sale is usually in late October. Call (909) 679-6612 for details. Another opportunity this month is the Fall Plant Festival at Huntington Botanical Gardens; call (626) 405-2141 for information.

☑ **PLANT COOL-SEASON VEGETABLES.** In coastal, inland, and low-desert gardens (zones 22–24, 18–21, and 13, respectively), continue to plant winter vegetables. Sow seeds for beets, carrots, chard, kale, lettuces, mustard greens, onions, peas, radishes, spinach and turnips. Set out transplants of broccoli, brussels sprouts, cabbage, and cauliflower.

☑ **OVERSEED BERMUDA.** Sow annual winter rye to cover up dormant Bermuda grass. Mow the Bermuda as low as possible first, then sow ryegrass at a rate of 1 pound per 100 square feet of lawn. Cover with light mulch and keep moist until seeds germinate.

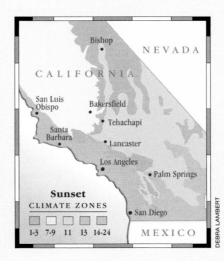

Sunset
CLIMATE ZONES

1-3 7-9 11 13 14-24

MAINTENANCE

☑ **PRUNE CANE BERRY PLANTS.** Cut back old canes of blackberry, boysenberry, and loganberry to the ground. Leave the smooth-barked canes that grew this year to bear fruit next year. Wait until December or January to cut back the canes of low-chill raspberries.

PEST & WEED CONTROL

☑ **SPRAY FRUIT TREES.** After leaves have fallen, spray peaches and nectarine trees with lime sulfur to control peach leaf curl, an airborne fungal disease. Rake up debris under trees before applying. Spray entire tree—trunk, branches, twigs—and ground under tree. Mark calendar to spray again at height of dormancy (around New Year's Day) and just before bud break (around Valentine's Day).

☑ **CONTROL SNAILS AND SLUGS.** Put collars or sleeves around vulnerable plants, and copper bands or screens around raised beds. Handpick pests evenings and early mornings. Or let tiny, conical-shelled decollate snails do the job. They feed on the eggs of brown snails, eat dead and decaying vegetation, and won't harm plants. Decollate snails are available at some nurseries. Or order from Mary's Decollate Snails in San Marcos (minimum order is 100 snails, $19.50; 760/744-9233).

☑ **STAY AHEAD OF WEEDS.** Pull out annual bluegrass, chickweed, spurge, and other weeds as they emerge. If they're prevented from setting seed, next year's weeding will be easier.

Mountain Checklist

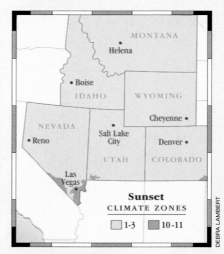

PLANTING

☑ **HERBS IN THE HOUSE.** Many herbs grow well indoors if they get five hours or more of bright light daily. In a sunny window, try oregano, rosemary, sage, sweet marjoram, and thyme. In a window with less light, try bay, chives, peppermint, and spearmint. Nurseries and some supermarkets sell herb plants in 2- or 4-inch pots; transplant these immediately into 6-inch or larger pots filled with well-drained potting soil. Allow the soil to dry slightly between waterings.

☑ **SPRING-BLOOMING BULBS.** Buy all kinds of spring-flowering bulbs and plant immediately.

☑ **WILDFLOWERS.** Sow spring-flowering kinds in weeded, prepared beds. Also sow a small amount of the same seed in a flat of sterile soil so you'll have a reference plot. Otherwise you won't know weeds from flower seedlings when they emerge next spring.

MAINTENANCE

☑ **DIG AND STORE DAHLIAS.** Stop watering a few days before digging dahlias, then carefully unearth them with a spading fork. Discard tops, brush dirt off tubers, and let them cure for a few days in a dry, frost-free place. Place tubers in boxes of peat, vermiculite, or sand and store at 45°.

☑ **GROOM LAWNS.** Mow and edge lawns one last time. Rake leaves off before they mat up and smother the grass.

☑ **MAINTAIN TOOLS.** Put an edge on all your tools, from hoes and spades to pruning shears, then wipe metal parts with machine oil and wood handles with linseed oil. Store in a dry place for the winter.

☑ **MULCH.** Spread a 3-inch layer of organic mulch around half-hardy plants, over bulb beds, and under trees and shrubs.

☑ **PLAN NEXT YEAR'S GARDEN.** While the layout of last summer's flower and vegetable beds is still fresh in your mind, draw up plans for next year's garden. To reduce the risk of soil-borne diseases, rotate your vegetable crops. For example, if you grew cabbage in a bed last summer, next year in that bed plant a completely different crop, such as tomatoes.

☑ **PROTECT ROSES.** After cutting back about half the canes, mound dry leaves over roses to insulate them (use screening to keep the leaves from blowing away).

☑ **PRUNE TREES AND SHRUBS.** After leaves fall from deciduous trees, start pruning ornamental varieties, but wait until spring to do stone fruits. Work on a mild day, removing dead, injured, and crossing or closely parallel branches. Then prune for shape.

Southwest Checklist

PLANTING

☑ **BULBS.** Zones 1–2, 10–11: Plant spring-blooming kinds immediately. Zones 12–13: Buy Dutch irises, hyacinths, and long-stemmed varieties of daffodils and tulips; they do better in the heat than short-stemmed kinds. Chill bulbs in your refrigerator for six weeks before planting.

☑ **COOL-SEASON COLOR.** Zones 12–13: Plant ageratum, aster, bells-of-Ireland, calendula, candytuft, clarkia, cornflower, foxglove, larkspur, lobelia, painted daisy, petunia, phlox, snapdragon, stock, sweet alyssum, and sweet pea. In shaded places, try dianthus, English daisy, pansy, primrose, and viola.

☑ **COOL-SEASON CROPS.** Zones 12–13: Sow or plant asparagus, beets, broccoli, brussels sprouts, cabbages, carrots, cauliflower, celery, endive, garlic, kale, kohlrabi, leeks, lettuces, mustard, parsley, peas, radishes, spinach, Swiss chard, and turnips.

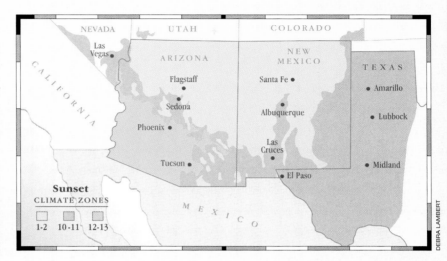

Sunset
CLIMATE ZONES
1-2   10-11   12-13

☑ **TREES AND SHRUBS.** Zones 10–13: Plant hardy trees, shrubs, and ground covers, including acacia, *Baccharis,* cassia, *Cordia boissieri,* desert spoon, fairy duster, mesquite, oleander, palo verde, *Salvia greggii,* and Texas ranger.

☑ **WILDFLOWERS.** Zones 10–13: Try blackfoot daisy (*Melampodium leucanthum*), desert bluebells (*Phacelia campanularia*), desert globe mallow (*Sphaeralcea ambigua*), firewheel (*Gaillardia pulchella*), and Mexican hat (*Ratibida columnifera*). Keep seed plots moist if rains are infrequent.

MAINTENANCE

☑ **CARE FOR ROSES.** Zones 12–13: Remove faded flowers, pruning lightly as you go. Then apply a complete fertilizer and water it in well to encourage a flush of winter flowers.

☑ **OVERSEED WARM-SEASON LAWNS.** Zones 12–13: Mow your warm-season lawn at about ½ inch, then overseed it with 10 to 20 pounds of rye per 1,000 square feet. You can use annual or perennial rye; the coarser-leafed annual rye needs more mowing than perennial rye. A month after sowing, fertilize the young grass to help it fill in quickly.

4-minute bouquets

Dress up your home for the holidays, almost instantly, with plants from the grocery store or nursery

BY KATHLEEN N. BRENZEL • PHOTOGRAPHS BY NORMAN A. PLATE

■ During the holiday season, most of us don't have time to make elaborate flower arrangements. Sure, you could order bouquets from a florist, or tumble out of bed on Thanksgiving Day to raid your garden for plant material before popping the turkey in the oven. Or you can create your own living bouquets like the ones shown here. They couldn't be easier: all you do is slip readily available plants into household containers such as baskets, bowls, or tureens, then cover their nursery pots with damp sphagnum moss. Once you've rounded up the ingredients, these arrangements go together quickly: the bowl pictured at right took only four minutes from start to finish.

Best of all, these arrangements can last for three weeks or longer. Then you can take them apart and give each plant a more permanent home in a pot or outdoors in a garden bed.

Choose a container first, then shop for plants to match its colors and size. (Take color cues from the decor of the room where the arrangement will be displayed.)

Many of the plants, including chrysanthemums, florists' cyclamen, kalanchoes, 'Needlepoint' ivy, and ornamental peppers, are sold in the gift plant section of grocery stores; buy them while you shop for your holiday meal. For a broad selection of bedding plants, stop by a nursery where you're likely to find fall-winter bloomers such as calendula, flowering cabbage and kale, Johnny-jump-up, pansy, primrose, stock, sweet alyssum, and viola.

While shopping, color-coordinate your plants, matching the flowers or fruit with foliage. For example, bright orange Rieger begonias or flaming kalanchoe blooms play off the orange blush of croton leaves beautifully.

Scarlet accent bowl

LEFT: Gather flowering cabbage and kale (one plant of each in 4-inch pots), stock (five plants from sixpack), violas (five plants from sixpack), and container (we used a bowl 9 inches wide and 7½ inches deep). **ABOVE:** Place the cabbage and kale (in their plastic pots) toward the front of the bowl, tilting them outward slightly (use plastic foam peanuts to raise plants just above the bowl's rim). Knock the stock and violas out of sixpacks, slip their rootballs into individual plastic sandwich bags, water soil, and arrange them behind and around the kale. To finish, tuck sphagnum moss around plants.

FRESH FROM the nursery, cabbage, kale, stock, and violas fill an elegant metal bowl.

You can display these bouquets temporarily in a warm, low-light area, but after the holidays, move them into a cool, bright location out of drafts and away from furnace vents. Water often enough to keep the soil moist, and regularly clip off spent blooms or fruits. In mild-winter climates, chrysanthemum, flowering kale, ivy, primrose, stock, and other bedding plants can go into outdoor containers or the ground.

Are holiday gift plants worth saving?

That depends on what they are and where you live. Kalanchoe can live for years with good care. Ornamental peppers can live for years and rebloom in the mildest parts of California, but they poop out in the deserts and cold-winter areas.

The pepper plants shown in the bouquet at left were gift plants last November. One of them is pictured below in August, covered with a new batch of blooms and young (still green), inedible fruits. To prolong their lives, last December we transplanted both plants into separate, slightly larger containers filled with fresh potting soil, placed them in a warm bathroom in bright light (a west-facing window), and watered them when the soil felt slightly dry. We snipped off shriveled peppers (fruiting continued well into June).

After weather warmed in late spring, we moved the plants outdoors onto a patio in filtered sun, and began feeding them every few weeks with dilute fish emulsion.

Each plant promises a second crop of bright yellow peppers this year. Not a bad rate of return for $3.

Sunshine in a soup tureen

Ornamental peppers (two plants in 4-inch pots), miniature chrysanthemums (two plants in 4-inch pots), and kalanchoe (one plant in a 4-inch pot) combine in an 8-inch-wide tureen. First, line the tureen with a plastic garbage bag, then set in the pepper plants. Add small mums and kalanchoe, or substitute English primroses or Rieger begonias. Cover any visible pot edges with sphagnum moss.

Autumn bounty in a basket

Adapt this design to fit any size basket. Croton (one plant in 6-inch pot), ornamental peppers (two plants in 4-inch pots), kalanchoe (two plants in 4-inch pots), Rieger begonia (one plant in 4-inch pot), and 'Needlepoint' ivy (six plants in 4-inch pots) fill basket tray measuring 9 by 21 inches.

First, line the basket with a plastic garbage bag. Place the croton toward one end, with the peppers, kalanchoe, and begonia around it. Use ivy to soften the basket's rim (to fit in more ivy, knock plants from pots and slip the rootballs into plastic sandwich bags). Camouflage pots and rootballs with moist sphagnum moss.

Post-holiday care for plants

Once their time in the spotlight is over, most of these plants will be happier if you dismantle the arrangement and give them the care they need. In mild-winter climates, plant hardier plants such as flowering cabbage and kale, stock, and violas outdoors in pots or garden beds. Follow the tips below for house plants and commonly available gift plants.

CROTON (*Codiaeum variegatum*). This gorgeous, leathery-leafed tropical grows outdoors only in frost-free climates—Hawaii and the Southern California coast (*Sunset* climate zone 24). Indoors, it needs bright light and regular misting (it does well in warm, humid greenhouses). Replant it in a larger pot if necessary. Water it regularly and feed occasionally during the growing season with a complete liquid plant food.

FLORISTS' CYCLAMEN (*Cyclamen persicum*). Grows outdoors in zones 16–24 (in warm-summer climates, it needs shade). In hot weather, plants will go dormant, but usually survive if soil drainage is good and they aren't overwatered.

THANKSGIVING AND CHRISTMAS CACTUS (*Schlumbergera*). Set the plants in a cool, bright spot out of direct sun. Don't let them dry out completely; water when the top ½ to 1 inch of soil is dry.

In a mild-winter climate, set cactus outdoors after flowering, or in a protected spot if light frosts are possible. Provide filtered sun. In cold-winter areas, keep cactus indoors until weather warms.

Starting in April, feed monthly with a complete liquid fertilizer. In late September or early October, cut back on watering. When a few tiny buds appear, resume normal watering.

KALANCHOE. In all but the warmest areas, keep plants indoors until all chance of frost is past. Indoors or out, place in bright light or full sun. Water when the top of the soil feels dry to touch. Clip off old blooms. Plants usually rebloom in late winter or spring. In fall, to force early bloom, set plants in low light for two months (don't overwater), then move them into brighter light.

ORNAMENTAL PEPPER (*Solanum*). See "Are Holiday Gift Plants Worth Saving?" on the facing page. ◆

Which living Christmas tree was the favorite among *Sunset* readers and nurseries around the West? The Colorado blue spruce, pictured here. For other choices—and tips on how to care for conifers in containers—see pages 314–316.

December

gardenguide

Go for gold

Yellow poinsettias make perfect pairs for house plants

■ When the holidays arrive, everything from dresses to decorations turns red. And that includes poinsettias. True, these beauties are festive when crowned with bright red bracts. But for a softer, more elegant color scheme, why not try a touch of gold this holiday season?

Poinsettias with bracts in light lemon yellow or cream pair beautifully with house plants with variegated foliage, especially when displayed in a large pot lightly brushed with gold paint.

For the arrangement shown at right, *Sunset* test garden coordinator Bud Stuckey combined a creamy lemon–colored poinsettia with cream-and-green-variegated dieffenbachia, 'Needle-point' ivy, and spider plant in a 24-inch-wide by 12-inch-deep terra-cotta pot that he'd spray-painted silvery gray and gold. The effect is soft and soothing.

To make your own arrangement, buy the dieffenbachia, ivy, and spider plant in 6-inch pots and a large poinsettia in an 8-inch pot. Also have on hand a 1-cubic-foot bag of potting soil.

Fill the pot with soil and add the house plants, setting the dieffenbachia toward the back of the arrangement and the ivy and spider plant toward the front. Plant the poinsettia in the center—plastic pot and all—so you can easily replace it with another 8-inch potted plant after the holidays.

Enjoy the arrangement indoors (or outdoors on a porch in mild climates) through the holidays; keep soil slightly moist to touch.

— *Lauren Bonar Swezey*

STRAPPY-LEAFED SPIDER PLANT and variegated ivy soften pot's front edges. Dieffenbachia, positioned toward the back, fans out beneath the poinsettia.

BACK TO BASICS

Caring for poinsettias

Much of the world's supply of flowering poinsettias comes from the greenhouses of Paul Ecke Ranch in Encinitas, California. Experts there offer these tips to keep plants looking their best during the holidays.

- Remove any decorative foil or wrap.
- Keep poinsettias away from heat sources; they prefer indirect or filtered light—not direct sun—and cool room temperatures (60° to 70° during the day, 60° to 65° at night).
- Don't overwater. When the top of the soil is just dry to touch, water plants in the sink and let them drain. Don't let plants stand in water-filled saucers. And don't mist plants or you'll encourage botrytis (a fungus).
- There's no need to feed plants in bloom.
- To avoid injuring plants, don't pick off faded bracts and leaves; let them fall, then dispose of them.

New 'Betty Boop' is all curves

Betty Boop, the saucer-eyed, bob-haired cartoon flapper, won America's hearts in the '30s. Now a new floribunda rose—a 1999 All-America Rose Selection winner—seems likely to do the same. Like its namesake, the 'Betty Boop' rose is all curves. Its flowers have ivory-yellow semidouble petals with lipstick-red, scalloped edges. The shrub, as wide as it is tall (approximately 3½ feet), has a naturally rounded shape.

'Betty Boop' is also a strong performer: "The first to bloom and the last to quit," claims Tom Carruth of Weeks Roses, who hybridized the rose. And so it is proving to be in our test gardens. (As is typical of sterile plants, 'Betty Boop' pumps out flowers nearly continuously in a vain effort to set seed.)

'Betty Boop's flowers last a long time on the shrub and also in the vase. And, as you'd expect from an AARS winner, the foliage is disease-resistant.

Look for 'Betty Boop' in nurseries this month, or order by mail from Petaluma Rose Company (707/769-8862) or Edmunds' Roses (888/481-7673).

— *Sharon Cohoon*

DEIDRA WALPOLE

GARDEN GIFT

Yuletide for hummingbirds

■ In winter, when few nectar-bearing flowers are in bloom, hummingbirds can draw nourishment from feeders containing a sugar-water mixture. Most of the feeders currently available are made of clear plastic embellished with red plastic flowers—they are serviceable but hardly elegant. Now a new line of handblown-glass feeders can bring the color and beauty of blown-glass Christmas tree ornaments to your garden.

Dew Drop feeders, designed by Mexican artist Alfredo García-Lucio for the Denver-based firm Parasol, come in two styles. The small Dew Drop is a 4-inch globe tinted with swirling shades of red, green, or blue and topped by a glass loop for hanging. Gardeners Eden carries the red model for about $35 plus shipping (800/822-9600). A large Dew Drop (pictured at left) measures 12 inches long and resembles a gourd. Its neck is curled to hang on a sturdy branch. It comes in cobalt blue, red, and red-and-gold swirl and costs about $75. A plastic feeding tube, rubber stopper, and optional metal hanger are included with either style. Both feeders also come with a recipe for stovetop nectar. Call (800) 879-6787 for a distributor of both small and large Dew Drops near you.

— *Dick Bushnell*

Decorate an ivy tree

■ An ivy topiary with just the right finishing touches makes a great gift or decoration for a holiday table. (In *Sunset* climate zones 7 through 24, container-grown ivy is also hardy outdoors year-round, so the trees can be used as handsome garden accents.) You can buy ivy trees already trained over wire trellises at nurseries for about $15 to $120, depending on the size. They range from 1 to 5 feet tall.

Four ways to decorate ivy trees

- Poke silver balls and red berries (such as holly, pyracantha, or nandina) into the ivy. Or use redwood tree cones and dried flowers.
- Wind decorative ribbon in a spiral down the ivy tree as shown at right. Start at the top and weave it in and out of the wire frame and the foliage.
- Spray-paint clay pots gold, silver, or green and set the potted ivy trees inside.
- Leave trees of variegated ivy undecorated and let the beauty of the foliage carry the show. Or enhance the tree at night with battery-operated white lights.

...and four ways to show them off

- Cluster three trees of the same height or varied sizes to create a miniature forest on a buffet table.
- Display a 5-foot-tall tree on each side of a door.
- Line up a row of small trees on a buffet table and surround them with wide hemp ribbon.
- Cluster three sizes of ivy trees together on the front porch, in a hallway, or on an end table.

Ivy tree care

To keep your tree healthy, follow these guidelines:

WATERING. Keep the soil moist but not wet.

NORMAN A. PLATE

FERTILIZING. During the growing season, feed plants with a half-strength dilution of a liquid house plant fertilizer every other watering.

SHAPING. Wind new growth around the topiary form and periodically pinch off shoots to keep the plant compact. Remove brown leaves regularly.

REPOTTING. Ivy trees grow best if transplanted into larger containers in spring. (If you leave them in small pots, the soil dries out too quickly.) Make sure the new pot is in scale with the plant; a container that's much too large can make a 1-foot-tall ivy tree look insignificant. Gain extra root space by selecting a container that's a bit taller, but not much wider, than the original plastic pot.

DECORATED FOR THE HOLIDAYS, 1-foot-tall ivy trees make elegant adornments for dining tables. Terra-cotta pots, spray-painted with metallic paint, camouflage plastic nursery containers. Wind 1- to 1½-inch-wide ribbon in and out of the wire frame, poke in ornaments, or leave the trees plain.

Pacific Northwest Checklist

PLANTING

☑ **AMARYLLIS.** Garden shops and nurseries will have amaryllis bulbs of all kinds, from classic big, red-flowered varieties to new dwarfs with cream-and-pink blooms. Buy several bulbs and pot them up at two-week intervals: you'll have plants in bloom from mid-December to Valentine's Day and beyond.

☑ **BUY CAMELLIAS.** Zones 4–7: Winter-flowering camellias will be available in full bloom. Slip them into decorative pots, planters, or big baskets to display on a deck or patio for the holidays (you can even string them with lights). When flowers fade, plant them out in the garden.

☑ **GROUND-LAYER EVERGREENS.** You can propagate evergreen plants such as daphne, hebe, mahonia, and rhododendrons by using a technique called ground-layering. Find a branch near the ground and scrape a bit of bark (about the size of a fingernail) from the underside. Dust the wound with rooting hormone and press the branch down into a shallow hollow in the ground. Cover the branch with a bit of soil and weigh it down with a rock or brick. Keep the area well watered. By next fall, the branch will have rooted; cut the new plant away from the parent and plant it in another site.

☑ **TREES AND SHRUBS.** Zones 4–7: Hardy kinds can go in the ground now. Water them generously at planting time.

MAINTENANCE

☑ **CARE FOR HOUSE PLANTS.** Give winter-blooming plants an application of fertilizer, but wait until April to feed the others.

☑ **COMPOST HOLIDAY GREENS.** Add withered greens from swags and wreaths to the compost pile. Cut boughs into 6-inch lengths to speed decomposition.

☑ **INSPECT STORED BULBS.** Look them over for signs of rot; throw out bulbs that have soft spots. Dahlia tubers are the exception: if they have rotten spots, cut the damaged parts out, dust the wounds with sulfur, and store them apart from other bulbs.

☑ **TEND GIFT PLANTS.** Christmas cactus, cyclamen, and kalanchoe will bloom longer if they are not allowed to dry out. They do, however, need perfect drainage. Remove foil wrapping or cut it from the bottom of the pot. Snip off faded leaves and flowers.

Northern California Checklist

PLANTING

☑ **CHOOSE CAMELLIAS. Zones 7–9, 14–17:** Select *C. sasanqua* and early-flowering *C. japonica* in bloom. Sasanquas are good choices for espaliers, ground covers, informal hedges, and containers. Some are upright, others spreading or vinelike; they tolerate a fair amount of sun. Choices include 'Egao', 'Rainbow', 'Shibori Egao', and 'Yuletide'. Japonicas are handsome as specimen plants and espaliers. Try 'Alba Plena', 'Daikagura', 'Debutante', 'Elegans' ('Chandleri Elegans'), 'Magnoliaeflora', 'Nuccio's Carousel', 'Nuccio's Gem', and 'Wildfire'.

☑ **SHOP FOR BARE-ROOT ROSES. Zones 7–9, 14–17:** Bare-root roses start appearing in nurseries this month. Shop while selections are good. If you missed the 1998 All-America Rose Selection 'Sunset Celebration' (with apricot-umber flowers), try again; nurseries should have plenty in stock now.

☑ **VISIT ROSES OF YESTERDAY. Zones 7–9, 14–17:** Roses of Yesterday and Today, which started in the 1930s and closed two years ago, is back in business as Roses of Yesterday. You can order roses on its Web site (www.rosesofyesterday.com), by phone (831/728-1901), or by visiting the company at 803 Brown's Valley Rd., Corralitos (between Santa Cruz and Watsonville). Hours are 9 to 4 daily.

Sunset CLIMATE ZONES
- Mountain (1-2)
- Valley (7-9)
- Inland (14)
- Coastal (15-17)

DEBRA LAMBERT

☑ **MAKE A LIVING ARRANGEMENT. Zones 7–9, 14–17:** Most nurseries have a good supply of 4-inch pots of color to cluster in large containers. Choose azaleas, calendula, Christmas cactus, cineraria, cyclamen, English primroses, fairy primroses, kalanchoe, pansies, *Primula obconica*, and snapdragons. Protect Christmas cactus and kalanchoe from frost.

MAINTENANCE

☑ **FEED ANNUALS. Zones 7–9, 14–17:** Even though the weather is cooler and foliage growth has slowed, annuals need nutrients for root development. Feed every two weeks with fish emulsion or once a month with a commercial fertilizer that's higher in nitrogen than the emulsion.

☑ **KEEP CUT CHRISTMAS TREES FRESH.** Look for trees that are stored in water at the Christmas tree lot. To prolong the tree's freshness after you bring it home, saw an inch off the bottom of the trunk, then temporarily store the tree in a bucket of water in a shady area outdoors. Before setting the tree in a stand, saw another inch off the trunk's bottom. Use a stand that holds water and keep the reservoir full.

☑ **WATCH FOR COLD WEATHER. Zones 7–9, 14–17:** You never know when the first freeze of the season will hit. Keep an eye on the weather report. If cold weather is predicted, move tender container plants under eaves and suspend covers over plants in the ground using four tall stakes (don't allow the cover to touch the leaves). Remove in the morning.

Southern California Checklist

PLANTING

☑ **BUY BARE-ROOT PLANTS.** Roses seem to turn up at nurseries earlier every year. Deciduous fruit trees, cane berries, grapes, and perennial vegetables such as asparagus and artichokes will start appearing later this month and early next. For the best selection, shop soon; plant all as soon as possible after purchase. If the soil is too wet for immediate planting, plant temporarily in containers.

☑ **PLANT FLOWERING SHRUBS.** Sasanqua and early-flowering japonica camellias are available in nurseries now. Other reliable winter bloomers to look for include breath of heaven (*Coleonema*) and New Zealand tea tree (*Leptospermum scoparium*).

☑ **REPLACE WINTER VEGETABLES.** If there are bare spots in your winter vegetable beds, sow chard, kale, leaf lettuce, peas, radishes, scallions, or spinach from seed. Healthy nursery cabbage, cauliflower, and broccoli plants can still be transplanted.

DEBRA LAMBERT

MAINTENANCE

☑ **PROTECT PLANTS.** Follow weather reports. When a temperature drop is predicted, move tender container plants under the eaves or indoors. Cover citrus and other sensitive plants in the ground with plastic or burlap supported by a frame that will keep the cover from touching the foliage.

☑ **FERTILIZE CYMBIDIUMS.** Feed cymbidiums with a bloom-promoting fertilizer, such as 15-30-15, until buds open up.

PEST CONTROL

☑ **PREVENT BEETLE DAMAGE.** Prune eucalyptus, pine, and other trees susceptible to bark beetles now, while beetles are inactive. Chip the prunings or cover the firewood lightly with a tarp to prevent beetles from laying eggs in the wood.

HOLIDAY CHECKLIST

☑ **CARE FOR CHRISTMAS TREES.** To prolong the freshness of a cut tree, saw an inch off the bottom of the trunk, then store the tree in a bucket of water in a shady spot outdoors. Before you bring it in, saw another inch from the trunk's base. Use a tree stand with a reservoir that holds plenty of water, and keep the reservoir full.

☑ **PRUNE FOR HOLIDAY GREENS.** Cotoneaster, holly, juniper, pittosporum, podocarpus, pyracantha, and toyon all benefit from a winter grooming. Use the cuttings for holiday decorations. Cut to side branches or to about ¼ inch above buds.

☑ **UNWIND AT A PUBLIC GARDEN.** One antidote to shopper's stress is the magic of a lighted nighttime garden. Quail Botanical Gardens in Encinitas, for instance, opens its gate for marshmallow roasting, carolers, horse-drawn carriage rides, and other low-key, spirit-restoring activities this month. Call (760) 436-3036 for the schedule. ◆

Mountain Checklist

PLANTING

☑ **PROPAGATE HOUSE PLANTS.** To start new plants of Chinese evergreen, dracaena, hoya, philodendron, and pothos, snip off leggy stems and immerse the cut ends in water. When roots form, transplant into fresh potting soil.

MAINTENANCE

☑ **CARE FOR GIFT PLANTS.** If you plan to keep small gift plants, give them plenty of light and regular water, and keep them out of drafts. Most plants will take poor conditions for a few days—as centerpieces in low-light places, for example—but give them optimal conditions again as soon as possible after the holidays

☑ **CHECK STORED BULBS, PRODUCE.** Examine stored summer bulbs, squash, and apples, throwing out any that show signs of rot. Dahlia tubers are an exception: cut out the bad spots, dust the wounds with sulfur, and store apart from the others.

☑ **MULCH.** It's not too late to put a 3- or 4-inch layer of mulch over perennial, bulb, and shrub beds that might be damaged by alternate cycles of freezing and thawing. Apply mulch on damp, unfrozen ground.

Sunset
CLIMATE ZONES
☐ 1-3   ☐ 10-11

DEBRA LAMBERT

☑ **PREPARE INDOOR CACTUS FOR BLOOM.** Allow spring-flowering indoor cactus to dry out from mid-December through February, then water regularly and fertilize lightly every second watering. If your cactus is growing in a bright spot, buds and flowers should follow.

☑ **PROTECT YOUNG TREES.** When the low winter sun shines on the trunks of young trees (any less than 4 inches in diameter), it can burn and split the tender bark. You can prevent this by wrapping the trunks with burlap or commercial tree wrap or by painting the bark with white latex (water base). Or make a protective collar by splitting white PVC pipe lengthwise and fitting it around the trunk. Use pipe that's slightly larger than the trunk so water will drain through the collar.

☑ **SAND ICY PATHS.** Sand is a better choice than salt for use around plants, since it's nontoxic and can be swept into the garden. But don't use sand on decks—it scars wood.

☑ **WATER.** When the temperature is above freezing, water dry spots in the garden and plants under house eaves.

PEST CONTROL

☑ **FIGHT RODENTS.** Hidden beneath snow and mulch, field mice and voles gnaw on the bark at ground level. To keep them from girdling landscape plants, put rodenticide around the base of garden trees and shrubs.

☑ **TREAT INDOOR PLANTS.** Sticky honeydew or fine webs on leaves are signs of insect infestations. Spray plants with insecticidal soap; it smothers the pests and washes off the honeydew.

Southwest Checklist

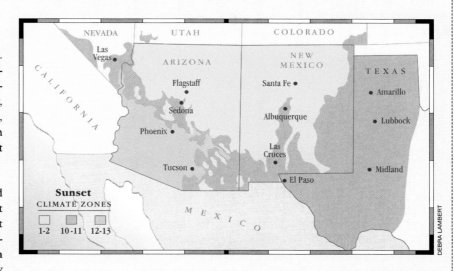

PLANTING

☑ **ANNUALS AND PERENNIALS.** Zones 12–13: Set out seedlings of calendula, candytuft, cyclamen, dianthus, Iceland poppy, larkspur, pansy, petunia, primrose, snapdragon, stock, sweet alyssum, and viola. In zone 13 (Phoenix), you can also set out bedding begonias and cineraria.

☑ **BARE-ROOT PLANTS.** Berries and roses are among the first bare-root plants in nurseries, followed by fruit trees and perennial vegetables, including asparagus. To keep plants from drying out and dying between nursery and garden, wrap them in damp burlap or place them in a sawdust-filled plastic bag. Plant immediately.

☑ **BULBS.** In early December, plant daffodil, gladiolus, ranunculus, and prechilled tulip bulbs (they need at least six weeks of chill in the refrigerator to perform well in the low desert).

☑ **NATIVE PLANTS.** Zones 10–13: Set out nursery stock, water in well, and mulch. If you don't get much winter rain, water regularly for the first year.

☑ **START PEPPERS, TOMATOES.** Zones 10–13: Sow seeds of peppers and tomatoes in a warm, bright spot indoors. They should be ready for transplanting around the end of February.

MAINTENANCE

☑ **CARE FOR GIFT PLANTS.** If you plan to keep small gift plants, give them plenty of light and regular water, and keep them out of drafts. Most plants will take poor conditions for a few days—as centerpieces in low-light places, for example—but give them optimal conditions again as soon as possible after the holidays.

☑ **FEED DECIDUOUS FRUIT TREES.** For trees at least four years old, apply 9 pounds of a complete fertilizer (10-10-10) this month.

☑ **MULCH.** Zones 1–2: Spread mulch over bulb and perennial beds and over the root zones of permanent shrubs, especially tender ones.

☑ **WATER.** When the temperature is above freezing, water dry spots in the garden as well as plants in containers and under house eaves. Well-watered plants stand a better chance of surviving a deep freeze than dehydrated ones.

Living Christmas trees to treasure

They can last for years, if you choose the right ones
and give them good care

BY JIM McCAUSLAND • ILLUSTRATIONS BY ALEXIS SEABROOK

■ Watching a Santa Ana wind desiccate a lot full of cut Christmas trees in Southern California one weekend, I was struck by how quickly the sawed-off trees dried out, their needles turning as crisp as toast before falling off. By comparison, trees in containers use nature's perfect hydration system—roots embedded in soil—to keep their foliage fresh. That's one reason living Christmas trees remain so popular.

Which trees perform best during their stay in containers and later in the garden? Which ones were favorites for decorating? To find out, we queried *Sunset* readers and surveyed nurseries around the West. Colorado blue spruce (shown at right) won the popularity contest, followed by an assortment of other conifers (see the facing page).

We also learned that people who grow living Christmas trees become very attached to them: they coddle them, play dress-up with them at Christmas, and usually move them to a place of honor in their gardens when the plants outgrow their containers and get too big to bring into the house.

BE A SMART TREE SHOPPER

Pick a conifer that's as well suited to your taste in garden plants as to your taste in Christmas trees. You can expect to use the same tree in a container for four to seven years, depending on how fast it grows. If you intend to plant it outdoors eventually, be sure the variety is one that thrives in your climate.

The nursery industry offers conifers in two basic grades: sheared, well-tapered trees grown for sale as living Christmas trees; and landscape-grade trees that receive no special care. You may not find both grades at every nursery, but when you do you'll notice a marked difference in quality and price between trees of the same species and size. Landscape-grade trees can be rangy, but they cost about a third less than sheared trees. In the long run, the

Colorado spruce
Picea pungens
'Glauca' is the standard Colorado blue spruce, but 'Hoopsii' is even bluer. Spruce aphid is a serious pest for all Colorado spruces in the Puget Sound area.
•*Sunset* climate zones: 1–10, 14–17
•Height: 80–100 ft.

Quick as a flash: A nursery pot cover-up

Need an easy cover-up for your living Christmas tree? You can make an elegant, yet simple, one by wrapping the container in aluminum flashing, as shown at left, around the base of a Colorado spruce. Available at hardware stores in silver or gold, flashing is sold by the foot and ranges in width from 8 inches (70 cents) to 20 inches ($2). Living Christmas trees are mostly sold in 5- to 15-gallon containers. Cut the aluminum to fit the size of your container and secure it at the back with silver duct tape. Shiny metallic flashing adds a festive touch, is easily removed, and can be safely stored for future use.

NORMAN A. PLATE

Best living Christmas trees for the West

Afghan pine
Pinus eldarica

Also sold as Goldwater or Mondell pine, this fast-growing tree has an open habit and long needles. Good choice for desert gardens.
- *Sunset* climate zones: 7–9, 11–24
- Height: 30–80 ft.

Aleppo pine
Pinus halepensis

Fast-growing tree with light green needles. Well suited for the low desert. Susceptible to dieback in Tucson and mites in Southern California.
- *Sunset* zones: 8–9, 11–24
- Height: 30–60 ft.

Alpine fir
Abies lasiocarpa

Slow-growing tree with bluish green needles. *A. l. arizonica,* which grows in the same areas, has blue-gray needles and creamy white, corky bark.
- *Sunset* zones: 1–9, 14–17
- Height: 60–90 ft.

Coast redwood
Sequoia sempervirens

Feathery leaves are green on top, grayish underneath. Relatively pest-free tree, as long as it gets enough water. A big seller in Southern California nurseries.
- *Sunset* zones: 4–9, 14–24
- Height: 70–90 ft.

Deodar cedar
Cedrus deodara

Nodding branches bear green needles with a bluish, gray, or golden yellow cast. Floppy top makes it hard to mount a star atop the tree. A good garden tree if you have room.
- *Sunset* zones: 2–12, 14–24
- Height: 80 ft.

Douglas fir
Pseudotsuga menziesii

Soft dark green or blue-green needles. Easy to grow and shape by shearing. *P. m. glauca* is a hardy form in the Rockies. A handsome Christmas tree.
- *Sunset* zones: 1–10, 14–17
- Height: 70 ft.

Giant sequoia
Sequoiadendron giganteum

Dense gray-green foliage; red bark. Widely adapted; able to tolerate colder, drier climates than coast redwood. Potentially huge tree.
- *Sunset* zones: All zones
- Height: 80 ft.

Korean fir
Abies koreana

Pyramidal tree with short, shiny green needles. Good choice for Southern California. Slow-growing, compact (seldom taller than 30 ft.).
- *Sunset* zones: 3–9, 14–24
- Height: 10–30 ft.

White fir
Abies concolor

Symmetrical tree with bluish green needles. *A. c.* 'Candicans' has bright silvery blue needles. Good container plant.
- *Sunset* zones: 1–9, 14–24
- Height: 30 ft. (eventual height when planted in the ground) ◆

How to keep trees healthy

INDOORS

• Keep the tree in its original nursery container at least for the first Christmas. You don't want to add the shock of transplanting to the stress of its indoor stay.

• Display the tree indoors for no longer than 10 days. Keep it away from heater vents and fireplaces.

• Decorate with small, cool bulbs.

• Water regularly. One easy way: Dump two trays of ice cubes onto the soil surface daily. As the ice melts, the water trickles slowly down through the root zone.

• In cold-winter areas, before you even bring the tree into the house—and before the ground freezes—dig a planting hole in the garden (the hole should be slightly larger than the container). After its indoor stay, ease the tree's transition from the house to outdoors:

First place it on a cool, bright porch for a few days; then move it to a protected place outside where the rootball won't freeze; finally, plant the tree, container and all, in the hole you dug. Spread a 5-inch layer of straw mulch over the top of the rootball to protect roots against freezing weather.

AFTER CHRISTMAS

• Water the tree regularly year-round. Trees in containers are much more vulnerable to drying out than trees in the ground, so check often by sticking a finger in the soil; if the top 2 inches of soil are dry, it's time to water. Always provide enough water so a little trickles out the drain holes.

• When new growth starts in spring, feed the tree with controlled-release fertilizer (a formula that releases nutrients over a six- to nine-month period is a good choice).

• Each spring, before new growth starts, gently slide the tree partway out of the pot

In hot-summer areas, protect trees in black plastic nursery containers from sun; overheated soil can injure or kill roots and eventually the tree. Transplant tree into a lighter-colored plastic, terra-cotta, or wood container. Or sink the nursery container into the ground.

and check the roots. When they begin to circle the inside of the pot, nip them back with pruning shears, rough up the rootball, and move the tree into a larger pot.

---

two grades will perform about the same in gardens. Trees of both grades are sold in various sizes in 5-, 7-, and 15-gallon plastic cans.

As you shop, you also may see trees tagged with the logo of Global ReLeaf, a tree-planting program sponsored by American Forests, the nation's oldest conservation organization. Global Re-Leaf encourages you to plant your tree outdoors after the holidays. For information on how you can plant your tree to save energy, visit the American Forests Web site at www.amfor.org.

WESTERN CONIFERS

Coast redwoods and giant sequoias are close relatives. Redwoods are greener and not as wide at the base as sequoias; they thrive along the coast and won't take extreme cold.

Sequoias grow more slowly than redwoods, and their foliage is a grayer shade of green. These trees do best in the Pacific Northwest, mountains, and colder interior climates.

Colorado spruces have stiff branches bristling with needles in shades from

bluish green to steely blue. 'Glauca' is the classic Colorado blue spruce, but its close cousin 'Hoopsii' has superior blue color and good form even when small, making it an ideal living Christmas tree.

Deodar cedar is one of the most graceful trees anywhere. Gigantic, lighted specimens line Christmas Tree Lane (Santa Rosa Ave.) in Altadena, California.

Douglas fir carpets the Pacific Northwest and grows wild down into Northern California and east to the Rockies. You can keep a Douglas fir dense and symmetrical in a container for many years using hedge shears.

Firs are classic cut trees; short-needled, well branched, and well formed, they fit everybody's mental image of a good tree. Some make outstanding living Christmas trees, but others are less than perfect as container plants: noble fir, for instance, is one of the most popular cut trees, but it has a hard time surviving in a nursery container.

Grand, noble, and white firs often don't do well when transplanted from field to pot, but more fibrous-rooted firs like alpine, balsam, cork, and Fraser

handle transplanting better.

To determine if a fir is container- or field-grown stock, ask the nursery staff or check for yourself by digging gently through the surface layer of potting soil to the rootball. If the rootball is covered with burlap, or if you find the roots growing in soil that's markedly different from the soil on the surface, the tree is field grown. If you find the same kind of soil throughout the pot, it's container grown.

Pines usually have longer needles than firs, and they often have a more open form. Most pines thrive in hotter, drier climates than firs and spruces.

Many nurseries still sell Monterey pine (*Pinus radiata*) as a living Christmas tree; if you buy one, keep it in a container and prune the roots annually to keep growth under control. Sadly, Monterey pine is no longer a viable choice as a landscape plant in California because the species is vulnerable to pitch canker, a fungal disease that has killed thousands of the trees in recent years.

For a chart of good living Christmas trees for the West, see page 315.

Article Titles Index

SUSANNE WEIHL

General Subject Index

SUSANNE WEIHL

If you are not already a subscriber to
Sunset Magazine and would be
interested in subscribing, please call
Sunset's subscriber service number,
1-800-777-0117.